D1552638

Life and Afterlife in Ancient China

Life and Afterlife in Ancient China

JESSICA RAWSON

UNIVERSITY OF WASHINGTON PRESS   SEATTLE

Text copyright © Jessica Rawson 2023

The author has asserted her moral rights

Original edition first published by Penguin Books Ltd, London

Set in 11.8/14.75pt Dante MT Std
Typeset by Jouve (UK), Milton Keynes
Printed and bound in the United States of America

UNIVERSITY OF WASHINGTON PRESS   *uwapress.uw.edu*

Cataloging information is available from the Library of Congress
Library of Congress Control Number: 2023942850

ISBN: 9780295752365 (hardcover)
ISBN: 9780295752501 (ebook)

Contents

Contents

List of Maps

Author's Note

Before the unification by the First Emperor in the third century BC, the territory we now know as China was not a single state. In fact, the word China was not used in the West before the expansion of European trade from the late Middle Ages onwards. The Chinese term Zhongguo, meaning Central or Middle Kingdom, derives from the name used in the Warring States period (475–221 BC) to distinguish the central states from those on the periphery. For simplicity, I will use China throughout the book, although we will not visit every corner of the present-day People's Republic. We will focus on the area that stretches from the Great Wall to the East and South China Seas, and westwards to the edge of the Tibetan Plateau. The history of China is not just the history of the central states and is informed by three major and distinct regions. First, the middle and lower Yellow River, and its tributary the Wei, were the heartlands of the Shang and Zhou dynasties (c.1500–256 BC). The Central Plains, the low-lying agricultural land east of the city of Sanmenxia, is used as a general term for this whole region, although it includes many areas, such as the North China Plain. I will call the mountains and valleys north and west of the Central Plains the Loess Plateau, although technically the name only applies to one part of a vast loess-covered landscape. This second region was and is an essential bridge between the agricultural valleys and plains and the steppe stretching from Inner Mongolia to the Black Sea and present-day Ukraine. The Yangtze basins, the foundation of China's prosperity, with their humid climate and rich rice fields, form the third region.

The development of China's civilisation – a mixture of social, cultural and environmental conditions – diverges from Western standards of social complexity. I have therefore recognised the distinctive, yet separate, features of China's early cities and states. In the millennia before a writing system was developed, China was occupied by many different regional groups. They are traditionally named as cultures of a region, for want of a better way of describing who those occupants were. The word dynasty is widely used for the major ruling houses of China from the Shang (*c*.1500–1045 BC) down to the Qing (1644–1911 AD). The territories held by these dynasties varied significantly, as did the nature of their governments. The rule of the Shang and the early Zhou into the eighth century BC was not large and involved a network of relations with elite lineage leaders, that is, the families belonging to a single patrilineal line of descent from a known individual, often within a larger kin-related group here called a clan. Some were relatives of the kings; others were powerful local landowners from different clans. Their territories will be called polities. The boundaries of territories were not marked nor stable and could (and did) move from one place to another. From the mid-eighth century BC, when the military power of the Zhou kings declined, numerous contending polities were gradually amalgamated into larger holdings, here called states. Their systems of government have been slowly revealed by a combination of transmitted and excavated texts. The peoples within such states are generally given the name of the state. Thus, for example, the state of Chu can be referred to as Chu, and its people as the Chu.

In among Shang, Zhou and non-Zhou clans and states were groups of people named in bronze inscriptions and later transmitted texts as Rong, Di, Yi and sometimes Hu, living primarily along the north and east of settlements. In due course, some people joined the Chinese ritual and material cultures; others did not and retained their northern customs. The terms northerner, newcomer and outsider are used for those whose presence we can identify by their tombs, communities who did not adopt the principal cultural norms propagated by the central dynasties and whose names we cannot know.

Efforts have been made to limit the use of Chinese names used for places, individuals, titles, practices, tombs and their objects. Current transliteration, named pinyin, has been used. Where other forms were employed, as in some quotations, the pinyin alternative has been substituted. For the Notes, as many references as possible in

English have been chosen. In all cases it is necessary to be aware that in China, with its different cultural foundations, some words inevitably have misleading meanings. For example, Western associations with the terms generally translated as state, king, temple, palace or even sacrifice do not necessarily reflect the practices of ancient China.

Chinese place names, usually polysyllabic, are referenced on the maps. Personal names are often monosyllabic. Traditionally the family name – usually a single syllable – comes before the given name. This form is used in the Notes unless the author is better known by an English form of their name when publishing outside China.

The tomb plans and objects are all based on drawings in archaeological reports. The originals have been redrawn for the purposes of this book, often to show the outer surface of the piece as a whole. Without the careful work of excavators, it would not have been possible to uncover the tombs in such detail.

Acknowledgements

'It would be a good idea to sort out the jades in the storeroom.'

When this suggestion was made to me in the 1970s, I was a junior curator at the British Museum and had just finished a second undergraduate degree, this time in Chinese, at the School of Oriental and African Studies. I was given the keys to a room alongside the loading bay, with a mass of stones, the famous Chinese jades. I soon realised that their history was little understood and that there was a lot to sort out.

I am grateful that my family had already lit my enthusiasm for languages with unusual scripts, especially Chinese. Dame Kathleen Kenyon, who accepted me as I left school to join her excavation in Jerusalem as a site supervisor, took me as far east as I could go in the 1960s. And throughout three seasons she built my interest in archaeology.

But I owe so much to the British Museum, its curators, several directors, most especially Sir David Wilson, exhibition designers, conservators and security staff. Above all, I had exceptional opportunities to see and learn about the multiple material cultures of Eurasia, often through working on interdepartmental exhibitions, including *7,000 Years of Jewellery*, *Animals in Art* and *Chinese Ornament: The Lotus and the Dragon*. A large project, cataloguing a major collection of bronze ritual vessels in the USA, overseen by Harvard University, gave me much-needed experience of China's extensive literature on its past. And into this whirl of cultures, jades came again in the form of Sir Joseph Hotung, with his magnificent jade collection at his house in Hong Kong. Joe transformed my academic life. His generosity in agreeing to my suggestion that he might not only kindly support the renovation of the Chinese gallery but add in the other half for the Indian subcontinent changed not only the Asian Department but also the whole Museum.

There is no way to sort out, indeed even recognise, ancient jades without examining them closely and holding them in your hands. Joe encouraged me to do this and so opened my eyes yet further. And as more excavations in China were undertaken and published, opportunities to travel to China expanded. During my years as Warden of Merton College (1994–2010) and later as a researcher in the School of Archaeology at Oxford, I made repeated visits to sites across much of the country. In this work, I enjoyed the enthusiasm for China of other colleagues in the School, most especially Chris Gosden and Mark Pollard. The openness and support of colleagues in the archaeological institutes and departments throughout China taught me everything I know today. Without this interaction with the excavators, scientists, curators and students, my understanding of ancient China would be much more limited. I am also indebted to the advice from colleagues during illuminating visits to sites and museums in the Russian Federation and Mongolia.

As China became better known, I profited, as did the University of Oxford, from the award of two major grants by the Leverhulme Trust. A first grant, for the Study of Contemporary China, was one of the major stimuli leading to the creation of the University's China Centre. And then, the Trust supported my research on 'China and Inner Asia, 1000–200 BC: Interactions that Changed China'. This was the foundation of my work on exchanges between the steppe and the central states by way of the Loess Plateau. I am very grateful for the visionary approach of the Trust. I have also benefited greatly over these years from students in the School of Archaeology, whose research and discoveries expanded what we know about key interactions across Eurasia. All their work has contributed to this book.

Although it is in the news every day, too few of us recognise the foundations of modern China. While Europeans inevitably look back to Greece and Rome and beyond to ancient Mesopotamia and Egypt, the Chinese are equally conscious of their long past and its contributions to their lives, their language and their values. I presented some of the ideas in the book at the University of Cambridge, where I was honoured to be elected as Slade Professor of Fine Art (2013–14) and must thank the Electors and the Fellows of St John's College Cambridge, where I enjoyed a fellowship for the year. I am grateful to Peter Straus at RCW for

encouraging and shaping my proposal and to Stuart Proffitt at Allen
Lane for accepting it. Two editors moulded my attempts to open up
a world shielded from us by distance, time and language. Ben Sinyor
suggested the focus on tombs and their contents; Alice Skinner held
me to this and worked tirelessly to help me realise the full breadth of
the book. I am grateful for their persistence and encouragement at
every stage. Many others at Allen Lane have made significant contributions along the way: Elizabeth Brandon, Amelia Evans, Sandra Fuller,
Matt Hutchinson, Shauna Lacy, Linden Lawson and Rebecca Lee.

Two others were indispensable. Dr Limin Huan worked with me
over several years on the role of horses, and on the loess region and
its tombs. Limin also drew the maps for the book and provided me
with a constant supply of information as I wrote the chapters and
built up its bibliography. However, without John, my husband, the
book would only be a shadow, as there would have been no drawings. He took a strong line. He believed that a book about tombs and
their objects had to have illustrations, so undertook all the drawings
of artefacts and many of the tomb plans. Unfortunately, he did not
live to see the book published, but his collaboration, visible in every
chapter, is a memorial to his continuous understanding and unfailing
support of my work throughout our married life, be it at the British
Museum, at Oxford or in China.

As the book covers such a wide area and long time period, I have
trespassed on the patience of many colleagues, who have been kind
enough to share their knowledge and to read one or more chapters:
Anthony Barbieri-Low, Roderick Campbell, Konstantin Chugunov,
Nicola Di Cosmo, Yegor Grebnev, Robert Harrist, Martin Kern, Maria
Khayutina, Maxim Korolkov, Jianjun Mei, Susan Naquin, Armin
Selbitschka, Jenny So, Alain Thote, Raphael Wong, Frances Wood,
Jay Xu and Yijie Zhuang. I am grateful for their comments and cor-
rections. Other colleagues have been so generous as to allow me to
make use of their translations of early texts. I am also indebted to
directors of archaeological institutes and museums and to archaeologists in China for providing me with some precious photographs and
granting the publisher permission for their use.

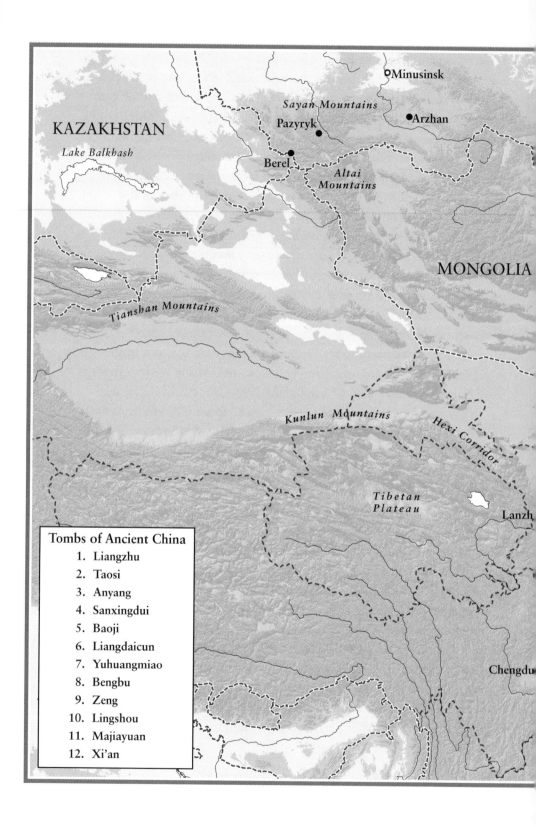

Minusinsk

Sayan Mountains

Pazyryk

Arzhan

KAZAKHSTAN

Lake Balkhash

Berel

Altai Mountains

MONGOLIA

Tianshan Mountains

Kunlun Mountains

Hexi Corridor

Tibetan Plateau

Lanzh

Chengdu

Tombs of Ancient China

1. Liangzhu
2. Taosi
3. Anyang
4. Sanxingdui
5. Baoji
6. Liangdaicun
7. Yuhuangmiao
8. Bengbu
9. Zeng
10. Lingshou
11. Majiayuan
12. Xi'an

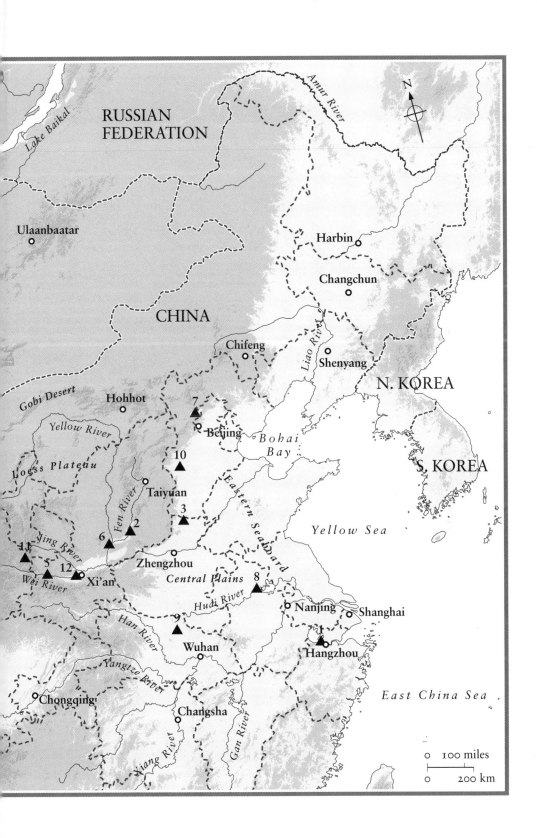

RUSSIAN
FEDERATION

Lake Baikal

Ulaanbaatar

Amur River

N

CHINA

Harbin

Changchun

Gobi Desert

Hohhot

Chifeng

Shenyang

Liao River

N. KOREA

Yellow River

7

10

Loess Plateau

Beijing

Bohai Bay

S. KOREA

Fen River

Taiyuan

3

Eastern Seaboard

Yellow Sea

Jing River

6

2

11

5 12

Wei River

Xi'an

Zhengzhou

Central Plains

8

Hudi River

Nanjing

Shanghai

Han River

9

1

Yangtze River

Wuhan

Hangzhou

Chongqing

Changsha

East China Sea

Xiang River

Gan River

o   100 miles

o   200 km

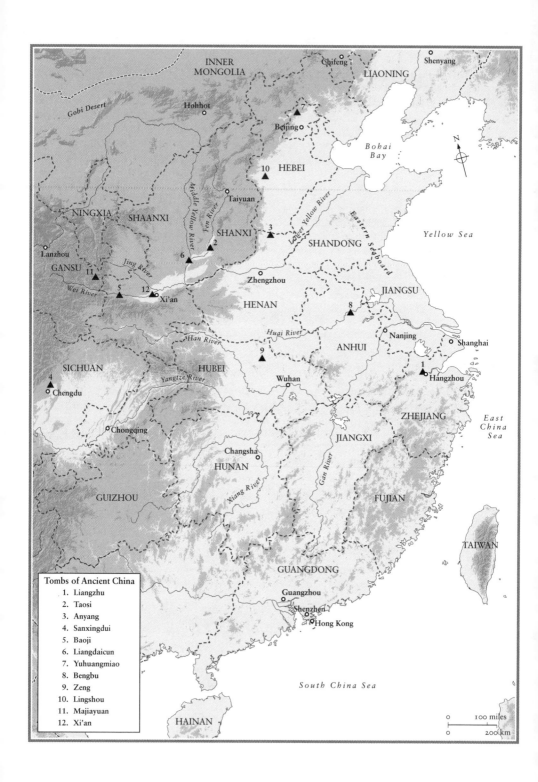

INNER
MONGOLIA

Gobi Desert

Hohhot ○

○ Chifeng

LIAONING

○ Shenyang

▲ 7

Beijing ○

Bohai
Bay

N

10 ▲ HEBEI

Taiyuan ○

Middle Yellow River

Fen River

NINGXIA   SHAANXI

SHANXI

3 ▲

Lower Yellow River

SHANDONG

Eastern Seaboard

Yellow Sea

2 ▲

Lanzhou ○

Jing River

6 ▲

GANSU   11 ▲

Wei River   5 ▲   12 ▲

Xi'an ○

Zhengzhou ○

HENAN

JIANGSU

8 ▲

Nanjing ○

○ Shanghai

Han River

Huai River

ANHUI

9 ▲

Wuhan ○

1 ▲

Hangzhou ○

SICHUAN

4 ▲

○ Chengdu

HUBEI

Yangtze River

○ Chongqing

JIANGXI

ZHEJIANG

East
China
Sea

Changsha ○

HUNAN

Xiang River

Gan River

FUJIAN

GUIZHOU

TAIWAN

GUANGDONG

Guangzhou ○

Shenzhen ○
○ Hong Kong

South China Sea

HAINAN

Tombs of Ancient China
1. Liangzhu
2. Taosi
3. Anyang
4. Sanxingdui
5. Baoji
6. Liangdaicun
7. Yuhuangmiao
8. Bengbu
9. Zeng
10. Lingshou
11. Majiayuan
12. Xi'an

○ ———— 100 miles
○ ———— 200 km

Introduction:
The World of the Afterlife

China plays a leading political and economic role on the world stage but, beyond its borders, the country and its history are not well known. In part, this is because its formidable language, its people and its landscapes are unfamiliar. We in the West rarely possess Chinese cultural literacy: in fact, a British newspaper recently commented that there was 'a severe national deficit' in our understanding of China.[1] A lack of empathy and even a perceived strangeness has obscured China's long and distinguished past. If we fail to acknowledge and value its history, which still informs not only its present but all our presents, we restrict ourselves in our engagement with a country that spans five geographical time zones and borders fourteen nations. China's modern leaders often refer to the 5,000 years of civilisation, built by distant ancestors, in order to underpin their country's position and role in the international community. This epic timespan gives shape and meaning to the individual and collective identities of the Chinese, their ethical values and their aspirations, and deserves our recognition and consideration. Yet even 5,000 years underestimates the millennia over which China emerged, distinct from much of the rest of the Eurasian continent. The unprecedented scale and sophistication of objects and writings that survive offer the Chinese themselves an authority in a world of much younger states in Europe and the Americas. We can only look at a small fraction of these millennia. Nevertheless, the 3,000 years before the establishment of the imperial Qin dynasty in 221 BC – a time of early cities and the first dynasties – provide the foundation for many of the distinctive cultural elements that are still in place in China today.

China embraces many extreme environments. Its territory stretches from the Black Dragon River, also known as the Amur, in the north, which freezes in winter at minus 40 or 50 degrees, to the subtropical island of Hainan in the south more than 4,000 kilometres away. Europe – from the most northern tip of Norway to the southern coast of Spain – is about the same size. In three immense steps, the land of China descends west to east, from the great plateau of Tibet at *c*.5,000 metres high down to the loess of the north and the mountain ranges of the south at *c*.1,500 metres, and then finally into the lowlands of agricultural valleys and plains. A vast northern area, the Loess Plateau, is covered with loess, a fine, often semi-crystalline dust blown from the Altai Mountains, the Tibet Plateau and the Gobi Desert over thousands or even millions of years.[2] This crucial land mass joins China to the grasslands of the steppe. In the centre and to the east, the middle and lower Yellow River flows over the plains on levees more than five metres high, and the Yangtze crashes south through the Three Gorges from the isolated Sichuan basin. This used to feed the great Yunmeng Marsh that, with the Dongting Lake, covered a basin south of the city of Wuhan, now drained as farmland, long before it reached the sea at Shanghai.

A map alone cannot convey this challenging terrain, stretching not only beyond the horizon but beyond our imagination and experience. The only way to understand this extraordinary country is to travel through it. In the 1970s and 1980s train journeys took me and many others at a deliberate pace, past loess hills with cave houses carefully dug into them to the bamboo groves in the south. Today the pace has rocketed, and all who can take high-speed trains or fly. China's diversity disappears in such haste. We need to slow down to see the drastic changes in the landscape and histories of the territories that were unified by the First Emperor in the third century BC. These territories were more compact than present-day China. They spread from the eastern edges of the Tibetan Plateau to the northern deserts and steppe, from the East China Sea and to the banks of the Yangtze Valley, with even more remote lands further south, where Hong Kong stands beyond more rivers and mountains. Although there was continuous travel and connections by sea down the eastern coast, the sea played a comparatively smaller role in ancient China than in the societies of the Mediterranean or the Indian Ocean.

Yet the ocean to the east does determine the climate of China and much of what we call East Asia. The Pacific Monsoon is a major flow of air that takes its moisture as summer rain. As these rains stall over the Loess Plateau and often do not reach the steppe, they set one of the most important boundaries in the world, a boundary beyond which crop-growing is possible, but limited. In the autumn the monsoon retreats, drawing the winds from the Arctic south over the steppe and much of northern China, spawning harsh winters. The monsoon is the source of China's long-standing wealth. It feeds the Yellow and Yangtze Rivers and their tributaries, bringing humid summers so different from those around the Mediterranean. The gift of rain also fuels the farming of native grasses, domesticated as rice in the south and millet in the north. Rice – the most nutritious grain exploited around the world – is very labour-intensive, whereas millet has a remarkably short growing season, from seed to harvest in forty-five days, and can thrive on higher ground. Both grains are boiled rather than ground to make bread, as in Western Asia and Europe, an Atlantic region characterised by dry summers and damp winters.[3] This major variance in environment has led to two completely different lifestyles and cuisines.

China also diverges markedly from the West in its farming practices. Although mountain sheep and goats grazed on the ranges of the north-west, they were not present in the river valleys. The early peoples of these valleys instead domesticated dogs and pigs. The result was the growth of a population that did not have to compete with animals for land needed for pasture. From 3000 BC to the present, China's huge population has been its central strength, enabling ambitious settlement projects and grand infrastructure, from the Great Wall, the Three Gorges Dam and the Forbidden City to high-speed railways, megacities and 5G internet. Early signs of ancient infrastructure lie in fragments of colossal buildings of rammed earth, city walls, dams and channels controlling the water necessary in the lands of the summer monsoon.[4] Rammed earth was such an effective building material that stone was not much used; indeed, it was often difficult to source. Bricks were not a major building material before the Han dynasty (206 BC–AD 220). So that, across China, we do not see many monuments equivalent to the stone temples of ancient Egypt, the high tells of Mesopotamia and Iran or the megaliths of Europe. The history of ancient China shows us that its peoples built their complex society in its own form.

As so much lies below ground, it has been easy to ignore the workforces operating in multiple groups within highly controlled enterprises.⁵ In due course, this adept subdivision of labour not only built cities, but created China's renowned bronzes and terracotta warriors and spread across the world. We see traces of these exceptional creations in the white ceramics in thousands of canteens that imitate Chinese porcelains and the ceremonial dress of European courts made from Chinese silk. Materials were favoured in China that required a distinct combination of large-scale production and specialised skill: jade, silk, lacquer and ceramics. It was a major undertaking to mine jade, rear the grubs and harvest silk from thousands of cocoons, source lacquer sap from forests or procure and mix the best clays. Hundreds of accomplished artisans were then needed to work the jade, turn fragile lengths of silk into weavable thread, treat lacquer and knead clay, collect brushwood and fire kilns. These workforces both inherited manufacturing traditions and developed new techniques, requiring disciplined production lines. And in among these bands of artisans were individuals with the particular prowess needed to create unusual objects, such as the king-*cong* of Liangzhu, the coloured ceramics at Taosi or the bronze man from Sanxingdui. Objects were not simply luxuries but rather signatures of China's culture, essential bonds between the living, their ancestors and the spirits in the millennia before *c.*1250 BC, when the first dynasties began to fully exploit writing.

Much of the early written history has come from the cities and rulers in the middle and lower Yellow River basin. Three dynasties – the Xia (possibly before 1500 BC), the Shang (*c.*1500–1045 BC) and the Zhou (*c.*1045–*c.*750; then 750–256 BC) – dominate what became the central narratives of China. Working with earlier records, the famous Han dynasty (206 BC–AD 220) court archivist, Sima Qian, writing in c.100 BC, described these dynasties in the first extensive history of his world and shaped much of the later writing on them.[6] Major ancient cities of the Shang and Zhou are recognised, but the settlements of the Xia have not so far been identified by archaeologists. The writings, ceramics and bronze vessels all drew attention to the Yellow River basin with a major capital at Anyang and the western capital city of the Zhou, near Xi'an. In the Spring and Autumn period (750–475 BC), the population grew and incursions from the north threatened the local Zhou lords who controlled the agricultural areas in nearly 150 polities. This led to political and military conflict, for which Confucius and other philosophers after him proposed resolutions. Increasingly deadly combat followed in the centuries of the Warring States (475–221 BC), as larger states swallowed up the smaller polities, until the Qin were faced by six states – Zhao, Han, Yan, Wei, Qi and Chu – which they eventually conquered.

This vein of riches, and the eastern area called the Central Plains, divert our eyes away from two other regions, on either side of the middle and lower Yellow River, which were essential to the creation of an overarching empire. To the north, the highlands of the Loess Plateau (plate 5) stretch more than 1,000 kilometres from Lanzhou to the Taihang Mountains (plate 19), with further loess spreading north-east far beyond Beijing.[7] The erosion of the Loess Plateau, with its cliffs and mounds – grey in colour but yellow in the light – gives the Yellow River its dense, opaque hue (plate 17). Rivers have spread this silt over basins and alluvial plains. Loess is an unusually stable geological phenomenon that enabled, even encouraged, people to dig spectacularly deep tombs, just as pozzolan – large accumulations of volcanic ash around and below Naples – was essential to set the concrete of Roman underwater harbour structures. The Loess Plateau was also at one and the same time both the edge of China's agricultural wealth and an intermediary with the steppe, that great reservoir of people, horses and herds. Over the millennia described in this book, interconnected mobile populations built one of the world's greatest routes of communication, across thousands of kilometres of mountains and grasslands, long before the sea lanes opened up. Through the Hexi Corridor in the west, a string of routes across deserts and oases led to Central Asia. From 10,000 BC, no single ruler claimed or controlled the loess lands, and instead they nurtured many different clans and aspiring invaders, occasionally even stockbreeders from the steppe. This pivotal position between two contrasting ways of life made the people of the Loess Plateau perpetual contributors to the history and indeed the expansion of China's material culture. The precariousness of their lifestyles contrasted with the agricultural prosperity further south, along the Yangtze, which supported several independent populations, who in turn built remarkably distinctive societies: we shall discover the jades in the Yangtze delta, bronze forests in the Sichuan basin, mounded tombs on the Huai River and writhing lacquer and bronze decoration south of the Han River. Before China was unified, and the Great Wall became its defensive line, the people of the Loess Plateau and the four basins of the Yangtze, while asserting their local customs, were slowly, step by step, drawn into the cultural practices of the Yellow River.

At first glance, China's trajectory, from agricultural to urban states, resembles the histories with which we may be more familiar in Western Asia, Egypt and the Mediterranean, regions whose development is too often regarded as the benchmark for 'progress' across the world. However, we can see fundamental differences if we step through the mirror and take the grandeur of ancient China on its own terms. What we have often arbitrarily called 'civilisation' – namely settled livelihoods dependent on wheat and barley, domesticated sheep, goats and cattle, metallurgy and writing that spread, almost like a contagion, from Western Asia around the Mediterranean and northwards into Europe as people moved, traded and migrated – could not be taken directly east.[8,9] Although these customs and skills did sometimes move south-east from Iran or Turkmenistan into the Indian subcontinent, vast mountains covered in thick jungle running south from eastern Tibet blocked further movement. The great height of this Tibetan Plateau, about 2,500 kilometres from west to east, made it almost impossible for people and their animals from lower lands to adapt and make the arduous journey across its centre: they had to move along its margins (plate 4). This is the foundation of China's independent civilisation. The summer growing season of rice and millet, the absence of herded animals, materials such as jade, lacquer and silk as status symbols before, and even after, metal was introduced via the steppe, and the relatively late creation of writing are all signs of China's independence. Even the Three Ages, a widely accepted trope for historic development from stone to bronze and then to iron, did not occur or spread in China in a remotely comparable way, nor in fact in other continents such as the Americas and Australia. We therefore cannot expect China's cities or early states to resemble those in Mesopotamia or ancient Egypt. Comparisons of diverse civilisations based on definitions, not just for cities and states, but also for rulership, rituals and beliefs, first identified for Western Asia, are misleading here when applied to regions beyond the Tibetan Plateau. The peoples in China took their architecture, their ambitions and their skills from their own environments.[10]

But China was never completely isolated. While straightforward routes across central Eurasia were barred for millennia by the height of the Plateau, contact, communication and encounter happened in other ways. The tectonic forces generated by the Indian subcontinent that drove up the Tibetan Plateau as it was thrust against Eurasia, elevated gigantic mountain ranges, forming the Hindu Kush in Afghanistan, the Pamirs, the Tianshan across Kazakhstan and China and the high mass of the Altai and the Sayan across north-western China, Mongolia and the Russian Federation (map 1). Mountains, reservoirs of minerals and water, were also important axes on the many paths of travel across Eurasia. The Altai-Sayan Mountains divide the western and the eastern steppe, and the tectonic movements give the eastern steppe additional height. These were the bridges around the Tibetan Plateau.

Geography is the single, outstanding reason why bronze was only widely taken up from the second millennium BC and iron from the eighth century BC (bearing in mind that the Hittites had iron weapons around 1400 BC): these metals were first discovered in Western Asia and the Balkans and became the tools of peoples who, with their animals, materials and technologies, began to travel eastwards over thousands of kilometres and over hundreds, even thousands, of years. Long before these novelties reached China, the peoples of its river valleys had developed their own objects, traditions, social hierarchies and beliefs; metallurgy could only be adopted when it was accommodated into this universe. The immovable Tibetan Plateau ensured that the steppe, the Pamirs, the Tianshan and the Altai-Sayan became the main passages between two early settled worlds. The Belt and Road Initiative, the 7,000-kilometre gas pipeline from Turkmenistan to Shanghai and the Siberian gas pipeline from Russia to northern China, remind us that these routes still persist today.

The extraordinary creativity and diversity of ancient China lie in its great tombs filled with objects for daily and ceremonial life. In all parts of the world, tombs have survived more completely and over much longer periods than palaces, ritual spaces and ordinary dwellings. And with the tombs, in so far as they were not looted, have come highly valued treasures and everyday possessions. These possessions always tell us something, but we need to be alert and sensitive to the range of social and religious meanings they may carry.[11] While the Egyptians built up, the Chinese built down. People on the dry Loess Plateau found that the geology of that region allowed the tombs to stand open as they dug seven, ten or more metres down without the shafts caving in. As the heights of the stone pyramids in ancient Egypt were symbols of power and realisations of belief in an afterlife, so in China the depth of tombs, and the installation of hoards of possessions, proclaimed the status of their owners and the future they expected to enjoy.[12] In no other part of the ancient world was a plethora of such enormous and rich tombs possible across a large region, built repeatedly over millennia. Loess – rather than rocks and stone – was the foundation for these underground palaces, mansions or houses for the afterlife and it fostered the extravagant banqueting vessels, weapons and other objects which tell the stories of their time. These tombs in the loess region and the valleys of the Yellow River, stimulated competition further south along the Yangtze and established a pattern that, unlike anywhere else, endured down to the nineteenth century.

To unearth China's history and to visit its afterlife, this book will explore twelve burials (eleven tombs and one large sacrificial deposit), twelve colourful triumphs of engineering, each from a particular moment in history, from that of a leader in a city 5,000 years ago to the famous tomb of the First Emperor, Qin Shi Huangdi, who in the late third century BC built an empire to rival that of Alexander the Great.[13] Most tombs were for men, but they were also granted to their spouses and concubines, making it possible for their inhabitants to continue to lead their lives fully and materially in the afterlife. These structures below the surface are the conspicuous celebration and vital extension of an individual's life. They were and are their futures. Each tomb – its structure and its objects – tells us who they were, how they lived and what they owned, showing an individual at the height of their power and giving us a glimpse into their family's aspirations for their after-life, framed within an ever-changing and often exuberant social life.

The tombs are found in twelve different regions: from the wet-lands of the Yangtze delta and the tributaries of the Yellow River to the arid landscape of the Loess Plateau and the mountains border-ing the open spaces of the northern steppe. This book is not about death, nor are the tombs uncovered symbols of death. They are what they claim to be: dwellings for the afterlife. These immense dwellings are not symbolic, and in all centuries existed within a wider universe. The tombs show how, over millennia and across broad geographical and cultural regions, the ancient Chinese developed their own cus-toms and beliefs, and then perpetuated them in the afterlife. Like a series of vivid scenes on a stage, the tombs are material evidence of life and reveal a wider history of how a diverse set of people became a relatively unified empire by c.221 BC. Although it has not been fully excavated, the tomb of the First Emperor, with the terracotta warriors arranged to defend him in his afterlife, is one of the most remarkable monuments in the world. Near Beijing are the later and more familiar imperial tombs of the emperors of the Ming (AD 1368–1644) and Qing (AD 1644–1911) dynasties, reflecting a tradition that goes back to long before there are surviving writings to explain what the ancient tomb occupants believed.

The history of ancient China will be told through the objects in the tombs. These objects allow us to enter a society, or societies, that can seem strange and are otherwise difficult to penetrate. Objects defined people's personal and political relationships and, to an extent, the ideology and performance of ritual. We all subconsciously construe the material world around us. The functions of various pans in our kitchens, the dress of individuals we meet and the shining golden mosaics that bring Heaven into Christian churches are all based on a received set of ideas and assumptions, and on specific artistic and technical traditions. Meanings attached to everyday and sacred objects are found in all societies. But only those brought up in or educated by the society can easily read such objects. As children, we are in fact given a language of objects as well as a language of words. From our early years, we in the West use spoons and then learn how to pick up food with knives and forks. These utensils are often still alien to Chinese children, as are the foods we need to cut with them. It is only too easy for those of us from outside China to work within our own language of objects, which is as much a barrier as our inflected alphabetic language when we try to read the multitude of characters in written Chinese. All we can do, as Neil MacGregor reminds us, 'when we venture in our own language into the thought worlds of others, is to acknowledge our inadequacy: we are discussing matters for which we do not have the words'.[14] As with words, objects do not carry a single meaning. It is more helpful to think of motifs, images and materials as holding associations that are built upon functions, customs and beliefs, only truly understood through experience.[15] As we move through the book, we will find that the tombs often hold inventories of weapons, ornaments and vessels belonging to not just one but to two or more languages. These reveal the multiple networks to which individuals belonged and the multiple identities they assumed and celebrated in their lives and afterlives. We have to develop a sensitivity and appreciation of these different languages, even if our interpretation can never be complete.

Many of the tombs are the consequence of binding religious and ritual practices, often summarily called ancestor worship. It is more appropriate, perhaps, to understand these practices as part of an ancestral cult, and this term will be used throughout the book. But even this fails to fully capture the full belief in the power of ancestors, and the ritual requirement to pay them respect by building deep tombs filled with a cornucopia of possessions and accompanied by regular nourishment through daily, weekly or annual rites. These are often named as sacrifices, but are not the kinds recorded in the Old Testament or Greek myths. They are in fact ceremonial banquets, offerings of lavish foods presented in multiple vessels of ceramic, bronze and lacquer, created with supremely sophisticated craftsmanship as some of China's greatest works of art.[16] This is a very different art form to the figural sculpture and painting that realised the Western Asian, Egyptian and Mediterranean religions. The beliefs to which these vessels belonged gave them an elusive quality that demanded the finest work in distinctive materials: 'their ritual functions gave them power only when the vessels were made and used properly by proper persons for proper purposes at proper times in proper places and in proper ways'.[17] Rituals were binding but not constraining, and should be seen as necessary but creative processes participated in willingly in the hope of a desired outcome. The ancestral cult developed and endured until the unification of China and continues in new ways today. It is a central component of China's social architecture, running through families, villages and cities. The rituals and banquets for ancestors were carried out and performed within a family. That family might be extensive, including relations by marriage, but no one outside the family could join or would have wanted to join the rituals of another family, as we learn from brief mentions in a famous text known as *The Zuo Tradition* or *Zuo Zhuan*, dating to the fourth century BC or later, which presents a commentary on an earlier sequence of annals of the eastern state of Lu:

The spirits do not enjoy what is not of their kind, the people do not sacrifice to those who are not of their lineage.[18]

In modern China the cardinal importance of ancestors survives, as do the same limitations on those who can share in the rituals. It thus restricts the most important community to the family, which is the foundation of all beliefs, ethics and ritual practices. As rituals are not shared between other families or neighbours, they do not build the same mixed, inclusive communities that we see in Christianity and Buddhism on religious occasions.[19] The privacy in which the ancestral cult is maintained has meant that the beliefs of most Chinese are little understood by those of us who live in countries that follow or are familiar with the culture, liturgies and public gatherings of so-called 'revealed' religions. Wall paintings and sculptures in Christian churches and Buddhist temples offer scenes of death and extinction. Chinese tombs do not. By contrast, they present and even create life. In any discussion of China, especially ancient China and its tombs, the ancestral cult – a religious belief with elaborate performance and veneration of the ancestors – is a central feature.

The private ancestral cult gave the family a powerful incentive to support and advance all its members. This was inevitable in any community where the welfare of the individual depended on their family. People turned to their ancestors for assistance against the sickness and misfortune that might come their way. Food was at the centre of the cult. There are no early writings before 1300 BC to explain these rituals. Ancient life and afterlife can only be discovered through material history, first in early tombs displaying vessels and then by examining inscriptions carved into bones for divination or cast into vessels in bronze. For later centuries, long bodies of writing set out how rituals for ancestors, spirits and ghosts should be followed. Tombs, filled with the objects of life, arose out of uninterrupted preoccupations with ensuring good outcomes for individuals and their families: wealth presented for the afterlife assured the ancestors of the success of their descendants.

This close bond between all members of a family, living and dead, had two other important long-lasting consequences. The first was that all forms of social hierarchy – in the family, in local organisations and in the state – were established by seniority, modelled on the sequences of the generations. Just as the seniority of the father above his son could not be defied, so all society was ordered in the same way. We also know from the earliest inscriptions that the same lineage structure was not only maintained, but forcibly proclaimed, by the first rulers, binding the state by the same principles as the family.[20] Within such structures all women came below men, but were still important marriage partners. From 1200 BC to the present, this social framework has not been challenged or radically altered by any alternative religious or community structures. The coexistence of distinct communities founded upon religious, aristocratic and commercial groups did not emerge in China, unlike in medieval and Renaissance Europe, where the Church and monasteries, landowners, governments, merchants and craftsmen's guilds jostled for power.[21] Even with the increasing popularity of deities such as the Queen Mother of the West from about the second century BC, or Guan Yu, a deified military leader of the third century AD, and the introduction of Buddhism after the fall of the Han, the ancestral cult and a hierarchical social structure remained ever present.[22] In the fifth and fourth centuries BC, the natural powers, which had been recognised from at least the late Shang dynasty (c.1250 BC) and were closely associated with divination, were also introduced into this ritual system. Later still the sun and the moon, heaven and the earth received offerings in ceremonial vessels at four altars that stand at the cardinal directions around the Forbidden City in Beijing. And while many tourists visit the Temple of Heaven today, they can hardly imagine, and never take part in, the grand annual court ceremonies that spread over the tiered marble platforms.

The China that grew upon these ancient foundations had room for many strong local traditions, which persist throughout our story. These did not displace the central practices of the ancestral cult and in fact many joined it, further emphasising the regional diversity embedded in China's geography.[23] As we examine tombs built over nearly

3,000 years, we see the growing features of a universe that was generated not by gods and spirits but by existing forces of nature, which were *part of*, not outside, that universe. During the fourth century BC, these concepts matured and were reinforced by the binary forces of Yin and Yang, originally the terms for the shady and sunny sides of a mountain, that describe the processes of a constantly changing world, branching out in sets of fours and fives: Four Seasons, Four Directions, Five Colours, Five Sounds and Five Tastes. These correlations, which were entrenched in the Han dynasty, were also linked to ancient searches for positive outcomes. And this search maintained a concern with auspicious signs, leading to some of the most accurate records of eclipses, and later a panoply of images – the lotus, peony and the pine tree.[24]

The ancestral cult lay within a widely shared understanding of the universe, binding the living, those inhabiting the afterlife and future generations in a continuing story of belonging.[25] The world of the living was overseen by ancestors, living in their tombs. Instead of a universe generated by God, as described by the Book of Genesis, or the pantheon of Greek and Roman deities ruling the heavens, the underworld and the ocean, the ancient Chinese universe was ordered by correlations and analogies, placing the powers of the ancestors in parallel with or above those of the living. Analogies have existed in other societies as ways to comprehend deities: for example, the power of God was represented by Him seated on a throne as a king in medieval Europe. And as we follow the gradual spread of the ancestral cult, we will also explore tombs expressing entirely different cosmologies through heterogeneous objects influenced by other cultural forces from the south and the world of the steppe.

Alongside the ancestral cult – interacting with diverse local customs – and a self-generating universe of correlations, a third essential element fostered continuity in ancient China: the remarkable script which we call Chinese characters.[26] These were employed widely by the late Shang dynasty and are still in use today. Based originally on pictographic and diagrammatic forms, Chinese characters each signified a single spoken word and were developed for a spoken language. Over time, the characters came to be pronounced differently by speakers of different dialects, but their semantic meanings only changed slowly. Although people may not have understood each other's speech, they could read and write the same characters, somewhat in the manner that speakers of English, French or Hindi understand written numbers – 1, 2, 3 – in the same way but pronounce them differently. The separation between meaning and pronunciation in Chinese, impossible in alphabetic languages, meant, for example, that edicts from the central government, despatched throughout the early empire of the Song dynasty in the tenth century AD, could be understood by all literate officials, irrespective of their local spoken dialect. Likewise, scholars, whatever their dialect, could read the same texts from earlier times. Apart from inscriptions on early bones used for divination and on bronze vessels used for ceremonial banquets, only a few surviving documents are contemporary with the individuals in the early chapters. The abundant transmitted writings, generally taken as the foundation of early history, were not usually from the same time as the events they described. They were compiled, sometimes centuries later, handed down and edited over hundreds of years. The objects in the tombs provide new ways to interpret the official written history of ancient China, often telling us about what was omitted or forgotten by these early documents.[27]

The tombs illuminate how three fundamental elements – the ancestral cult, a universe of correlations and analogies and a shared script – were taken north and south outside the middle and lower Yellow River basins. The Loess Plateau and the basins along the Yangtze originally fostered ways of life, cultures and beliefs very different from each other *and* from the dynastic rule of the Shang and the Zhou in central China. And even as peoples in these two regions adopted these practices and beliefs, they retained their local customs. Throughout, the Loess Plateau serves as an essential buffer zone between the pastoralists of the steppe and the farmers of the settled river basins. The mixed populations of agriculturalists, herders and, from *c.* 800 BC, stockbreeders who brought horses from the steppe, granted them considerable cultural influence and even political power. These northerners, as we shall see, did not follow the rituals of the ancestral cult. But they were important agents bringing new materials and technologies into central China. Over centuries, communities moving south with their horses to live alongside the states were only accepted if they too adopted the ancestral cult. We can identify those who did from the objects in their tombs, and thereby also those who remained outsiders.

The peoples of the Yangtze basins also had objects and beliefs unlike those of the Yellow River. There was communication but little direct movement by southerners into the centre. However, as the competition between the central states spread from the eighth century BC, many groups and clans from the south and east were attracted to and eventually did join the political power bases and religious framework of the central states. Their adoption of vessels for the offerings to ancestors and of written characters was significant, even while they retained many of their own traditions. Over the last thousand years described in this book, the lords of the Yellow River also expanded both north and south. Despite this growth of an official and organised state, the multitude of landfalls, steep mountains, piled swathes of loess and rich, but ever flat, plains encouraged a medley of cultures. In the tombs we meet a China replete with a bewildering diversity that is still familiar today. Their inhabitants contributed to the long-term development of one of the world's greatest civilisations, and a world view that was formed as much by interactions across a multitude of environments and among local cultures as in the heartlands of the Central Plains.

PART I

Building and Dwelling, 3200–1200 BC

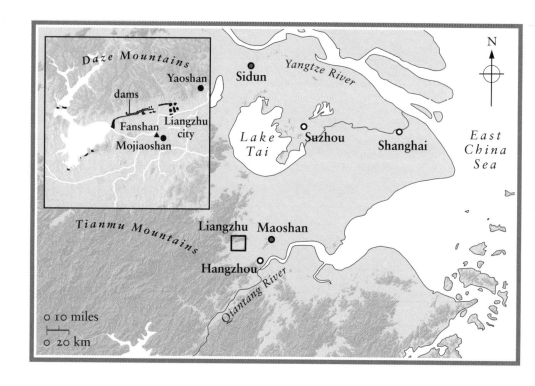

Liangzhu and the Yangtze delta

I.

The Mystery of Jade

If one material represents, even embodies the values and expectations of China, it is jade. This hard, almost translucent stone, cold but with a soft, silky touch, is the most treasured material throughout the whole of China's history – from the jade peaches of the garden of the Queen Mother of the West and the wisdom of sages, often carved in jade among craggy mountains, to the auspiciousness of jade dragons, phoenixes and the *bixie*, a leaping creature that, with its one horn, can protect from ill. For all familiar with jade, it carries an unspoken quality of perpetuity, even immortality. For two millennia, from the time the Han armies moved into today's Xinjiang province in the first century BC, jade has been unquestionably associated with the western mountains of the Kunlun, the northern edge of the Tibetan Plateau.[1] This origin story was reinforced by anecdotes that were eventually recorded in the seventeenth-century encyclopaedia by Song Yingxing, *The Exploitation of the Works of Nature (Tiangong Kaiwu)*, on the manufacture of a range of materials, including woodwork, paper and ceramics. The passage on gems describes jade as being collected from the rivers that descend from the great heights of the Kunlun Mountains along the north of the Tibetan Plateau:

> Crude jades [or jade-containing rocks] are not buried deeply under the earth, but instead are formed in places where precipitous mountain streams rush by. Because of the swiftness of the current, however, miners do not obtain jade from its original deposit. Rather, they wait until the streams are swollen in the summer, when the crude jades will be carried away by the current and can be gathered from the river, perhaps 100 or even 200 or 300 *li* from their original

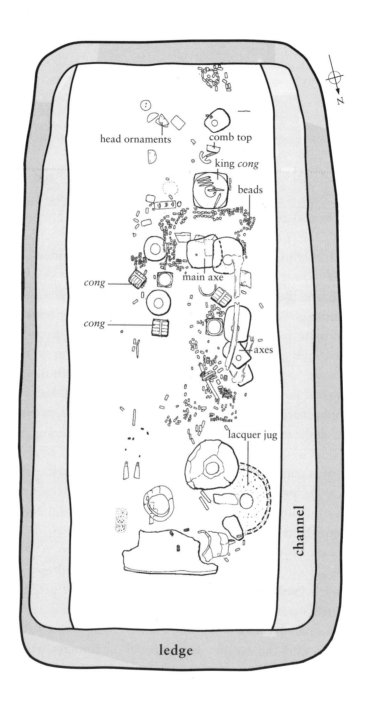

head ornaments

comb top

king *cong*

beads

cong

cong

main axe

axes

lacquer jug

channel

ledge

The tomb at Fanshan, Liangzhu. Length 3.1 m, width 1.65 m, depth 1.1 m.

deposits. Since jade is formed by the shining essence of moonlight, those who gather it along the river banks often keep watch there under the autumn moon. When an especially brilliant light is spied, there crude jades are sure to be found. After travelling together with the current [for a considerable distance], the jade-containing rocks are still mixed up with ordinary rocks in the shallow water and must be picked up, examined and identified.[2]

If this is the case, why turn to the small town of Liangzhu, near the great city of Hangzhou on the Qiantang River? Although some mountains embrace the scenery, these are not the great peaks of the Kunlun. Moreover, Liangzhu is on a huge delta, not where valuable rocks are usually discovered.

The Yangtze River is only surpassed in length by the Nile and the Amazon. It rises on the Tibetan Plateau and travels more than 6,000 kilometres to the sea at Shanghai. As the East China Sea rose and advanced inland at the end of the last Ice Age, some 15,000 years ago, the river laid deposits of silt at its mouth, creating a delta. Nanjing, for a time the capital of the Ming dynasty in the fourteenth century AD, stands on the southern bank. Other famous cities, most especially Suzhou, a jewel of exquisite gardens, lie near Lake Tai at the centre of this triangular spit of lowland the size of Wales.

The Yangtze delta is home to more than 140 million people in the densest concentration of towns, cities and megacities in the world. It is a region of great agricultural, industrial and international trade, extending south as far as Hangzhou, today a landmark for its prosperity and for being the home of the technological giant, Alibaba. The shimmering Lake Tai, the mists and the intense humidity are traces of a different and ancient world. The delta is the hinterland of one of China's most outstanding ancient cities, named after Liangzhu. It dominated for over 1,000 years, from about 3300 to 2200 BC, and is set in a curved basin, with some higher land to the east protecting it from surges along the Qiantang River; the Tianmu range guards it to the north-west. Despite the growing influence of the industries at Hangzhou, Liangzhu is still remote. A bus is the only way to travel into the early history of jades. In the late 1980s, fields of rice stretched over the whole basin. Now a town flourishes, a sign of China's recent prosperity. The basin and all the land to the north was once covered by sea.[3] After the sediment deposits from the Yangtze and Qiantang, much was covered in brackish water. In due course it became a freshwater marsh. As the waters retreated in the fourth millennium BC, people began to make a living here. Predecessors of the Liangzhu people, named by archaeologists as the Songze, gradually moved south across the whole region from c.4000 BC onwards.[4]

To celebrate Liangzhu, an archaeological park – freshly planted with trees – was opened in 2019. If we are to understand how jade came to dominate Chinese culture, we need to follow the intriguing discs, tubes and beads that have cropped up in the area since 1936 – signs of a city where jade had been at the centre of the lives, the deaths and the beliefs of its leaders. The first major tombs were discovered in the 1980s, but it was still hard to envisage a vast city as no buildings have survived above ground. Everything that remains is below the surface of mounds covered in vegetation. The immense walls of the city and numerous water channels were first fully excavated in 2006–7;[5] only then did scholars begin to recognise the remarkable traces of a whole vanished society, supported by rice agriculture.[6] In China walls are a sign of urbanism; in fact the Chinese character for wall is also used for a city. Liangzhu not only had huge walls, but was the central settlement across the delta. We do not know who lived there, nor how the population was organised, but the success of the society can be measured in the scale of its water management, which marks the landscape, its huge harvests of rice and its sophisticated jades. These were not the achievements of a series of small villages. Liangzhu must have been the seat of power, a great city, even if it does not resemble the ancient cities of Mesopotamia. More has been discovered since 2013, as archaeologists moved into the mountains and across the flood-plains.[7] These campaigns revolutionised our understanding of the history of ancient China, and that of the wider world. In 2019, the water management around Liangzhu, as well as the city itself, became a World Heritage Site.[8]

Along with the archaeological park, an intensely angular museum offers an introduction to this underground city. It is a series of low, brilliantly white blocks of windowless galleries. Designed by the British architect David Chipperfield, it is faced entirely with travertine stone from Iran. The strength of the stone is awe-inspiring. The entrance is through a long glass façade. Inside, a wide atrium is open to the sky. Great white discs, with central holes, appear to float like waterlilies on a dark pool, echoing ancient jades. On display are similar discs, much smaller of course, and axes so smooth and beautifully curved they hardly look like weapons. And most strange of all are jades of varying heights, square in section with a central, circular hollow column, a kind of tube, with traces of eyes at their corners. Eyes appear again on a rectangular plaque from one of several cemeteries at Liangzhu; it rises to a central point along the upper edge with two outward-sloping sides and has three holes along the bottom to attach another part of what was an ancient comb.[9] Its creamy surface is marked with sloping bands and is wonderfully soft to the touch. These dark grey-green bands almost hide the engraving cut into the surface. Jades were clearly more than trinkets to the people who lived at Liangzhu until *c.*2200 BC. And two pairs of eyes, small round circles near the top and extended ovals with circular pupils lower down, are on many Liangzhu jades, as are the two bird-like creatures in the corners. But what is jade?

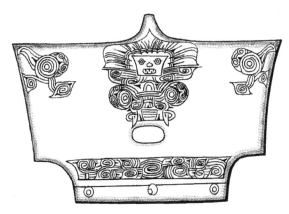

The head of a jade comb, just 5.8 cm high and 7.7 cm wide.

The answer is not at all obvious. In English, the term jade is used for a variety of green, grey, white or darkly clouded minerals, of which the most significant is nephrite. Others include forms of serpentine, and another stone called bowenite. Similarly, in Chinese a single word, *yu*, is used for several minerals. Rarity is the hallmark of jade. For the Chinese the most highly prized *yu* is also nephrite, and the majority of the Liangzhu jades are of this mineral.[10] Nephrite can be found in many cloudy colours, from pure white to a green so dark that it is almost black. Regardless of colour, nephrite is exceptionally difficult to work: because it is formed under great pressure and heat over ancient geological time, its tiny, needle-shaped crystals become interlocked and matted. This means it does not fracture into its crystals as, for example, diamonds or emeralds do, nor can it be cut by metal. As early inhabitants of Liangzhu explored the nearby mountains and made contact with the world around them, they probably found a good source of jade. We do not know its location – an essential part of why the discovery of so many jades on a delta remains a mystery.

Nephrite is usually mined from seams often fractured among other minerals and rocks. Someone must have discovered rocks with translucent veins and attempted to extract them, which is not an easy task. First, nephrite had to be removed from the surrounding rock with stone tools (the only ones available), although some rocks may have been split with heat to extract the jade. Then bigger sections were cut into smaller slabs and chunks; it had to be ground with a brittle sand, such as corundum, applied with a tool, such as bamboo, in which the corundum can easily be embedded.[11] This combination creates an ancient form of what we recognise today as sandpaper.[12] Finished jade feels smooth to the touch because it has been repeatedly polished: a seductive, tactile quality that has always attracted owners to wear small ornaments against their skin. While jade is hard and cold, silk is soft and warm. The feeling of both is almost impossible to describe, yet inherent to the value of many objects in China. The same silkiness is found in lacquer, in Song-period ceramics, whose grey-green glazes reproduce jade, and even in later Ming furniture. One result of cutting blocks of jade in this way was constant flat surfaces that could be modified and polished. When cutting the stone into pieces, many offcuts were inevitable, which could then be skilfully shaped to make objects such as the comb head we have just seen, and small decorative pieces and beads. We do not know how the fine lines depicting the eyes of a man and the strange creature were incised into this hard mineral; small fragments of a silica, rather like flint (widely distributed across Europe), may have been used.[13] Liangzhu must have had unusually plentiful sources, as there was enough nephrite to create broad axes, discs and numerous tubes.

Nephrite does not disintegrate and disappear over time. When buried, traces of chemicals in the surrounding soils and humidity sometimes turn it a chalky white, but it often does not change much at all. Permanence is one of its defining qualities. The scarcity of nephrite ensured that, once it had been worked, only the highest-ranking members in early societies could own it. Its rarity raises a profound question. How did it become so embedded in Chinese culture, so widely accepted as part of its social and ritual landscape? Jade and the many ancient shapes into which it was worked here at Liangzhu are completely unfamiliar to everyone outside China. Even when we hold a piece of jade, the many threads woven into its history lie far outside our grasp. It is our first meeting with a material and its forms that belong to an unknown cultural language.

In fact, even for Chinese scholars, the low-lying, waterlogged area around Liangzhu looked like the last place where such an abundance of ancient jades would be found. Throughout written history, from at least about 1000 BC, jade had been mentioned in inscriptions on bronze ritual vessels and in transmitted documents. People acquired ancient jades and made many copies, not knowing anything about Liangzhu. In the following centuries, especially after the fifth century BC, these antique pieces were given names. The huge discs copied in the atrium at the museum had traditionally been given the name of *bi*. The tube with a square cross-section and a central vertical hole was given the name *cong*. These names cannot have been used at Liangzhu; their owners would have had their own names, in their own language. As the people of this ancient city are not likely to have developed writing, we, tantalisingly, have no way to discover what these could have been. The terms *bi* and *cong* became standard in the Warring States period of the fifth to third centuries BC.[14] During a time of almost continuous conflict, ritual specialists and scholars attempted to retrieve and to follow the ritual practices of their predecessors, the kings of the early Zhou dynasty (*c.*1045–750 BC), regarding them as models of righteous, upright rule. Specialists strung together a list of names for jades and then added what they believed they signified. A summary of these, including the *cong*, was set out in a famous ritual text, the *Rites of Zhou* (*Zhou Li*), collected and compiled in the third to second centuries BC:

> Jade is used to make six ritual implements for ceremonies to Heaven, Earth, and the four directions.
>> The blue *bi* [disc] for offering rituals to Heaven,
>> The yellow *cong* [tube or cylinder] for offering rituals to the Earth,
>> The green *gui* [sceptre] for offering ritual to the East,
>> The red *zhang* [sceptre] for offering ritual to the South,
>> The white *hu* [tiger-shaped pendant] for offering to the West,
>> The black *huang* [arc-shaped pendant] for offering to the North.[15]

All of these (with the exception of the *hu*) were much older than the Zhou dynasty. The *cong* probably predated the Zhou by 2,000 years. Before jades began to be excavated at Liangzhu, the origins of their shapes, given names by much later ritual specialists, were just not known. Associating jades with the Zhou dynasty gave them prestige in a culture that valued writing and its history, but this was totally misleading. Ancient jade forms, profoundly meaningful for those on the southern edge of the Yangtze delta, who built an enormous city surrounded by water channels and rivers, had been taken over and put into someone else's story. This is a very human activity, and throughout history there is a persistent tendency to identify sources of, or attribute meanings to, objects. People in a completely different urban society living more than 2,000 years later in the middle and lower Yellow River basin – with different types of burial, possessions, aspirations and beliefs – could not have had any knowledge of Liangzhu. These Zhou societies had developed a universe of correlations, which over time became part of a later and much wider philosophical endeavour, formalised in the Han dynasty. And then this list was memorised and guided subsequent owners, scholars and jade traders. Attributes of the universe were organised into tables, with the opposing forces of Yin and Yang, the Five Phases of wood, fire, earth, metal and water, and the Five Directions – North, East, South, West and Centre – connected with the five colours of black, green, red, white and yellow. For example, *Yang* signified brightness, heat, dryness, hardness, activity, masculinity, Heaven, sun, south, roundness and odd numbers, and *Yin* darkness, cold, wetness, softness, quiescence, completeness, femininity, Earth, moon and north, squareness and even numbers. The square section of the *cong* appeared, misleadingly, to offer a way to understand the world as square beneath the *bi*, the circular heaven above.[16] The *cong* and other jade forms of the Liangzhu people had been reappropriated and become embedded in a different society. This transformation has added to the mystery of jade. Even though we are now able to recognise two unconnected systems of belief, it remains difficult to truly appreciate what we are looking at. The roles of the jades have become blurred, and it is very hard to bring their original meanings back into focus.

Discoveries at Liangzhu took ancient China's jades back further by several millennia to long before the Zhou, and indeed to before the rise of dynasties in the Yellow River basin. The jades showed that the area between the Yangtze River and Hangzhou housed a particular group of people with skills in working jade and beliefs associated with this precious stone. The real turning point was an excavation in 1986, when a cemetery of eleven tombs at Fanshan was revealed in the Liangzhu basin.[17]

One of the most interesting tombs is over three metres in length, about one metre in depth and has two channels along its length on either side of the central section. These are sometimes identified as the foot of a wooden chamber, within which was a smaller coffin. More distinct traces of wood have been found at other sites of the same period. Given the acidity of the soil, very little remains of the skeleton of the male occupant. Clothes or items made of textile or other organic materials, which may have been with him, have not survived either. Looking down into the tomb, we can see that jades and stone axes were spread over the length, obviously to cover his body. He must have had an intense preoccupation with jade in death – 647 jades are listed in the excavation report. They were clearly of very high value and will lead us further into jade's history. Although elegant ceramics have been found at many other Liangzhu sites, there were only four in this tomb at Fanshan, alongside a red lacquer jug inlaid with small jade fragments. The red colour was derived from the mineral cinnabar. A long loop of jade beads would have encircled his neck or shoulders; others hung much lower down. Above the man's head were several finely carved jade plaques, a form of insignia attached to a hat or a band worn around his head. Positioned where his chest would have been was a jade axe, with several stone axes on his left side. A massive, square block of jade, of the type named today as a *cong*, was near his left shoulder. So remarkable is the size of this piece and its multiple engravings that it is sometimes called the 'king-*cong*'. Numerous miniature jades – plaques, long spiky pendants, beads and ornaments that could be strung together – were also the signatures of a powerful man. A different set of ornaments are thought to have been for a woman. We know nothing about the relative status of women at Liangzhu. But if some of the tombs were for them, then they too had a high standing. Buried with such a striking display in jade, the man and his peers at Fanshan were certainly among the leaders of the city.

The man's jades are in three categories: tools and weapons, such as axes; objects of personal adornment attached to his clothes or hung around his body, which displayed and reaffirmed his identity; and *cong* tubes, which like *bi* discs served no obvious function, but almost certainly were of ritual significance.[18] The jade axe is the centrepiece. It is of great elegance and beauty, not made to cut down

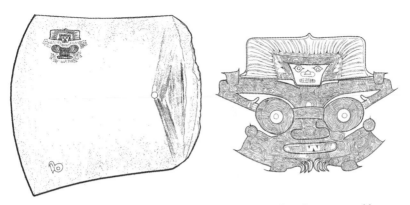

The jade axe, length 17.9 cm, width 14.4 cm, engraved with a man and beast.

a tree or to behead an enemy. Its sheen and careful finishing are for a weapon of might, not of war. For a jade it is substantial, with a curved cutting edge and swelling surfaces on the two sides showing off the efforts of sophisticated craftsmen with extensive experience in the jade tradition. At Liangzhu, on easily flooded land, which required the management of great populations to build its huge walls, this axe must have served as an emblem of authority. A small hole near one edge allowed it to be tied to a wooden staff that carried attractive jade ornaments top and bottom. On both sides, in the upper corner, is another sign of the axe's power. A sharply angular face with tiny circles for eyes peers out of an enigmatic, almost human figure. A narrow mouth shows clenched teeth. The small face is overwhelmed by a feather headdress, rising to a point at the centre. The other face below, also in relief, has two oval eyes with circular pupils, surrounded by a dense sunken pattern which covers the bridge above the nose. This combination of relief and sunken design suggests that the two beings are emerging from within the jade itself. In the lower corner, on both sides, one eye of the monster has been turned into a bird.[19] We do not know who or what these entangled figures and the two pairs of eyes, one for a human figure and one for a more animalistic monster, portray. But the intensity of their stare and their repetition on many jades underline the fundamental role that they played in the Liangzhu universe.[20]

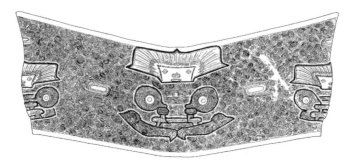

The engravings on the sides of a jade fitting for a staff,
drawn and presented together, height 5.72 cm, length 8.4 cm.
The edges repeat the embroilment of the man and beast.

The eyes appear again on a band wrapped around a small, semi-rectangular jade. Their force is yet more intense. This piece of jade, less than six centimetres in height, has a slot on the underside and, like the axe, may have been fitted to a wooden staff. It is covered in spirals and criss-crossing bundles of lines. Every inch is filled with movement. On the two outer edges are the man with his headdress and the fanged monster with its bent legs and claws. The engraved figures had to be stretched around the wide edges and were transformed by the curved surface. The dense lines surrounding the two figures suggest that they are hidden beings who only appear occasionally. Perhaps these are mists of another realm, or the clouds of visions and dreams. What this fantastical creation signified we do not know, but its decoration is the measure of its effectiveness in joining its owner with a mythical past or the powerful spirits of the universe, a bridge to an unseen world. This is the only example of such a piece found to date. The owner must have been celebrated for possessing so special an object. That it could only be seen from up close further emphasises its value.

Small ornaments attached to a person define their age, gender and role in society. People across the world have used metal crowns for leaders, chains and medals for office, rings for marriage and necklaces and brooches to signify wealth or endow status. In the West such ornaments are usually in shining gold or silver, decorated with sparkling cut gems. In China the tone and style of jade ornaments are completely other. The many thousands of years for which it has been mined and carefully worked have given jade a supreme status. Such was the continuity that during the Ming dynasty men wore belts with jade plaques and carried, as sceptres, tablets based on the shapes of ancient jades, and women wore jade flowers in their hair.[21] If we are to appreciate the power of the man buried at Fanshan with his magnificent *cong*, we must look next at what is known of the remains of the ancient city; the world in which he lived.

Liangzhu is one of the very largest early walled settlements, that is, a city, in ancient China. With its inner area of three square kilometres and an outer one of some eight square kilometres, the excavators of Liangzhu have compared its estimated population size with Uruk in southern Mesopotamia (*c*.3300 BC) and Harappa in the Indus Valley (*c*.2500–1900 BC).[22] Yet it is not its size that awards Liangzhu its prime place in the history of China, but the achievements of its people in managing their landscape and their creation of a distinctive identity and cosmology. When evaluating early cities, historians have often turned to those in Mesopotamia and Egypt, where wheat and barley fed populations. Until recently, the lives and the sophistication of societies built upon rice-farming have been little considered. Domestication of this native grain was probably achieved between 6000 and 5000 BC.[23] And rice cultivation was at the heart of Liangzhu's success. It would have been difficult to create a settled life in south-eastern China without rice. The low-lying lands brought wealth but also hazardous sea surges and flooding rivers.

Remains of flooded rice fields fed by channels of water from rivers and ponds have been found outside the centre of Liangzhu, at Maoshan.[24] Complex irrigation systems, which must have needed constant manipulation and repair, render rice one of the most labour-intensive of all domesticated grains regulated by the seasons.[25] From May to June the Pacific Monsoon sweeps across the whole of southern China, which remains humid throughout July and August. Rice must be sown, and the sprouting seedlings planted as the rains arrive.

Winter meant fewer farming demands, so people turned to building the irrigation channels needed to provide water and drainage. In this tough environment, large-scale infrastructure would have taken a long time to develop. Every stage required many groups to fetch almost unfathomable quantities of earth to create channels and dams. And as control of the water was essential to rice-farming, its management required careful planning.

This was a world in which small bands of people were coordinated to realise an important project. Today, as visitors walk along the planked paths over marshy land and numerous small tributaries, it is no surprise to learn that Liangzhu had canals inside and outside its walls – fifty-one small canals within the ancient city and eight water gates. Remains of wooden posts suggesting docks for boats and traces of what may have been canoes and paddles have also been discovered.[26] Walls of rammed earth with foundations of rocks, sometimes as wide as 120 metres, enclosed the central area. Controlling the water in and around the city was not enough. Before the city reached its present form, levees and dams had been constructed across much of the basin. This is an indelible imprint of human activity, and also a clear sign of the skill of the leaders at Liangzhu in managing giant projects.

Sections of the enormous line of banks and levees can still be identified at the foot of the Tianmu Mountains. They protected the city from precipitous flows of water coming off the steep slopes at the height of the monsoon. Before they used their labour force to build city walls, the leaders at Liangzhu deployed their population to build not just the lower levees, but also additional defences deeper in the mountains. Several high dams held back canals, restricting the flow of water down on to lower land. It has been estimated that perhaps 3,000 people worked for over eight years to set up the system.[27] It may have taken much longer, and there were probably earlier attempts. The dams were made of ancient sandbags of local mud wrapped in reeds and grasses. These have intrigued archaeologists as they show a highly advanced understanding of engineering: the dams – between 20 and 50 metres in length and up to 7 metres in height – were not experimental. Many smaller dams had been made before the more ambitious constructions. After all, if they failed, they would catastrophically flood the land below.[28] Lower-level dams held back lakes of fresh-water for agriculture. As small sea surges forced brackish water into the channels that were vital to the management of rice fields, back-up sources of good rain and river water were valued by the community. We know that the organisation of water for the rice fields produced huge quantities to feed the population. A great store of charred rice, weighing more than 13,000 kilos, was found at the centre of the city, probably from granaries destroyed by fire.[29] There were no rice fields within the city or nearby. Instead, this supply was commanded by leaders able to demand and extract rice from more distant agricultural lands.

Liangzhu certainly grew over the 1,000 years of its existence. Its population inevitably had to create higher areas on which to live. Mounds were found around the city, and people may have occupied them and parts of the walls.[30] Detailed surveys and excavations have brought to light additional areas fenced with sandbags.[31] The sandbags and rice fields demanded a continuous input of human labour to shift the earth and transform the landscape. Other contemporary cities in various regions across the Yellow River basin, at Taosi in the north and in present-day Shandong province, must also have relied on subdivided labour forces to build rammed-earth walls and platforms.[32] Liangzhu is one of the original examples of the Chinese architectural tradition of wide earthen platforms supporting lighter wooden columned buildings. We still see this today in the Forbidden City. There, the earthen platforms are hidden by elaborate stone facings. This decoration makes us immediately realise how much we have lost of ancient Chinese cities. Not only are we missing the wood and bamboo that formed the structures of the halls and houses; their roofs of rush and reeds are also gone, and we can no longer see the texture and carving of building decorations. What we have is telling. But it must always remind us of what has vanished.

Mojiaoshan, a platform of between 10 and 15 metres in height on a small hill at the centre of Liangzhu, must have supported buildings with wooden columns. Excavators estimate that some 2,280,000 cubic metres of earth were moved to create it and compare it with the transfer of the 2,500,000 cubic metres of stone to build the Khufu Pyramid in Egypt some 300 years later in *c*.2500 BC.[33] The rectangular area, 630 by 450 metres (about 74 acres), held further platform foundations, possibly for palaces, ritual temples or administrative centres. Mojiaoshan is indicative of the centralised leadership of this great city. The Fanshan cemetery, on its own platform, is just north-west of Mojiaoshan. When we reflect upon the achievements of Liangzhu, we see that the people buried at Fanshan must have been crucial to those efforts, being laid to rest at the centre of the city and at an elevation that corresponded to their commanding position at the top of society – a position also expressed by the jades they took with them to the afterlife.

But the size and infrastructure of Liangzhu do not totally explain the presence of extraordinary jades. High levels of organisation and skilful management of water would not have necessarily led to the working of fine jades with mysterious faces. Nor can jade production have happened all at once.[34] Very few societies have made use of jade – other notable examples include the Olmec and the Maya in Central America and the Maori in New Zealand, but none on the scale nor with the antiquity we find in China. By the time that the man was buried at Fanshan, jade had been known for at least 4,000 years. For jade to have been widely used, the sources of the material, the ways of working it and, most importantly, the *notion* that these stones were desirable had to have developed and spread. This was not a single idea, invented in a single place.

While there is no direct source of its spiritual qualities, jade has a long history among multiple peoples along China's eastern seaboard, from the far north near the Amur River down to the Yangtze delta and on further south. Joined by the sea and many waterways, extensive lines of communication had been developed. The translucent stones were venerated by people living during the last Ice Age, the Late Palaeolithic (30,000–10,000 BC), who also used mammoth ivory and animal teeth for ornaments.[35] These materials were scattered across forests and tundra and along immense frozen rivers in today's Siberia, bordering Heilongjiang province. The earliest nephrite in the territory of present-day China has been found at an ancient burial ground just south of the Amur, in a cemetery of small stone mounds holding jade ornaments, dating from approximately 7200–6200 BC.[36] We do not know the histories of these people but we have a much fuller picture of how jade was taken up further south, in the areas north-east of Beijing in Inner Mongolia and Liaoning from the seventh millennium BC. Here too jade appeared as personal ornaments, especially for the ear, as slit rings. These, together with thin square plaques with rounded corners and a central hole, were very popular and repeatedly made and copied down the eastern seaboard among many small societies across a huge area. We find the peak of this second stage of jade-working in graves of the Hongshan culture, outlined with stones and embedded in spreading stone mounds, at a site called Niuheliang, built around 3500 BC. These turned a natural landscape of rolling hills into one filled with monuments for people with particular beliefs and rituals.[37] The dead were given jades as they entered the afterlife.[38] Here, as at Liangzhu, the presence of jade expressed beliefs in the powers of the material to join the worlds of the living and of the afterlife.

Among the several jades buried by the Hongshan people, a heavy coiled creature is the most important. It is often of a bright, translucent green stone (plate 22). This thick circle, about 10 centimetres high, with a horizontal slit across one side, is a magnified version of the earlier jade ear ornaments. The surfaces are smoothly curved, and above the slit is the face of a creature with prominent, rounded ears. Some see this as the head of a pig, the primary animal domesticated in ancient China after the dog. But below the ears are two wide eyes, one on either side of the ring. These staring eyes are a far cry from the intricacy of the Liangzhu faces. This is a parallel, but very different, choice of an unrecognisable creature, a being beyond daily life, whose form and material probably offered authority to their owners. To create it the jade craftsmen exploited a rare material which they could bring to life with a glowing surface.

Faces will appear again and again in our story. And we must never expect these faces to have borne the same meanings across time and place. Some objects were transported over long distances by exchange or picked up as chance finds by travellers; objects do not, and often cannot, take their original meanings with them. For that to happen their makers and owners have to travel too, and successfully communicate their beliefs. We in the West put Chinese vases decorated with bats on our tables and mantelpieces, but we do not know that, for the Chinese bats bring prosperity. Twisted pine trees, on the other hand, celebrate wisdom and endurance in old age. These porcelain motifs have travelled, but the significance they hold for those who made and owned them has not. Despite different meanings and styles of production, the Hongshan jades confirm that, in eastern China, as at Liangzhu, elites used jade to express their powers, and to be in close communion with the invisible.

Although the Hongshan people lived more than 500 years before Liangzhu grew to its full size, we find traces of contact over more than 3,000 kilometres along the eastern seaboard and by sea. The Songze, predecessors of Liangzhu in the Yangtze delta, produced jade carvings resembling turtle shells, a human figure with raised arms, and the coiled 'pig dragon', all of which had prototypes in Niuheliang.[39] Bangles and rings may have travelled to the Songze. Some were damaged, some were recut. This abundance of jade over 1,000 years built what could be called a Jade Corridor.[40] The Liangzhu people created jades echoing distant memories of the Hongshan dragon, with similar small coiled dragons with prominent eyes.[41] The spread of rings and bangles drew these faces into the Liangzhu repertoire, but two major changes were made, in effect reinterpreting the creature. The heads were turned 90 degrees and framed within a rectangle. This was the first important step towards the monster faces on the *cong*. Workers had at the same time found that silica, or another stone, could cut into nephrite, and now made these ancient motifs using a new technique. This second step transformed the rounded lines on the Hongshan dragon into the dynamic figures engraved into Liangzhu jades. While the faces within the raised rectangles on rings or bangles retained the eyes, nose and mouth in relief, the jade workers

A small coiled dragon from Liangzhu.

now incised numerous fine lines to provide a dense patterned background.[42] The human-like figure was also added, with its arms and the bent clawed legs of the monster carved at a lower level into the surfaces. These features were a sign that the relief and the flatter designs have different sources. The jade workers had thus brought into being an original motif with new meanings and purposes. As we follow those steps taken over many centuries, the transformation of

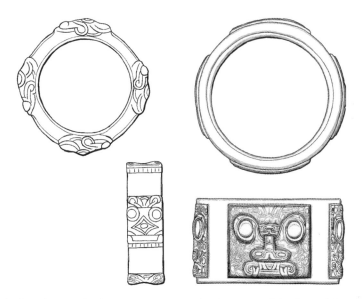

The bangle (*top left*), diameter 8.2 cm, is a development of the face of the coiled creature in plate 22. The faces have then been rotated and elaborated, highlighting a surge in craftsmanship, in the bangle (*top right*), diameter 7.95 cm.

the original creature as it interacted with local ideas, we are tracing an ancient journey with parallels in many societies, including our own.

It is not surprising that we do not know who worked the nephrite to make the *bi*, *cong* and ornaments carrying these strange faces, nor what their meanings were. There are no records, neither oral nor written down. Some archaeologists have suggested that the owners of the fine jades were the craftsmen themselves, which gave them a unique cultural status among the population as a whole, the authority to command and demand. But as many other craftsmen were employed, for example for ceramics and lacquer, and probably also for textile-weaving, it is likely that all enjoyed a favourable social standing. Something yet more unfathomable today must have been behind the possession of jade in life and the afterlife.

The king-*cong* lay to the left of the head and shoulder of the man in the tomb at Fanshan. This was a significant, even major statement about his identity and role in society. At first sight, the *cong* is simply a square block (plate 1). If we could pick it up, we would suddenly find that it is very heavy, weighing more than six kilos – a sign of high value for a rare material. A wheel or a drill, and perhaps pieces of hollow bamboo with corundum, were used to make a central hole through the *cong*, technically a forerunner of a diamond-tipped drill used today. As for all Liangzhu jades, the hole was worked from the two ends, forming a tiny step in the middle where the drilling from both directions did not meet precisely.[43] We can find the step by feeling inside with our fingers.[44] Using a wheel, the top and bottom of the man's *cong* were shaped as discs, with a few millimetres cut away at the corners to leave a lower surface. These circular layers, part of the *cong* itself, have a hole at the centre and therefore look almost like the discs today known as *bi*. However, they were not, at this stage, arbitrarily paired with the *cong*; their meanings and purposes were clearly beyond the reach of the Zhou literati. There are only a few insignificant *bi* in the tomb with this *cong*. Another tomb in the Fanshan cemetery has forty-three *bi*, many of which still show signs of the rotating cutting wheel, but no *cong* as impressive as that next to the man's shoulder. The *cong* and *bi* jades have no obvious practical function and must have had two different ritual attributes within the customs of Liangzhu as part, along with the other jades, of a structured system of beliefs about the universe. If they are a mystery for us, that is because they expressed beliefs so personal and profoundly important to their owners that they are beyond our comprehension. If we step into a shrine or a temple of a religion with which we are unfamiliar, we cannot interpret what we see. The same is true here. By opening the tomb and seeing the jades we have stepped into a universe far more remote than the correlative system of colours and directions of the later ritual texts.

We must also look at the four sides of the king-*cong*, each divided into three vertical sections. In the slightly sunken central section are two examples of the human figures with the feathered headdress, gripping the eyes of the creature below, complete with its fangs and claws. A definitive interpretation of what these figures would have meant to the owner is impossible.[45] However, this sinuous engraving makes this *cong* one of the most important ritual jades ever found. Almost all other *cong* do not display the full, let alone repeated, engravings of two figures combined with abbreviations of eyes at the four corners. Eyes appear on many other *cong*, but this motif was first seen at Liangzhu. The figures may have also been displayed on other materials – ceramics, lacquer and clothes, for example – now lost.[46]

If we were able to run our fingers over one side of the *cong*, we would find that while the central vertical section is completely flat, the two sides of each corner have been cut down lightly, creating a wide angle and giving them gently curved surfaces which were certainly not made by chance. These curved sides form a broad rectangle across each corner, giving the eyes of the man and beast joined across the corners a frame and presenting the faces in three dimensions. The man and the monster are emerging from the jade, pressing towards us, yet remaining distant and aloof. The patrons of the jades and their workers wanted an almost square cross-section, convenient to carve and impressive to look at. At the same time they used the curved corners to recreate the two figures, the man and the beast. They are not simply representations: they are part of the jade and exist within

The king-*cong*, height 8.9 cm, width 17.6 cm, weight 6.5 kg.

it. And this effect would have given the owner of the *cong* access to another part of his world. Jade implements were a way to communicate with beings outside and beyond the everyday, yet at the same time were always present within it. Jade, and the manner in which it had been worked, was the instrument. These early jade workers perceived power within the stone. This was the central value of jade for the ancient city of Liangzhu and even for later Chinese societies. The burial of this *cong*, extraordinary even in its own time, meant that the jade would continue to be there with its owner after death. To remove from life such a magnificent carving is undeniable evidence that it, and the multitude of small jades with the same motifs, were as important in the afterlife as in life. The *cong* is one of the most prominent landmarks of the creative eastern Jade Corridor. It is also the ancestor of other, later *cong* discovered elsewhere and one of only a few that we can still see and hold. Without the exceptional imagery on this particular *cong*, we would not recognise the presence of similar, but simplified, faces on other jades.

The *cong* retrieved today from cemeteries around Lake Tai are of a later and more familiar form, also displayed in many museums. The square section is emphasised, the curved corners lost. The detail of the faces is reduced. Often only the small eyes of the human-like figure remain, below narrow raised bands. As usual a central column is hollow. These *cong* come in different proportions, some short, some tall. And many are of a brown or striated green stone, a variant of serpentine. Their different shapes and stones cloud the situation even more. If the *cong* at Fanshan, a pinnacle of craftsmanship, belongs to an early stage, who owned these much more standard pieces? Are they products of a growing society in which size mattered more than detail? They are the footprints of a shared belief system travelling between people who had mastered a specialised craft and technology, and who required a rare material. As such *cong* are much more numerous than the precious piece belonging to the man at Fanshan, it is not surprising that later scholars and connoisseurs were overwhelmed by the stolid, squarer, often darker jades. They just accepted the *cong* that they had found and placed them in their different correlated universe; they did not look back and imagine more distant origins. These relatively simplified versions of the *cong* spread and were found later in other parts of China.[47] When we see the broad and heavy *cong* in the man's tomb at Fanshan, with its exquisitely carved motifs, we are being let in on a secret, but a secret barely whispered.

It was the loss of the walls and dams of Liangzhu that left later generations without information with which to untangle the story of its jades. How did the city disappear? And how did some jades survive to be copied, adapted, preserved and interpreted in different contexts? These questions are not often asked, but are key to the legacy of the *cong* and of other jades. We now know that major environmental challenges disturbed Liangzhu.[48] The landfall in this region was dangerously low. It had been covered by the sea in its more remote history and rainfall was sometimes very heavy. After a dry spell in the latter half of Liangzhu's ascendency, two long but separate periods of rainfall caused catastrophic flooding. At first the fallout may have taken effect slowly; there seem to have been several phases of flooding across the whole Yangtze delta, precipitating rising sea levels. Then

the city vanished. Traces of these problems are only visible archae-
ologically. Dense, thick sediments of barren earth covered layers of
habitation.[49] In some areas, small seashells have been found near or in
the rice fields, a further sign of incursions of the sea.[50] If this destruction happened gradually at first, groups of people probably moved
both south and north along the eastern seaboard looking for higher
land.[51] *Cong*, or fairly accurate copies of them, have been found in
this wider sphere of Liangzhu. But the relocation of a massive city,
a population of thousands, large-scale infrastructure and extensively
cultivated land, was impossible. Liangzhu was strangled by water.
A number of people returned to the region fairly quickly, but only
during the Han period (206 BC–AD 220) did this area of China become
populous again.

When people left the fading city, some took their jades with them.
A few, particularly small pendants, would probably have evaded burial
and been passed down over generations and mislaid, only to be found
centuries later. Other jades were buried, subsequently to be retrieved
as people dug ditches, cut out terraced fields and farmed land, or
when flooding or looting opened tombs. The remarkable, unchan-
ging nature of jade, especially nephrite, ensured that the stones had
an afterlife, surviving in most cases without evident signs of decay.
The impact of the relics from Liangzhu on the history of jade was
great, and copies of the *cong* shape reappear in ritual deposits as far
away as eastern Gansu and the Sichuan basin, each more than 2,000
kilometres west.[52] This distinctive object, square in section with a central hollow column, cannot have been completely reinvented. If we
map the places in China where the *cong* appears in the second millennium BC, still well before the Shang dynasty ruled on the Central
Plains from about 1500 BC, we find both squat and tall versions, all
ultimately derived from Liangzhu archetypes. Some carried copies of
the small circular eyes, others just the circles, and some had no eyes
at all. Other jades also travelled, especially the *bi* discs.

Liangzhu was not the only ancient city of jade to be affected
by flooding. Further west along the Yangtze was another prominent city, Shijiahe, where people had occupied areas of lowland over

hundreds of years and had built enormous moats. The community also expanded, with settlements on the highlands encircling the city. As flooding once more undermined this society, those remaining there turned to producing fine jades, which they buried in urns around 2000 BC. These are a departure from the jades we have seen, but, as with the Liangzhu *cong*, they also were disseminated: people leaving the area carried jades with them that survived and were collected in later centuries.[53]

Huge rivers with immense tributaries inevitably flooded and contributed to legends surrounding the mythic hero, the Emperor Yu, who is said to have founded the Xia dynasty.[54] An account, probably dating to the fourth century BC, describes Yu's conquest of the water and his control of the land in a cosmic pattern of nine divisions that came to symbolically delineate regions of China's culture.[55] Flooding, but also severe drought, affected areas around the Yellow River basin. China's history is charged with such traumatic moments and even today the Yangtze repeatedly floods. The wide range of jades in different shapes along the Jade Corridor often evaded destruction and in due course were rediscovered.[56] This fortuitously took jades across the whole of northern and central China, to be reused over several thousand years. And the reappearance of jade from the earth enhanced its miraculous qualities. In the Loess Plateau, metals were unknown or remained rare as the layers of earth made it almost impossible to discover ore, but jade as it travelled was frequently buried, later to be found by chance. It became a much-prized, highly valued material, occupying the position taken by gold in many other societies.

If we turn our attention to the eastern seaboard, to the sites around and north of Niuheliang and to Liangzhu and its surroundings, we face away from the much later western sources in the Kunlun Mountains on the edge of the Tibetan Plateau. A change in geographical focus is essential if we are to appreciate jade's penetration across a vast landscape. This crucial shift alters our understanding of how jade emerged and spread to other eastern cities, especially in Shandong, which also declined and disappeared.[57] Their jades added to the melting pot of ancient pieces that moved and were then reused in later history. The dispersal of jades ensured that the stone's elusive power and obscure forms would survive down to the present, accepted without interrogation of its origins, and valued beyond all other materials. As Liangzhu was forgotten, so too were some of the most impressive ancient jades in China.

Excavation has restored this history. Societies in eastern China from at least the eighth millennium BC had created an abundance of pieces to be uncovered in later millennia. Jade had even been known and used much further west among early societies in Gansu province; but only a few pieces have been found at excavated sites.[58] The great *cong* from Fanshan, with its beautiful, carefully smoothed corners and engravings, enables us to recognise but not to read the language of the many other *cong* with abbreviated faces. Far-reaching lineages of these jades were established as many different ancient shapes were retrieved, imitated, owned and displayed in the afterlife by the leaders of the first dynasties. These later *cong* (plate 20) acquired new purposes, deflecting efforts to understand the ancient forms of the *cong* and others listed in the ritual texts. The *cong* representing the earth and the *bi* the sky were not new explanations but added layers of mystery. A famous description attributed to Confucius added another layer, with jade entering a completely different social, political and cosmological universe in the hands of the people of the Warring States:

> Anciently superior men found the likeness of all excellent
> qualities in jade.
> Soft, smooth and glossy, like benevolence
> Fine, compact and strong, like intelligence
> Angular, but not sharp and cutting, like righteousness
> His pendants hanging low to the ground, like humility
> When struck, its sound clear, elevating and expansive, like music
> Its flaws not concealing its beauty (and its beauty not its flaws),
> like loyalty
> With an internal radiance issuing from all sides, like good faith
> The aura of a pure rainbow, like the heavens
> The spirit of hills and streams, like the earth

Standing out as symbols of rank, like virtue
Esteemed by all under heaven, like truth and duty.[59]

At Hangzhou, the capital of Song China in the twelfth and thir-teen centuries AD, no one knew what lay beneath the surrounding fields of rice. They nonetheless made copies of *cong* in green-glazed porcelains.[60] Ample supplies of the stone, often from distant Xinjiang province, were offered to the emperors and officials of the Ming and Qing dynasties. Brush washers and rests, small sculptures of auspi-cious creatures, as well as copies of ancient *cong*, *bi* and arc-shaped pendants, were worked to satisfy growing demand. These culminated in massive jade mountains depicting legends of the kingdoms of the immortals for the Qianlong Emperor (AD 1735–95).[61] And the main character, Baoyu, meaning 'precious jade', in one of China's most famous novels, the *Dream of the Red Chamber* (*Honglou Meng*), writ-ten in the eighteenth century, was born with a piece of the luminous stone in his mouth. The complex story of his life and that of his family ultimately ends as the jade disappears.[62]

The legacy of the man at Fanshan is not just a set of exceptional jades exhibited in a museum. It is something else: the owner of the king-*cong* and his peers built up a great walled city at the summit of a powerful society with its own distinctive beliefs. A series of ruptures scattered ancient jades from Liangzhu, Hongshan and even older soci-eties across China, creating new histories, the bedrock upon which new beliefs were built, modified and then again rebuilt. The physical-ity of jade ensured that it continues to offer potent protection. The early jades of the eastern seaboard, which had bridged life and after-life in ancient China, also bridge China's past and present.

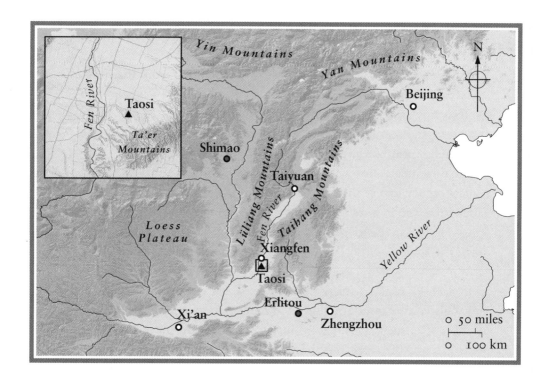

Taosi and the Loess Plateau

2.

A Disrupted Banquet

The Loess Plateau, stretching more than 1,000 kilometres from Lanzhou across high land to the Taihang Mountains (plate 19), is an extraordinary landscape that played a central role in China's evolving history and culture.[1] It pairs with the powerful Yangtze River and its tributaries to the south as they, together, border both sides of the later famous dynastic cities on the middle and lower Yellow River and the Wei River. Like the Yangtze delta with the great city of Liangzhu, the southern borders of the Loess Plateau supported large walled settlements which flourished before the Shang and the Zhou. The loess is yellow-grey sediment, blown over millions of years from mountains and deserts to the west by the Arctic winds and the Westerlies, especially during the winter.[2] In most areas, the loess is very fine and can compact into high-standing, grainy cliffs.[3] The region has an arid climate, but its minerals supported crops and animals. Few visitors make their way into this strange landscape of enormous dust storms and harsh winters. The Plateau diverges from the standard images of China – the Forbidden City, the terracotta warriors and the rice fields. In fact, many do not know that it is there. It is one of ancient China's hidden strengths.

The heavy loess deposits lie over a relatively flat plateau, rising to between 1,600 and 2,000 metres above sea level. This determines the route of the Yellow River. As it leaves the Tibetan Plateau and passes through the city of Lanzhou, it is forced north around great mounds of loess, filling with opaque silt until it reaches its Great Bend, north of the deserts and hills of the Ordos region. Here it turns south suddenly, cutting through the loess, dividing the provinces of Shaanxi, with its capital Xi'an, from its neighbour, Shanxi (plate 17). The Yellow River then enters a small basin of lowland where the Fen River joins

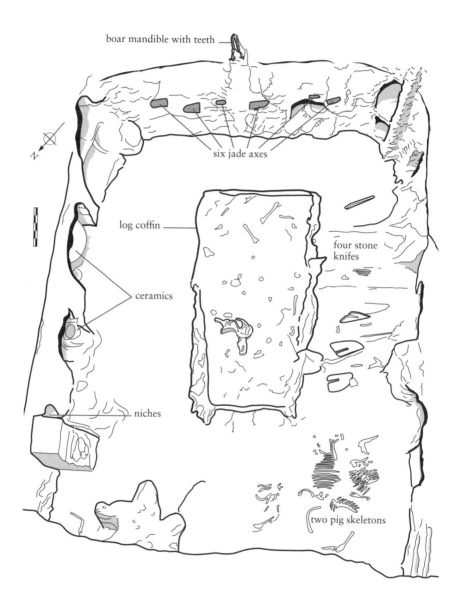

boar mandible with teeth

six jade axes

log coffin

four stone knifes

ceramics

niches

two pig skeletons

N

The vandalised tomb – 5–5.3 m long, 3.7 m wide, and 7–8 m deep.

it from the east. Further south, where it meets its most important tributary, the Wei, it changes direction sharply again, this time flowing east. Associated with this abrupt turn is a mythological mountain, the Dragons' Gate, where a massive waterfall cascades down. It is said that if a carp leaps over this waterfall it becomes a dragon. The river then makes its way through several narrow mountain passages, known as the Pass, before it arrives at the Central Plains, sweeping the silt on to rich agricultural land. This unique combination of the great mounds of loess and the twists of the Yellow River and its tributaries was the setting for some of the most famous events in early China's history.

Continuous erosion from wind and water has excavated crevasses and canyons in the deposits of the Loess Plateau, which its inhabitants have worked into terraces, roads and fortifications, precipitating further erosion. A satellite view reveals a multitude of ravines and dry riverbeds as numerous and dense as the veins of leaves. This is a rural area of labyrinthine valleys and terraces – precious refuges that have always attracted people confronted by fierce winters – that burn pale ochre in the unrelenting summer heat (plate 5). Villages and towns with layers of cultivated land pepper the horizon. The principal crop was millet, which is suitable for the high, dry land. Today it is supplemented by wheat, maize and some pastoralism.[4] Over millennia populations have lived in caves, which could be dug in tiers without collapsing, almost resembling today's tower blocks, as an American described as he travelled in the 1920s:

> In fact, cave dwellings had become almost universal, and were to remain so for many days to come; villages, whole towns of caves, stretched in row after row up the face of great loess cliffs, like the terraced fields that covered every foot of the mountainous world from river-bottom to the crest of the farthest visible range. In all this tumbled landscape often the only touch of colour was the persimmons, like big orange-tinted tomatoes.[5]

Most famed is the village of cave houses at Yan'an in Shaanxi province, where Mao Zedong and his comrades sheltered in the 1930s from the

Japanese and from Nationalist forces led by General Chiang Kai-shek. Protected by the geography, Mao and his followers planned the future of China. Although the environment and climate were often challenging for agriculture, the loess regions hosted some of China's early farming communities from before 5000 BC.[6] In subsequent centuries, their inhabitants were denigrated for their lack of cities and writing. The agricultural people south of the Loess Plateau both feared and disregarded their neighbours, yet had to accept their repeated intrusions, which were crucial to the development of ancient China.

The lie of the loess lands offered three routes from further north for people moving towards the agricultural basins. The most direct route from Central Asia and the mountains in present-day western Mongolia came down the Hexi Corridor, a narrow band of land between the Tibetan Plateau and the steppe. Alternatively, far to the east, the steppe of eastern Mongolia is separated from the agricultural land south of Beijing by the Yan Mountains. This route crosses the Great Wall, built in sections from the fifth or fourth centuries BC. The third route, and the one that concerns the ancient city of Taosi, ran south from the Mongolian steppe down the Yellow and Fen Rivers.

North of what became the Great Wall, and beyond the loess, China joins a flow of communication along the whole steppe across the Eurasian continent. To the west the land rises high to the great node of the Altai Mountains; beyond, the steppe races on, a sea of grass and mountains open to hunters, then migrants from further west, and mobile pastoralists moving by season from lowland to higher pastures and then down again, and on to the Urals and the lands of present-day Russia and eastern Europe. The pastoralists travelled with their herds of sheep, cattle and, later, domesticated horses, first traced in the western steppe and Western Asia.[7] And along this unending, almost continuous, route people had links with more settled societies to the south in Anatolia, Mesopotamia and Iran before contact with China was made. The rulers of the agricultural basins of the Yellow River could not and did not know what lay to the north and north-west. Even today, routes around the Tibetan Plateau, this incredible ecological and geographic barrier to direct trans-Eurasian communication, are hard to imagine. Yet new people, new animals, new materials and new technologies moved up mountain corridors and along the grasslands over the loess to reach central China.

Climate changes seem to have provoked movements southwards. Over millennia, the northern boundary of the Pacific Monsoon shifted, affecting peoples in search of a secure livelihood. During the third millennium BC abundant rain encouraged settled farming in the north of the Loess Plateau. But during the second millennium BC the boundary moved south, rain was less frequent, and so too farming communities and pastoralists moved south.[8] North of the Loess Plateau the steppe grasslands were more arid, suitable for hunting and herding, with small, diffuse pockets of agriculture. The north–south movement of people between the grasslands of the steppe, over the Loess Plateau towards the agricultural basins of the Wei, the Fen and other tributaries of the Yellow River, led to recurrent cultural encounters and exchanges, but also instability. In the increasing dialogue between the inhabitants of the steppe and those of the settled villages, towns and cities of the major valleys, the people across the Loess Plateau were essential intermediaries. The discovery of Taosi, a large settlement – or even a city – in the valley of the Fen in the 1950s caused great excitement among archaeologists hoping to find evidence of the Xia, the first dynasty mentioned in ancient writings.[9] In traditional stories of China's remote past, the Xia followed the period of the mythical Sage Kings and were eventually displaced by the well-documented Shang dynasty.[10]

The principal Sage Kings – the Yellow Emperor, and the Emperors Yao and Shun – are renowned figures in the foundation myths of China's culture. Detailed accounts of their lives appear in *The Book of Documents* (*Shu Jing*) with some material handed down, often orally, from the ninth century BC, but also with many accounts no earlier than the fifth century BC.[11] The passages on the Sage Kings incorporated into the *Historical Records* (*Shi Ji*) by the court historian Sima Qian around 100 BC celebrate the virtues and achievements of rulers now believed to have been mythical.[12] Although Taosi may not provide traces of the Xia dynasty it shows that, well before the Shang came to power, agriculture in valleys just to the south of the Loess

Plateau witnessed the establishment of cities. As each new city is discovered, we learn that ancient China was more diverse than we could ever have conceived.[13] Almost everything we shall examine at Taosi was completely unknown in the first half of the twentieth century.[14] The cities themselves, and the connections between them, open new doors on to China's past long before the invention of writing.

Taosi is in a valley, near the small town of Xiangfen. It was a key junction, joining activity along the Yellow River and the Fen. Between the third and the first half of the second millennium BC the area lay within the monsoon belt. Fertile land supported agricultural communities that flourished for 300 or 400 years from c.2300 BC until their populations declined around 1900 BC.[15] Over this time, Taosi grew from a minor settlement into a small city of less than two square kilometres, making it one of the first cities on the borders of the Loess Plateau. It was far inland, in a different environment from Liangzhu. These environmental and climate variations are essential contributors to the richness of China's culture. The valleys of the 'Yellow Earth' were and are just as important as the rich rice fields on the Yangtze delta. The nearby valleys south of Taosi, those along the Yellow River and the basin of the Wei, are often considered part of the Central Plains, the areas of farmland east of the Pass. However, while Taosi flourished, the lands beyond the Pass were likely unknown to its inhabitants. And we will understand China more completely if we recognise the special qualities of the Loess Plateau.

As at Liangzhu, we have to look at the walls, buildings and tombs to discover Taosi. From its early phase (2300–2100 BC) the city was surrounded by ditches, which in due course were replaced by walls of loess. Loess was exploited for walls across northern China and remains a staple there.[16] Its unusual strength and stability, and the speed with which it could be rammed inside wooden planks, explains why many settlements were built in this way and why there was little use of stone in early millennia.[17] As each section of a wall was completed, the planks were moved up and another section pounded. Collecting, quarrying and shaping stone would have been far more labour-intensive, and did not fully enter the building repertoire until the late nineteenth or twentieth centuries AD. The absence of stone buildings and sculptures has often led to unfavourable comparisons with ancient Egypt. But this is to miss the point. China's exceptional ability to create walls, platforms and tombs at great speed was an effective expression of political and hierarchical power, but one that has not been properly appreciated. Rammed loess walls are also easy to overlook as they sink back into the ground. And as they were built and rebuilt throughout the centuries, their dates and their purposes are not always easy to identify. But they became one of the defining architectural practices of China, an enduring tradition, readily repaired, replaced and extended.

A great structure, often called a palace, lies at the centre of Taosi. Substantial platforms or foundations must have required gangs of workers. The platforms gave space for the repeated development of intricate buildings in wood with which we are still familiar today. A massive cemetery, south of the walls, with more than 10,000 tombs – 1,000 of which have been excavated – gives us an inkling of life in the city.[18] Six significant tombs display the material wealth and social status of the occupants, as well as their beliefs about their universe. They were buried with sets of storage jars, serving dishes and bowls so that they could enjoy foods on ceramic or lacquered wooden platters on high stands in the afterlife.[19] The large numbers buried are a measure not only of the mastery of clay and wood, but also of the agricultural prosperity of an elite population. These practices continued into the second phase (2100–2000 BC), when Taosi grew to cover 2.8 square kilometres, enclosed by a new wall. Taosi's affluence expanded, and more extravagant ceremonial buildings, walls and tombs were constructed, as well as smaller dwellings, indicating, as in the early phase, a growing hierarchical society. A long central road divided the city and connected it to a hinterland of villages, which eventually developed into towns. In the third phase (2000–1900 BC), the city changed dramatically, and the earlier planning was overturned as buildings were destroyed, the tomb of a major leader of the second phase was vandalised and tombs of commoners freely distributed across the city.

Such destruction is rare in China's archaeological record. Houses and grander buildings of loess readily collapse and disappear unnoticed. They do not leave the traces of farmed land, mud brick, or stone buildings found in other parts of Eurasia. Taosi's ruins are therefore valuable evidence of great affluence.

A vandalised tomb has, however, drawn attention to a major calamity. It was found not in the main cemetery but in the south-east quadrant of the walled city.[20] The area around it had its own wall, which also enclosed an unusual structure, currently understood from its semicircular foundations by the principal excavator, Professor He Nu, as an observatory for reading the heavens.[21] The crescent foundation may have supported a row of pillars framing the views towards the south-east in the direction of Chongshan, a prominent local peak in the Ta'er Mountains. The pillars may have been positioned to offer accurate observations of the sun's movements. The excavators reckon that a long pole, coloured in sections, perhaps demarcating measurements, which was found in the vandalised tomb, had something to do with this monument. They tentatively suggest that the man buried was also connected with it, as both were destroyed. We can of course speculate about how a structure, named by the excavators as an observatory, might have been used by the elite in their management of the city. And we should not let our ideas overrun those of people no longer here to speak for themselves. The destruction of the loess buildings at Taosi is far removed from the water, canals and dams of Liangzhu. A different world with a different fate. Taosi expands our understanding of the multiple ways in which early cities were built, flourished and declined.

The destroyed tomb is one of the most interesting burials in ancient China for its position, its size and its eventual destruction. It is the most substantial discovered so far in pre-Shang China, and marks the gathering impetus for great tombs. Dug down to almost eight metres, it is believed to be deeper than earlier tombs at Taosi, although this is difficult to assess as the ground level may have changed.[22] To achieve this tomb, the allies or family of the tomb owner had made use of the loess. Depth was to be prized in all areas with loess: the more important the owner, the deeper the tomb. The stability of loess was the principal driver for the development of these underground mansions across the whole of northern China. The fine, grainy soil allowed immense tomb walls to stand open, without threat of collapse, while the funeral and burial were carried out. Alongside the objects within, the tombs themselves were displays of authority.

The vandalised tomb approaches in size and depth the major tombs at Anyang in the next chapter, long considered the grandest in Shang China. The male occupant must have been a very significant individual when Taosi was at the height of its power, and we can justifiably refer to him as a leader. Burials with fewer grave goods surrounded him and are thought to have been for members of the elite – his clients and valued subjects. In turn, these tombs were accompanied by smaller ones, in which individuals assumed to have been attendants were interred with jades and cowries.

In his coffin the leader lay with his head to the south-east, orientated towards Mount Chongshan. Unusually, his coffin was boat-shaped, carved from an immense tree trunk. Around the coffin, at the base of the shaft, the faded yellow walls were cut to create niches for objects, again possible because of the stability of loess. The niches may have mirrored those used in life in cave houses to store food and possessions.[23] Both the log coffin and the niches are traits from elsewhere, perhaps further north in the Loess Plateau. This was a surprisingly unprecedented burial, whose origins we cannot trace today. Tomb-building, at all times determined by those carrying out the burial, was intimately connected with the identity of the occupant. The depth and design of this tomb must have been intended to express the leader's origins. Unusually, he was likely to have come from beyond Taosi, probably bringing with him new skills and knowledge, and was awarded a magnificent funeral. We do not know anything about his life, but he may have been admired for his background in a distant and now unknown society. Cinnabar, the ore from which mercury can be extracted, was also found within and around his coffin. Huge quantities were later mined in the Qinling Mountains, south of the Wei River.[24] Cinnabar was probably scattered over the leader's body when he was buried. With its brilliant red colour, cinnabar in lacquer is eye-catching. Red later represented a positive force and, in due course, was correlated with the south and the warmth of the sun. Alongside the cinnabar, traces of small tiles of turquoise add another shade to the visual environment. These tiles were found inside the coffin along with one cowrie shell. We know what this combination may have looked like from a band embedded with a turquoise mosaic plaque, with one cowrie at the centre, recovered at a nearby site.[25] This type of ornament, perhaps a form of protection, had probably been brought to Taosi by people from far west of the city.[26]

A slight, smooth, square jade *cong* with a cylindrical hole was found in one of the niches. *Cong* in other Taosi tombs have similar squat proportions, and some refer to the original form with horizontal ridges. At the time of the leader's death, several hundred years after the height of Liangzhu jade production, *cong* had been taken from the eastern seaboard via rivers to settlements south of Taosi to be copied or reworked.[27] Further encounters and exchanges with jade-using people from Shijiahe on the Yangtze had brought another type of jade to Taosi – a small plaque shaped as a rather abstract head or face, topped by a crest and wide wing extensions, perhaps with eyebrows above elongated holes that may signify eyes, and a circulate hole as a mouth.[28] The leader had acted, it seems, as a magnet, drawing jades from different directions to his burial. He also had several more axes or tablets in fine agate, and other jades are reported to have been found in the earth back-filling the pit.

Jade is unlikely to have been mined close to Taosi. There are no sources in the wind-blown loess. Mountains hundreds of kilometres

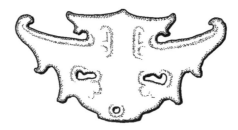

A slice of jade, cut to create an intriguing face, 6.4 cm wide, is typical of the jade culture of Shijiahe from the late third millennium BC.

to the north-west contained the nearest seams, but these cannot have been known to the people of Taosi.[29] Archaeological discoveries steadily reveal the previously uncharted contacts between people of the Yangtze basin and the tributaries of the Yellow River, a connection that fostered widespread enthusiasm for jade and new ideas about its auspicious, ritual and even supernatural qualities, long before metal was introduced from much further west. This leader at Taosi cannot have had any knowledge of Liangzhu or Shijiahe, nor of the routes by which jade had reached him. We do not know how the jades were used, but they confirmed his exalted seniority. Beautiful stones may have been associated with spirits, especially polished jade axes on short, red lacquered staffs, prominently displayed on the east wall of his tomb: three on each side of a wild boar mandible. This could have signified martial power, as did later European displays of halberds or spears on castle walls. The leader also had a set of bone arrowheads and a bow, suggesting that he may himself have hunted and killed the boar.

In addition to ritual objects and weapons, the leader was given provisions for banquets in the afterlife. Feasts – with multiple dishes, tastes and flavours – which varied region by region, even village by village, are quintessentially Chinese. At Taosi, we see how this tradition had become embedded in the afterlife. The first signs of banqueting are skeletons of ten pigs (two are shown on the tomb plan), split in half lengthways, ready for cooking. The boar and pigs were central to the economy of ancient China and especially to the lives of the wealthy. At the time Taosi was established, only two animals had been domesticated in China: pigs and dogs.[30] Though dogs were no doubt sometimes eaten, pigs were valued above all for their rich, fatty meat. Pork remains the most popular meat in China and the source of political unrest when disease causes supplies to run low. A description of a market in the twelfth century AD gives pigs a central place:

The pigs destined for slaughter arrived in the city [Kaifeng] through the Nanfeng Gate every day from morning until evening. None of them broke away, although the herds sometimes numbered over ten thousand animals with only a few drivers in charge . . .

Three to five men stand next to each other at the table, wield their knives, and joint the meat into big pieces, cut into chunks or small strips, or pound it to suit the customer's wishes.[31]

The pigs were clearly for consumption and the remains of several wooden chopping boards lay next to them. Also placed nearby were hefty V-shaped stone knives, the upper section to be grasped in the hand. Such knives ranged in size from 15 to 60 centimetres long, probably designed to produce different cuts of pork. The important contribution of pigs to the posthumous well-being of the leader must have been understood by the vandals who ransacked his tomb: although they left some jades behind, they destroyed the carcasses, as if to spoil his feasting in the afterlife, denying him the preferred food of the day.

By comparing the leader's tomb with other graves from Taosi's first phase, we can assume that one side would have been used for the final preparation of food to be served, rather like a Peking duck brought to the table in a restaurant and carved in front of guests.[32] In all the principal Taosi burials, the pigs to be prepared, the chopping boards and the stone knives were not simply the remains of a funerary banquet; they point to a belief in feasts in the future.

If the pigs and the utensils were there to provide for the leader in the afterlife, we need to imagine audiences, living and dead, for these preparations. First of course were the living relatives and attendants of the leader, presiding at his funeral; but another invisible audience of spirits and ancestors was also present. We cannot say whether the occupant enjoyed feasting solo in the afterlife or whether he was expected to entertain others, perhaps departed members of his family. Without doubt, however, he took with him all he needed for his future banqueting. In his tomb, banqueting sets and the foods and drinks they were to hold were parts of a vital line of communication, connecting the living who prepared the burial, the occupant, and other denizens of the afterlife. We see vessels and their contents taking the role occupied by jade at Liangzhu: their physical presence was a way to reach the world of the spirits. It is almost certain that the feasting menus in life and in the afterlife were similar. We see a much later example of food employed as one of the ways to tempt back the soul of a dying man in *The Summons of the Soul (Zhao Hun)*, from an anthology of poems from the state of Chu dating to the fourth or third century BC:

O soul, come back! Why should you go far away?
All your household have come to do you honour; all kinds of
　　good food are ready;
Rice, broom-corn, early wheat, mixed all with yellow millet;
Bitter, salt, sour, hot and sweet: there are dishes of all flavours.
Ribs of the fatted ox, cooked tender and succulent;
Sour and bitter blended in the soup of Wu;
Stewed turtle and roast kid, served up with yam sauce;
Geese cooked in sour sauce, casseroled duck, fried flesh of the
　　great crane;
Braised chicken, seethed tortoise, high-seasoned but not to spoil
　　the taste;
Fried honey-cakes of rice flour and malt-sugar sweetmeats;
Jade-like wine, honey-flavoured, fills the winged cups;
Ice-cooled liquor, strained of impurities, clear wine, cool and
　　refreshing;
Here are laid out patterned ladles, and here is sparkling wine.[33]

This classic example of how delicacies were thought to please the dead makes the desecration at Taosi all the more shocking: the vandals who ruined the provisions for feasting, like malicious party crashers, knew they were doing grievous harm to the leader, whose death did not render him invincible to further misfortune.

The original intention of those who prepared the tomb was that meat from the ten pigs was to be cooked in basins or pans, not roasted as we might imagine from European images of carcasses being turned on spits. Grains and vegetables accompanied the pork. Like rice, millet had to be boiled or steamed. Differences between the hard or crisp bread of Western Asia and Europe and the softer millet and rice in China, often served as a gruel, marked a clear boundary between the cuisines.[34] Wide basins on high, hollow conical legs were the standard cooking vessel at Taosi, though their legs were a new development.[35] Changes in cooking pots should not pass unnoticed. They indicate contacts and exchanges and are always a measure of prosperity and the surrounding agriculture. We do not know what stimulated this change in the late third millennium BC, but it was shared across much of the Loess Plateau and down into the river valleys also covered in waterborne loess silt. Separate and perhaps competing societies, with different ceramics for cooking and feasting, often with tripod legs and lobed pouring ewers, thrived to the east, in present-day Shandong province; these may have stimulated the changes in the shapes of the cooking vessels at Taosi.[36]

We find another, striking pot at Taosi with three separate legs shaped like rounded sacks or pouches, joined at the top by a shallow neck to make a lobed container, much heavier than the elegant ewers of Shandong. This pot was used not just for cooking, but also perhaps for the fermentation of grain and is known today by the name *li*.[37] People further north and at Taosi also used a steamer, a pot with a container joined to three lower lobes. Steamers had been developed much earlier and remained fundamental to Chinese cuisine. Both the *li* and the steamer were later copied in bronze for the ritual vessel sets of the Shang and the early Zhou dynasties. The ceramics across northern China set a pattern for later bronze casters, who were also to make use of loess for their moulds.

A tomb, especially one of this great depth, was a dwelling for eternity, not a kitchen. Fragments of big pots for the cooking or reheating of food have been found in surrounding ash pits and in the debris of houses across the city. Tomb owners were assigned stoves on which a pot with a pointed or rounded base could be balanced. Small models of granaries were often included. Foods for the day and for the

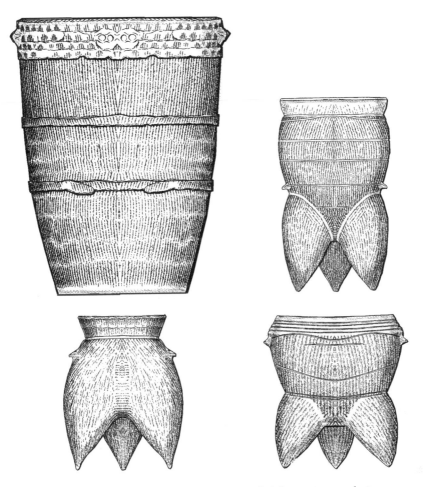

A large vat, height 60.8 cm, two steamers, heights 37.6 cm and 28 cm, and a cooking vessel, height 26.8 cm, reconstructed from excavated shards.

future were stored in vats, some squat, some tall. These retain some of the rough impressions of the cooking pots but were also painted around the neck. Colourful jars and serving vessels, and later vessels in bronze, required cooks and servants in the kitchens of the afterlife to prepare the banquets. Later attempts to recreate earlier rituals, as set out in the *The Rites of Zhou (Zhou Li)* of the third to second centuries BC, provide lists of the numbers of cooks, assistants and overseers needed in the kitchens of kings.[38]

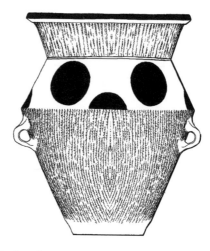

Tombs were supplied with stores of food, probably grain and vegetables. The rough grooves on the lower body are signs that this is a storage vessel, but with bright-red patches to make it suitable for the banqueting hall, height 34.6 cm.

Banquets were spectacular as well as delicious. Brilliant colour was an idiom by which the leader and his predecessors demonstrated their influence. Taosi had an unusually vivid repertoire, its own form of art. Multiple, abstract motifs on flasks, cups, dishes, bowls and platters, with their deliberately varied proportions and silhouettes, brought a visual symphony of rhythms, alternations and inversions of shapes, scrolls and flowing lines. As different courses were served, the various tall stands and wide basins would have been raised and handed from a servant to the host, producing other swiftly moving sequences intended to catch people's eyes. A cup on a curved foot and two small ledges is one of the painted ceramics that escaped destruction (plate 2). It still shows off its faded red background on which black and white lines make clear, horizontal patterns. In the upper row are what the excavators call feathers, but these could also be pairs of animal horns outlined in black. Contrasting black and white lines fall in angular patterns that are surprisingly close to some of the patterns used on later Central Plains bronzes. The same narrow bands appear on a small flask, above an undecorated base. Such pieces look almost modern in their abstract compositions. Platters belonging to other

A group of jars showing the inventive painted designs at Taosi. Heights: 23.6 cm (*top left*), 24 cm (*top right*), 28.1 cm (*bottom left*), 25.4 cm (*bottom right*).

owners, decorated with coiled serpents, also painted in black and red, are among the most conspicuous of these energetic designs.

Alcohol, perhaps in the form of a beer, was drunk at Taosi.[39] Slender flasks were for drinking, while tripods and other vessels with conical legs may have been for heating the beer. These are the foundations of the later ceremonies for departed ancestors recorded in the earliest poetry, first written down around 600 BC but transmitted orally over many centuries:

> Abundant is the year, with much millet, much rice;
> But we have tall granaries,
> To hold myriads, many myriads, of grain and millions of grains.
> We make wine, we make sweet liquor,
> We offer it to ancestor, to ancestress,
> We use it to fulfil the rites,
> To bring down blessings on each and all.[40]

The first painted ceramics discovered were shallow basins
with serpents or dragons. This one is 40.9 cm in diameter.

With some of the world's most nutritious grains, societies across
the great river basins could feed populations and support manufacture alongside agriculture. Ancient China was a world of many skills,
as well as many hands, to fashion objects of clay, reeds, bamboo or
wood, often painted with the lacquer that was popular at Taosi. The
excavators have skilfully recovered traces of wood within the fragile
soil, now part of the earth. Years of experience excavating in loess
have trained archaeologists to recognise decayed wood within it: the
lacquer usually survives in traces of black and red flakes that alert
them as they dig through the earth.

While alcohol and food were clearly essential, what is even more
striking is the emphasis on performance. The wish to preserve
prosperity may have stimulated such display. Taosi's sumptuous
combinations of cups, basins and platters filled with different foods
continue uninterrupted today. Feasting is a trait in most societies, yet
few others buried whole banqueting sets. The high-ranking members of Taosi were by no means alone in China in taking groups of

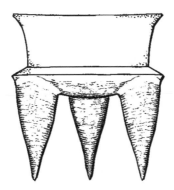

This alcohol vessel (height 19 cm), later known as a *jia*, was made by the same method as the cooking pots. Three holes were cut into the underside of a shallow basin, into which three slender pointed lobes were fitted.

elegant eating and drinking vessels with them into the afterlife. These sets have been dug up in tombs at settlements and cities of the third and early second millennia BC and had much earlier predecessors.[41] In each region diverse skills brought to life ceramics from the earth. Among the most renowned today are black cups on tall stands, with complex silhouettes in strands of clay or with numerous holes pierced in their columns, found further east in Shandong. These fragile cups accompanied ornate ewers in buff or white clay, a completely different aesthetic.[42]

Just as the ritual jades at Liangzhu belonged to China's eastern seaboard, so Taosi was part of a wider series of cultures in which ceramic banqueting vessels were essential for ritualised feasts. Bowls and serving dishes were expressions of identity, impressive in life where feasting built relations within and between members of related clans.[43] The ancestors of the leader would also have recognised his wealth from the exciting designs. The magnificent ceramics at Taosi (and elsewhere) were not a passing phase. They pioneered the ever-increasing virtuosity of China's ceramic tradition and developed the role of feasts in life and the afterlife. They were also forerunners of the bronze banqueting vessels we see in the tomb in the next chapter.

China originated the world's earliest ceramic cooking basins and food storage jars: 18,000 years ago, hunters living in caves in central

China left behind shards of pots that they had used for boiling their game and tall basins for stews of game and fish cooked with plants.[44] As peoples of both the north and south began to discover the potential of the grasses we now call rice and millet around 6000 BC, extensive ceramic output was launched, as the grains had to be boiled. Communities of the rich, river-based settlements and villages shared not just a delight in the presentation of multiple dishes but also in the creative uses of the many different clays. The ceramics were part of the cultural and economic life of these societies. Loess provided exceptional clays in different parts of the Plateau and the river valleys, which are famous for some of the most strikingly painted basins and bowls.[45] The visually enticing vessels at Taosi required labour to source and prepare materials and expertise to fashion and decorate them. Potters inherited craft traditions and passed on their experience over centuries. By the time that Taosi potters painted their ceramics, a wealth of artistry had piled up. Pottery always had clear utilitarian purposes, but at Taosi many deliberately spectacular ceramics were made (plate 3). Such distinctive innovation suggests that ceramic-making was both a functional and a creative art, relied upon to form bonds across groups within a society.

New combinations of plants, grains and meats, as well as the development of culinary flair, inspired the manufacture and decoration of an ever-growing range of ceramic cups, ewers and platters: the art of the cook and that of the potter reinforced one another. Complex sets of jars, basins and dishes were effective ways of emphasising the variety and abundance of what they held. A medley of many dishes was to become the preferred cuisine of China. In any assessment of the history of China's culture, we must remember that food and feasting lie at its heart. When, for example, we survey the list of fifty-eight different dishes for a banquet to celebrate a high-level appointment in the early eighth century during the Tang dynasty (AD 618–906), we realise that the display of foods was inherent to the success of the event but also an endorsement of the man's appointment.[46] It is tempting to question the continuity of China's cuisine. Can food customs really last so long? Yet the basic practices shown in the surviving ceramics from Taosi are the early formulations of heating foods,

The dazzling designs on a deep bowl, height *c*.20 cm.

steaming grains and presenting them in seductively decorated basins and platters.[47] They were an appetiser for a long tradition of ceramics and glazes that lay ahead.

Visual displays of status and wealth are part of the structures of many societies around the world. All societies make choices, perhaps often by chance, and associations become attached to these choices, creating a visual language recognised only by members of that society. The sophistication of the ceramics is easy to ignore. Their role in performances is brushed aside. In fact, Chinese ceramics are one of the great artistic traditions of the world, too often placed below Western sculpture and painting. Such elaborate ceramics, foods and burials have not been found among smaller villages in more rural areas outside Taosi. They required assemblages of people for workshops and reflect the social activities of more urban environments.[48] In life, the leader at Taosi would have hosted extravagant banquets to impress his followers and to gain allies. The need to provide for the afterlife was an added impetus to create ceramics of the highest aesthetic appeal. Everything from the cultivation of grain to the preparation and presentation of foods was essential. Banquets were significant to the social life and political negotiations of the elite in all periods. The leader in his tomb was probably competing with his peers, as well as his ancestors.

Music was also a means of communicating with spirits. Rounded drums, with a tall neck above a bulging ceramic body, found in several

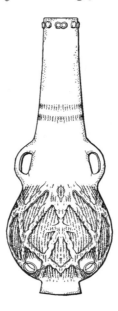

A ceramic drum, height 81.4 cm. The small holes at the base
are for releasing the sound generated within the rounded belly.

tombs at Taosi, would have produced a thundering noise.[49] Chime
stones, some of which were nearly a metre in length, sounded by
a mallet, added more sonority. A skin was held over the mouth of
the drum by small studs around the neck. Recovered fragments of
alligator scales are the remains of such skins. The alligators were
not necessarily local. Traces of their scales have been found at the
pools in Shandong and along coasts in the east, although it is possible
that they also moved up the Yellow River. As with the jades, alligator
skins were undoubtedly a luxury. Throbbing drumbeats and clang-
ing chime stones were perhaps not just pleasant accompaniments
during the meal; they suggest some sort of announcement, possibly
to summon spirits to take a seat beside the dead man.

We do not know how long after the burial the tomb was looted. The
food was spoiled, the jars and dishes broken, and the wood left to
decay, thus eliminating any possibility that the dead could continue to
live fully in the afterlife. The robbers gained possession of his means

of survival, thereby driving away protective spirits and undermining their potential to interfere in the lives of his rivals. As a new regime seized Taosi, vandalism may have been an explicit part of a political revolution in the city's third phase.

The whole of Taosi was razed and almost all the major buildings destroyed. Much of the area of the second phase was covered in houses for common people over the third phase from 2000 BC, until the city ceased to have any occupation from 1900 BC. Taosi's intensely hierarchical society appears to have been overwhelmed. In the process, the leader's tomb was opened. It is even possible that the burial, and its neighbouring observatory, were the target of this dramatic assault. The city wall was also torn down, and the area within disorganised. The palace and places for ritual offerings were destroyed or abandoned. Cattle horns were driven into the bodies of women, who were tossed into trenches and pits.[50] The observatory was broken up and a pit dug at its centre which filled with water. The body of a person who had met a violent death was buried here. Traces of horns and animal and human bones were also found.

The bones of herded animals and cattle horns were new. Neither sheep nor cattle had yet been domesticated within the territory of today's central China. Therefore, we need to turn north to a different part of the Loess Plateau, the city of Shimao, 500 kilometres away, in the county of Yunlin. Shimao was only excavated in 2012 but is an essential part of Taosi's story.[51] It may have been an almost exact contemporary over the period 2200–1800 BC or possibly grew later, down to 1600 BC. And people there were familiar with sheep and cattle. Animal herders were moving from west to east across the steppe to inhabit and in due course dominate grasslands north of the Loess Plateau. Without this stream of movement, sheep and cattle would not have reached the Hexi Corridor further west. These herded animals had been first domesticated in Western Asia around 8000 BC. The transformative moment for Shimao, Taosi and other early cities came when mobile herders from west of the Urals began to move, bringing with them their tents, wagons and burial rituals, and building stone and turf mounds, known as kurgans. This was a major migration of people and animals over an astonishing distance of 2,000 kilometres to the Altai Mountains.[52] From there, herding spread not only across Mongolia and Inner Mongolia, but along the three routes into the Yellow River basin, along the Hexi Corridor, through Shimao and to the north-east.[53]

The arrival of pastoralists may have been one of the conditions that led to the success of Shimao and its surrounding villages.[54] Unlike all the earthen constructions of other ancient Chinese cities, including Taosi, Shimao was enclosed by stone walls. Even though the people of the region often lived in cave houses within the loess, they had turned away from it as a major ceremonial building material and instead used local stone. Stone structures are a specific feature that links Shimao to nearby northern regions and across the steppe.[55] Traces of stone walls had been mistaken by earlier archaeologists for part of the Great Wall. It turned out that these stones protected an area of four square kilometres. Even more impressive is a massive stone structure on the north-western cliff edge, with a series of rising stone terraces. These stones were individually shaped and are banked against a small natural hill covered in loess. To hold the stone walls against the loess, whole tree trunks were thrust into the banks.[56] Strange stone face carvings fill the walls at irregular intervals. The other unprecedented discovery at Shimao is a complex set of gateways joining up the walls, with human skulls buried in pits nearby.

The purposes of the earthen platforms at Taosi and the stone terraces at Shimao are almost impossible to define without any written history. They are likely to have been foundations for buildings for rulers, religious leaders and other powerful organisers. But as we have no way of knowing how these buildings were used, or who built and occupied them, we are unable to give them names without imposing a misleading vocabulary with such terms as palaces or offices, as deployed in Mesopotamian and Mediterranean societies. This is even more difficult when we turn to religious or ritual behaviour. Names such as temple or shrine are not applicable, as these conjure up the worlds of ancient Greece and Christian Europe. But, with the elaborate stonework and skulls sacrificed at the eastern gate, we can be certain that there were powerful beliefs about the supernatural across a vast region spreading from further north in Inner Mongolia and south from Shimao.[57] We do not know how or when contacts between the northern stone-built settlement and Taosi came about, nor who was the leader and who followed. We can, however, see that despite the distance, the people of Shimao shared many cultural features with those of Taosi: coloured plastered walls, pottery drums, chime stones, small pottery bells, bone instruments – known to us as a Jew's harp – and skulls in pits.[58] Even more indicative of contact between Taosi and Shimao in the lifetime of our leader was the similarity of the ceramics used for cooking and feasting: basins with hollow conical legs and jars with angular profiles and trumpet-shaped necks.[59]

The animal bones and horns thrust through bodies mark a clear and devastating fissure in Taosi's history. While the two imposing cities shared parts of their cultures, they were located in two disparate environments. Shimao, on rolling hills and grasslands, was perfect for stockbreeding. As we shall see, the lower lands and the agricultural basins of Taosi turned out to be unsuitable for pastoral communities and their herded animals. The cattle horns are signs that the arrival of animals and their herders had reached Taosi and may have destabilised its economy. Perhaps the power of the leader caused unrest. Nu He argues that an internal rebellion was responsible for this sudden upheaval, inaugurating the third phase.[60] This is one possibility. Another may have been the unsettling influx of northerners from Shimao, but also potentially from other settlements in the northwest. New burials, dug after the devastation, include tombs in which a man is accompanied by a woman laid on her side. This is a practice found among the settlements around Shimao and in Inner Mongolia.[61] As tombs are good indicators of identity, when such double burials suddenly occur at Taosi, it seems almost certain that people had arrived from further north.

In addition to sheep and cattle, small metal objects found at Taosi are a complete novelty. The ores needed to produce metal, found buried in mountains, could never be discovered in areas covered in huge deposits of loess.[62] Like the domestication of herded animals, copper and bronze metallurgy had originated in Western Asia and extended into the Balkans and around the Black Sea. From there it travelled across the steppe and over huge mountain ranges.[63] Knowledge of metallurgy could only have journeyed with pastoralists. Without their herds, people could not have travelled far; nor could they have settled over the huge mountains and across the steppe. The herders carried practical bronze tools, such as knives, useful for working with animals, and wore bronze ornaments.[64] Until archaeologists recognised the long-distance movement across the steppe, the questions of how the herded animals and bronze-casting had arrived in China had gone unanswered. The extraordinary creativity at cities such as Liangzhu and Taosi had not been factored into the conversation. Jade had muffled the desire to search for other green stones, such as malachite, which had led to the discovery of copper in Western Asia and in due course the alloys we call bronze.

In the strenuous and often confusing work of excavation it is easier to pay attention to a piece of metalwork than to the debris of broken bones. Yet in reconstructing the history of Taosi, bones are vital:[65] the animals had been companions of the carriers of metal. Among the finds at Taosi is a small bronze disc with a notched edge. Similar pieces have also been found at Shimao. When first retrieved, the disc suggested to some a connection with a mechanical operation, perhaps even belonging to the so-called observatory. It was discovered in a relatively compact late burial, the bronze glued, perhaps with a resin, to a jade bangle – clearly an updated form of ancient adornment. Analysis of the metal added to the surprise. Other small bronzes were also found, of which the most interesting was a bell.[66] It is hollow and

This notched disc, diameter 12.4 cm, is one of
the earliest bronzes found in ancient China.

so would have required a clay core, as well as an outer clay mould, as hot metal was poured to make its full form. Despite this advanced casting method, the bell, like the disc, came from a modest tomb, found in a bag on the body of the occupant. Pottery predecessors of this bell had been found in several burials and also near Shimao, all with small holes in the top from which they could hang. Their ringers have not been identified. Where the bronzes found at Shimao and Taosi were cast is not settled upon, but they clearly indicate connections westwards across the Loess Plateau.

The animals' bones and horns and the tiny metal objects are signs of a major transition along several major routes into north-western China.[67] While both Shimao and Taosi shared in the movement of herded animals and metals across the steppe, other parts of the loess regions also saw these developments. Alien practices, materials and technologies, namely the herding of oxen and caprids by mobile stock-breeders, met a large and wealthy settled society at Taosi that offered banquets to the dead. In this encounter, which also affected numerous regions of the north, these innovations were almost seamlessly adopted and adapted to the new environment.[68] Abundant agriculture and a well-organised population proved dominant. Neither stockbreeding nor the use of metals for small knives and ornaments was taken up in the valleys of the lower Yellow River. Instead, the herded animals supplemented animal sacrifices and provided bones in a growing use of scapulimancy for divination.[69] Metal triumphed because it proved to be more desirable and useful as a display of status than ceramics.

Taosi is one of the hinges between the steppe, the Loess Plateau and the Central Plains.[70] Although the tomb was ransacked, the city destroyed and the region abandoned, Taosi and the leader established new forms of afterlife ritual that were to endure. The vandalised tomb looked like the end; it was in fact a beginning. One extravagantly deep tomb had been destroyed, but ever greater tombs were to follow. One banquet had been disrupted, but the banquets of the afterlife continued.

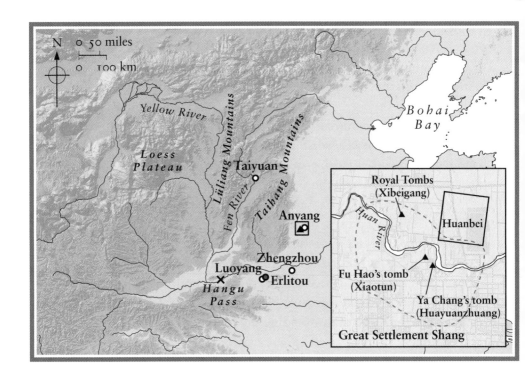

Anyang and the western edge of the Central Plains

3.

The Warrior with the Bronze Hand

The ancient city at Anyang was the capital of the late Shang dynasty (1250–1045 BC) and has been under excavation for almost 100 years.[1] It lies in what has traditionally been thought of as the heart of ancient China. Unlike ancient monuments and cities in the West – such as Stonehenge, Thebes or Rome – no structures remained above ground to tell the archaeologists where the city had been. What we encounter instead is a modern metropolis of tower blocks and motorways and, beyond it, the North China Plain. Huge, flat agricultural lands radiate from the gap where the Yellow River emerges from the Pass which protects the Wei River basin. At first the river encounters land around Luoyang, among lower hills and ridges. It is impossible to identify any ancient structures across these unending fields and villages. As the agricultural land widens out, the Yellow River flows east and then north-east to the Bohai Bay, on levees up to four or five metres, and sometimes as much as eight metres, high over the surrounding fields and villages. The river's course has dramatically shifted several times and its rich yellow silt has made an enormous fan of fertile soil that stretches from Beijing to Shanghai. Flooding remains a constant danger. When the levees were deliberately broken during the Japanese invasion of 1938, hundreds of thousands of people drowned. Yet the prosperity of all China's dynasties has rested on this region, from the rise of the Shang around 1500 BC to the fall of the Qing in 1911.

The Loess Plateau is concealed by the Taihang Mountains, which in turn are out of sight to the west from Anyang. The inhabitants of Anyang living 3,000 years ago knew that threats lurked among the mountains – peoples who might suddenly emerge to seize their crops or attack their villages – but they almost certainly had no sense of

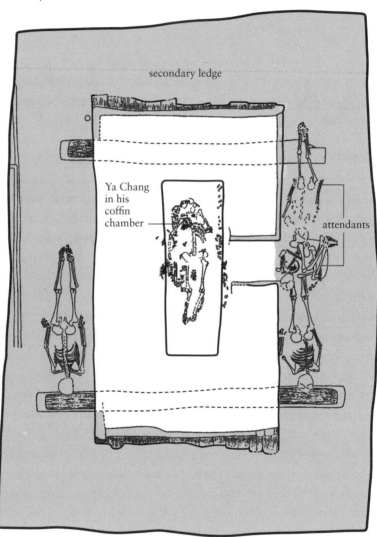

N

secondary ledge

Ya Chang
in his
coffin
chamber

attendants

Ya Chang's tomb. Length 6.03 m, width 4.4 m, depth 5–6 m.

the enormous lands spreading to the steppe. Equally unfathomable were the southern basins on the banks of the lower Yangtze, with the copper mines that contributed to the great bronze workshops which emerged at Anyang. The Shang were part of a long-distance network of alliances and material cultures, connected through the loess hills with the north and by copper ore and tin to both north and south, but along routes they did not know in our geographical terms.[2] They must have depended on people moving along paths and rivers to gain these materials and others such as turtle shells. The Shang could not even have begun to control the expanse of agricultural land on the lower Yellow River, some 409,500 square kilometres, as a single territory. Over 500 years, from c.1500 to c.1045, their capitals were relocated several times. Concentrations of populations settled and then disappeared again. The last Shang capital, covering perhaps 30 square kilometres, is now within an archaeological park. This was known in its day as the Great Settlement Shang. Later it was described as the Ruins of Yin, or Yinxu. But as it is often simply called Anyang, we will do so too.

Roughly bisecting Anyang is the Huan River, which cuts across from west to east. On its southern bank lie the temple-palace buildings at Xiaotun; on the northern, raised on a small elevation, the royal cemetery at Xibeigang. This was the hub of one of the most famous and powerful of ancient China's ruling dynasties. Continuous excavation at Anyang has revealed cemeteries of the major lineages, groups with a known line of patrilineal descent.[3] Recent excavations have also discovered an earlier settlement at Huanbei, east of the royal cemetery, surrounded by a neat defensive wall. Surprisingly, as far as we know the Great Settlement had no such defences. Below ground, foundations of the ancient city made of rammed yellow earth remain, on which a web of buildings of wooden columns once stood on platforms – the most substantial was 85 metres long. These were structures for the living: residences and temples for kings, their diviners, and military commanders, though the presence of sacrificial pits near or beneath them shows that ritual activities were also part of daily life. Immediately south of Xiaotun was the village of

Huayuanzhuang and it is here – not in the royal cemetery north of the river – that our warrior is to be found.[4]

The form of his tomb is standard for the Shang: a rectangular pit aligned on a north–south axis and dug down five to six metres, depending on where we take the surface to have been. While typical at Anyang, six metres would be very challenging, even impossible to achieve in Europe, where the pit walls, of stone, gravel and soil, retaining water, would cave in. The base is about 24 square metres – significant, but nowhere near the size of the burials in the royal cemetery. There the tombs are massive rectangular pits, dug more than 10 metres down, with some even cutting down to 14 metres, and more than 15 metres square, each with four ramps in the cardinal directions, a measure of how far tomb-engineering had now advanced.[5] The four ramps could be 50 metres in length or much more. Both the size of the tombs and the creation of the ramps were impressive additions. The sheer walls, revealed in excavation, must have inspired awe in all who saw them, labourers or members of the royal lineage alike (plate 10). For us they are a mark of new ostentatious rituals now possible due to the stable loess at Anyang, extending east from the foothills of the Taihang. One ramp would have helped the removal of earth from the pit, but four were superfluous for this function and must have instead aligned with ritual and religious beliefs. Indeed, all the enormous ramps may have been used in the funeral rites. Unlike the royal tombs, the warrior's lacks a ramp. Inside his wooden outer chamber, level with a secondary earthen ledge – typical of the majority of Shang and Zhou burials – was his coffin, also made of wood and long ago disintegrated; only lacquered fragments decorated with a snake or a dragon remain. Two strong beams of wood held the coffin chamber above the earth of the pit, which has also collapsed, as the shaft had been backfilled. The warrior was buried during the reign of King Zugeng or King Zujia, the second and third of the Shang kings to rule from Anyang. He (and it is certainly a he) died violently around 1200 BC, probably in battle. A deep cut on the left femur appears to have been caused by a spear or axe, and further damage is apparent on his left-hand ribs. He died shortly after these injuries were inflicted since there is no sign of any healing of the bone. The blow which cut straight into the right side of the ilium, the site of a major artery, was likely the fatal one. His right hand is missing altogether. The man has, however, been given a replacement: a bronze hand, 13 centimetres in length, complete with a socket that may have allowed it to be attached with a wooden staff to the body. Although it is tiny, the size of a child's hand, it seems to have been a kind of prosthesis that restored him to wholeness for the afterlife (plate 11). Such a careful burial for someone who had presumably been killed on the battlefield is highly unusual, and the bronze hand is unique. We know from much later writings of the fourth and third centuries BC that individuals who had died in battle were viewed with dread and often not accorded a full burial.[6] Clearly, this man was exceptional.

Seemingly at odds with this, however, is the position of his body: prone, facing downwards into the floor of the coffin. The principal burial posture in this region before, throughout and after the late Shang dynasty was the opposite: supine, with the individual laid on their back.[7] There are other prone burials at Anyang, but the majority are of persons evidently less esteemed, and many of them sacrificial victims. The warrior's death was the inevitable consequence of warfare with clans who challenged the Shang. One earlier tomb in the same cemetery has a prone male accompanied by a supine female. Both are orientated east–west, typical for prone burials.[8] Joint burials were characteristic of the peoples living in the borderlands to the north of the Loess Plateau.[9] In the life and death of this warrior we see the early stages of a persistent dialogue between the peoples of the Yellow River basin and the pastoralists further north. As encounters could be violent, the settled peoples – in this case the rulers of the late Shang – had to find ways to engage with and absorb northerners within their agricultural world. The number and quality of the warrior's possessions are unequivocal evidence of his high rank and accommodation by the Shang rulers.

If we look down into the outer chamber, we see thirty-eight intricate bronze vessels clustered above the head and below the foot of the coffin. Scattered over the whole area were multiple weapons: spears, arrowheads, axes and imposing knife-like blades. The weapons cannot have been installed like that. Most were probably displayed on long wooden shafts that have decayed over time, leaving them to drop down at random. Two bowed bronze arcs had fallen near where an enormous chime stone, almost triangular, rests. Many of the bronzes have characters cast into their surfaces: the title 'Ya' and family name 'Chang'. Ya Chang's numerous weapons and those of another man, Ya Zhi, buried further south in the Great Settlement, suggest that Ya is a military title.[10] During the late Shang, names, undoubtedly always used in many forms and in earlier languages, were for the first time carefully recorded.

Our warrior is not alone. Killed, but not sacrificed, to be buried with Ya Chang are fifteen attendants – exceeding the number generally found with other members of the elite Anyang lineages. Six are stationed inside the base of the coffin chamber, presumably as guards. Others lie on the secondary ledge. Where their skeletons are adequately preserved, we can see that many of them, like the warrior himself, are prone.[11] Beneath the warrior's coffin is a dog, presumably also a guard or companion. Thirteen other dogs lie around the coffin to accompany the attendants – an indication that they were important supporters or comrades of Ya Chang.[12] Regular burial of dogs with the late Shang elite has never really been explained. As in most societies, dogs were for hunting and herding. Several divination inscriptions on bones found at Anyang record royal hunts:

Crack-making on *yiwei* [day thirty-two]: 'Today if His Majesty hunts [at] Guang, he will capture [game]' [then follows the verification]: [He] really did capture tigresses 2; wild buffalo 1; Lu-deer, 21; pigs, 2; Ni-deer, 127; tigers 2; rabbits, 23; pheasants, 27. Eleventh moon.[13]

Attendants with their dogs give us a glimpse of Ya Chang's life and afterlife among the upper echelons of society. And his goods are also indicative of his wider connections.

When archaeologists first arrived at Anyang in the late 1920s, the ancient city was invisible. The palaces, settlements and tombs had all been destroyed by the Zhou as they defeated and displaced the Shang around 1045 BC.[14] What remained was eventually smothered in loess. For thousands of years farmers had grown and harvested their crops there, unaware of what lay beneath. For the first 1,000 years of the Zhou the area was known as the Ruins of Yin, and down to the Han dynasty (206 BC–AD 220) the Ruins were noted in the official histories as in those by the historian Sima Qian. He had full access to the archives of the Han court and his accounts – enlivened with legends, anecdotes and rhetorical speeches – are useful, though not always accurate.[15] After the Han, however, the Shang and the Ruins fell into the shadows. The Zhou were instead heralded as a beacon of righteous governance to which later rulers would turn for inspiration.

It was the chance discovery of some inscribed bones that spotlighted the Shang once more. In the winter of 1899 a servant brought some 'dragon bones' to Wang Yirong, President of the Imperial University, as he lay in his sickbed in Beijing. Before the bones could be ground up as medicine, Wang recognised the carvings on them as forms of Chinese characters and sent the servant back to the shop to buy up the rest.[16] Although Wang perished the following autumn, when the Western Allied Forces invaded Beijing, the bones were rescued and published. Other scholars followed the trail and found that the inscribed bones had been retrieved by looters at Anyang, and published surveys in the final years of the Qing dynasty. What the looters had fallen upon were archives of divination records, carved into ox scapulae and turtle plastrons, made for or by the late Shang kings. The Shang bones had brought back from the distant past China's earliest corpus of writing.[17] The Shang may also have written documents on materials such as silk or bamboo that have not survived. Written records perhaps existed in China before the late Shang, as suggested on a variety of ceramic fragments, dating as far back as the third and second millennia BC found at several sites.[18] But we cannot look to these for definitive accounts of the dreams, fears or rituals of their makers.

The characters on the bones are the antecedents of those used in China, and later Korea and Japan. Chinese characters are not directly tied to specific phonetics, so they have been adapted for different forms of the language and regional dialects over millennia.[19] The overall structure of the graphs would be familiar to anyone who uses characters. With some practice all past writings are also comprehensible to people in the present. The Zhou successors of the Shang took on this writing system, probably even before their conquest. And over the next 500 years or more, clans and groups who aspired to join the political and ritual systems established by the Shang and the Zhou gradually adopted the script too. The characters began to connect the whole of central China. Along with the jades of Liangzhu and the banqueting sets at Taosi, the characters are one part of the essential framework of ancient Chinese culture.

For more than 1,000 years, divination by scorching deer, pig and possibly sheep scapulae had been practised in the north. The earliest traces are in the north-east, today's Inner Mongolia, far from the later agricultural centres. There a process had emerged in which hollows were cut into bones and a heated tool or burning wood was applied to cause a crack.[20] With the arrival of herded animals at Taosi and other parts of the Loess Plateau, more and larger bones, such as the scapulae of oxen, were now available. At Anyang too, small depressions were drilled into the bones and heat applied to create the crack. The crack was the message to be interpreted by diviners. When carried out by or on behalf of the late Shang kings, records of the propositions and responses were sometimes inscribed on bones.[21] The character which opens the inscription on hunting was written as a vertical straight stroke with the second stroke representing 'the crack' branching to the right. The characters that Wang Yirong spotted were the questions or statements and responses. Decades of excavations at Anyang have recovered more than 100,000 inscribed fragments. The divination bones offer a wealth of information and are China's equivalent of the texts written in cuneiform on hundreds of thousands of clay tablets in Mesopotamia.[22] Some of the Mesopotamian tablets record economic transactions. In China the divination archives record daily, weekly and annual ritual cycles and are transactional in a completely different manner, revealing the anxieties and desires of the Shang kings and their quest for good fortune through offerings to their ancestors. While their purposes differ, the oracle bones show that this too was a highly ordered society. The numbers of bones alone indicate the presence of a significant administration at Anyang. Rulers there had oversight of what they regarded as the key operations of the state: agriculture, weather, misfortune and war. Through the questions posed on the bones we can see all this in detail, from the numbers of men conscripted into the Shang army to the casualties they inflicted upon their enemies, from the various animals they offered in sacrifice or caught in hunts, to the cycles of the calendar and frequency of harvests.[23]

Long before the late Shang, the dead had been thought to require the nourishment and entertainment that they knew in life.[24] In the centuries after the disappearance of Taosi around 1900 BC, cities grew on the Central Plains – one excavated at Erlitou, near Luoyang, dating from *c.*1700 BC, has sometimes been seen as a possible site of the Xia dynasty.[25] Walled settlements, of which the most substantial was the city at present-day Zhengzhou (*c.*1500–1300 BC), show us early Shang power.[26] With the move to Anyang, first to the smaller capital Huanbei and then to the Great Settlement Shang, more formal rituals developed under King Wu Ding, the first Shang king to rule from this city. The names and succession of the Shang kings are known from the oracle bone inscriptions. Many refer to ancestors who lived before the foundation of Anyang and who must have been buried elsewhere. Some name the founder of the Shang lineage and record offerings to other specific Shang kings:

> On *dingsi* [day fifty-four] divined: 'In performing the *you*-cutting sacrifices and Great Exorcism [for the king to the ancestors] from Shang Jia [on down], [we make] this ritual announcement to Da Yi [first king]', *Cracked in the temple of Father Ding* [king twenty-five].[27]

To achieve success, the kings also sought the support of Shang Di, the High God. Other powers were those of the natural world: the Winds, the Earth, the Mountains and the Rivers. But the third group, the ancestral founders of their dynasty, were of overwhelming importance to the Shang. The divination inscriptions were set out in a strict formula, recording the day in the Shang calendar when they were made, the subjects for which support was sought and the powers whose attention was required. Cumulatively, the oracle bones illustrate a tightly planned system of ritual offerings, following a sixty-day calendar. The programme was organised over a ten-day week, with buildings assigned for the rituals for specific ancestors.[28] The Shang kings made regular offerings to gain their ancestors' assistance in their lives and those of their families, in sickness and childbirth, and to ensure abundant harvests. The lives of all members of the court, the ritual specialists (including diviners), the administrators and the military leaders, and indeed all the Shang elite, were regulated by the rhythms of multiple rituals, offerings and sacrifices. These are mirrored in the impressive royal cemetery at Anyang, a memory of the intense drama of Shang burial.[29]

In the eastern part of the royal cemetery is a tomb with four ramps surrounded by small pits crammed with human and animal sacrifices. The 2,000 pits lie in neat rows. Some hold between ten and forty bodies, often decapitated. It is estimated that during the two and a half centuries of late Shang rule, 30,000 people were killed as offerings, primarily to the ancestors of the Shang kings, to ensure good outcomes.[30] Distinct populations living near or among the Shang, called the Qiang, are frequently described as being captured for this purpose.[31] Assistance was essential to achieve victory over enemies and thus reinforce legitimacy. A typical inscription on an oracle bone gives the posthumous titles of three deceased kings and enumerates the offerings made to them:

> Offering to Da Ding, Da Jia, Zu Yi [three deceased kings] hundred cups of wine, hundred Qiang prisoners, three hundred cattle, three hundred sheep, and three hundred pigs.[32]

With such offerings the rulers garnered their ancestors' favour. Court ritual and the cyclical ceremonies honouring past rulers continued to regulate the lives of emperors of all dynasties.

Today the area seems peaceful; the outlines of the tombs are marked by neat hedges in the swathes of grass. But over the 200 years of late Shang occupation Anyang was a hive of ritual activity: the pits had to be dug, formal burial rituals carried out, a mass of grave goods installed, and then the tombs had to be refilled. The pits and ramps would have fostered elaborate processions and rites intended to please the ancestors before they were closed forever. The whole society was structured to achieve positive outcomes for the rulers and their lineages under the gaze of the ancestors. This was part of a long history in which auspicious signs determined good days and bad days.[33]

Neighbouring Ya Chang, east of the temple-palace, is another remarkably lavish burial, that of a royal consort of King Wu Ding. Her name is Fu Hao and oracle bone inscriptions reveal that she was a military leader – a decidedly unusual position for a woman.[34] The graph Fu designated the wives of Shang kings, with the second graph referring to the polities from which they came. In the ancestral cult, as recorded in the oracle bone inscriptions, women only received veneration with their spouses.[35] Yet there is no known Hao with which to associate Fu Hao. Wu Ding is thought to have had more than sixty wives, among whom she was undoubtedly an important spouse.

Why do we have another eminent individual also not buried in the royal cemetery? Are the minor graves nearby part of Ya Chang's lineage, or indeed Fu Hao's? They don't appear to be. But their location must have been deliberate. After all, the location, depth and contents of all major tombs would have been decided by the court's ritual specialists. Ya Chang's and Fu Hao's dwellings are the largest and richest found undisturbed in the whole of Anyang, though also, revealingly, they come nowhere near the size of the kings' tombs. They had a different role in the life of the city.[36]

Ya Chang's future was assured by his bronze banqueting vessels. Bronze-casting, a new technology for small ornaments and tools introduced from further north and west, had been almost seamlessly assimilated into a long-standing pattern of belief which produced ceramic banqueting vessels. Yet while many rituals are mentioned in

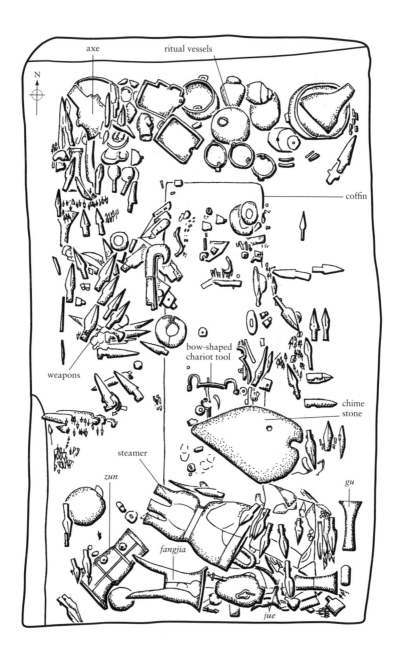

Ya Chang's bronzes spread over the chamber. At the head and foot are
ritual vessels. Weapons – especially spearheads – line the sides.
Across the centre of the coffin is an arched bronze, a rein holder for a chariot
driver. Just to the right below it is a large chime stone.

the oracle bone inscriptions, we do not know whether any of them referred to offerings in the form of ceremonial banquets. Nor do we know whether offerings by the living made it possible for the dead, using their vessels, to literally dine alongside their ancestors and descendants. We do know, however, that these bronzes were not primarily made for burial. In the succeeding Zhou period, hoards of the most valuable vessels, buried either to preserve them in times of danger or as offerings to spirits, tell us that bronze was always highly prized in the hands of the living.

An angular, four-legged alcohol vessel known as a *fangjia* illustrates the transformation of earlier ceramics that the bronze casters

A *fangjia*, height 66.6 cm.

could now achieve. Its four spear-like legs and angular cross-section replaced the three conical legs on the alcohol vessel, the *jia* at Taosi. This is now an imposing object at 66 centimetres in height and 20 kilos in weight.[37] Its square body, accentuated by vertical projections (often called flanges) contrasting with curved legs, an arching handle crowned by an animal head and two posts on the upper lip carrying small pinnacles, are further examples of the potential of the metal. Exceptional skill in casting produced detailed animal faces on each of the four sides. These diverse animal face motifs are all called a *taotie*, but how it fitted into Shang belief and ritual is unknown.[38] Such designs and the bronze itself must have been auspicious, as emphasised in inscriptions in the following centuries.[39] The bronze is also decorated with triangles and abstract patterns, and above the face is a narrow band with pairs of tiny dragons confronting each other. All are surrounded and intensified by angular spirals in relief; their delicate massed lines are almost as detailed as a fingerprint.[40]

These vessels were the product of a sophisticated bronze-casting system developed on the Central Plains, almost as bewildering to us as the jades, in the eyes of the Shang, that appeared to emerge out the loess. Bronze-casting was not advanced primarily for tools and weapons but to meet long-standing ritual demands. These do not follow the traditions of a Western Bronze Age, where weapons were highly prized. The casters and their patrons had completely different priorities. From about 1600 BC, when the metallurgy we saw at Shimao and Taosi was practised at Erlitou, the standard ceramic shapes for feasting were radically modified to be cast in bronze.

A yet more substantial alcohol vessel, called a *zun*, shorter than the *fangjia* at 51 centimetres in height, but much heavier at 27 kilos, is a new version of the flasks seen at Taosi, reproducing their sharp outward-sloping mouths and clear shoulders. Two different forms of the *taotie* face spread over the body and the foot. These are also defined by the same dense spirals. Inside the trumpet mouth are two copies of the two graphs for the name Ya Chang; the cross-shaped graph at the top is read as Ya and the one below as Chang. It was very unusual to cast two copies such as this on a single vessel and to place

A *zun*, height 51.9 cm.

them inside the neck. The typical position for an inscription was inside the foot. Were the inscriptions suddenly adopted in response to Ya Chang's sudden death?

Art flowed from ancient ceramic skills and the ambition for aesthetic perfection. Flasks, rounded cups and shallow basins were replaced by bronzes with sharp profiles and some quadrangular sections, ornate handles, animal heads and complicated legs, making them intriguing and almost otherworldly. The Anyang vessels were a major step in the steady creation of ever more beautiful objects. Ritual, hierarchy and artistic prowess were the foundation of the most exacting and enticing objects of Shang society. The most exquisite, but also the largest, were acquired by members of the royal court. After all, vessels were the means by which to communicate with the world of ancestors and spirits, who could both harm and support their descendants, and who shared the same concern for social hierarchy.

73

Very few vessels from the royal tombs survived the Shang defeat by the Zhou. Among those that did are two rectangular *ding*. Their conspicuous animal heads, a stag on one (plate 13) and an ox on the other, herald changes enticed by contacts with northern pastoralists.

Unlike many other ancient bronze societies, the peoples of the Central Plains did not opt for forging – heating metal until it became malleable and working it into the desired shape – or lost-wax casting. Instead they developed ceramic-based techniques.[41] First, a model of the vessel to be cast was made in loess clay. Though the word clay is often used to describe the models and moulds, research has shown that much of the clay had been washed out of the loess, instead leaving a fine-grained sand-like material in which to create extremely detailed motifs.[42] A mould was formed by impressing a wrapper of loess around a model. Some parts of the designs were first cut into the model and thus appear in the reverse on the wrapper. The loess wrapper was then cut off the model, rather like removing the peel from an orange. The wrapper became the mould sections (embedded in a stronger outer layer) which could either be touched up or significantly altered before being reassembled around a core. It is miraculous that this extraordinary technology was invented and spread so successfully: the moulds were clearly fragile and great skill was involved in creating them, deciding on how many sections were needed and how they were to carry the decoration. We still do not know how much of the design was produced by impressing the moulds on the model, nor how much was cut or added as craftsmen worked directly on the moulds. Many moulds survive, but no complete models. Fragments of bronze kept the core and the moulds apart as molten bronze – an alloy of tin, copper and often lead – was poured into the gap. Without the strange geology of the Loess Plateau, the minutiae in the decoration on the Shang bronzes may not have been possible.[43]

As metal ores were not accessible across the vast areas covered by loess, well-organised, centralised efforts must have been devised to source metals from distant mines, some as far away as the lower Yangtze. Smelting, alloying and then casting required the coordination of work by many craftsmen,[44] who had to collaborate in workshops, with one or more overseers directing them. In turn, the overseers must have followed some centrally recognised schemes for the types of bronzes required. The shift to bronze had brought a good deal of standardisation in the presentation of foods in vessels. Each project must have been clearly delineated so that the craftsmen completed specialised tasks. Like all great arts, Shang bronze-casting involved work at the edge of the possible, with constant risk: hazards in constructing delicate moulds, holding them in place as molten metal was poured in, then finishing the final pieces and removing the last traces of the ceramic. This is how the people of ancient China chose to produce inventive works of art. There is no bronze-casting in other parts of the ancient world, founded on such a ceramic-based technology, with equivalent scale, coordination, technique and artistry.[45]

The most common vessels were narrow flasks with a trumpet mouth, known as *gu*, accompanied by small spouted cups on three narrow legs, known as *jue*. Ya Chang had nine of each. These were for a drink similar to beer. Ya Chang had three other rather unusual bronzes for alcohol. One of these takes the shape of a magnificent buffalo, another – a lidded jug called a *gong* – was of an imaginary animal and a third, a rectangular box with a roof-shaped lid, is known as a *fang yi*. While alcohol was a major element in banquets, it was always balanced by food. Ya Chang had accompanying food vessels: six tripods and two with four legs for cooking, a tall steamer and four basins. The alcohol and food vessels were all made in standard sets. If we recognise them as such, rather than as individual pieces, we can compare them in different contexts and identify which pieces were routine and which were rare.[46] A knife, fork and spoon would be a more familiar set to us. Each piece has a specific function and contributes to the whole, and the set can be expanded or condensed as the occasion demands – think also of a tea set. Even if we were ignorant of toast, jam or milky tea, we would know from looking at a set that different items were intended for liquids or solids and used at specific moments in a ceremony.

Most traditional vessels are symmetrical. But the buffalo and the imaginary animal-shaped jug, the *gong*, have a different kind of symmetry: their heads form a centre point, and the two sides of the creatures are identical.[47] The buffalo has a rather blunt face, with wide flat horns, distinct eyes and a robust frame standing on four stubby legs. Its body is packed with creatures. The most striking is a tiger, one on each side of the belly, with vicious claws. Similar tigers appear on the chariot fittings in the royal cemetery and bring to mind the hunt. Tigers were threatening in a domestic context where cattle and sheep were penned. This wild tiger on a buffalo's belly cannot just have been decorative, but its meaning has not travelled through time. Another tiny tiger runs beneath the buffalo's eyes, with a fish at the front of its lower jaw and a bird behind. A *taotie* lies between the horns surrounded by small dragons. The *gong* on four, pointed, almost dancing,

Ya Chang's buffalo, length 40 cm, and a pouring vessel,
a *gong*, height 18.7 cm, hold auspicious meanings.

feet also bears on each side a *taotie* face with all its features – eyes, ears, horns and claws – rendered as separate islands against a delicate background of rectangular spirals. The main creature on the lid is a bottle-head dragon, and the vessel is also animated on its sides by an elephant and a bird.[48]

Vessels in the shapes of real or imaginary creatures were a distinctive introduction at Anyang and highlight networks across long distances into the south, where realistic examples of elephants and boars in bronze have been found. Fu Hao must have been aware of this fashion: her pair of owls and her two sheep pouring vessels (plate 12) are even more majestic than Ya Chang's. In fact, her collection of bronze exceeds comparison. She has 200 items to his thirty-eight, and fifty-three *gu* and forty *jue* to his nine of each.[49] Fu Hao's mass of bronzes go far beyond what was needed for the principal ritual ceremonies. The collection displays her authority, as it includes many vessels that were, according to their inscriptions, originally made for others. Typically, her possessions are associated with her status as a royal consort. But she was an unusual consort, chosen it seems from a northern community, perhaps to cement a strategic alliance. She took with her into the afterlife four northern mirrors, which were not made or used in the Central Plains in *c.*1250 BC.[50] Her bronzes may have been a diplomatic device, a gift to gain her loyalty and that of her wider clan. That we can make some comparisons of Ya Chang's bronzes with those of Fu Hao is a mark of the seniority he was accorded in death.

The vessels were more than personal trophies: they had a vital role in Shang society and the ancestral cult, being essential to bring success and indeed 'happiness'. The fact that they were buried with high-ranking people underlines not only their value but their eternal significance. Bronzes were required for the world of the dead as it mirrored that of the living. Once again the material was a bridge between both. We can see the power of the ancestral cult in asserting the Shang social structure beyond Anyang. The leaders of several settlements across the lower Yellow River basin were found buried with ritual vessel sets. A shared practice supplemented or even replaced military coercion in joining together Shang dependants.[51] The bronze vessels also connected disparate communities. They were instruments of politics *and* ritual. This profoundly influenced the culture of the next dynasty, the Zhou, who similarly managed lineages across an even more expansive territory.

A great stone chime, almost triangular in shape with a small hole in the upper corner, sits above Ya Chang's feet, where it had fallen from a wooden stand. It seems to have lost its two sharper lower corners. Such a stone would have vibrated with a deep sound when struck by a wooden hammer. Three bells of different sizes lie below; turned into position, with their oval openings at the top, they would have stood on their short shafts. They would also have been struck on the outside, each producing different notes to complement the chime. Their shape was a modification of smaller, earlier bells from Erlitou.[52] The earliest bronze casting found at Taosi was a similar oval bell, but unlike that bell, which had a clanger, these late Shang bells were probably struck with wooden mallets. Much heavier bells were cast in the Yangtze valleys, some as tall as 50 centimetres, but the relationship between the late Shang bells and the southern ones is not easily traced. We do not know how the practice of striking them from the outside, as gongs, came about; perhaps musicians adopted the style from chime stones. Over the next 1,000 years bells became central in ritual performances. In Ya Chang's day, both music and bronzes created an increasingly

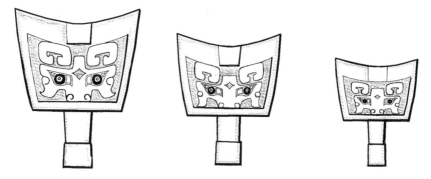

In the late Shang, bells were cast in sets to provide
the music for feasting, heights 17.6, 14.4, 9.6 cm.

extravagant ceremony. Ceramics were still used in kitchens and store rooms, but less frequently displayed among sets of bronzes, which were often accompanied by lacquers.[53]

As a military commander, Ya Chang needed weapons to defend himself against enemies in the afterlife. He did not have a sword; there were no swords in Shang times. Instead, in the top corner of the coffin chamber, above his left shoulder, was a massive axe. It is relatively thin with a long, curved cutting edge and an extended rectangular flange, which would have been pushed through a wooden staff. His name appears at the centre of this flange between two dragons, their heads facing downwards. Axes had been the primary weapon over millennia, from before the time of the Liangzhu leader. Just as swords in the West gain legitimacy through longevity, so too, it seems, did axes in ancient China. The Shang had taken the original jade and transformed it into bronze. Ya Chang's axe weighs nearly six

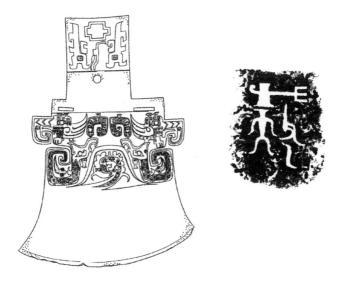

The axe, height 40.5 cm, bears Ya Chang's name. The two graphs are identical with those on the *zun*. The inscription (*right*) shows an axe beheading a victim. In it are the graphs for 'father', Fu, and his posthumous name, Yi. Rubbings were recorded and collected from the Song period, tenth century AD. This rubbing is from a famous compendium made in the late nineteenth and early twentieth centuries by the scholar Luo Zhenyu (1866–1940).

kilos.[54] It could behead adversaries, as shown by a clan sign on some other bronzes found at Anyang featuring an axe above a decapitated victim.[55] Reports of heads collected in battle, counted in divination inscriptions, reveal that decapitation was not practised only sacrificially in the royal cemetery. The axe is the weapon of a leader, even though this highly decorated one was probably more a sign of military status.

Almost all of the important Shang axes we have – Fu Hao possessed three – bear their own individual decoration. Ya Chang's displays a pair of birds with curved beaks projecting beyond the outer edge, well placed to tear the flesh of a victim. Below them are more dragons, jaws wide to swallow prey, and a small one coiled within what looks like an open mouth. Menacing jaws, often with bared teeth, recur. A raised circular hole in the centre of two of Ya Chang's bronze axes recalls the apertures on ancient jade discs. Shang jade workers repurposed many ancient discs by cutting down two of their sides to create teeth, giving these smooth surfaces a ferocious appearance.[56]

Jade weapons had qualities unlike those of bronze. They were often chance discoveries or spoils of war – signs of a kind of value gained by favours from the king. We also speculate that jade was thought to deter foes in the afterlife. While there is no manual left behind for us to explain the power of jade, the consistent placement of jade on the bodies in tombs demonstrates its importance. Ya Chang had seven bronze axes for warfare in life, and six jade and stone axes for defence in the afterlife. There were also some jade spearheads elegantly mounted in bronze. Ya Chang and Fu Hao had 175 and 755 jades respectively. By contrast, the military leader Ya Zhi had just thirty-three.[57] This discrepancy is more startling once we recognise that the Shang, by reworking so many ancient pieces, may have suffered from shortages of raw nephrite.

Seventy-eight more ordinary bronze spearheads and seventy-three dagger axes, often called halberds, make up the majority of Ya Chang's arsenal. Both weapons were mounted on long staffs for fighting at some distance. The halberds were set at a right angle to the staff with a narrow, bronze flange thrust through the wood. They are early iterations and by Ya Chang's time halberds of a new kind, with a vertical hole for the staff, had arrived – and only these carry his name. This advanced method of mounting and securing the halberds can be found in the nearby sacrificial pits and was inspired by axes with tubular shaft holes, popular on the Loess Plateau and the nearby steppe beyond. Ya Chang commanded the armoury of a leader in the Shang army, but as we look closer we find traces of a northern identity among his possessions.

The weapons make us wonder who the enemies were. The oracle bone inscriptions record orders to raise troops:

> On *dingyou* [day thirty-four] divined: 'His Majesty will form the three armies, Right, Centre, and Left.'[58]

From the bones we also know that the Shang fielded armies of 3,000 to 5,000 men, sometimes as many as 10,000.[59] The names of several leaders in these campaigns, including Fu Hao, appear in the inscriptions:

> Making cracks on *xinsi* [day eighteen] Zheng divined: 'In the present season, if His Majesty raises men and calls upon Fu Hao to attack the Tufang, [we] will receive abundant assistance.' Fifth Moon.[60]

Ya Chang's name is missing from the divination archives but an object, an unassuming bronze arc placed atop his coffin, reveals his contribution. If we could pick up this curved bar, tapered at each end into a hook with a hollow ball at the tip, we would hear a jingling sound. This is not a weapon but rather a tool. Ya Chang had six: four with jingles and two with horses' heads. These are rein holders for a chariot driver to attach to his belt. The reins of a pair of horses could be wound around their hooks, freeing the chariot driver's hands to wield a weapon or cut loose an injured horse.[61] Tiny slivers of turquoise decorate the arched surfaces with animal heads and cicadas, and one of the holders bears Ya Chang's name inlaid with the stone, telling us that these special tools were for him and his attendants to use. The same turquoise displayed his name on his small axes, intended for combat. Turquoise inlays were a rare luxury.[62] By the late Shang, it seems turquoise was primarily for fittings, tools and weapons belonging to charioteers, but rarely for vessels. Such inlay was delicate and would have worn away in battle, so the equipment may well have been fashioned specially for the burial. Although the reign holders were almost certainly made at Anyang, the jingles and horse heads referenced a northern tradition. The bronze workshops must have received specific instructions to create such items for Ya Chang. Fu Hao too was a chariot leader: she also had rein holders with jingles and horse heads, hers embellished with dragons. As with the stag on the royal *ding*, the percolation of northern tools, armour and motifs among the bronzes owned by the Shang elite is testimony to their wide geographical reach and the skills of their workshop organisers.

To see the kind of vehicle that Ya Chang commanded we need only look a little further south of the temple-palace, where five burial pits contain chariots.[63] Two chariots, carefully placed inside one of the pits, had oval baskets made of a vertical frame, possibly of wooden stakes woven together with organic materials such as leather, to carry a driver and perhaps a warrior too. Later these were replaced by bigger rectangular boxes, which were also woven. Both varieties were fixed directly on to the chariot's axle. This connected two wooden wheels, more than two metres in diameter, with between eighteen and twenty-six spokes apiece, which sat either side of the basket. These were sophisticated vehicles – the tanks of their day. A shaft with a bronze

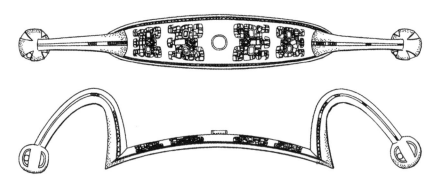

Ya Chang's rein holder, length 36.6 cm.

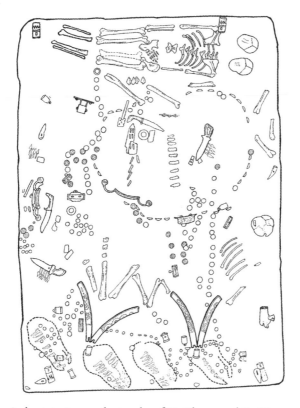

A chariot pit near the tombs of Ya Chang and Fu Hao.

animal head ran forward from the basket to a yoke bar, from which hung V-shaped yoke-saddles for the two horses drawing the chariot. Four horses were buried in this pit (their heads are visible along the bottom of the plan).[64] The pit also housed two chariot drivers, both orientated east–west and buried prone, though an incomplete skeleton of another individual was also found. The chariot drivers were equipped with Anyang-made rein holders, animal-headed knives and a number of other weapons such as spearheads and halberds, confirming that their purpose was war, and war in the afterlife, not just transport. The chariots and horse harnesses were extensively decorated with bronze fittings inlaid with turquoise, often in the shape of stars. But something more fundamental was at play here. Chariots had not been invented at Anyang, nor were they inherited from any previous ruler in ancient China. They were brought from elsewhere, and the horses with them. Their arrival was a transformative moment in China's history.

There are constant references to hostile peoples around the Shang, designated with the suffix *fang*, referring to areas beyond the borders of Anyang.[65] Persistent divinations about attacks from the *fang* register a clamouring anxiety. From the reign of Wu Ding onwards, northerners from the Loess Plateau ventured south to raid Shang lands with distressing regularity. To meet their northern enemy on their own terms, the Shang had to incorporate chariots, horses and chariot drivers into their armies – and into their rituals too. The threat was also the solution. By the late thirteenth century BC, chariots were buried alongside rulers to defend them in the afterlife. Chariots had become part of the Shang world. Yet this development passes without mention in the oracle bones and can only be traced through the tombs. Indeed, the very character for the vehicle itself is sporadic in the divination archives. The graph, which looks like a chariot seen from above, appeared in clan names and was only used occasionally.[66] In Shang inscriptions, chariot forces are thought to be designated by the term *Duo Ma*, 'the many horse (officials)'. Horses were not generally ridden at this time, so it is likely that the *Duo Ma* were managers or drivers of the chariots:

A Shang chariot.

Making cracks on the *bingshen* day [day thirty-three] divined: '[We] will deploy the Horse [chariot officers] – the left, right and centre – 300 [of them].' Sixth moon.[67]

The name Ya, which we recognise from Ya Chang's title, is sometimes appended to make *Duo Ma Ya*, or 'leader of the many horse officers'.[68] But elsewhere in the divination archives the graph for horses is joined with *fang* to describe hostile peoples in chariots.

The shared character is telling. Chariot leaders were now in the Shang army but could also drive in an opposing army. Perhaps due to encounters with the *Ma-fang*, the Shang equipped themselves with new machines, new animals and new skills and imported chariots, horses and their drivers. Ya Chang was undoubtedly part of this Shang enterprise. At the same time, these acquisitions brought challenges into the day-to-day management of the Shang militia. Horses were a prime instrument of war as they powered the chariot. The need to obtain horses, to capture or engage people to train them, to pasture herds and to build the chariots – which, as they were repeatedly buried, had to be continually replaced – was a significant drain on Shang resources.

The proximity of Ya Chang's tomb to the temple-palace, with a throng of attendants, weapons and chariot fittings, reinforced by the presence of the royal consort Fu Hao and the chariots they both commanded, marks him out as essential to the protection of the Shang king. His role extended beyond the battlefield, however, to the acquisition and management of the horses. Relationships were built with horses from a young age and honed over a lifetime. Ya Chang is also part of the wider story of horses becoming crucial military partners, not just for the Shang and then the Zhou, but for entire armies across Eurasia. As the Shang were pushing back the incursions from the north, the Egyptian Pharaoh Ramses II was engaging in chariot battles with Hittite forces from Anatolia. Famous wall carvings from the Assyrian palaces parade the virtuosity of their king in driving chariots in the well-known Lion Hunt.[69]

The horses that drew the Shang chariots were not the local *Equus przewalskii* that still roams, albeit scarcely, on the Mongolian steppe, but ancestors of the breed we ride today, the *Equus caballus*.[70] Such horses had probably been domesticated far to the west, before spreading east. They moved along similar routes to the people who brought metallurgy and cattle, sheep and goats to China.[71] Their passage, and those of the early chariots – light wooden carts with spoked wheels invented in the eastern Urals – can be mapped by rock carvings strung along the steppe.[72] Across the sweeping grasslands and mountains are hundreds of megaliths, known as deer stones, first erected around 1400 BC and continuously carved for several centuries.[73] These tall stones pay homage to important figures. A few actually have a human face at their summit. More often they are engraved with rings, such as might be worn around a person's temple or ears, thus suggesting rather than representing a human head (plate 8). Giving these slabs their name are layered carvings of stags, their antlers trailing behind them, swimming upwards across all sides of the stones. The carved stags reproduce tattoos or appliqués on clothes. Engraved around the lower part of the stones is a belt from which would hang weapons, tools and rein holders, identical in function and style to those belonging to Ya Chang. He also owned a curved knife, with a stag's head and a protruding eye, which may even have come from Mongolia.[74] The deer stones introduce a new phase of interaction between the steppe and the Central Plains. These moments of encounter and exchange are also signalled by new weapons and armour, including bronze helmets in the royal tombs.

In the same era that the deer stones were erected, horses were celebrated in sacrificial rituals on the steppe, their heads, hoofs and bones buried ceremonially in deposits around khirigsuurs – stone-fenced monuments – which were visited and supplemented year after year.[75] Here is the physical record of a different cosmology threaded through lives in which horses were essential partners.[76] In this demanding environment horses were treasured and bred in large numbers. In the winter they could sweep away the snow, allowing other herded animals to feed. When freezing rain turned the grasslands to ice so that not even the horses could clear it, the steppe people were frequently driven south. At Anyang, the chariots they introduced were without precedent. Initially, chariots can only have been crafted by carpenters familiar with the best wood for the felloes, which make up the circular rim of the wheels, and the technique of heating it so that it could be bent without fracturing.[77] The first chariots made in the Shang lands were likely built by northerners captured in battle. The woodworking technology could be copied and learned, but the animals which powered them were another matter. Horses had not been bred or broken in central China before the late Shang period, let alone trained in pairs.[78] The Shang needed people with roots in, or at least close contact with, northern hinterlands. They also had to gain access to a constant supply of strong horses from present-day Mongolia and Inner Mongolia. We can imagine that the intruders soon became members of Shang society, bringing their own traditions with them, such as prone burial, which was practised precisely in the regions where the horses came from.[79] We cannot know whether or not Ya Chang and the others buried prone at Anyang had themselves

A rubbing of the four sides of a deer stone on the steppe at
Uushigiin Ovor in Khovsgol province (*c.*1400–700 BC).

made the journey south as part of the *Ma-fang* threat.[80] Their fore-bears may have led the way, and then they found themselves in the Shang's employment, not only as chariot commanders but also as the keepers and trainers of horses for the Shang army.[81]

This was not a single episode. Even when horses were introduced to central China they could not be properly bred there. Long before the arrival of domesticated herds, the human population of the agricultural basins of the Yellow River had grown too extensive to turn their grain-growing land over to pasture. Horses deprived farmers of land and required too much fodder.[82] The peripheral land was marshy, and the high temperatures and humidity of the summer monsoon were not suited to rearing horses.[83] A further difficulty seems to have been the lack of certain minerals in the soil of the agricultural areas, especially selenium, which is required for bone and muscle development in cattle and horses. This deficiency also has grievous effects on bone development in humans, known as Kashin-Beck disease. An extensive region extending in a great arc from the southern Tibetan Plateau in the south-west, across the Yellow River and northwards to eastern Siberia and north Korea, has this deficiency. All central regions dominated by the Shang and in due course by the Zhou were challenged by these problems, which of course they could not recognise.[84] As horses bred in the lower Yellow River area proved too weak to match those of the northerners, the Shang had to turn to their neighbours again and again. Bronzes made by the Shang, possibly exchanged for horses, have been found far into the Loess Plateau where the wind-blown deposits, and the neighbouring grasslands, offered much better geological and climatic conditions, putting the rulers of the central states in the unenviable position of relying on the herders and stockbreeders.[85]

The Shang chariots and their horses were clearly the status symbols of military leaders. They were also essential parts of the burial ritual. The 300 chariots mentioned in one inscription would have demanded 600 horses. Consequently, the passage of horses over the Loess Plateau and down the Yellow River would have been a thriving project, encouraging a small but steady migration of northerners familiar with their care. Over the next 3,000 years this stimulated a continuous interdependence between northerners on the Loess Plateau with direct steppe contacts and the rulers on the Central Plains.[86] The people within these landscapes remained distinct. However, the burials of Ya Chang and Fu Hao are early signs of some assimilation.

The late Shang recognised and accepted people from diverse backgrounds and, to rule successfully, they quickly adopted the war machine of their neighbours and absorbed some of them to drive it. And, in return, their rich and ordered agricultural world allowed newcomers to follow its ritual and writing customs. This dialogue was of profound significance to both sides. The need for well-bred horses fostered a never-ending relationship. The peoples of the settled basins continued to develop strategies to obtain horses. And even when great steppe groups dominated China after the fall of the Han dynasty in the third century AD, they in turn found themselves pragmatically adopting the rituals of the ancestral cult for the afterlife.[87]

Ya Chang's bronzes now look very different. The casting is outstanding, finessed in Anyang's most prestigious workshops, and indicative of his high social standing. But his banqueting set seems to be incomplete. There are no water vessels, not even a typical water basin. At the burial, the organisers seem to have enhanced Ya Chang's personal set – the inscribed vessels – by adding five uninscribed pairs of *gu* and *jue* to the existing four to bring the total number up to nine.[88] The alcohol vessels, the *fangjia* and the angular flask, *zun*, were usually cast in pairs, yet here we see only singletons. The double inscription within the neck of the *zun* is also very odd. Were all the bronzes granted after Ya Chang had died in battle? Or did he initially own an incomplete set? The latter seems rather unlikely. More plausible is a degree of haste to make sure that Ya Chang, a chariot leader connected with the north, had magnificent bronzes for the afterlife. It seems that every effort was made to create a set for his funeral in recognition of the loyalty and bravery that he had shown, and the knowledge and skill that he had brought to the Shang army.

Ya Chang had 157 large jade beads wound around his head and body, along with 1,472 cowrie shells. These must have been sewn on to the shroud or clothes in which he was buried. Fu Hao likewise had over 100 jade beads and 7,000 cowries.[89] The jades and the cowries were presumably gifts from the court. At the same time, however, they suited the tastes of northerners across Eurasia where shiny materials – first animal teeth, shells, small, fine stones and later gold – were the favoured accessories of mobile peoples. Ya Chang's beads and cowries wove together the two aspects of his identity – as a member both of the Shang elite and a descendant of northerners who served them – as did small, delicate scraps of gold found with him, a further sign of a material associated with the north, almost invisible due to corrosion from adjacent bronzes.

The closer we look, the more we see. Ya Chang seems at first to be unmistakably a high-ranking member of Shang society, offered a suitably deep tomb. His set of banqueting vessels, bells and weapons carrying his name all confirm that the ritual specialists considered him their equal or superior. As warriors, he, Fu Hao and the charioteers were poised to defend the temple-palace in the afterlife. Ya Chang's authority was enhanced by his wounded body being buried prone, acknowledging his northern origins and equine expertise. To honour Ya Chang's victories the ritual specialists had carried out a hybrid burial, which involved creating a standard tomb but placing his body in a position that was typical of his ancestors. The overseers of the workshops that made the bronze weapons and vessels – cornerstones of Shang ritual – did the same. When they produced his rein holders and knives they incorporated northern refrains – jingles and horse heads. In these formative centuries between 1300 BC and 1045 BC, the late Shang accepted not only new military technologies but also the traditions of the individuals who managed and drove horses. An outstanding commander such as Ya Chang was venerated with a dwelling adjacent to the seat of Shang power. And his bronze hand enabled him to once again pick up the reins and command the convoy of the king's chariots.

PART II

The Language of Objects, 1200–700 BC

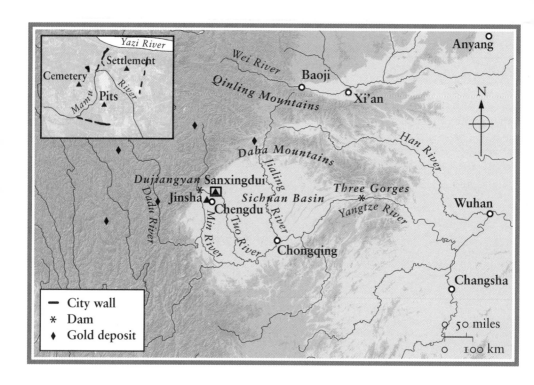

Sanxingdui and the Sichuan basin

4.

Sacrifices in a Hidden Land

The road to Shu is hard, harder than climbing the Sky.

Li Bai, *The Road to Shu is Hard*
(the ancient name for Sichuan).[1]

The Sichuan basin is hemmed in by soaring mountains. The eastern ridges of the Tibetan Plateau are an almost impenetrable barrier. They stand like an enormous fence at between 3,000 and 4,000 metres above sea level, no more than 300 to 400 kilometres from Chengdu, the provincial capital of Sichuan. The Yangtze rising on the Tibetan Plateau first runs south before turning east within the basin. It is prevented from running further towards south-east Asia by high land. The river, to find a way out, has cut a deep and perilous gorge, or rather Three Gorges, in the east, taking it to Wuhan, where it is joined by the Han River for the remainder of its long journey to the sea. Three winding tributaries – the Min, the Tuo and the Jialing – flow into the Yangtze from the north. The Jialing can be followed upstream, northwards towards the Qinling range, south of the agricultural land along the Wei River, offering another, less punishing route out of the basin. Alternatively, the nearby eastern ranges can be traversed into the Han River basin. The Yangtze basin is separated from the Yellow River by these northern mountains, creating a boundary between the two rivers and the lands they water. The whole Sichuan basin lies within the summer rain belt of the Pacific Monsoon. While the Yellow River creates a continuum along its length, and the wind-blown loess a shared rural life to the north, the basins along the Yangtze are distinct from one another, often cut off from the next by mountains, lakes and marshes.

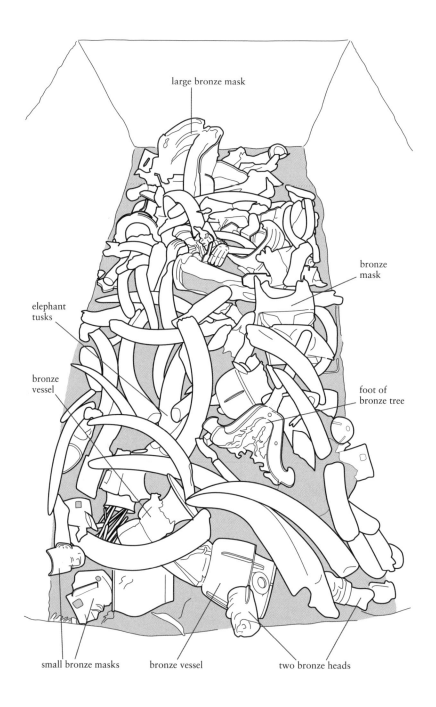

large bronze mask

bronze
mask

elephant
tusks

bronze
vessel

foot of
bronze tree

small bronze masks   bronze vessel   two bronze heads

The pit is 5 m long and 2 m wide.

The Yangtze delta and the Sichuan basin are nearly 2,000 kilometres apart, with different landscapes and independent early histories.

Today, with a population of over 100 million, Sichuan is one of the most prosperous regions in China, yielding agriculture and industry. It is now integrated into the rest of the country by long-distance trains and airlines, but until the Qin armies annexed the basin in 316 BC, as they moved east to conquer the Kingdom of Chu, interaction with the other parts of China was limited. The ancestors of the First Emperor and his Han successors, with their capitals at Xi'an on the far side of the Qinling Mountains, built or repaired the first 'planked roads'. Planks supported on cantilevered wooden beams and narrow channels cut into the mountain rock along steep river valleys finally connected Xi'an and Chengdu. As with the earthen walls of Liangzhu, this formidable engineering feat demanded a long-term and, in this case, conscripted labour force.[2] The effort was driven by Qin ambition, as were attempts to prevent the Min River from flooding the plains near Chengdu.[3] Under the direction of Li Bing in 256 BC, the power of the river was subdued by leading it through three newly dug channels. Renovated many times, this system is still a major tourist attraction. Known as the Dujiangyan, the project reflects the fear of flooding that simmered among local officials. During the nineteenth century, great iron turtles and oxen were retrieved from riverbeds, originally buried to protect against the rivers rising drastically.[4] This method of flood prevention emerged out of the correlative thinking that spread widely from the fourth century BC, in which iron was understood to control water.[5]

In *The Hard Road to Shu* (*Shu Dao Nan*) Li Bai (AD 701–62) described the difficulties in reaching the basin and the dangers of crossing the planked roads:

When the earth collapsed and the mountains crashed
the muscled warriors died.
It was after that when the ladders to heaven
were linked together with wood and stone.
 Up above is
the towering pillar where six dragons turn the sun,

Down below on
the twisting river colliding waves dash into the turns,
The flight of the yellow crane cannot cross it;
Gibbons and monkeys climb in despair.[6]

The challenges of the road were reaffirmed in poems and paintings of the flight of the Tang emperor Xuanzong (AD 685–762). In AD 755 he faced rebellion and was forced to abdicate, abandoning his capital near Xi'an and escaping via the planked roads to the sheltered basin of Sichuan (plate 14).[7] The other route in and out of the basin was along the Yangtze River but any brave traveller had to pass through the Three Gorges, nearly 200 kilometres of perpetual peril. With torrents tearing down the river in spring and summer, winter was the only possible time to attempt to go upstream. In all seasons, the force of the current was immense and sailing was impossible, so the boats were hauled by men, with enormous bamboo ropes, clambering along narrow paths cut into the mountains. Rocks below the swirling water and lurking rapids destroyed many boats and drowned hundreds of passengers. The Gorges appear in Li Daoyuan's (d. AD 527) lyrical account, *Guide to the Waterways with Commentary (Shui Jing Zhu Jiao Zheng)*:

The two banks are chains of mountains with nary an opening. Layered cliffs and massed peaks hide the sky and cover the sun. If it is not midday or midnight, the sun and moon are invisible. In summer, when the waters rise up the mountains, routes upstream and downstream become impassable . . .

When winter turns to spring, there are frothing torrents, green pools, and crystalline eddies that toss and turn reflections. On the highest peaks strange cedars grow in profusion, hanging springs and waterfalls gushing from their midst. Pure, luminous, towering, lush – there is so much to delight.

Whenever the weather clears or the day dawns with frost, within forests chill and by streams swift, one hears the long cries of gibbons high above. Unbroken and eerie, the sound echoes through the empty valleys, its mournfulness fading only after a long time. For this reason the fishermen [of the area] sing: 'Of Badong's Three Gorges, Wu Gorge is longest; when the gibbon thrice cries, tears drench your gown'.[8]

The Yangtze became more frequently travelled in the nineteenth century with the arrival of European steam shipping. But Isabella Bird (Mrs Bishop), aboard a traditional junk in 1898, still found the Yangtze dangerous:

> The river-bed, there forty feet below its summer level, is an area of heaped, contorted rock-fragments, sharp-edged, through which one or more swirling streams or violent rapids pursue their course, the volume of water, even at that season, being tremendous.[9]

Rocks and shoals were eventually dynamited in the twentieth century to forge a clear passage for sailboats and coal steamers and the Three Gorges Dam was finally completed in 2008. It is 185 metres high and spans 2,309 metres, creating a reservoir stretching for hundreds of kilometres behind it.[10] Yet even with this modern infrastructure, the Yangtze still floods many a year across cities and farmland to the east.

In the second millennium BC, as the charioteer Ya Chang was defending Anyang, a society at the ancient city of Sanxingdui was flourishing. The presence of jades and bronze technology suggests intermittent moments of encounter despite the physical barriers, but the materials found at Sanxingdui bear no relation to the prevailing burial rituals or ancestral cult of the late Shang capital. The people settled along the Yellow River were not the only cultural force in ancient China. Sanxingdui, some 40 kilometres north of Chengdu, is proof of the cultural diversity that arises from environmental diversity, an individuality caused by (comparative) isolation. The population at Sanxingdui had a very different understanding of life and the world of the spirits.

People whose material culture is named as belonging to the Baodun, an earlier rice-farming society, first built several walled cities in the late third and second millennia BC to the west and south of Sanxingdui.[11] The characters for Sanxingdui read as Three Star Mounds, yet while bits of pottery and jades have been stumbled upon since 1927, archaeologists only realised in 1985 that the mounds were the remains of a city wall.[12] The walls had long sloping sides on their faces, probably to protect against flooding and land erosion. They resemble those found at ancient cities further along the Yangtze, implying that people must have moved here from the east.[13] Walls to the east, west and south of the Yazi River, a tributary of the Tuo, surrounded traces of houses and workshops. These walls were incredibly thick: about 40 metres wide at the base and about 20 metres at their remaining height. Two rectangular pits were discovered by builders from a local brickyard digging clay.[14] The corners of both pits pointed to the cardinal directions and were neatly cut into virgin soil and sealed with tamped earth. The first pit excavated was originally thought to be a few decades older than the second, although both are contemporary with late Shang rule. Pit 1 was 3.5 by 4.5 metres at the top and smaller at its base. It held a substantial hoard: 200 bronzes, among which were four vessels, thirteen human heads, 107 rings and forty-four triangular serrated blades. There were 200 jade and stone items, including sixty tools and seventy blades, and four gold objects including a tubular sheath for a staff. There were thirteen elephant tusks near the top and heaps of cowrie shells underneath. The pit was also filled with three cubic metres of burnt animal bones and ash.[15] If the contents of pit 1 were remarkable, the discoveries in pit 2 were astonishing. Pit 2, which lay 30 metres away, was longer and narrower, but about the same depth. It was filled with jades, bronzes, stone implements and gold pieces in three layers. Pit 2 stored forty-four more of the bronze heads, of which at least six were wrapped in gold masks. There were also twenty faces on U-shaped bronzes, 4,600 cowries, sixty-one gold objects, sixty-seven elephant tusks and three animal masks. Most unexpected was a full-sized figure in bronze.

These pits were not tombs – they were sacrifices or ceremonial offerings by a clan whose name we do not know in a ritual language we do not recognise. In pit 1, the depth of bones and ash suggests a sacrifice of animals with the burning of wood or bamboo, before the wholesale destruction and burial of precious goods. This second mysterious pit was more formalised, as the objects were carefully arranged. Jade, bronze, gold and ivory had been buried in aligned pits and confined to the ground, never to be seen again in the lives of their makers. Just like the meticulously prepared tombs, the pits were consigned to another part of the universe. With new excavations in 2021, we now know of six more pits, further evidence of a great destruction of wealth.[16]

The pits set out in bronze, gold and jade the distinctive world view of the people who made them. Without any accompanying written records, this is a language of objects that is challenging to decipher. And it does not match the language of the objects at Anyang. The tall man cast in bronze, interred with a store of precious materials, was undoubtedly a central figure in this society. His discovery in today's Sichuan province astonished the whole of China. When exhibited in Germany, London, Seattle and New York, the man also captivated the world. Standing on his pedestal, he is more than two and half metres tall, weighing 180 kilos. The man's name and history remain unknown. He was found broken in two, with the parts widely strewn.[17] We do not know why he had to be shut away for ever. His life and power were deliberately destroyed; clearly he was not just a decorative statue, but an essential member of the Sanxingdui world. The man is slender, his body emphasised by a long robe drawn in above the waist and brushing his ankles. He has a strong chin and his brow, above the heavy ridges of his eyebrows, is bound by a headband that secures the remains of a flaring headdress. Like other heads found in the pits, his protruding eyes are almond-shaped, and below them pronounced cheeks spread from a broad nose. The ears are oversized and holes in the lobes must have been for earrings. From the base of his pillar-like neck two arms extend horizontally, bent inwards at the elbows, ending in monstrous hands that must have encircled an object now lost. These open hands are too massive to hold even an elephant tusk. Whatever he grasped, the man must have been an awesome sight. His profile is still striking, his stern, unseeing gaze mysterious (plate 16).

In contrast to the enormous, almost clumsy, hands the man's robe is decorated with a network of fine detail, with intricate dragon patterns cast into two of the three layers of garments. There is a division marked by a horizontal line between the shorter upper garment and the longer inner robe. This robe falls to below the knees and has two hanging tails, one on each side. Another, less decorated inner garment is visible at the sleeves. The man stands on a square pedestal, supported on all four sides by elephant heads, one at each corner with their trunks curled up, above a plain base that may have been sunk into the ground. Although the man appears to have been made in a single casting, he, his stand and his base were assembled from at least eight pieces, cast individually. While the craftsmen at Sanxingdui were able to cast simple bronzes in one pour, their ambition to create complex figures led them to cast several pieces separately to be joined together.[18] At Anyang, when casters wanted to join separate pieces, for instance fixing the handles to a basin, they often cast the handles first and then inserted them into the mould for the whole piece. As the hot metal was poured into the mould it joined with the precast handles, or the basin was cast first and the handles cast on, leaving a trace of additional metal on the surface. But the casters in the Sichuan basin were masters at creating several separate parts and then soldering them together.

Are we looking at a king, a priest, a deity or some being beyond the limits of our imagination? Was he an imposing guardian to ward off evil? Or a mythic figure to be venerated? The pits are the only way into this universe. The Sanxingdui casters were able to realise a particular vision in a permanent form. And as this vision was shattered, their society was eliminated. Future discoveries may yield new surprises, but for now the man is unique in the entire inventory of ancient Chinese archaeology. He is the only person in the late centuries of the second millennium BC we have in bronze, standing at full size. On the Central Plains and beyond there was no tradition of large-scale sculpture.[19] Further north, beyond the boundary of the Pacific Monsoon,

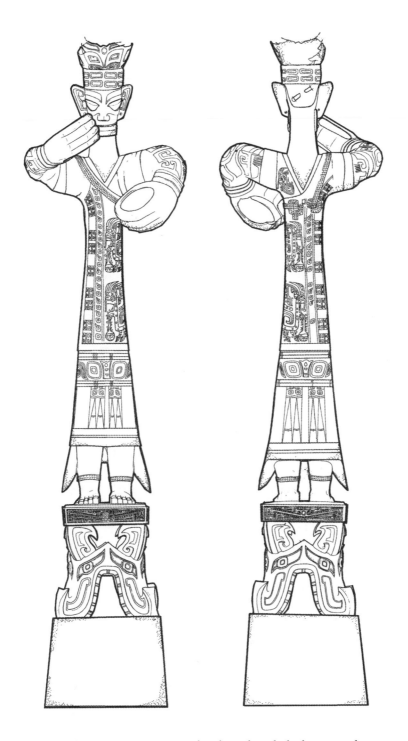

The towering bronze man is 1.72 m in height and, with the base, stands at 2.6 m.

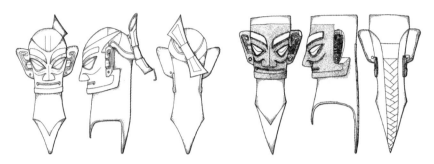

(*left*) A bronze head with a textile band at the back, height 51.6 cm.
(*right*) A head with a mask of gold foil, height 42.5 cm. The flat top suggests
that such heads were originally made from trunks of slender trees.

concentrated in present-day Mongolia but spanning the steppe, we
have encountered powerful warriors commemorated on deer stones
(plate 8). But these do not resemble the man at Sanxingdui in any way.

We are still startled by a direct encounter with him. His compelling presence appears to come out of nowhere. We are unable to
name him, or describe his society or his beliefs, yet he challenges
and enriches our interpretation of ancient China. Like the tombs at
Liangzhu and Taosi, these sacrificial deposits take us far outside typical narratives told through the relics of the Shang dynasty, revered
over generations in China and interpreted through textual histories
inscribed on the oracle bones and bronzes. Bronze vessels had been
thought to be a beacon of Shang achievement. Yet here, in the Sichuan
basin, is something so different. Linear patterns of dragons in profile,
with tiny legs and rounded claws, on the bronze man signify his prestige. This was an independent, rich world whose people exploited
their landscape to realise their own beliefs.

The two pits together contained over fifty bronze heads, many
between 30 and 50 centimetres in height, but others smaller at 15 centimetres. The uniformity of the facial features show that the heads were
not portraits of individuals, though it is possible that they represented
a specific population group.[20] The bronze heads also wore a variety of
ceremonial hats, headdresses and hairstyles, probably following the
ritual dress of their makers. A long plait of hair often hangs down the

back of those with high, flat heads. A rounded head has a ribbon tied behind. Other heads bear bands in bronze like that on the full figure. Some headdresses were simple, and these may have had textile hats or crowns which have since disintegrated. This was an extensive and varied community of historical or mythological figures, who perhaps also once wore diverse real clothes. At least six of the heads have a layer of gold foil over their faces, giving them an additional aura and perhaps religious rank. A full face in gold and a large fragment have also recently been discovered at Sanxingdui and another at the later capital at Jinsha (plate 15). The glow of gold hardly known elsewhere in ancient China, and certainly not among the Shang, was obviously prized for its intensity compared with the softer sheen of bronze. As the people of Sanxingdui formed their own cultural framework it is not surprising that they chose gold, which was readily available to mine in mountains north of Chengdu.[21]

The strong faces and repetitive forms were most likely earlier carved in wood. Instead of ceramics and the loess, which were the foundation of the casting technology on the Yellow River, here in the Sichuan basin wood may have been the dominant material. Cutting and carving it in curving lines would have stimulated the sloping brows, giving the heads force and intensity.[22] The deep cuts leaving protruding eyes, with two surfaces at different angles, could also have been made with a sharp tool. Without pupils, the staring eyes have an inward-looking aspect. Pupils were almost certainly once painted on them, as traces of a black colour appear on some of the eyebrows.[23] A line below the cheek looks as though it was again cut by a tool, as if following a wooden prototype. A horizontal mouth with two tight lips has small circular holes at the two corners, as if copying earlier examples, when a sharp drill was inserted at the corner and then cut across the wooden face to make the lips, shown when the man is viewed in profile (plate 16). The chin and the equally level line around the upper forehead look as though the trunk of a narrow tree was cut straight across.[24] The neck was not always neatly finished, as if it was to be covered later with other materials.[25] The fact that the bronzes were made by people familiar with wood sculpture is indicative of a history that pre-dated bronze. If so, the cutting and carving must have been done with stone tools, a sophisticated technology.[26]

We can imagine a period of experiment when the representation of their cosmology evolved from wood to metal.[27] This may have been only a decade, or it may have taken longer. The bronzes cannot have been the first attempts, but rather the culmination of practical experience. Complex beliefs may also have been physically realised in bamboo and textiles. By the time bronze-casting arrived in the Sichuan basin, not directly from the Yellow River basin but passing through other hands in the south, both the figurative styles and the beliefs that they supported had probably existed for some time. If there had been an earlier phase, when the primary material was wood, the figures could have been stationed within clearings, making an inhabited forest. While the heads are complete, their necks taper to a point, as though to be fitted over a long body, perhaps a tree trunk. In this context the bronze man was a more substantial version of these heads, for only he had a complete body in bronze from brow to feet. If more than fifty figures had bronze heads and wooden bodies, this would have built a whole community, be they ancestors, heroes, deities or spirits. Once more the regions of ancient China overturn our assumptions of what a Bronze Age might look like. Bronze weapons do not seem to have been of great significance here, although they certainly existed and have been found; nor were bronze banqueting sets used, though their ceramic counterparts appear. Instead the arrival of bronze was an added bonus – a novel way to make fabulous landscapes.

If all the heads rested on tall wooden bodies and carved pedestals, clothed in textiles and then assembled in a group, the effect must have been breathtaking. The approach of a museum visitor – only able to see individual heads – loses sight of the worlds which the people inhabited, governed by ritual cycles and explained in words, chants, dance and song. It is likely that some of the figures, such as the bronze man, had dramatic outstretched arms. This is made more probable by a smaller, damaged figure also found in the same pit, with an unusual headdress, arms in the same position and his hands

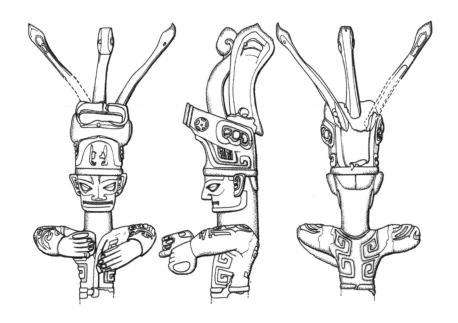

A man with an unusual headdress survives, height 40.2 cm.

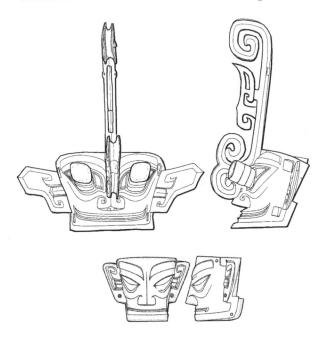

A U-shaped bronze face, height 84.3 cm, this time
with protruding pupils and a trunk.
(*bottom*) The same strange face, height 15 cm, to be attached
to a column or tree trunk.

grasping something.[28] U-shaped bronze heads, often termed masks, with similar facial features also peopled this imagined forest. Some are very wide, with broad menacing smiles, rod-like pupils projecting from the eyes and flaring ears arcing downwards. The most substantial mask from pit 2 is 138 centimetres in width and 66 centimetres in height.[29] Square holes on the forehead and either side could have been used to attach it to wooden structures. It would have been unsettling to see such a face emerging from a column on a building or even possibly a trunk of a tree. Two of the faces have a plume extension rising from the nose to well above the head and curving slightly forwards.[30] The large U-shaped bronzes were also built of several parts cast separately and then soldered together. Masses of bronze eyes and pupils excavated from the pits may have adorned other faces now lost. Another mysterious bronze, which must have been attached to something else, is shaped like the steering wheel of a machine. It may have represented the sun, or embodied a special symbol, or was perhaps a distant reference to a chariot wheel.[31] At this stage all possibilities remain open. The bronzes, fitted in buildings or attached to trees, belonged to a world of strange, venerated beings.

As well as incorporating existing trees in their world, the Sanxingdui people also added lofty, straggling bronze trees. One, badly broken, was retrieved from pit 2. A vertical pole, held on a ring by a tripod, forms the trunk. From it hang three sets of bow-shaped branches. On each branch is a flower on which perches a bird, and another flower flourishes from the branch tip. A dragon with a long rising tail lurks at the foot of the trunk. Other bronze ornaments, such as bells, probably hung from the branches. One bell has flanges like those on the early bells from the Central Plains; another has a curved knife with a ring on the grip, as a tiny clapper, like tools from the Loess Plateau. The tree bursts with life. It is a portal that must have figured in ritual. Its great height suggests that it stood at the gate or in the centre of a high building or open space. It was large enough to walk among, and was probably recreated in many more materials: first wood, and then perhaps also in bamboo and textile. A much smaller, damaged tree base had kneeling figures around it: participants in a

A tree, over 4 m in height, with birds perched on its drooping branches.

ceremony or denizens of the universe to which the dragon under the tall tree also belonged. Together they would have planted a forest. As so much in the pits was seriously damaged or deliberately broken, it is difficult to reconstruct every detail. More trees (sections were discovered in the recently excavated pits) filled with birds with peacock tails, one like a farmyard cock, anthropomorphic figures and creatures such as snakes undoubtedly also embellished these arboreal landscapes. We do not know where the trees and the figures were placed, but they must have stood together. While the use of elaborate materials to create and communicate with another aspect of reality is by now familiar, the consequence in this part of ancient China was entirely different. The people at Sanxingdui had their own distinct conception of the universe. Nothing like this has been found anywhere else in the world. The very strangeness is important and revealing. Sanxingdui shows us how difficult it is to engage with a world so unfamiliar,

An elephant bears people or spirits to an unknown destination, height 53.3 cm.

and how dependent we are on a lifetime of education in our physical, ideological and religious environments, which enables us to interpret things around us and express (at least a part of) that interpretation in words. Yet at the same time we are privileged to be able to assemble, if gradually, all the different parts of this universe for ourselves.

We can move closer to a clearer vision with a few more bronzes in miniature. When restored, they compress representations of anthropomorphic figures in new contexts, with a conspicuous winged creature. They have faces exactly like those we have already looked at, wear wide hats and patterned textile tunics and have rather stumpy legs. Their hats carry a four-petalled structure, with four long-necked heads acting as additional props.[32] Balanced on the triangles of the petals is a box containing rows of figures. Atop this box loom two eagles in profile. A pacing animal holds up the men. It has clearly delineated hoofs or bony toes on squat legs and its body is marked by two spirals. Flapping ears and a curved horn, or perhaps a trunk, rise above the head, and it has both a long tail and a pair of wings.[33] On its wide-open snout is a small circular petal. The beast and miniature men must have been participants in, or embodiments of, a myth that we cannot reconstruct today. The complexity of the composition suggests that, at ceremonies and rituals, people would have banded together to recreate such scenes. The creature has already appeared (p.105 above), with a trunk and spreading ears balanced as a headdress on the miniature figure.[34] It seems that tiny tusks were placed in the open snouts of the intriguing compositions. We are looking at elephants. Given the vast number of tusks in the sacrificial pits, we can deduce that elephants played a key part in religious life at Sanxingdui in the twelfth century BC. Even today, elephants are native to the forests south-west of Sichuan, in present-day Yunnan province. And we can now see that the ears and trunks of the masks combine elephantine and human features.

The standing man and other bronze figures had no parallels in the late Shang world, nor did the central role of elephants, despite the value of their ivory. Ya Chang and his peers communed with the afterlife in ritual banquets that they performed themselves, not by making representations of ancestors or supernatural beings. At such ceremonies, a relative may have acted as or taken the place of a recently deceased ancestor. We cannot use our experience at Anyang to understand Sanxingdui. The heads, the figures, the huge masks and the trees would, if placed together, have built a dramatic stage for ritual activities. The plain stand of the tall man even suggests that it was buried in the ground, making him immobile. The bronze trees and the masks attached to buildings or trees did not move either. They were not active in the ceremonies. The figures and trees were what we can still see, inhabitants of an otherwise invisible part of the universe, made visible for the people of Sanxingdui. By carving them in wood or casting them in bronze, it was possible for their makers to engage with them physically, to participate with them in rituals more fully and to welcome the figures into their community.

The bronze man could not have come into being without casting technology reaching Sanxingdui. Extracting small droplets of copper from rocks, assembling adequate quantities by smelting and creating alloys of copper, tin and lead for casting are not intuitive techniques that a metalworker could suddenly invent. After metallurgy was first discovered in Western Asia, it took many centuries for it to travel east and to reach the advanced levels we see in Sanxingdui. Even in northern China, where bronze-casting was extensively developed, it took around 400 years to achieve the level of casting that we see here. The use of metal alloys at Sanxingdui, alongside the piece-mould system of the Central Plains, tell us that bronze-casting arrived at this ancient Sichuan city fully developed. Did agents of the Shang come south-west looking for ores and bringing new skills? If the principal introduction of bronze-casting had come from Anyang, we would expect more attempts at making vessels. Instead we see a replication of wood-carving, including occasional examples of a mortise and tenon system, typically suited to carpentry, joining the separate pieces of the man's stand. Despite the seclusion of the basin, the importing of such a specific piece-moulding technique is, nonetheless, conspicuous of links beyond Sanxingdui. This includes an alcohol flask, *zun*, nearly 60 centimetres in height and about 50 centimetres in

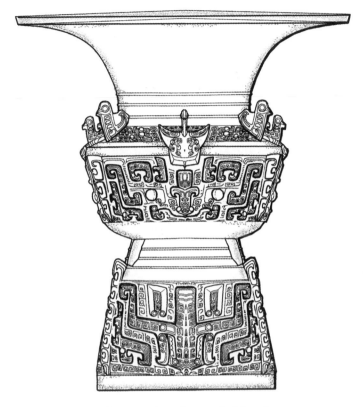

A southern version of a *zun*, height 56.5 cm.

diameter at the mouth, from the second pit, that immediately echoes Ya Chang's flask and the casting of the Yellow River basin.[35] Yet its proportions, a shallow body on a high narrowing foot and a trumpeting mouth, hooked flanges that divide decoration on the body and foot, small birds on the shoulders and large semi-rectangular holes in the foot, show that it was not cast at Anyang. Both body and foot carry versions of the *taotie*, but those on the foot have long, slender compressed jaws with narrow teeth, somewhat like a crocodile. This *zun*, along with six other vessels and three other alcohol containers called *lei* (restored from fragments in the pits) were distinct from those made on the Central Plains.[36] As the bronze vessels meet the bronze heads and trees, we realise that we are witnessing the result of a web of communication across vast areas. Today we might call this globalisation. The driving force behind these networks was the transfer of the useful technology of bronze-casting, adapted for several independent purposes.[37]

At Sanxingdui and other places in the Yangtze region many vessels held cowries, jades or stone implements, important in regions to the east of the Three Gorges in present-day Hunan.[38] Here we can see traces of the network that leads back not just to Anyang but to earlier bronze-casting at the Shang capital at Zhengzhou.[39] Moreover, southern casters developed their own traditions exploiting the copper mines along the lower Yangtze.[40] Encounters – trade, exchange or simply command and demand – brought bronze technology south as the copper ore went north. Although the principal Shang shapes served as inspiration, they were modified to southern tastes and to local customs and beliefs.

The extraordinary richness at Sanxingdui is inexplicable without this network that fostered not only casting but also a bounty of jade. The hazardous journey up the Yangtze may have been one avenue of contact. Another was probably the Han River, joining routes from the north over the mountains.[41] Jades found in the pits may have come this way and were clearly revered, as they were woven into the bronze man's woodland landscape.[42] We can appreciate the role of jade in the figure of one kneeling man, now missing his head, holding out a forked blade, a typical form usually made in jade. He shows us how some of these jades were presented at Sanxingdui. The man and his sceptre are likely to have belonged to one of the intricate scenes cast in bronze. Jade sceptres may have been carried in ceremonies or placed in front of the figures or masks. The sceptre is a copy of a well-known jade called a *yazhang*, or toothed *zhang*, especially popular at Shimao.[43] Instead of the carefully notched teeth on blades from Shimao and later Erlitou, those at Sanxingdui were strongly made in local jade-like stones.[44] Other weapons, some in stone and some in bronze, were also found in the pits. Aggressive, scalloped bronze blade edges would have painfully severed human flesh. Yet unlike in the contemporary Shang societies, warfare and death do not seem to have been celebrated. The *zhang* sceptres have not been found at Anyang, but they

A tiny bronze figure, height 4.7 cm, wields a jade sceptre.

clearly circulated – another example of how Sanxingdui lived beyond the reach of the late Shang. At Sanxingdui, sceptres were transformed and reinterpreted. In several examples the notch at the top was lengthened down into the body of the sceptre, with the sides drawn in to create the shape of a fish head. Here the teeth become fins or part of a tail. One has a bird perching, as on the bronze tree, in the fish's mouth.[45] The sceptre takes us back again to the Han River. There, much smaller versions were cast in bronze with the same deep fork, unlike many early forms of this sceptre made further north.

Another rare sceptre from Sanxingdui is carved with four rows of figures, all of whom have faces very like that of the bronze man. The figures stand on flat surfaces, above mountains. On either side of the two inner rows of hills are tiny engraved forked blades, the *yazhang*. They even show the notches on the sides. We are given a landscape setting as the stage for the rituals involving the jades. Early examples of the sceptre, as with the *cong*, have been found further east along the Yangtze or much further north at Shimao. They were carried along many routes threaded across China. We will probably never know who had the right to bear jades to new places. Nonetheless, such a proliferation of a single form, the *zhang*, is evidence of shared techniques and a widespread fascination with jade established outside the late Shang dynasty.

While the sceptres were often dark in colour, the pits also interred paler, almost white dagger-shaped jades, versions of the halberd, the primary Shang weapon.[46] However, like many jades buried far beyond

Detail from a jade sceptre.

the Central Plains or in tombs of a much later period, the people who acquired, looted or were gifted these jades attributed to them powers relevant to their own rituals and ideas of the universe. While traces of contacts by way of the jades remain visible, most of the bronzes belong solely to the people at Sanxingdui. The trees, the elephant masks, the tall man and his fellow heads are unique. If these had not been made, and if they had not been interred in pits but instead melted down, this community and their beliefs would have vanished. When we gather all the bronzes and visualise them in a landscape, we picture the world that the people of Sanxingdui saw for themselves.

The miniature scenes show us a well-established set of ceremonies, frequently performed by ritual specialists and routinely witnessed by the community.[47] Such a setting would have taken many years to accumulate, even if the arrival of bronze-casting in the thirteenth or twelfth century BC was relatively new. The destruction may have been either an attempt to obliterate some aspect of the vision or a step towards regenerating it. The pits and their contents look like an offering to placate spirits, or a sign of despair as the people of Sanxingdui turned away from their

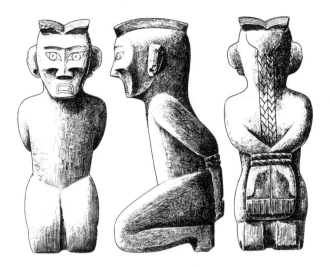

A captured figure in stone from Jinsha, height 21.7 cm.

world to build a new one. As we do not know how their society was constructed nor what language they spoke, we are haunted by ideas but cannot say why the landscape and its objects had to be shattered.

We do know that some people continued to live in the basin at the separate city at Jinsha, which became a great settlement. The city was built, without walls it seems, soon after Sanxingdui around 1100 BC and survived for some centuries. Houses, public buildings, workshops and kilns have been found, as have less formally arranged pits packed with extraordinary jades, gold and bronze. Jinsha continued the material culture of Sanxingdui.[48] Further destruction in the Jinsha pits is also a sign of immolation or distress. But although Jinsha had abundant jades, including some half finished, and pieces of spectacular gold, its bronzes do not reproduce the forest of Sanxingdui. Instead there are small stone sculptures of kneeling figures with their hands tied behind their backs. The faces, with their strong cheekbones, remind us of the bronze heads. The deep lines, which could originally have been cut in wood, are now exaggerated in stone. The plait of hair hanging down their backs also recalls one of the Sanxingdui hairstyles in bronze. Are these prisoners sacrifices, an attempt to stave off devastation, or perhaps warfare or invasion?

Sacrifices embody dread. Recent archaeological discoveries reveal that the two pits at Sanxingdui were part of a much larger sacrificial offering: the bronze man was surrounded by yet more intriguing and unsettling compositions.[49] Was he destroyed by others who did not want to accept his authority? It is possible that the city of Sanxingdui was first threatened and then overwhelmed, in part at least, by flooding. Was the flooding exacerbated by the growth in population and an extensive use of wood in ritual? Cutting down forests would have accelerated torrents in a rainy season. Were the offerings to halt the rising water? Yet we do not find sediment traces or flood remains, nor skeletons that might tell us of disease or raids. We simply do not know enough.

If the rituals and objects of the Shang and early Zhou had little impact in Sichuan, the role of the bronze man and his landscape at Sanxingdui likewise did not move north and east. There, banquets forged connections between life and the afterlife. As this world was occupied by those relatives whom they had known from life, the Shang may have felt no need to create new images of them. A landscape of life-size figures in a forest did not feature in the world-building of the succeeding dynasties and their settlements. We can therefore reason that Sanxingdui and Anyang did not know much about each other. Both, however, had extended their experience of the world to create a satisfying explanation of the universe that they knew and inhabited.

The pits at Sanxingdui are filled with tangible realisations of this wider universe. Their destruction therefore sought the opposite. The fragmented bronzes, the interred jades and gold, took this world and its spirits away. For some overwhelming reason, the man and his wooded surroundings had to be eradicated. This reminds us that outsiders have always struggled to reach this hidden realm of forests and elephants. Who the man in bronze was remains an enigma, and it is probably fitting, as the Sichuan basin itself stood aloof and inaccessible until the Qin laid the planked roads.

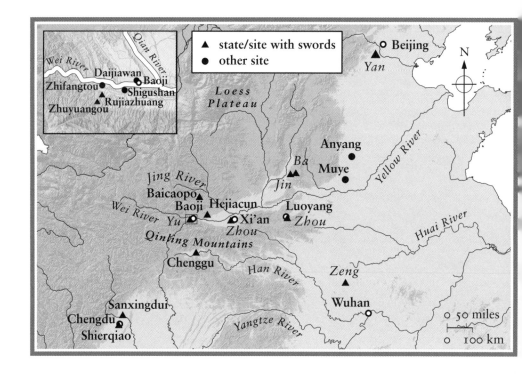

Baoji and the Western Wei Valley

5.

The Gift Economy at Baoji

As we move to Baoji, more than 800 kilometres west of Anyang, we find ourselves among the early allies of the Zhou. The modern city with its glinting high-rises conceals a much more significant feature of its history – long-distance communication. The city straddles one of the principal routes across Asia and today is an entrance to the New Silk Road of the Belt and Road Initiative. In the past, it was a key junction of roads from the west, the north and the south, leading people down into the Wei River Valley, then on east to the Central Plains. It was and is a vital point on the crossroads of China. Modern railways and motorways move eastwards through the Pass, on to the Central Plains. Baoji holds the western end, Xi'an the eastern.

Baoji faces away from central China along the principal road to Central Asia. The land rises steeply in nearby Gansu province towards its provincial capital at Lanzhou, at 1,500 metres above sea level. Beyond Lanzhou the Hexi Corridor, between the Tibetan Plateau, the Gobi Desert and the Mongolian Mountains, has always been an important passage. Protected to the north by hills and to the south by mountains, the Wei Valley is often treated as part of the enormous agricultural land further east. But this description disguises the fact that this narrow valley is bounded by high land, as a traveller there in the 1920s described a view to the south:

All morning long Huashan, second only to Taishan among the five sacred mountains of China, walled off the southern horizon with its series of jagged ranges, shaped not unlike a mammoth sleeping elephant, the sunless northern slopes like a great perpendicular

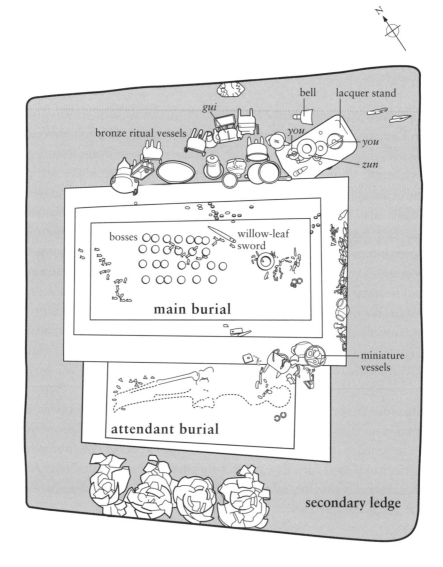

N

bell   lacquer stand

gui

bronze ritual vessels

you

you

zun

bosses   willow-leaf
sword

main burial

miniature
vessels

attendant burial

secondary ledge

The tomb of Yu Bo and his attendant, length 3.75 m,
width 4.4 m at the head, depth below today's surface 2.8 m.

wall of beautiful blue-grey colour, topped by a wonderful, fantastic skyline.[1]

Few travelled the roads south out of the valley, which provided vital links with neighbours and encouraged occasional exchanges, including with the people at Sanxingdui.[2] The Qinling Mountains, among them Huashan, stand in the way, and today's railway line travels through more than 300 tunnels and 1,000 bridges on its journey towards Sichuan. The route going north, the fourth branch of the crossroads, which enters the Loess Plateau, is completely hidden to the modern traveller. This middle ground is wedged between the pastoralists of the steppe and the farmers of the valleys. Inevitably, the promise of a more comfortable life in the fertile Wei River basin encouraged the repeated migration which drove China's political life over millennia. With harsh winters and limited rain, people further north were tempted by the land falling south and east to move into the Hexi Corridor, and then the upper Wei and Qian Valleys, taking them directly to Baoji. Movement south was not a single event, but cropping in the north seems to have become particularly difficult in the last centuries of the second millennium BC and many seem to have made the journey.[3]

The Zhou, who ousted the Shang in c.1045 BC, were among a number of groups who took the chance, arriving near Baoji earlier in the eleventh century BC. They then turned yet further east, first to a settlement below the Qishan Mountains, which became their ritual centre (now named Zhouyuan), before founding their residences at Xi'an. It was the Zhou who initiated Xi'an's long history as a dynastic capital down to the tenth century AD. We have hints of this journey from pastoral life and organised agriculture to settlements and cities in some of the very earliest Chinese verse. In a volume known as *The Book of Poetry* (*Shi Jing*), assembled from oral material around 600 BC, we learn of the first farming, led by a Zhou ancestor, Hou Ji:

Truly Hou Ji's husbandry
Followed the way that had been shown.

He cleared away the thick grass,
He planted the yellow crop.
It failed nowhere, it grew thick,
It was heavy, it was tall,
It sprouted, it eared,
It was firm and good,
It nodded, it hung –
He made house and home in Tai.[4]

Another poem records the next stage, the building of the first small settlement by the leader Danfu, grandfather of the first Zhou king, Wen (1056–1050 BC), father of King Wu (1049–1043 BC), who defeated the Shang:

So he halted, so he stopped.
And left and right
He drew boundaries of big plots and little,
He opened up the ground, he counted the acres
From west to east;
Everywhere he took his task in hand.[5]

There are few written sources which tell of the origins of the Zhou. While these poems may seem modest, they are far from it. They are vital evidence of the arrival of the Zhou from outside the agricultural lands before they defeated the Shang.

The Zhou were some of the most influential rulers in the ancient world and their 800-year reign is as much a part of China's identity as the Greeks and Romans are of many in the West. Zhou governing principles are still evoked, albeit in different words: the successful conquest and formation of a single united territory, the importance of a virtuous ruler concerned with the welfare of the people and the legitimation of history. And Zhou bronze vessels were copied as incense burners in temples of all periods across China, Korea and Japan. Today, copies stand in the halls of the major offices of the Chinese state and a 'Zun of Peace' was gifted to the United Nations in 2015.

From 1045 BC to the mid-eighth century BC the royal Zhou palaces were at or near Xi'an; then they moved to their secondary capital at Luoyang further east. This first period is known as the Western Zhou; the second half, down to their demise in 256 BC, leading to the ascendancy of the Qin in 221 BC, is called the Eastern Zhou.

The Zhou drew together many clans who have disappeared from history and only return to us in the tombs at Baoji. The fate of one group, the Yu, was tied to that of the more famous Zhou; they seem to have followed the Zhou and established themselves at Baoji, as we know from their three cemeteries. The Yu are just one of many shifting populations affiliated with Zhou military success. Their moves accompanied the first years of Zhou occupation of the Wei. The tomb of the earliest member of the Yu lineage in a cemetery at Zhifangtou was destroyed, with only some of its bronzes retrieved. But another Yu cemetery at Zhuyuangou, with most of the twenty-two tombs still intact, has been fully excavated. A third cemetery, at Rujiazhuang, offers us the last known generation of the Yu.[6]

The earliest burial in the Zhuyuangou cemetery was that of a man we shall call Yu Bo, recognising him as a leader of the Yu lineage. His tomb was impressive in size and assertive in layout. It was almost square, narrowing to the foot. At the centre was a wooden chamber with two inner coffins. A pit dug nearly three metres into the loess with a coffin chamber echoed what we saw at Anyang, but it was shallower, as he was not a member of the Zhou clan. Yet there is a striking deviation. Yu Bo had a female companion, a spouse or a concubine, alongside him. Burial with a companion, installed at a slightly higher level, was not an accepted custom on the Central Plains or in the Wei Valley. Yu Bo and his female companion were also aligned approximately east–west, deliberately avoiding the usual north–south convention. Building a tomb with a ledge for valued grave goods was a deliberate imitation of the practices of the Central Plains, indicating that Yu Bo wished to show his ancestors that he had risen in Zhou society. However, he had preserved some of his own traditions.

Yu Bo and his immediate ancestors were presumably new to Baoji, or at the very least had only recently taken up aspects of the ancestral cult. As joint burials were not favoured in the east, we have to look north to the Loess Plateau for the genesis of the Yu lineage, where, for example, joint burials were used in the north-west.[7] By contrast the Zhou, in setting up their rule in the Wei Valley and extending into the Central Plains, had followed Shang conventions, taking over tombs with a single occupant buried supine in a north–south orientation. Yu Bo's double burial was also adopted by later lineage leaders in the same cemetery – their traditions held good over several generations. He had a group of twenty-one bronze ritual containers for food and alcohol, a ladle and a bell, strung out alongside the coffin chamber on his right. Three further pieces were allocated to the woman and lay near her head, marking her status. Yu Bo also had rows of bosses on the lower part of his body, perhaps from his boots or shield, and a short sword.

We recognise Yu Bo's authority as a lineage leader from the size of his tomb relative to the twenty-one others at Zhuyuangou.[8] The last lord, buried in the cemetery at Rujiazhuang towards the end of the tenth century BC, also had a double tomb. Although the original structure was destroyed, we have some of the ritual vessels that belonged to the first known Lord of Yu buried nearby. Together the three cemeteries at Zhifangtou, Zhuyuangou and Rujiazhuang, and a clear sequence of leaders, are signs of a strong and wealthy community. Yu Bo and his heirs would have been surrounded by their clan or supporters, both as an army and as labourers working the fields. His achievements in life were not only realised in the size of his afterlife dwelling and its contents, but also reinforced by his descendants, who were able to offer ceremonial banquets to him with their own ritual sets. Each generation in turn thus assured their ancestors of the success of the lineage. From the Shang and probably earlier, down to the early twentieth century, families were bound by the ancestral cult to their forebears and descendants in a hierarchy determined by generational sequence. Wealth and status were fundamental markers within the hierarchies. As a result, the imperative to achieve wealth, to ensure the success of the lineage, has imprinted on China the importance of the wider family, to which all members are expected to contribute.

We know the name of the lineage not from Yu Bo's bronzes but from other bronzes nearby. We take it from an inscription on an impressive *gui*, a basin for ritual food offerings, in a tomb of Yu Bo's predecessor at the cemetery at Zhifangtou. The flamboyant decoration, perhaps referring to the pastoral life of the north, is of a real creature, an ox, with its horns projecting away from the surface, unlike the more usual *taotie* motifs, and a tiger grasping its head on the handles, anticipating the predator scenes later displayed on steppe weapons and belts.[9] A modern version of the character for Yu Bo's name is not used today, although it can be constructed. It is composed of the graph for a bow, combined with one for fish, or *yu*, from which we take the pronunciation Yu.[10] In the eleventh century BC the pronunciation would have been different. The word Bo is not a name, but a title for a senior member of a lineage who was a direct descendant in a single patrilineal line and thereby distinct from the wider clan and its branches into further lineages.[11] While none of Yu Bo's vessels bear his name, we can assume that he took the same title as his predecessor, for his tomb shows that he was the most eminent figure in the lineage of his day.

This *gui*, height 31 cm, was cast for an ancestor of Yu Bo. It bears an inscription (*right*) of six characters in early Zhou script. The first character, top right, is the character for Yu, with the graph for a bow (*left*) and a fish (*right*). Next to it is the character for Bo. The next four characters read 'made the treasured ritual *gui*'.

His name does not appear in the long inscriptions on other bronzes, nor in the copious later transmitted writings. The Yu lineage's renown did not spread. Having moved to Baoji, the Yu were clearly one of several local regional groups who assisted the Zhou at the beginning of their conquest. These early encounters may have led the Zhou scribes to give them a name for which a character could be devised. But the Yu did not subsequently command the attention of patrons and scribes working for the Zhou kings at their primary residences at Xi'an. The absence in the written history implies that the Yu were *early* allies, when the action was here, in the west.[12]

We actually learn more about the situation at Baoji from the *lack* of records. The Yu, and many others buried in tombs at the present-day villages of Shigushan and Daijiawan, and further east at Hejiacun and into the Loess Plateau at Baicaopo, display an abundance of northern weapons and tools, alongside ritual vessels from the Western Zhou.[13] The weapons are distinct from the armoury used by the Shang and in due course by the Zhou. They are sometimes compared with weapons from the steppe: daggers, axes with tubular shafts and maces. But they have not come directly from the steppe and are a local iteration of a style from the Loess Plateau.[14] Military forces had moved south and attracted rewards. Though we have no way of knowing whether the Zhou had settled yet, even temporarily, in this region, we see that the numerous clans were their allies.[15]

The sets of tiny bronzes arranged above Yu Bo's head, and the woman's stored in a larger basin, show that he was from elsewhere. Miniature jars with a pointed base, and deep ladles with a round body and a thick, upturned handle, belong to a different ritual tradition. Flat trays that imitate wood complete this intriguing group. None of these have parallels in bronze or in ceramic on the Central Plains. Miniatures are in themselves always significant and are used by many societies to recall objects and events long ago, or even imagined: the creation of a crib at Christmas, for example, or a doll's house. Accompanying combs and hairpins have led some to suggest that the bronze jars and ladles were an embellishment or for personal comfort; but it is entirely possible that they had other purposes. As they were placed in many of

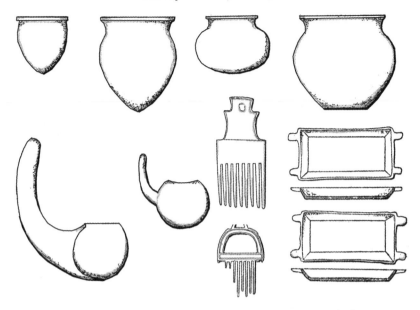

Miniature bronze vessels, none of which were typical of
Wei Valley culture. The smallest jars are less than 5 cm high.

the principal tombs at Baoji they must have had a role in marking the
origin and continuation of the Yu lineage. Moreover, unlike the full-
sized ritual vessels, the composition of the metal was different: these
objects were local, rough castings. The miniatures, replicas in memory
of other forms, had been made to complete the afterlife of Yu Bo.[16]
This is something we all do. We retain contact with people and places
that we have known in the past, collecting photographs of our relatives, or shells from a beach on a happy summer holiday.

The miniatures were copies of much more substantial ceramic containers, a row of which stood next to the woman's coffin, before they
were crushed by the weight of the earth as the pit was filled. These
had no connection with cooking or food storage, as east of the Pass,
and have often been compared in rather generic terms to the ceramics from the Chengdu basin over the Qinling Mountains.[17] Yu Bo also
had jades and carnelian beads around his neck and bronze pendants
on his tunic or robe. The jades emerged from the mainstream Shang
tradition. He also had a wider appreciation of ornament: the tiny

beads are from the steppe, where beads, gold and bronze were sewn on to clothes, and the carnelian, a bright-red agate, may have come from the Gobi.[18] The simple beads owned by Yu Bo, and later by other members of his clan, were in succeeding centuries extended into long hangings, especially for women, among the polities and states on the Yellow and Fen Rivers. This was a region with many ancient roads, so the people around Baoji may have had good connections to Sichuan, and even to Sanxingdui; but clearly their chief links were to the Loess Plateau. Yu Bo and his companion had gained prestige under the oversight of a new dynasty, but they remained loyal to their heritage and their history.

Led by their King Wu, the Zhou had attacked the Shang at the Battle at Muye, south of Anyang, around 1045 BC.[19] They had overturned a major dynasty and taken possession of their territory. A great deal about the conquest has been written down, but by no means everything. The decision to move against the Shang was linked with an alignment of the planets, offering a bright light in the sky. This auspiciousness is congruent with world views inherited from the Shang but, as it was recorded long after the conquest, may have been framed in much later terms.[20] In hindsight, the moment is remembered as a dramatic and immediate victory:

> It was the first month, *renchen* [day twenty-nine], the [day of] expanded dying brightness [of the moon]. On the next day, *guisi* [day thirty], the king then in the morning set out from Zhou and went on campaign to attack the Shang king Zhou. On *jiazi* [day one], five days after [the day] after the dying brightness [of the moon] of the following second month, [they] arrived in the morning and defeated the Shang, thence entirely decapitating the Shang king Zhou and shackling [his] one hundred evil ministers.[21]

The same text, *The Collection of the Leftover Documents of the Zhou (Yi Zhou Shu)*, then records, summarily, a ritual exorcism, an inspection tour and a sacrifice to King Wen, father of King Wu. Next the account turns back to captives and to the ears taken from dead enemies, before proceeding with a further ceremony:

> On *xinhai* [day forty-eight], presentation of the captured cauldrons of the Yin king. King Wu reverently displayed the jade tablet and the codice, making an announcement to the heavenly ancestor Lord on High.[22]

This is how the Zhou wished to be remembered: as a strong military power with due ritual diligence, who honoured their ancestors and so ensured that their deeds were known not just among the living, but among the spirits. There are strong proclamations about the inherent evil of the Shang government and the righteousness of the Zhou. In due course they underpinned their claim to rule by stating that they had been awarded the Mandate of Heaven, with kings from the late tenth century BC being titled the Son of Heaven, recorded in a few bronze-vessel inscriptions. How quickly these claims were made we do not know. Many more descriptions of Zhou achievements are recorded in *The Book of Documents*, to which the *Yi Zhou Shu* is a supplement.[23] Most of the narratives were composed 100 years or more after the battles and subsequently edited. Few people in later centuries would have given much thought to places in the west, such as Baoji. Taking up the mantle of the Shang, the Zhou had turned their focus east, where there was rich agricultural land. While heroic claims to legitimacy are captivating stories, as was probably intended, discovering what actually happened during the Zhou conquest requires further investigation.

Baoji was not a backwater, nor were the Yu minor figures on a frontier between the Central Plains and the Loess Plateau. For the Yu and Zhou, the people around Baoji were probably not on the margins, but central to the Zhou, as they gathered troops from several different lineages and prepared their invasions from the Wei Valley in the eleventh century BC. Ritual sets of the eleventh and early tenth centuries BC are evidence that several clans meaningfully contributed to the success of the Zhou and were thus endowed with gifts or were allowed to seize loot from Shang graves. For Yu Bo and his companion, the twenty-four vessels, one ladle and one bell were probably among the booty offered by the Zhou to the Yu. They were prestigious trophies within the framework of long-standing offerings to ancestors. If Yu Bo and his lineage were, from the perspective of those on the Central Plains, newcomers, they had been easily persuaded to adopt both deep tombs and the paraphernalia of the ancestral banquet.[24] They had borrowed, for the time being, the language of the Zhou and of the Shang before them. Such small regional groups would have had little or no capacity to cast such fine bronzes; their participation in the ancestral cult was made possible by the Zhou. Initiating Yu Bo to their norms was a political gesture, but also a ritual and religious one which in turn legitimised themselves.

Yu Bo's set prioritised food containers, now popular with the Zhou, as part of a gradual shift away from the primacy of alcohol during the Shang. Yet it was mismatched. The vessels are not a standard group. There are seven *ding* for food, of which five are tripods and two have four legs supporting deep rectangular bodies, but only three of the vessels are food basins, *gui*, which usually corresponded in number to some degree with the *ding*. One of these is a somewhat subdued

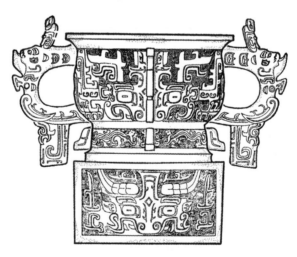

One of Yu Bo's three *gui*, height 25.9 cm.

version of the inscribed *gui* of his predecessor, with the oxen head flat against the sides of the base and a less realistic tiger head grasping a bird's crest in its jaw. Inside the stand is a little bell, which must have tinkled as it was moved. Neither the square stand or provision for a bell are features of Shang casting, but were popular in the eleventh and early tenth centuries BC among other clans, who were probably also allies of the Zhou.[25] Yu Bo's main alcohol set, lying on the secondary ledge opposite his head, consisted of a central tubular flask (*zun*), with two tubular buckets (*you*) encircled by horizontal borders, often described as being shaped like sections of thick bamboo. They had their own tray, perhaps of lacquered wood, now decayed. Very similar examples were found in late Shang tombs on the Central Plains, and Yu Bo's may have come from there. A final alcohol vessel looks to be an unnecessary addition. A single bell, of the type seen in Ya Chang's tomb, clearly lacks two more to make a musical set. The woman had three rather ordinary vessels for the necessary functions – food, alcohol and water – which also do not make a complete set. This imbalance indicates that the bronzes had been collected from several sources before being given to or acquired by the Yu.

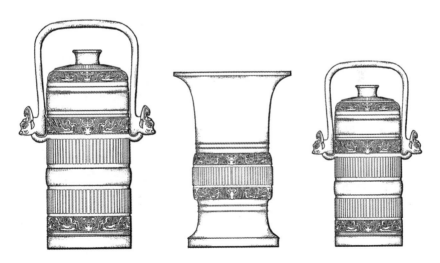

(*middle*) A flask, *zun*, height 25.4 cm, and two alcohol buckets, *you*, heights 33.3 cm (*left*) and 27 cm (*right*), make up a set.

A neighbouring village, Shigushan, on the same southern river terraces, has also produced a surprising number of even earlier eleventh-century BC bronzes gathered from several places and then buried. Unlike the Yu tombs, those at Shigushan have niches in which the bronzes were placed, showing that these owners came from elsewhere, again almost certainly the north.[26] The bronzes are ostentatious, with hooked flanges projecting down their sides and animal-headed handles (plate 18). All are earlier than those of Yu Bo, but their basins on square stands and sets of flasks with two alcohol buckets were part of the same tradition. Some are now famous for their intriguing birds with spiky plumage or pronged horns. Many inscriptions show that they had had previous owners. Surprisingly, it is likely that some were cast at Anyang.[27] Closely related pieces were found in the twentieth century at Daijiawan, signalling a gathering of powerful individuals. All these high-quality castings were either gifts from the Shang to the Zhou or made under Zhou auspices and given to their dependants in the Baoji area.[28] And there are other discoveries further north, among the Jing River's tributaries, including at Baicaopo, where lords again had ritual sets, gifted from the Shang and Zhou. Clusters of clans had congregated at Baoji to make gains in league with the Zhou.[29] Yu Bo and his lineage stand out as they proved more successful than many others in controlling territory and commanding influence over several generations.

The well-formed characters inscribed on Yu Bo's vessels confirm that the bronzes he now possessed had been cast at metropolitan centres, where the scribal tradition of the Shang and the early decades of Zhou rule was more established than at Baoji. We do not expect that Yu Bo was able to read the inscriptions. We know from cuneiform tablets in Western Asia that scribes were trained systematically. Likewise, in ancient China scribes, with official positions, will have been a select, highly qualified group. Given the extensive inscriptions on bronzes from the Zhou period, leading families may have had their own ritual specialists who could read the characters, usually honouring the family's predecessors, at the ceremonial banquets. Nonetheless, literacy will always have been limited and highly prized. Even now, mastering a useful number of characters is an intimidating task. Yet today,

China boasts a higher level of literacy across its gigantic population than many Western societies.

A rather sudden appearance at Baoji of Shang or very early Zhou vessels – distributed to members of Zhou forces – points to a major transfer of political and military power. In Asia this watershed is as renowned as the Fall of Rome and the coronation of Charlemagne are in the West. But as it happened nearly 2,000 years earlier, much of the detail recorded in writing is retrospective. The significance of those who settled in the Baoji region is commemorated in a speech attributed to King Wu of the Zhou, just before battle:

> [The time was] the grey dawn of the day *jiazi*. On that morning the king came to the open country of Mu in the borders of Shang, and addressed his army. In his left hand he carried a battle-axe, yellow with gold, and in his right he held a white ensign, which he bran-dished, saying, 'Far are you come, you men of the western regions!' He added, 'Ah! You hereditary rulers of my friendly states, You man-agers of affairs, the ministers; of instruction, of war, and of public works; the many officers subordinate to them: the master of my bodyguards and captains of thousands and captains of hundreds; and You, oh men of Yong, Shu, Qiang, Mao, Wei, Lu, Peng and Bo; lift up your lances, join your shields, raise your spears, I have a speech to make.'[30]

These evocative words were subsequently written down, probably after the seventh century BC, referring to bureaucratic structures that did not yet exist in the mid-eleventh century. At the same time, this passage, possibly a distant memory, records that the Zhou brought armies from the west.[31] By that time, the west was probably simply a general term for regions beyond the Central Plains.

The overthrow of the Shang was cemented by the looting of the royal cemetery at Anyang. A rebellion by the Shang two years later was soon put down. Zhou contacts and control spread eastwards across the Central Plains as separate polities of agricultural land were established – the most significant led by members of the royal Zhou family, the Ji clan.[32] These polities did not, however, form an uninterrupted political realm. As we discover several centres of authority through the inscriptions on their bronzes, we realise that they too were drawn into the Zhou sphere of influence by gifts from the court workshops. The Zhou had been remarkably swift in taking over Shang practices. Not only were they clear followers of the ancestral cult, they had also adopted Shang tomb structures. And, most importantly, they took over the system of writing in characters. For that they must, over the decades before the conquest, have employed scribes, well versed both in the form of the characters and in the language that they expressed. The Shang oracle bones' inscriptions reveal that a people called the Zhou were already known to them.[33] Over those early years in the eleventh century BC, living along the Wei (as the poems described), the Zhou must have observed that the agricultural land offered wealth. They also became aware that both the ancestral cult and the script were vital tools in the hands of the Shang. They were just biding their time.

Bronze vessel-casting is a complex skill, relying on prescriptive and repetitive training. Rather ordinary, sometimes rough vessels were made by the Zhou before the conquest. But the high cultural barriers of casting and written inscriptions indicate that the majority of ritual bronzes in Yu Bo's and his neighbours' tombs must have been cast at Zhouyuan and Xi'an, or even at Anyang under late Shang or early Zhou command. Scribes must also have been educated during the first decades of Zhou rule and employed in the bronze workshops to compose the lengthier, more informative inscriptions. The distribution of inscriptions shows us which areas were important during the early days of the new dynasty. In these inscriptions we can see the Zhou presenting their court lives. Only about eight among the hundreds of surviving inscriptions mention the conquest, and then merely in passing. One of these is on a bronze food basin known as the Li *gui*:

King Wu campaigned against Shang; it was *jiazi* [day one] morning. [King Wu performed] *sui* and *ding* sacrifices, and was able to make known that he had routed the Shang. On *xinwei* [day eight], the King was at Jian Encampment and awarded Chargé d'affaires Li metal [bronze]. [Li] herewith makes [for] Duke of Zhan [this] treasured sacrificial vessel.[34]

The Li *gui* was excavated in a hoard to the east of present-day Xi'an. It was probably brought there from elsewhere. Li may have taken part in the campaign against the Shang led by King Wu, making it possible for us to date the bronze to his reign or shortly thereafter in the eleventh century BC. Li's choice to cast the vessel for his ancestor shows that these offerings were already well established among the Zhou and their followers. The vessel has expressive *taotie* faces on its rounded basin and on its square stand.[35] It aimed to 'make known' the conquest to the spirit world by offering food to and communing with the ancestors. The inscription also connects the head of the Li lineage to the Zhou court and rituals. Yu Bo, who, as we know, also owned a *gui* on a square stand, was bound in the same way.

Very few early vessels inscribed with events have been found near Baoji. This is in part because the burials were created at a time before the Zhou had fully developed longer inscriptions. A *zun* belonging to a leader, He, found in this western area is an exception. It is famous for naming the two early kings:

In the fourth month, on the day *bingxu* [day twenty-three], the king made a proclamation to the junior sons of the ancestral shrine in the Lofty Chamber, saying: 'Formerly your pious patriarchs were able to approach King Wen. Thereupon King Wen received this [Great Mandate]. Later on, King Wu conquered the Great Settlement Shang and, from the courtyard [of a palace or temple] made a proclamation to Heaven, saying: "I shall reside in this central region and govern the people from here!" *Wu hu*! You are but junior sons having no knowledge. Look to [the examples of your ancestors], the patriarchs, have merits before Heaven, carry out commands, [and] respectfully offer sacrifices.'[36]

The inscription on the He *zun*. A hole inside the vessel has damaged the character usually translated as Heaven's Mandate. The inscription includes the name for Chengzhou, the Zhou capital at present-day Luoyang, the names of King Wen and King Wu and characters for the 'central region'.

The characters for the 'central region' are often taken as an early reference to a name still used today for China, Zhongguo. The vessel is 38.8 centimetres high and weighs nearly 15 kilos. Its decoration and the style and content of its inscription place it in the reign of King Kang (1005–978 BC), (who followed King Cheng (1042–1006 BC), the son of King Wu), or his successor King Zhao (977–957 BC) in the early tenth century BC.[37] The rams' horns on the principal *taotie* face were favoured in the Baoji region and also occur on the flask and two alcohol buckets belonging to Yu Bo's immediate successor, Yu Bo Ge (we do not know why this third character for his name was chosen) of the

The flask, *zun*, belonging to Yu Bo Ge,
height 25.8 cm, was paired with two *you*.

early to mid tenth century BC, who would have used them in his offerings to Yu Bo. By this date, the Zhou had started declaring a direct
relationship with Heaven. They also emphasised the importance of
their Mandate through the merits of their ancestors. These reinforced
the standing both of the Zhou and of all ancestral lineages, including
that of the Yu. A hierarchy based on seniority by generation was thus
embedded at Baoji by the ancestral cult. Further, formal recognition
of the lineage as the foundation not only of the family but also the
state gave it an essential role in Zhou rule, as recorded in numerous
bronze inscriptions that relate specific lineages to the Zhou kings,
emphasising the importance of their loyalty and military support.[38]

As they brought the achievements of the past into the present,
the Zhou established history as a legitimating force. It is remarkable that within a few decades even a bronze vessel, the He *zun*, cast
not by rulers but by a high-ranking member of the elite spread these

notions to their lineage: to the living, to their descendants and to their ancestors. Like He, Yu Bo would have participated in supporting such claims. This was an immensely powerful political system, replicated through a ritual cult. All facets of it were reinforced in the cycle of ceremonial banquets, repeated by lineages across the territory of the Zhou and reiterated in inscriptions. A network loyal to the Zhou was built up through ritual customs and was not, therefore, dependent on continual military coercion. Moreover, as the ceremonial banquets took place in given cycles of weeks, seasons and years, the ideological bond was repeatedly made visible to all participants.[39] Even with the decline of the Zhou, the conjunction of the ancestral cult with political legitimacy was an important cohesive force among diverse groups of people.

The ancestral cult was taken up in new forms during the upheavals of the eighth to third centuries BC, known as the Spring and Autumn and Warring States periods. The propositions are included in the later texts in *The Book of Documents*, which came to be included in the *Five Confucian Classics*, as they are known in the West. In Chinese they are the foundation of classical learning. From at least the Song dynasty onwards (960–1279 AD), these writings had to be memorised by would-be officials, aspiring to civil service posts in government via a rigorous examination system.[40] Zhou authority was carved into China's culture and sustained the view, over the millennia, that one unified state was inevitable, founded upon the memory of the virtues of its great past.[41] This is why so much attention has been paid to the Zhou. Yet without the unsung efforts of Yu Bo, of his descendant Yu Bo Ge and of his many contemporary clans, the Zhou conquest might never have happened, nor would Zhou culture have been so thoroughly embedded in China.

We all like to record our achievements. The Zhou were no different. But what of the situation on the ground: the complications of landfall and the huge distances from the Wei Valley to the Great Settlement Shang? Before the Zhou could make proclamations about their legitimacy, they had to win some major battles. Yu Bo's military role in

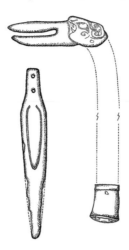

The short sword, length 26.8 cm, and the bird-head for a staff,
13 cm long at the top, were fundamental to the identity of the Yu lineage.

the history of the Zhou is embedded in his small sword, known as a willow-leaf sword. Lying on his right side, a mere 26.8 centimetres in length, the sword has two important features. Both sides are cutting edges and there must have been a grip in a material such as leather, or more probably wood, to cover the narrow end, in which there are two holes. It is a signal of the identity of several regional groups upon whom the Zhou could draw for military support. At Baoji it was a key weapon for almost all the known men of the Yu lineage, a signature of their individual contribution to combat, as well as their shared origins. Swords had not reached the Shang, nor had been invented by them, although they had borrowed and copied some single-edged northern knives and a few doubled-edged daggers. The willow-leaf sword had to have come from outside the Central Plains. Long and short swords are prime thrusting weapons for hand-to-hand fighting or for killing and skinning animals. They were essential for all stockbreeders, most especially on the steppe. Yu Bo's sword was a close relative of these Eurasian weapons. In ancient China, swords did not become widely popular until the sixth century BC, still 500 or 400 years away.[42] The standard weapon for the elite was the axe and their armies carried halberds or spearheads mounted on long staffs. The Yu, who all owned and used these swords, stood out as distinctive, even alien, in the military context of their day.

The earliest relevant comparisons for willow-leaf swords have been found in the Altai Mountains and the grasslands further north-west.[43] The popularity of this weapon in the Western Wei basin is surprising, but it is not the only weapon which has a clear association with the steppe. Yu Bo also had an axe with the head of a man wearing a plait, hinting at some contact with Sichuan, a mace and a mattock, well known on the Loess Plateau.[44] Bone armour fragments, a technology from further north-west, were also found in Yu Bo's tomb, as were the remains of an unusual staff. A prominent bird beak in bronze, with an animal head grasping it, to hold a flag or banner, was matched with a hoof-shaped cap to fit on the other end. All the principal leaders of the Yu lineage were buried with similar ones.

These bronze weapons are evidence that the Yu had military associations with other groups allied to the Zhou. This is a revelation, and a tantalising indication of the peoples on whom at least some of the Zhou's military success depended. We can see from their diverse burial structures, northern weapons and carnelian beads that many of the sword owners were, like Yu Bo and his lineage, joining the Zhou in combat. We also find communities in Sichuan and on the western Han River with the same sword, forming a remarkable chain south of the Qinling Mountains meeting Baoji in the west.[45] The most surprising southern discovery is in tombs of the early Zeng state in Hubei province, east of Sichuan. One tomb has two willow-leaf swords and another the bird-headed standard. These cannot be there by chance. They are traits that the people at Zeng shared with Baoji. And, like the Yu, the Zeng were powerful allies, attracting scores of bronzes cast at metropolitan centres under direct Zhou control. At the same time, they either employed warriors from the Baoji area or were integrated with them through marriages or other relationships.

A similar connection with the Yu is uncovered in a wealthy cemetery in the Fen River basin, a tributary of the Yellow River further north-east. The leader of this regional group, who named themselves the Ba, built lavish, very deep tombs with niches, a northern tradition.

The earliest tomb in this cemetery had several willow-leaf swords, some even with decorated scabbards and a bird-headed standard fitting. The Ba lord also had an extraordinary number of beautifully designed and inscribed bronzes, indicative of Zhou patronage. In fact, one vessel records a marriage treaty with the northern Zhou polity of Yan, near Beijing, where willow-leaf swords were also found.[46] In retrospect, both the Zeng polity in the south and the Ba on the Fen River look more significant than the Yu. But we are underestimating Yu Bo and his lineage: in his day the Yu may have drawn together influential neighbours in a common cause. They are the source of this combination of the willow-leaf sword and the bird-headed standard. Interrelated groups of regional powers were clearly significant contributors to the fall of the Shang.[47]

Yu Bo not only took his sword and standard into the afterlife. He made sure that he had his prime weapon, his chariot. An animal head with blunt horns and duck and buffalo heads topped with birds, all in bronze, are fittings for one or more chariots. Given their fine casting, these too must have been gifts from the Zhou. Chariot forces were essential at the Battle of Muye and in later displays of power. Before the conquest, if the Yu had driven chariots, they must have been vehicles without bronze decoration. But now Yu Bo owned bronze chariot fittings, including one long axle cap typical of the late Shang and early Zhou, and three pairs of lynchpins with animal heads. These indicate three chariots, as pairs of lynchpins would have fixed the axle caps on their two large wheels. Six jingles on vertical supports, which would have stood on the yoke bars, also represent three vehicles. Yu Bo and several other leaders were also supplied with socketed axes and spades for the repair of wooden chariots. And a Shang rein holder has been found with Yu Bo's successor. The chariots may have been in an adjacent pit or may even have been too valuable to bury.

The Zhou were fearsome opponents. They or their allies brought a new form of chariot, one with four horses, to the Central Plains.[48] As with the Shang two-horse chariots, those with four horses had first been used in the steppe, seen in petroglyphs on rocks in the Altai Mountains.[49] The Zhou did not drive them across those distances, but must have acquired them gradually as they moved south. Adding two horses, which were not tied to the yoke bar, demanded sophisticated horsemanship:

> We yoke the teams of four,
> Those steeds so strong,
> That our lord rides behind,
> That lesser men protect.
> The four steeds so grand,
> The ivory bow-ends. The fish-skin quiver,
> Yes we must always be on our guard.[50]

While archaeologists have concentrated on chariots, which are very testing to excavate, they have sidelined the horses. The solid, square cheekpieces, with a central hole for a bit and two tubes for the harness, at Baoji confirm that the chariot drivers there knew and adopted steppe harnessing methods.[51] These were standard at Anyang and were still employed at the time of conquest by the people buried at Shigushan. A curved bronze also tells us that the Yu and their contemporaries had themselves brought horses south. This tiny object is a vital link between the Yu and northern horse breeders. A neat, narrow bronze, curled over at the top and pierced by three holes – one for the

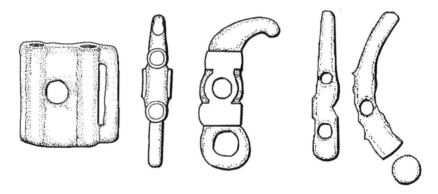

Horse cheekpieces, from Shigushan (*left*), height 7.5 cm, from the tomb of Yu Bo Ge (*middle*), length 10.1 cm, and from the tomb of last Yu lord (*right*), length *c*.10 cm.

bit and two, at right angles, for the harness – had displaced the square cheekpiece.[52] Eight examples of this new harnessing of the early tenth century BC were found with Yu Bo Ge. This bronze version, no doubt developed in the Wei Valley or nearby, closely copies antler-horn cheekpieces, also with three holes, universal across the steppe. The Yu must have been in touch with northerners, and through them learned of new developments in horse-driving.[53] These bridles show that the Yu lineage and many other allies of the Zhou, including the Ba, who also had many antler cheekpieces in their tombs, continued to use horses from the north. Only close relationships between peoples in the Loess Plateau and the Wei Valley with northern stockbreeders would have generated four-horse chariots and these specific cheek-pieces. Such command of horses added to the military prowess of the Baoji region, but above all to that of the Zhou, a chapter often left out of the story of conquest. The close relations of the Yu, the Ba and many others with horses for chariot warfare are as much evidence of their northern origins as are their unusual tombs, the miniature bronzes and their weapons. Gifts of ritual vessels often overshadow these much smaller bronzes, but they now remind us that, as with Ya Chang, we need to be aware of the dual heritage of their owners.

A search for northern horses that began in early Shang had now expanded and was to remain essential for all the dynasties that followed. Later texts, including *The Zuo Tradition, Zuo Zhuan,* a commentary of the fourth century BC on earlier annals, show that, over centuries, this connection with the north was well recognised:

The northern territory of Ji is where horses are bred, but no domain [political authority] has ever arisen there [northern Hebei and Shanxi]. Since ancient times it has been true that one cannot achieve true security by relying on natural defences and horses. For this reason, the former kings cultivated their reputation for virtue in order to bring ritual entertainment to the spirits and the human ancestors. One never hears of their having devoted themselves to natural defences and horses.[54]

And yet even here the writer plays down the role of the horses, subordinating their supply to a rule by ritual and virtue. As the people of the Central Plains had no way to penetrate the environmental and agricultural reasons that limited them in breeding strong horses, they resorted to methods of alliances and bargains, while proclaiming their own right to rule. Given such restrictions within the Wei Valley, the role of chariot drivers at Baoji and the gifts to Yu Bo now look even more significant. North-west of the modern city of Baoji lies good pasture, a favourable climate and the necessary nutrients, such as selenium, for rearing horses.[55] In fact, these very conditions explain the presence of Yu Bo and his lineage, probably favoured by the Zhou for their access to strong horses and their ability to drive chariots. They may even have established herds to pasture on the nearby hills. Numerous cheekpieces at Shigushan and a horse head buried at Baicaopo highlight other pockets of local expertise. The tombs, modified versions of those on the Central Plains, show us that the Yu had not only taken part in the Zhou conquest but that they had been encouraged by gifts of ritual vessels to settle at Baoji and adjacent areas to raise and drive horses, and to guard the Wei Valley against others who might invade from the north.

As the Zhou claimed more land, their demand for horses increased, as did pressures from the northerners. Invaders, named by the Zhou as the Rong, harassed their lands. Some inscriptions on bronzes describe intermittent warfare.[56] Others commemorate the bronzes, jades, chariot equipment, including the decoration on yokes and shafts, fighting apparel and banners offered by the Zhou kings to lineage leaders in exchange for military assistance in the occupation of newly conquered land over the tenth, ninth and eighth centuries BC.[57] Many inscriptions are cast into massive tripods, the *ding*, the largest and eventually the most renowned of all Zhou bronzes. Among the late Western Zhou tripod inscriptions, the Mao Gong *ding* records:

> I award you one ewer of fragrant fine ale, a jade staff and inlaid ladle for libations, crimson knee covers with an onion-green belt, jade circlets, jade [treasures], metal-decorated chariot with handrail

and decorated curtain, crimson suede girth straps and neck décor, tiger canopy with dark lining, yokes with painted straps, painted leather straps [connecting the carriage to the axle], metal shaft, an inlaid yoke crossbar . . . fish-skin quiver, four horses, bits and bridles, metal horse head ornaments, metal breast décor, crimson pennant with two small bells. I award you with these gifts for use in the annual sacrifices and in executing government.[58]

While the bronze vessel and its inscription speak of Zhou power through the ancestral cult, the four horses, their highly decorated harness and chariot speak of an urgent need to keep the high-ranking lineages on side, to work with them against the Rong. Such gifts remind us continually of the challenges the Zhou faced. In concentrating on the Zhou's skill in crafting a history and a system of rule, it is sometimes easy to overlook the military component of their gift economy and to underestimate the contributions of Yu Bo and his contemporaries in holding back the Rong, especially in the western Wei Valley.

The Yu lineage flourished in the eleventh and tenth centuries BC, but they seem to have disappeared by the beginning of the ninth century BC after the death of the last Yu lord, who probably lived in the reign of King Mu (956–918 BC).[59] The Baoji region may no longer have been of interest to the Zhou kings, now concentrating on expansion eastwards. For Yu Bo and his successors in the cemeteries at Zhuyuangou and Rujiazhuang this was a tragedy. They were buried with valuable ritual vessels with the expectation that they would receive sustenance after their death through the ceremonial banquets offered by their descendants. The ancestors were in effect abandoned and could no longer reciprocally support their descendants. This was catastrophic in the moral universe of the afterlife.

We know that the activity of the Zhou court ceased in the Baoji area as no ninth-century BC sets of ritual bronzes have been found there.[60] We can only assume that pressure from people on the Loess Plateau had overwhelmed the Zhou and their allies and edged them out. One chariot fitting from a chariot pit, belonging to the last

Yu lord, foreshadows the difficulties on the horizon. It is a central, chariot-shaft ornament cast with a tiger's head on one side and a man grasping it on the other. Seen from behind, we find that the crouching man has long strands of hair hanging down his back, very like the plait on the head of the axe belonging to Yu Bo. He wears a belt and has decorated straps around his leg, which tied his leggings. This was a form of northern costume, unlike that of the Central Plains, where tight belts were not part of the dress. It was the uniform of chariot drivers and horse managers, as we saw on the deer stones. A pair of stags are displayed on his back, their heads turned to look towards their tails. These were either tattoos or appliqués on his clothes. While the tiger's head and the man were undoubtedly cast, the stags have a slightly jagged outline, as if they were incised in the bronze *after* the casting was complete. The last Yu lord was also buried with exquisite jade carvings of stags, as was his female companion (plate 6). These stags belong to the same language of objects expressed by people in the north, especially from the steppe. The stags also complete the miniatures and weapons we have already seen. We have in Yu Bo's tomb, in its shape, structure and bronzes, verification that he and his lineage were drawn as allies of the Zhou to settle near Baoji. The

Back view of the ornament for the front of a chariot shaft,
from a pit near the tomb of the last Yu lord, height 13 cm.

146

distribution of the willow-leaf sword and the bird-headed standard holder in areas outside the main strongholds of the Zhou show us that the Yu were one of a number of regional groups useful in warfare, with a background in chariot-driving and horse-training. The Yu's northern heritage is confirmed by the elegant jade stags in the tomb of the last member of the lineage. The excavations at Baoji and elsewhere give us a greater understanding of the foundation of the Zhou dynasty, enhancing the picture that they constructed and that has been perpetuated. The Yu inform us of the role of chariots, horses and their drivers in the Baoji area. Yu Bo and his lineage also offer significant examples of a dual allegiance, expressed in objects, both to their place of origin and to the Zhou.

For all the proud statements of the Zhou, the lands around Baoji were eventually lost. The defensive efforts of the Yu lords and their Zhou kings had been in vain. Transmitted writings and even a few bronze inscriptions show that there was trouble, often attributed to competition and factional infighting at court.[61] The more likely sources of instability were peoples from the Loess Plateau, the Rong, incessantly raiding the Zhou settlements. The intense problems that they caused show just how successful Yu Bo and his lineage had been in their time at fending off similar invaders from the southern end of the Hexi Corridor. The Zhou had had every reason to court the Yu and others at Baoji in an attempt to block the Rong or others on chariots using this gateway to central China. The important position that the Yu and others filled is made more apparent by Zhou efforts from the tenth century BC onwards to block the gap. We learn from Sima Qian in a chapter, 'The Basic History of the Qin' ('Qin Ben Ji'), in his major work *The Historical Records (Shi Ji)*, that as the Zhou moved east in the eighth century BC the Qin, because they raised good horses, were offered land in the Wei Valley.[62] We can infer that Yu Bo and his contemporaries had provided the same protection in their day. Newcomers were needed to replace the Yu, who had been defenders of the back door into the region that the Zhou claimed. Blocking an advance of stockbreeders and herders from the north and the north-west was to remain an essential task for future dynasties.

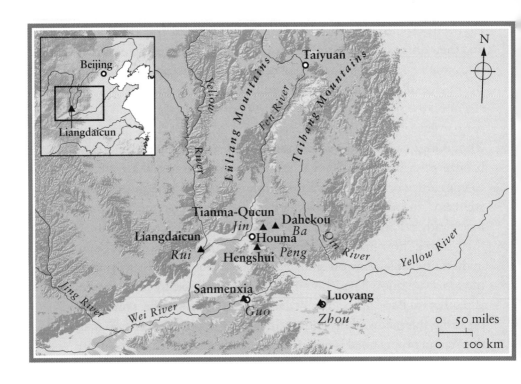

Liangdaicun and the meeting of the Yellow, the Fen and the Wei Rivers

6

Innovations and Heirlooms

A radically different political situation guided the Lord of Rui as he prepared his afterlife in the mid-eighth century BC. His tomb is in a cemetery at Liangdaicun, nearly 400 kilometres east of Baoji. The Zhou lost control of the Western Wei Valley in the late tenth century BC; over the following 100 years the Rong, an assortment of mobile agro-pastoralists from the Loess Plateau, repeatedly invaded, precipitating political disputes at the Zhou court and leading to a move east to the secondary capital at Luoyang, south-east of Liang-daicun. Some of this turbulence can be traced in the written history, recording, for example, an unusual succession to the throne, an uncle following a nephew.[1] Other conspiracies ensued, with a continu-ous backdrop of military combat. These writings leave much to be inferred. Well-established scribal practices meant that difficulties were rarely officially explicated. It was thought that emphasising misfor-tune might bring on more bad episodes. A close connection between spoken or recorded accounts, including images, that might affect the future was, it appears, widely accepted. Both the invasions by the Rong and the divisions at court are chronicled, but probably only in part. Causes and consequences were not fully explored and thus many aspects of the upheavals in the eighth century BC are difficult to unravel.[2]

Liangdaicun is today a small village on the southern edge of the Loess Plateau, standing high above a ravine on the west bank of the Yellow River. If the Rui had travelled from their original home in the western valley along the Wei River and then turned north up the south-flowing Yellow River, they would have been on lowland throughout. The cemetery and presumably their settlement, near the

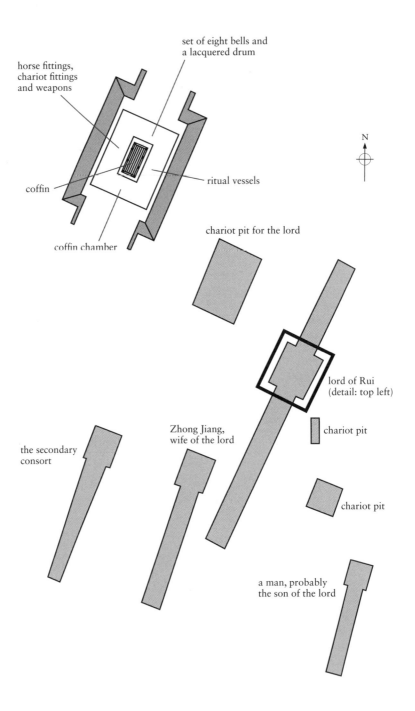

horse fittings, chariot fittings and weapons

set of eight bells and a lacquered drum

coffin

ritual vessels

coffin chamber

N

chariot pit for the lord

lord of Rui (detail: top left)

Zhong Jiang, wife of the lord

chariot pit

the secondary consort

chariot pit

a man, probably the son of the lord

A plan of the cemetery at Liangdaicun with the tomb of the Lord of Rui.

modern town of Hancheng, stood at the point where the agricultural land narrowed and the hilly loess extended northwards. The local peasants knew nothing of the distant stockbreeders and herders that lived 500 kilometres or more further north. Almost directly opposite, the Fen River, also flowing south, joins the Yellow River. This was a key position. The lords here could farm the land around these basins and at the same time defend them against pastoralists moving south.

The Zhou had quickly noted the perils of this junction. A son of the victorious King Wu, Tangshu Yu, thus a member of the royal Ji clan, had been despatched sometime after the conquest to the Fen River basin to found the Jin polity and defend the region.[3] Jin was to grow substantially to become one of the major contenders for power from the eighth century BC. The activities of the Jin are well documented in the histories, and on account of this fame two large Jin cemeteries have been thoroughly excavated, one of which held the lords and their spouses.[4] The Jin followed the standard Zhou burial pattern, with graves oriented north–south and owners laid in a supine position. The difficulties of holding the region are apparent, however, from the presence of rival regional groups, favoured by the Zhou, newcomers from further north in the Loess Plateau, who founded their own polities nearby: the Ba at Dahekou, to the east of the Jin, and the Peng at Hengshui, beyond a small ridge of mountains south of the Fen.[5] In their cemeteries, some individuals were placed prone and adopted the alternative east–west/west–east pattern we found at the Yu polity in Baoji. A few had ramps and a number were exceptionally deep, reaching 10 or more metres below the surface; some also had the northern feature of niches. One of the tantalising aspects of China's past is this exchange of burial practices, despite tomb-building being an intensely private ritual. Plentiful bronze vessels and cowries tell us that these non-Zhou clans were also allies and had received gifts from the Zhou court.

For over 100 years from *c.*1045 BC, the Zhou successfully built a secure defence on the border between agricultural land and the Loess Plateau. However, their foothold was fraying in the eighth century BC, when the head of the Rui lineage, also from the royal Ji clan, created his tomb at Liangdaicun. His name, inscribed on bronzes belonging to his senior consort, is Huan Gong, where Huan is his name and Gong his title. The term Gong used to be translated as Duke, the highest honour in the Zhou ranking system, but this is a misleading attempt to align ancient Chinese titles with much later Western ones. We shall instead call him the Lord of Rui. His impressive tomb is more than 13 metres in depth, in evident competition with his neighbours among the Jin, the Ba and the Peng. It was demonstrably a lot more prestigious than that of Yu Bo – with two enormous ramps sloping in, one 34 metres in length from the south and another nearly 18 metres long from the north.⁶ The sheer sides of the shaft and the massive ramps seemed, even when I saw them in the twenty-first century, supernatural. When the tomb stood open the ramps added to its impact, declaring the lord's high social standing and wealth during the funeral rites, which were greater than that of the other tomb owners at Baoji.⁷ The lord was after all a powerful member of the Zhou clan. In the afterlife, his ostentatious tomb established his position among his ancestors. The only other tombs with ramps that we have met are those of the Shang kings, who each had four, recognising the cardinal directions. As the movements of the sun, planets and stars, and natural events, such as earthquakes, were closely monitored, a wider cosmology undoubtedly existed, but was not formally recorded at this relatively early date.⁸

The Lord of Rui's two main consorts and another Rui lord, who may have been his son, lay adjacent to him. As the two women and the later lord were of lower rank, their tombs had single ramps and were smaller. Nearby was a rectangular pit for chariots and horses. Another, smaller pit was next to the other lord's tomb. We know the name of the principal consort, Zhong Jiang, from inscriptions on her bronzes. The lord's three coffins, one inside the other, were at the centre of a large chamber. A substantial wooden outer one had been bound with ropes passing through a series of bronze rings around its rim, which still survive. Traces of fabric used to cover the coffin were found in several other burials within the cemetery. We can assume from the way in which a nearby coffin was originally surrounded by a suite of narrow wooden posts, which suspended a canopy with two layers of textile on horizontal frames, that the lord's coffin was arranged in a similar way.[9] Tiny strings of beads, combined with cowries, were attached to the wooden crossbars.[10] Then tall standards of forged bronze were placed on top of the frame. These standards, termed *sha*, often topped with birds in profile, give the impression that for the funeral they replaced a textile flag or banner used in life.

The chamber is filled with bronze vessels on one side and weapons – chariot fittings and bronze armour – along the other. Looking into the inner coffins, we are astonished by the array of jades and gold (plate 20). As the skeleton has not survived, these stand out against a red layer of cinnabar. This is the first time that we have come across a person with gold woven among jade. Glittering over what would have been the lord's waist is a row of gold rings shaped like dragons, with pairs of curved lines bearing massive heads filled with long teeth; and another six rings have dragon's heads on solid bodies. They belong with two openwork gold triangles, which form the remains of one or two belts. This is a groundbreaking discovery as belts, especially gold belts, belong to an entirely different culture, that of the steppe. In the context of Shang and then Zhou life on the Central Plains, belts with extravagant ornament were a complete innovation, and so too was this lavish use of a material not popular in earlier centuries.[11]

The Lord of Rui could only have obtained troves of a rare metal through unusual relationships with local allies. Gold was coveted by all on the steppe. We have seen belts as part of the dress of chariot drivers and riders from the north, from which to hang their weapons, but the lord's belt was something else. A belt of gold plaques placed the lord alongside the great leaders of the steppe, whose richly furnished burials under vast kurgans have been excavated at the world-famous site of Arzhan, in the Tuva Republic of the Russian Federation.[12] The fashion for gold belt plaques, with gold ornamented quivers, daggers and ornaments, often figuring horses and stags, is better known in the West among later steppe peoples, such as the Scythians around the Black Sea. Yet this tradition, which stretched the length of Eurasia, is likely to have been founded on the eastern steppe, with the gold sources in the Altai Mountains.

The earliest Arzhan kurgans were built a century before the Lord of Rui was buried. As gold belts were indispensable expressions of the authority of steppe leaders, and nothing like them was known among the echelons of the Zhou elite, the lord must have enjoyed access not only to gold but to news of changing symbols of power. In this tumultuous period, with constant threats from the Rong, the lord's close engagement with the loess pastoralists and steppe lords is confirmed by his gold scabbard, again distantly following the model found at Arzhan.* Before the eighth century BC, gold was not a material that had been favoured by the Zhou or their followers; indeed it could not be recovered, deliberately or by chance, in the depths of loess or beneath the loess silt of the river valleys.[13] When found among the Shang, it is almost always associated with northern horse decoration. But that is not how the lord saw gold. He clearly desired it for himself. In the style of a steppe lord, he had gold discs for his dress, boots and tack, enhanced by small gold oxen heads with rings through their snouts, and gold stags' heads as buckles for decoration. Bangles made of a spiral of gold wire would have adorned his wrists. He also had thumb rings used in archery in both gold and jade.[14]

The lavish display is unparalleled among his contemporaries in the agricultural valleys. The northern groups were clearly infiltrating. Behind this development loomed the growing strength of the steppe lords, who now commanded large numbers of pastoralists and stockbreeders as clients and allies. They had also taken to mounted riding in raiding and war.[15] This new threat may have pushed some less powerful neighbours southwards, in turn generating a new wave of intrusion into the Loess Plateau and interaction with the Zhou polities, as at Rui. Some of the regional allies of the Zhou, such as the Ba, had copied traditional jade forms in gold and buried them with them in their tombs.[16] It was through engagement with these powerful people that the Rui may have learned how to exploit this foreign metal.

That his own personal weapon, the dagger, was of jade and not

---

* Chinese culture has always given gold a lower status, and in archaeological reports gold items are always listed after bronze and jade.

of iron shows us that the lord was still bound by ancient customs of the afterlife, relying on the protection of jade. But he did have several small knives with iron blades held in bronze grips. These are almost the earliest iron blades in central China. Like bronze and gold, iron-working was not a technology developed on the Central Plains.[17] Iron was used from at least the fourteenth century BC by the Hittites in Anatolia. It was not independently identified, nor was its potential detected, in China's agricultural valleys. Stockbreeders with iron weapons had travelled from Western Asia across the steppe. Iron may also have reached the lord across the oases and deserts of Central Asia. Small iron-bladed knives show that the Lord of Rui kept abreast of the latest technologies.[18] And he was obliged to be up to date. The Loess Plateau was on the move, and the Zhou king had headed east to Luoyang. To keep hold of his land and ensure the success of his lineage, the Lord of Rui had to become the equal of the newcomers around him, whose tombs with their impressive shafts proclaimed them as powerful competitors with the Zhou lords.[19]

The lord was obviously a skilful negotiator and had utilised other strategies to meet the increasing cultural and military challenge. We

Six vessels found in the tomb of Zhong Jiang. The box (*top left*) is 10.6 cm high.

see these in a group of elegant bronzes belonging to his consort, Zhong Jiang. A small openwork frame which may have decorated a rectangular box has four feet in the shape of small tigers, with wheels between their front paws. It was clearly meant to roll. Much more conventional, on the other hand, is a miniaturised rectangular food *ding*. We have met *ding* before, but this vessel is different. It is held up by four feet in the shape of kneeling men. Inside it is another similar vessel. A small basin on a high foot is the ancestor of the many cauldrons employed in later centuries on the steppe. And three others are also unusual, one featuring a creature with a human head perched on the lid. These are much more carefully cast than Yu Bo's miniatures. And they certainly do not follow the shapes of a typical ritual vessel set.[20]

Miniatures have also been found with other women, including consorts of the Jin lords, in cemeteries in the Fen River basin.[21] All these women had probably moved from regions further north as the consorts of powerful leaders intending to use marriage alliances to help defend their agricultural lands. Marriage was a frequent manoeuvre to reinforce political and military relationships, as both fathers and prospective partners knew well. There are, of course, no personal writings by men or women on these arrangements. Some ritual vessels, however, carry inscriptions to show that they were gifts either from the wife's family or her new partner. In a few cases a woman from the royal Ji clan became the spouse of a lord from the Loess Plateau, as in the nearby state of Peng. Women who had travelled from the Loess Plateau brought into their lives large cooking or storage vessels on three lobed feet and a tall basin with a wide-open neck;[22] these originated around the Great Bend of the Yellow River, as we have seen at Shimao and Taosi.[23] Marriage alliances across cultural and territorial boundaries to aid the ambitions of the Zhou and their allies involved migration, negotiations in war, exchanges and economic transactions.[24] But newcomers also introduced new cultures.

We see more evidence of the Lord of Rui's reliance on his northern networks in the mass of small red beads which threaded together jades in traditional shapes. This extravagant hanging dressed him from his neck to his knees and matched Zhong Jiang's exotic beaded strings, which were hung on long strings from a substantial trapezoidal jade plaque, drilled with rows of small holes (plate 23). Carnelians alternated with bi-conical faience as ball-shaped and rectangular stone beads formed horizontal rows over the body, an exaggerated version of ornaments hung on either side of the head of women on the steppe.[25] The Lord of Rui was obviously keen to harmonise with his spouse. His own hangings of beads and arcs in jade must have been a method of self-aggrandisement, to prove that he could outdo his well-dressed neighbours and to show off his connections which spread far and wide. The idea of using such a brilliant red came ultimately from Western Asia.[26] The magnificent strings of beads worn by the lord and Zhong Jiang are, as with the gold belt, improvisations on the customs of the steppe. It is almost impossible to imagine that the Lord of Rui and Zhong Jiang could have walked in life wearing so many beads and jades. The couple could, of course, have sat formally, with attendants, at a reception or ceremonial banquet.

It is, however, likely that the gold, jade and carnelian hangings were above all intended to impress the lord's ancestors in the afterlife. A visual impact carried a strong message: new alliances had been established between the northerners and the Rui. If we look back at Shimao and the vandalised tomb at Taosi, we see the first phase of northern contact with the introduction of herded animals and metallurgy. And under the Shang and early Zhou in the tombs of Ya Chang and Yu Bo, horses, chariots and beads came to central China by way of mobile peoples from outside settled agricultural society. These new materials and technologies seem to have been unconsciously absorbed within an existing cultural framework, just as bronze had been adopted into an existing ancestral cult. Integration was a fundamental trend as, again and again, societies on the Central Plains co-opted new technologies – bronze for ritual vessels, iron for casting weapons and even cattle-raising for sacrifice and scapulimancy – for their own purposes. The Lord of Rui was a member of the royal Zhou clan. Yet even as an insider, he seems to have deliberately chosen to assert his equivalence with others using the inventory originating in the steppe. He had added gold and carnelian beads to celebrate his august standing and his alliance with people from the Loess Plateau, who had acquired gold, iron and beads from the north. [27] The lord expected competition between the Zhou and the Rong to continue in the afterlife, so took with him the necessary markers of his rank and influence.

The jade dagger hidden in the Lord of Rui's gold scabbard has a more subtle message. If the gold belt was a translation of the steppe language, the jade dagger was a reversion to the traditional objects of the Central Plains. Its form is, however, that of a northern dagger. Quite different jade blades were laid over the lord's body. These are jade versions of the principal Shang weapon, the bronze halberd blade. Mounted at right angles on a long wooden staff, the bronze version had been carried by Shang foot soldiers over 400 years earlier. By the mid-eighth century BC, this shape had fallen out of fashion. Shorter, sharp blades, with a long vertical extension against a staff to hold them steady in the fray, were now popular. The Lord of Rui had his own bronze versions. He and his attendants preparing the burial must have understood that the jade halberds did not duplicate current weaponry; they were ancient. As enemies existed as spirits in the afterlife, however, the blades may have offered important protection.

The Lord of Rui and Zhong Jiang took a vast number of jades into the afterlife which could not have been acquired at random. Four small *cong* are conspicuous around the lower part of his body (plate 20). Something more than jade's value was at stake. They had to have come from somewhere, or from somebody. There was no jade-working in the middle Yellow River Valley. Many of the jades in the Rui tombs were in ancient shapes, such as the *cong* and halberds, or of ancient age, but with decoration added in the tenth century BC. They could have been found by chance, as weather eroded the loess. But these jades had probably been looted from the Shang by the Zhou army more than 200 years earlier, especially the large halberd blades, some of which were copied and decorated later. For us, these jades are part of the uncharted spread of very ancient pieces across China. The Zhou rulers may have gifted them to the Lord of

1. The king-*cong*, with the remarkable engraving of the man and fanged monster, a motif recurring among the jades in the ancient city of Liangzhu, which dominated the Yangtze Delta from *c*. 3200–2200 BC.

2. A surviving cup from Taosi, one of the few decorated ceramics retrieved from the vandalised tomb, *c*. 2000 BC.

3. A painted basin from another tomb at Taosi, *c*. 2000 BC. Its sharp, angular profile looks almost contemporary, and anticipates similar geometric forms in bronze.

4. The altitude and size (*c.* 2500 km) of the Tibetan Plateau impeded communication with the Iranian Plateau and further west and led to the development of Silk Roads to the north across the deserts and steppe of Inner Asia.

5. Farmed terraces of loess in southern Shanxi province.

6. A jade stag from northern China which echoes the animal designs of steppe culture, tenth century BC.

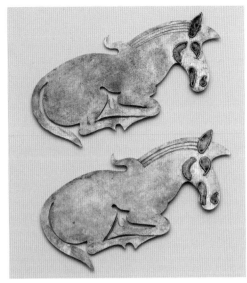

7. Two of a herd of four golden horses, sewn onto the caps of the couple in the principal burial in the kurgan, Arzhan II, the Valley of the Kings, South Siberia, Russia, seventh century BC.

8. A deer stone (*c.* 1400–700 BC) on the Mongolian steppe which commemorates an individual, his face at the summit. Tools and weapons hang from his belt. The monument is carved with stags, from which such stones take their name.

9. A gold deer with a griffin's beak and horns and tipped by raptor heads, fourth–third century BC. The same horns were added to horse bridles buried at Pazyryk in Siberia, evidence of far-reaching contact across the steppe.

10. The shaft of a late Shang tomb in the royal cemetery at Anyang, with sheer walls of loess that are over three storeys deep, *c.* 1200 BC.

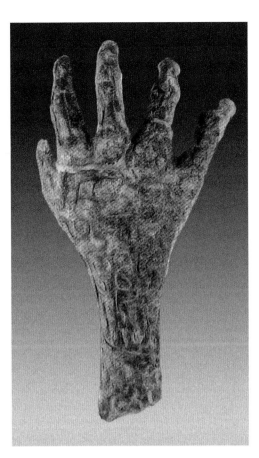

11. Ya Chang's bronze hand, which was buried with him near the temple and palaces at Anyang, enabled him to defend the late Shang capital in the afterlife.

12. One of Fu Hao's bronze ritual vessels, an imaginary animal with rams' horns and large wings folded at the rear, *c.* 1250 BC.

13. A rectangular offering vessel for food, *ding*, from the foot of a royal tomb at Anyang. The stag motif was popular with the Shang's northern neighbours.

14. The Tang Emperor Xuanzong's perilous flight to the Sichuan basin (712–756 AD), when he abdicated in the face of rebellions. Painting on silk scroll, ninth–tenth century AD.

15. An imposing gold mask from the ancient city of Jinsha, Sichuan Province, twelfth–eleventh century BC.

16. The torso of the mysterious bronze man borrows its form from a tree trunk. Sanxingdui, Sichuan Province, thirteenth–twelfth century BC.

17. The opaque colour of the Yellow River as it runs south, winding in huge bends around the piled loess landscape along the border of Shaanxi and Shanxi provinces.

18. A set of bronze ritual vessels for alcohol from Shigushan with spikey heads and exuberant flanges. They were designed for a bronze stand (height 20.5 cm, length 94.5 cm).

Rui and his immediate family to ensure their loyal support as the incursions of the Rong continued. The Jin rulers and their consorts received similar bequests.[28] Ancient pendants, arcs or discs, such as those in the lord's hangings, were among the donations. The heaviest and most unusual ancient piece was a large coiled 'pig-dragon' from the far north-east among the Hongshan people of 3500 BC, or it may have been a copy (plate 21). It was placed near Zhong Jiang's head.[29] These pieces were not celebrated for their age or distant origins, but rather, were interred with the lord and his consort for their auspiciousness and as records of alliances. Chance discovery of jades or bronzes in the ground was probably also considered fortunate. We do not have written formulations of these ideas: they are simply part of the unspoken beliefs that we have already encountered. From the fourth century BC onwards, when more had been recorded, clouds in the shape of dragons or phoenixes, emblems of benign spirits on front doors and gifts from eminent figures are recognised as helpful contributions to mitigate or even avoid the disasters that bad weather, sickness or evil forces might inflict.[30]

We can assess the majesty of the lord's jades, even if the Zhou had no exact idea of how old they were, from a single piece. It is a quarter of a Neolithic blade, with only half a hole at the top. It has been cut vertically, straight down the centre, from a Neolithic axe. This jade blade is very thin because the original piece had also been sliced, all the way from the top to the bottom, between the front and the back, probably to create two new items. One ancient axe had thus been cut to produce four new jades to be embellished, a sign of both the high value and the shortage of nephrite. The quarter that the lord owned had been carefully worked so that the incised motifs on the back and the front join to make a single subject. At the top is a pair of birds facing one another. Below, traversing the two halves, is a semi-human creature in profile. He has long hair hanging from the top of his head. His arm, bent at the elbow, has claws like a bird, as does his large stocky leg. A dragon at his waist fills the space below his arm and a long tail runs across. The edge of the original jade was cut with angled small prongs so that its profile is submerged. This is

A rubbing of the two decorated sides of a sliver
from an ancient jade axe, length 18 cm.

not from the eighth century BC. It was an ancient carving reworked
in the tenth century BC; as with so many of the jades at the Rui and
Jin polities, it is an antique.

The jades are remarkable for their age, quality and quantity. But
more extraordinary is the fact that the lord and his consort had them
at all. Only very few people in the history of China have had the
privilege to be buried under such a display of this precious stone. In
the Shang period the highest elite, Ya Chang and Fu Hao, had jades
strewn on their bodies. And before them, the leader at Liangzhu is
one of the very first instances of this practice. The later jade suits of
the Han imperial princes in the second and first centuries BC are cor-
responding examples.[31] No one would have buried jade if it were not
understood to provide safe passage for its owners, a way to communicate with spirits and ancestors.

Jade and bronze were stores of social and ritual capital. During the
uncertainties of the mid-eighth century BC, the Zhou kings seemingly
felt compelled to expand their gifting culture with jade. The wealth of

the Lord of Rui and his lineage indicates that the political situation was not improving but getting more fraught. But as times had changed, so had the positions of the lords and their relationships with their superiors and neighbours. As core members of the clan, the Lords of Rui and Jin were expected to fight for the Zhou king and defend the Wei Valley.[32] The Lord of Rui was hedging his bets. He realised that he needed to court his northern neighbours by declaring his relationships with them, even as he promised loyalty to the Zhou.

We know from the archaeological record, as well as from some inscriptions and poems, that the peoples named as the Xianyun and the Rong were not allies. The loose names do not specify how many different groups they refer to, but we can call them newcomers or identify them as pastoralists as, unlike the Yu, they do not appear to have been respected within Zhou political systems.[33] Their presence explains the preparation for warfare in the afterlife as well as in life. Some inscriptions on bronze vessels explicitly tell us that, from the latter part of the ninth century BC, the Zhou had been at war. An inscription on the Duoyou *ding* describes chariot warfare:

> On the *guiwei* [day twenty], the Rong attacked Xun and took captives. Duoyou pursued to the west. In the morning of the *jiashen* [day twenty-one], [he] struck [them] at Qi. Duoyou had cut off heads and captured prisoners to be interrogated: in all using the ducal chariots to cut 2 [X] 5 heads, to capture 23 prisoners, and to take 117 Rong chariots; [Duoyou] liberated the Xun people captured [by the Xianyun].[34]

This chariot battle, taking place in the late ninth or eighth century BC, was part of a wider conflict in which throngs of horses were captured. Naturally, victories were always emphasised, but the northern allies of the Zhou were now tested by steppe warriors on horseback as well as those using chariots. This new horse warfare created an unusual borderland where Zhou traditions of the Central Plains butted up against those of northern regional groups.

Carefully excavated and restored fragments of thin bronze sheets stacked around the west and south end of the coffin chamber of the later Rui lord are sections of armour for men and horses.[35] This tomb had sets of armour to cover the head and neck of horses or teams of two pulling chariots. For men, the armour consisted of scaly plaques held together with small strings of bronze to make a tunic. The use of armour, especially for horses, must have come from outside the agricultural plains. Bone and antler armour had been used for centuries in the steppe, and there horses were probably protected with leather.[36] The first traces of bronze armour – helmets at Anyang – arrived alongside the chariots from the steppe.[37] Bronze armour may also have come from Central Asia. But only in the hands of the sophisticated and wealthy societies of the Loess Plateau and the Yellow River basin, where bronze was plentiful, were whole suits of armour now forged. The *sha* standards of forged bronze atop coffin lids probably came into fashion at the same time. Simple horse harnesses – bronze bits and cheekpieces – were also buried among the Lord of Rui's possessions. Much more impressive however was his chariot pit, the core of his army. This has not been fully surveyed, but we can turn to comparisons at the cemetery of the Jin lords at Beizhao, just over the Yellow River, where one enormous pit held nearly fifty chariots and a host of horses.[38]

Armour for a horse's head, with a small square hole for the eye and the rounded section below for the muzzle, length 43.8 cm.

While the Zhou kings demanded practical support in war, they had another essential requirement: all lineage leaders had to adhere absolutely to the rituals of the ancestral cult, cementing the legitimacy of Zhou rule. The Lord of Rui and all contemporary and later lords had accepted an expansion in the numbers and a limitation in the shapes of the vessels they now used. Although no writing tells us this, the vessels themselves bear the signs of a major revolution. The Lord had seven tripods, *ding*, identical in profile but in descending size – ranging from 32.3 centimetres down to 22.4 centimetres in height – and six basins with lids, *gui*, all of similar size at a diameter of 23.5 centimetres. The bodies of the tripods are almost hemispherical, with legs braced in a curve, standing on small hoofed feet. Decoration had been scaled down generally to a single band, with simplified scrolls replacing earlier, more complex *taotie* and dragons. The lidded basins are circular and have wide horizontal grooves borrowed from ceramics. Relics of earlier bird motifs remain on two large alcohol flasks, poised on the surface within binding, which reproduces leather or cords. A steamer was also provided in a new shape and water vessels were added. Significantly, the main alcohol drinking vessels – cups and goblets (*jue* and *gu*) – had vanished.

A dramatic change in design and practice had taken place. The variety of vessel shapes belonging to Yu Bo at Baoji had been replaced by regular repetition. In Liangdaicun, identical vessels in a set were valued. The second lord and the secondary consort had almost identical vessels in fewer numbers and reduced sizes to denote their lower position in the Zhou hierarchy. Surprisingly, Zhong Jiang had larger and heavier ones, exhibiting her value to the lord through marriage. Vessels at the settlements of Jin and the regional clans in the nearby Fen River basin bear witness to the same repetition. Later texts set out, mainly as a form of explanation, the numbers of tripods and basins to be allocated to lords of different ranks. By this time *ding* had taken a leading role. Some were enormous. Seven tripods were to distinguish the lord, as nine, in theory, were allocated to the Zhou kings. Other writings suggest that the kings might have had twelve. This numerical regularity between ranks may only have been described in retrospect

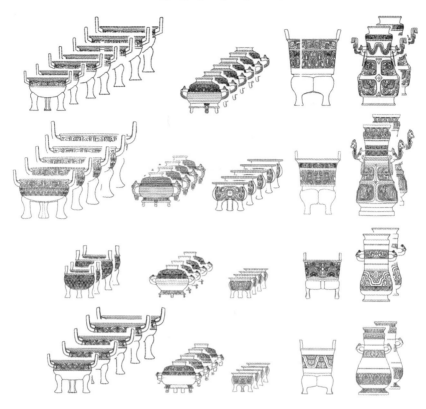

Part of the standardised ritual sets of the four family members.
Top row: the Lord of Rui's set, flask, *hu* (*far right*), height 49.1 cm, weight 14.1 kg.
Second row: Zhong Jiang's set, *hu*, height 53.3 cm, weight 14.9 kg.
Third row: the secondary consort's set, *hu*, height 38.6 cm.
Fourth row: the set of a son or another man, *hu*, height 40 cm.

and was not applied consistently. But an attempt to order the vessel numbers by status and physical and visual impact was part of a new ritual regime. When the Zhou took over the territory from the Shang, they had kept most of the ancient system of ritual banquets in place, with a few changes to emphasise the food vessels. Now, at a time of military and political instability, they set up a revised system.[39]

The arresting sets of duplicate vessels must have resulted from a central decision. They mark a formal change in the design, the cost of the metal and the performance of ritual banquets. The bronzes are grander in scale and scope than those owned by the Yu lords. And each Zhou generation was buried with his or her own set. So the lord buried next to the Lord of Rui had commissioned his own new set. The Zhou had thus developed a method to regulate relationships between generations in a patrilineal clan, thus organising the lives of the principal aristocratic lineages.[40] The Liangdaicun bronzes are much less intricate than those of Ya Chang or Yu Bo. On the other hand, the easily recognisable shapes would have been more impressive to a larger lineage or clan standing at a distance, taking in their bulk. The level of craftsmanship had declined and the cost of bronze had risen steeply. In high-ranking sets, we no longer see haphazard additions of vessels. The new system applied across all the lands over which the Zhou exerted control, to both Ji and non-Ji members. These complete sets were not allocated to, nor obtained by, the Rong at this date. Therefore we realise that, in areas where these new vessel sets are not found, as at Baoji, Zhou authority and even influence had burned out. Ninth- and eighth-century BC sets were in the hands of valued members of the Zhou community. This situation, however, would soon rapidly change again, as many local groups claimed political recognition with displays of ritual vessels.

We also need to consider the actual performance of the banqueting ritual. The vessels were part of a theatrical display, attended by members of the lineage and their ancestors. With heavier vessels and fewer types, the sequences in which food and alcohol were offered to the participants must have altered. I became interested in the inevitable changes to the performances when I worked in the British Museum. At times, when it was necessary to move particular bronzes to a new display cabinet, it became apparent how heavy the Lord of Rui's new vessels were. The mighty alcohol flasks, which were now standard, were far more difficult to move than the earlier ones; full of liquid they would have been even more cumbersome. The two alcohol flasks in the lord's set weigh over 28 kilos together. Those of his consort were even heavier, at 30 kilos the pair. The set of three owned by Yu Bo weigh just under 8 kilos.[41] The later repetitive sets added gravitas and even pomp as servants, attendants or junior members of the family must have been present to move and offer them, in the correct order, during the ceremony.[42] As before, the ritual banquets, fulfilled on a predetermined cycle, continued to make visible the family and political structures.[43]

The Lord of Rui would have been familiar with the presentation sequences. But this move to a rigorously enforced uniformity, palpable to all who took part, including the spirits of the ancestors (who were certainly aware of the changes), shows us that the Zhou court and the regional lords had accepted a significant and costly overhaul of their rituals. They were now committed to a new, shared, self-conscious understanding of the ways in which the offerings were to be performed. Differences between the vessels of one person and another would have been in size and number, rather than in design. If we look back to the Yu polity we see that the vessels in each tomb would have led to diverse performances, even between members of the same lineage. Standardisation at Liangdaicun was a way to ensure that the ritual performances followed a prescribed system. As the legitimacy of the Zhou depended on their ancestors, especially the early Kings Wen and Wu, it is not surprising that the shapes and numbers of vessels for the ancestral cult were now ordained.

Changes in ritual vessels had not happened all at once. Some simplified vessel types, such as lidded basins, had been introduced in the late tenth and early ninth centuries BC and used alongside earlier ones, which continued to be cast. These looked as though they were made of ceramics; was this some sort of call for simplicity? Then more homogeneity was established in the mid to late ninth century BC, perhaps by force or by decree, or by some means we cannot reconstruct. We know that the change had taken place well before the Zhou left the Wei River basin, as sets in the new form were buried in the hoards at the ritual centre west of Xi'an as families abandoned the valley.[44] The vessels of the ninth century could not have gradually evolved to make up a new set. The changes in shape were too far removed from the earlier vessel types. A plan must have been made. As there are no written records of this change, with the new vessel types appearing in the ninth century BC, an alternative proposal has been made by

Professor Li Feng, based on textual analysis. He suggests that ritual changes occurred in the tenth century BC, before they were manifested in material terms. This difference in dating of what was clearly a major upheaval is a useful indicator of the ways in which archaeology and written history offer rather different perspectives.[45]

The vessels in his tomb indicate that the Lord of Rui and his attendants were willing to conform to this ritual revolution. At the same time, knowledge of the earlier vessel types was retained, conveying a continuing respect for the achievements of ancestors. We know from the hoards buried west of Xi'an that some early vessels were preserved, often for their important inscriptions.[46] With the move eastwards, these ancient types were often left behind and instead usually replicated in poorly cast miniatures.[47] The lord, however, was in an unusual position. His lineage had kept and brought some ancient pieces with them. An alcohol bucket or *you*, an imitation of an eleventh-century BC bronze of the form and decoration seen at Baoji, was found in his tomb. Decorated with birds with spiky plumage, and

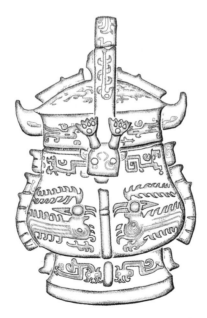

The *you* from the Lord of Rui's tomb, height 25.4 cm.
It closely resembles the more extravagant *you* at Shigushan (plate 18).

167

with a rudimentary antlered head where the handle joins the body, it closely resembles some of the finest bronzes found at Shigushan (plate 18). Although probably ancient, this *you* is not an original piece. The principal decoration is blurred, with rather rudimentary treatment of the handles. No small scrolls fill the background of the principal motifs, unlike the dense decoration on the Shigushan vessels. It is a detailed but much less accomplished copy. It must have been commissioned in the tenth or ninth century BC, perhaps to replace a lost bronze. A caster must also have known how to make a realistic version of an older bronze. The fact that the family wanted to reproduce this form and decoration, still in use at Baoji, tells us how much they valued their traditions and their identity. A flask or *zun* of the type that might have accompanied such a *you* was also allocated to the lord. It too is probably a copy, but less conspicuously so. Relatives of the lord must also have brought three earlier bronzes to Liangdaicun, with the one or two copies. The originals include a slender flask or *gu*, made in the early Western Zhou, a variant on the very fine Shang cup or *jue*, known as a *jiao*, and a middle Western Zhou basin, *gui*.[48] They do not recreate an earlier set and, as singletons, cannot have been used with the new set.

All members of the Zhou elite appear to have been aware of this radical change in the vessel shapes, numbers and sizes now deemed essential for ancestral banquets. While the lord followed this court-determined practice, he also retained the antique pieces from his family history. He and his retinue may even have seen the vessels as a tribute to their ancestors. An ancestor of the Lord of Rui buried in the same cemetery during the late Western Zhou had a set of miniature copies of the earlier vessel types, alongside a tripod or *ding*, a typical vessel of his time.[49] Lords had needed to swiftly replace personal, diverse bronzes that they had inherited with the standard set. While we cannot trace the directive, the acquaintance of the lords with the new requirements, and their copies of earlier vessels, tell us that the message had been received.

The Lord of Rui owned heirlooms, items of his heritage, due to his seniority. In the period from King Wu to King Kang (the eleventh to the tenth century BC), the Rui held important offices under the Zhou. A few records of inscribed bronzes naming the Rui survive. Among them are two *gui* vessels on square stands, one with a loop for hanging a bell underneath, comparable with basins from Yu.[50] While we do not know where they came from, the stands suggest that they were intended for the Rui when they held land in the Baoji region. Their polity may have been there. It would have consisted of a group of dwellings surrounded by land farmed by people who owed allegiance to the leader. Small Zhou polities, and later larger states, often moved as the politics demanded. It is unsurprising that the Rui had left Baoji and settled to the north-west of the Jin state from the ninth century BC at this critical point in the tussles with the Rong.

Political and military tumult must have been behind the revision of ritual sets. Embodied in this new, plain presentation was an entire web of decisions and constraints about managing bronze production. Someone must have given orders to the workshops, the patrons and the lineage lords. More bronzes needed more metal from the mines. More craftsmen had to be trained and more finished bronzes had to be transported. We have nothing in writing to show us this chain of command. A complete overhaul in how the banqueting vessels were designed, made, inscribed and distributed was not a minor

The inscription inside an impressive *gui* states that
the vessel was made for Rui Bo.

169

development. As this reform took place during a period of precariousness, the Zhou were very unlikely to have recorded it. They did not
do bad news. This may be why our picture of events, often framed by
how the Zhou wanted to be remembered, is slanted in a positive direction. One of the most famous, and misleading, accounts is a long
inscription on a basin buried in a hoard in the Wei Valley as the Zhou
moved east. It states that

> Vast and substantial was King Zhao! [He] broadly tamed the Chu
> and Jing [southerners]; it was to connect the southern route.[51]

What the scribe does not tell us is that, on this campaign, King
Zhao (977–957 BC) was routed in battle and may have drowned in the
River Han. We learn of this alternative version from the annals of
the Zhou preserved on bamboo strips discovered at a site of the third
century AD. King Zhao's defeat was the beginning of a long period
of turbulence: infighting in the Zhou court and raids from both the
north and the south. These upheavals encouraged the Rui polity to
move nearer to the Yellow River. With the revision of the banqueting set, the Zhou must have wanted to maintain a sense of continuity
with the achievements of the first kings, and would not have proclaimed any sort of divergence from previous stability. The belief
in the ancestors as guardians of their descendants had not shifted.
But the ways in which banquets were arranged and sets were buried
certainly had.

If we look at the evolution in religious practice and belief that
has taken place in Christian rituals over millennia, in papal bulls and
ecumenical councils, we recognise that this level of transformation
must have involved central coordination. It was probably also disturbing. Such a universal change could not have been made without the
involvement of the Zhou king and his advisers. The newly reformed
vessels at Liangdaicun are a deliberate sign that the Rui had accepted
the new sets, a political message of unity in the face of disorder.[52]
The Lord of Rui's weapons, chariots and armour are evidence of his
role in military defence, while his gold, iron and carnelians show that

he had, himself, taken the initiative in forming bonds with northern neighbours to defend his lands and to gain both horses and horse managers to bolster his own forces.

Martin Kern's reinterpretation of the major Zhou chronicles and early poems provides some important background to the dynasty's fading power from the tenth century BC. He argues that the transmitted writings, which set out the early history of the Zhou and their political claims, namely *The Book of Documents*, *The Collection of Leftover Documents* (*Yi Zhou Shu*) and *The Book of Poetry*, were gathered together late in the ninth to seventh centuries BC, during the later Western Zhou period or even in the early Eastern Zhou.[53] He calls the texts 'idealising artefacts', identifying them as propaganda rather than factual registers. In parallel with the standardisation of the ritual vessels, the objective behind the assembly of this material was not just to record the early Zhou conquest but to present a carefully curated version of it. Zhou claims to the Mandate of Heaven and the virtue of the early kings would have been expanded at this moment of transition: a time when military pressures increased, when new cultural patterns emerged, when the Zhou moved east and when new forms of ritual vessel were disseminated. We know from the bronze inscriptions that these notions of grandeur had been around for a long time. But the Lord of Rui was living in the shadow of a new order when the difficulties of the day had led the court to demand renewed allegiance. The Zhou do not mention the pressures of the northerners, but the lord's gold belt vividly invokes their influence. Such cultural interaction may even have stimulated the urge to affirm the Zhou identity.

A number of hymns in *The Book of Poetry* emphasise the models of the early kings and of blessings that the ancestors will offer their descendants:

It is the Mandate of Heaven,
How majestic and not ending!
Ah, greatly illustrious –
How pure the virtuous power of King Wen!
[His] fine blessings flow to us in abundance,

May we receive them!
[He who] grandly gives us favours is King Wen –
[His] distant descendants will strengthen them.[54]

The lineages of the eighth century BC had inherited this celebration of the past and were extending it into the future, emphasising their longevity through repetition. Other hymns addressed the lords, perhaps assembled in a temple, to whom the kings had offered land and military charges. The ancestors were informed that the Zhou kings continued to follow the example set out by Kings Wen and Wu, which the lords and future generations are exhorted to observe.[55] And, as these charges were inscribed on bronze vessels, the political and military relationships on which the kings depended were reiterated in ceremonial banquets. This repetition was both visual and oral, and echoed in rhythmical song.

The Zhou poems appear today as deliberate efforts to stabilise their kingdom. In this context we can reconsider a frequent topic of discussion in *The Book of Documents*: the decadent hedonism of the Shang, manifested in their excessive consumption of alcohol.[56] Admonishments to avoid such deleterious drunkenness appear in several of the main speeches attributed to the early Zhou kings. It seems that in the ninth century BC, and later, the Zhou were giving a more official shape to their history. It is not surprising, therefore, to see the alcohol drinking vessels, current in the late Shang and early Zhou, as at Baoji, eliminated in the ritual reform. At the same time, the value and role of the ancestral offerings were preserved by the hymns and poems. Recitations chanted at the banquets, of which the verse below is a later version, may have merged several traditions, leading to a shared norm, just as uniform casting had fostered a shared identity:

The furnace managers are attentive, attentive,
Making the sacrificial stands grand and magnificent:
Some [meat] is roasted, some is broiled.
The noble wives are solemn, solemn,
Making the plates grand and numerous.

With those who are guests, with those who are visitors,
Presentations and toasts are exchanged.
Rites and ceremonies are perfectly to the rule.
Laughter and talk are perfectly measured.
The divine protector, he is led to arrive,
He will requite [you] with great blessings –
Ten thousand years longevity will be [your] reward.[57]

The standardisation of vessels was also accompanied by changes to the musical instruments. The Lord of Rui had a set of eight bells, a more advanced form than Ya Chang's three bells or Yu Bo's singleton. In place of these earlier bells, which had stood with the oval mouth pointing upwards, the lord's were now hung the other way up, by a small loop on the vertical stem. Longer now in proportion to their width, the bells carried rows of bosses that are thought to have affected the sound they made. This change had probably come about in the Yangtze Valley in the south and had then travelled north in the tenth century BC.[58] But as with the earlier bells, they are oval in cross-section and were sounded as before, struck with a mallet or a staff on the outside, at the centre of the mouth and at one corner, producing two different notes. Ancient chime stones had also now been expanded into a large set. The original shape of a flat stone rising to a

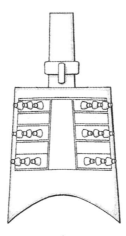

One of a set of eight bells, the largest at 39.9 cm high.

point, where the hole was drilled, was now modified, with an uneven angular top and a flat or curved base. The stones descended in size, just like the bells, to offer a rising scale of notes. Both the bells and the chimes required stands, probably in lacquered wood, as the poem below describes. The Lord of Rui also had a wooden lacquered drum. Animal skins were used for drums in ceramics, wood or bronze, with bamboo perhaps for flutes and pipes. A similar spectacle is recorded in *The Book of Poetry*:

> There are blind musicians, there are blind musicians,
> They are in the courtyard of the Zhou [temple],
> [We] have set up the boards, we have set up the vertical posts [for
>   bells and drums],
> With raised flanges, planted feathers,
> The [small] responding and introducing drums, the [large]
>   suspended drums,
> The [little] hand drums, chime stones, rattles and clappers –
> All prepared and now played.
> The pan-pipes and flutes are raised –
> *Huang-huang* is their sound.
> Solemn and concordant [their] harmonious tune –
> The former ancestors, these are listening!
> Our guests [the ancestors] have arrived.
> For long [they] observe the performance.[59]

The ritual revolution had taken place well before the Lord of Rui died around 750 BC, and indeed before the Zhou had moved east to Luoyang. The Jin, the Rui's Ji clan neighbours, also adopted this wholesale change. Offerings to ancestors were an integral instrument in Zhou political theatre as they attempted to hold together their lands north of the Yangtze River. The newcomers were no doubt unperturbed. The lord had to accommodate himself within the southern Loess Plateau and potential enemies of the Zhou. His ancestors would have immediately recognised his high status from his massive tomb, with its long ramps, filled with riches. As an ancestor himself, he would have joined the ceremonial banquets prepared by his son and his family, ensuring the continuity of both his lineage and the Zhou state. From this new vantage point, he would have witnessed the increasing challenges to his clan and polity. The growing impact of the Rong and others fostered a cultural symbiosis that invariably adapted their materials and technologies to the practices of the Central Plains. The golden belt is a milestone, but we have to look much later to the Tang dynasty (618–906 AD) to find belts finally taken into the heart of official life.[60] Tang emperors and their highest officials were assigned belts with jade plaques; gold plaques, in line with China's values, were reserved for the rank below. Two forces were at work on the Lord of Rui, which were expressed in his objects. The pressures from the north were displayed in the elaborate dress that he wore for the afterlife. And the unwavering authority of the ruling court manifested itself in his standardised sets of ritual vessels and in the heirlooms that had been passed down to him by his forebears.

PART III

Converging Cultures, 700–300 BC

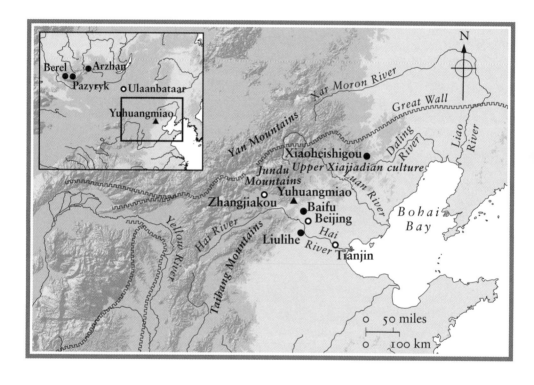

Yuhuangmiao and the Yan Mountains

7.

The Steppe Frontier

Herded animals have to be kept on the move to find new pastures and to leave areas that become overgrazed. Horses were essential companions of prosperous stockbreeders who, in the early seventh century BC, brought their mobile existence on to the south-facing slopes of the Yan Mountains. These slopes are very different from the lands along the Wei and the Fen. There, hundreds of miles of the Loess Plateau acted as an obstacle, blunting the impact of the Arctic winds and impeding the movement of people coming south. But here, the most northern place we have visited so far, the plain is exposed to the seasonal climate of northern Eurasia. High summer was a time of wealth, as the grasslands flourished and supported a livelihood of meat, milk and sheep wool, but beyond the mountains the pastoralists on the steppe always had to endure the winter's cold winds, which were drawn south as the Pacific Monsoon pulled away from China. The meeting of divergent landforms – plains, river basins, deserts and open grasslands – on the two sides of the Yan Mountains, and the continuous movement of people it encouraged, were always challenges for the rulers of the Yellow River basin. Yet they were one of the defining features of ancient China.

The low, wide plains stretch east to the coast near the modern city of Tianjin. The Yan Mountains also extend towards this coast, but permit a route to the north along the fertile basins of the Liao River to an enormous expanse of land, originally forested, beyond the Xar Moron River and today bordering Russia's eastern provinces. This major route is matched to the west by a pass over the Yan peaks from the direction of the modern city of Zhangjiakou. These are the main roads between two worlds, separated only by mountains and subsequently by the Great Wall. The stone-faced walls and turrets which

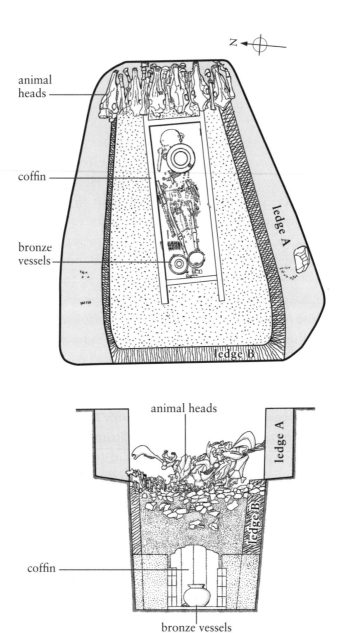

N

animal
heads

coffin

bronze
vessels

ledge A

ledge B

animal heads

ledge A

ledge B

coffin

bronze vessels

The earthen pit of the Mountain Rong leader, more than 3 m in length and
2.66 m in depth, is arranged east–west, narrowing at the eastern end to
1.6 m and widening at the west to 3.6 m, almost taking the form of a vehicle,
perhaps a chariot or a boat.

we see today were mostly built or restored under the Ming dynasty (AD 1368–1644), after the Mongol dynasty of the Yuan (AD 1260–1368) was driven out. Earlier, a rammed earthen wall had been strung along the northern borders. The buffer here was much narrower than the Loess Plateau, exemplified by the tomb of a man who crossed the boundary from one world to the other. He shows that it was much easier to move between two lifestyles and environments than the fortifications might suggest.

Over decades, even centuries, the Zhou rulers had used the wealth of the Central Plains to attract and convert potential enemies into allies. The eighth and seventh centuries BC were the turning point, as they had to give up some of their land in the west around Baoji and their authority in the Yellow River basin had weakened. At the same time, the people on the steppe had grown stronger, more numerous, more prosperous and had, in some cases, taken to mounted warfare.[1] We should not be led astray by the usual propaganda: that peaceful, refined settlements were invaded by uncivilised pastoralists. The new arrivals had their own sophisticated ways of life. As China was fostering a shared culture along the great valleys, so too a shared, but an utterly different, culture was spreading across the grasslands. Engagement, integration and even accommodation were always possible via the Loess Plateau, as northern groups accepted gifts of banqueting vessels, adopted the ancestral cult and its associated burial practices and contributed to the political and military objectives of the Zhou.

The Zhou had quickly recognised the dangers that lay on the northern fringes of the lands they intended to control. They must have rapidly surveyed land south of present-day Beijing and decided to station loyal members of their clan there to subdue and manage the area. Members of the family of Shao Gong, one of the brothers of King Wu, were sent to the north to establish the polity of Yan.[2] This probably comprised settlements surrounded by farmland located, we believe, near Liulihe, as a cemetery has been excavated there dated to the tenth century BC.[3] This outpost completed a sequence of military settlements, intended to secure inroads from the north along the three main routes: the first at Baoji with non-Zhou clans, among them Yu

Bo, the second on the Fen River with members of the Ji clan at the Jin and Rui polities, and the third through the Yan Mountains. When northern stockbreeders settled beneath the Yan in the early seventh century BC, traces of the late Western Zhou occupation were missing. The people who fostered the cemetery at Liulihe had died or moved on. We find the tomb of a prominent new leader in a cemetery on the slopes of one of the lower ridges, known as the Jundu Mountains. Among three cemeteries there, Yuhuangmiao is the most extensive, with some 400 of the 600 total tombs.[4]

The three most impressive tombs in Yuhuangmiao must have belonged to clan leaders. They all had an unusual shape. They do not correspond to the tombs of the Zhou and their allies. This alone was a declaration that the people at Yuhuangmiao did not belong to the Zhou and did not aspire to join them. As each tomb was dug in an east–west orientation, a thick ledge was left in place, less than a metre from the surface at the eastern end and around the two slightly longer curved sides north and south. Digging down somewhat further, another, thinner ledge was left around the deep central area, in which the coffin was placed. In each, the leader lies, head to the east, in the remains of a wooden chamber cut into the surface at the base of the tomb. All his possessions – weapons, horse harnesses and gold below his neck and on his ears – were laid directly on his body within the coffin and identify him as a wealthy stockbreeder, a role that continued in the afterlife. None of his possessions were placed on a wide secondary ledge, as would have been typical of a Zhou burial. The weapons indicate that the person buried is a man, for weapons are rare in the tombs of women in this cemetery.

The Han historian Sima Qian identified a group of newcomers as the Shan Rong, meaning the Mountain Rong. We do not know whether he had any knowledge of the people at the Jundu Mountains. This name was, however, selected and applied by historians and archaeologists working on the cemetery. So while the name is convenient, it is arbitrary. The name Rong matches the terminology that the Zhou used to describe northerners approaching, somewhat threateningly, the Central Plains. We do not know what these people called themselves. We do not even know how many different clans or groups were involved in the persistent movement southwards and were then clumped together by the Zhou. The term Rong was simply a general designation of 'other', with violent overtones. They certainly did not all belong in one single group and the term means that differences between them became blurred and lost. The name Rong has also made them seem insignificant, without the individual lineage names afforded to the Yu or their contemporaries on the Fen River, the Ba and the Peng. Yet the many members of the Rong had a huge impact on the Zhou. Over the eighth century BC, some moved not only into many areas of the Loess Plateau, but actively and effectively infiltrated the Zhou polities and settlements. It is likely that they occupied scrub land and less fertile areas in the interstices between the agricultural settlements. Several Rong groups had become participants in the daily politics of settled communities, now divided into competing small polities and some larger states. Chronicles, including the *Bamboo Annals* (*Zhu Shu Ji Nian*) and *The Spring and Autumn Annals* (*Chun Qiu Ji Nian*), together covering the period from the late ninth century to the middle of the sixth century BC, and commentaries, including the *Zuo Zhuan*, record almost yearly attacks and skirmishes.[5]

The constant danger that the pastoralists posed, as they returned again and again to encroach on their settled neighbours, is remembered in a famous comment by a minister addressing a leader of the eastern state of Qi in 661 BC: 'the Rong and the Di are jackals and wolves and cannot be satisfied'.[6] This is an oft-repeated notion. But it is hyperbolic, designed to denigrate and to even obscure their power. As Sima Qian writes in his chapter on the later eastern pastoralists, the Xiongnu, who threatened the Qin and the Han: 'in periods of crisis they take up arms and go off on plundering and marauding expeditions'.[7] Yet incessant warfare was not the only, or even the main, contribution of these intruders.[8] They had considerable uses too; they had horses, they had gold, they had iron tools and they had interesting weapons. And all underscored, as we saw in the tomb of the Lord of Rui, new cultural developments. Though never mentioned in historical texts, this cultural dialogue was of immense value to both sides.

And perhaps the settled inhabitants of the river basins made the greatest gains. As the populations of the northern states expanded, they could use iron tools to open up more land. The dual movement of the pastoralists and stockbreeders migrating south and the agriculturalists spreading north led to the construction of the first walls, from the fourth and third centuries BC, primarily by the Zhao and Yan states.[9]

Significantly, the tombs on the Jundu Mountains house people whom, unlike Yu Bo or the Lord of Rui, we can identify as having *direct* steppe connections. They had arrived to make use of the land, at least for seasonal spells of occupation and for burial. The surprising tomb structure at Yuhuangmiao indicates that this group came from further north. An east–west orientation is quite typical for the northern reaches of the Loess Plateau, or even the steppe, but the wide, almost chariot or boat shape of the bigger tombs has no parallels elsewhere. It may even have been unusual in its time, aiming to give prominence to the leaders among a wider population. Most other people were buried in rectangular graves with an oval pit for the body, also orientated east–west. The curving perimeter and varied levels of platforms are not found in the less elaborate tombs. The tomb owner and his followers appear to have brought several traditions together: a steppe tomb orientation, an otherwise unknown shape with ledges and a wooden chamber or coffin – a misinterpretation of Zhou practices.

There is a pile of animal heads and bones at the east end of the tomb on an additional high platform, level with the upper ledges. We have not seen this before. The animal jaws face east, as if pulling the tomb towards the rising sun. There are sixteen horse heads with sixteen leg bones and their hoofs. At the bottom of the pile, six of the horse heads are paired with twelve leg bones and their hoofs. The animal bones, alongside a few sets of bronze harness rings, immediately remind us of similar ritual deposits around the stone khirigsuurs in Mongolia. A further ten horse heads are laid over the rings, with the heads and bones of three cattle, seven caprids (sheep and goats) and four dogs. The bones are not only a ritual offering. They are a record of a pastoral life led among animals.[10] The man was also laid on a broad animal fur and a layer of felt made from sheep's wool.

These skins were essential for the clothes and tents of stockbreeders as they moved through the seasons. The 600 tombs in the three cemeteries indicate that a vast herding community, or several communities, of men, women, children, horses and herds regularly occupied the Jundu slopes.

The activities of the pastoralists and the extent of the steppe were beyond the grasp of settled Eurasia. The unknown is always disconcerting, and newcomers and stockbreeding neighbours were often given unflattering names. 'Barbarian' (and its equivalents in other languages) unhelpfully disguises the prowess of the pastoralists – they gained huge areas by migration and occupation and later posed some of the most significant military threats that the settled world was to know. Even the term 'nomad' is inaccurate. To call a group nomadic implies an unregulated movement of people, without any form of social organisation. We now know, both from anthropological and archaeological research, that this was not how pastoralists managed their lives.[11] Pasture was essential. But it was not open to all. A clan had to reach some sort of agreement with other neighbouring herding groups. Bargains, concessions and disputes certainly took place. A key negotiating tactic was long-term occupation. Gatherings for regular festivals also probably drew multiple populations together, allowing marriages and exchanges of animals and valuable materials. Cyclical movement was critical to make full use of the environment. In summer, the herders took their animals up hills and mountains to find fresh pastures. In the autumn they returned to their winter camps in valleys and basins to shelter from the northerly winds. The Mountain Rong leader, as we shall call him for convenience, must have followed this pattern of life.

As time would tell, the inevitable mobility of herding and stockbreeding was impossible to integrate into the agricultural basins of the Central Plains. Genghis Khan is said to have thought that the fields in the valleys should be turned over to grass for his herds. But neither he, nor his entourage, nor the settled farmers for that matter, could have known that the rain-fed plains were not suitable for herding and

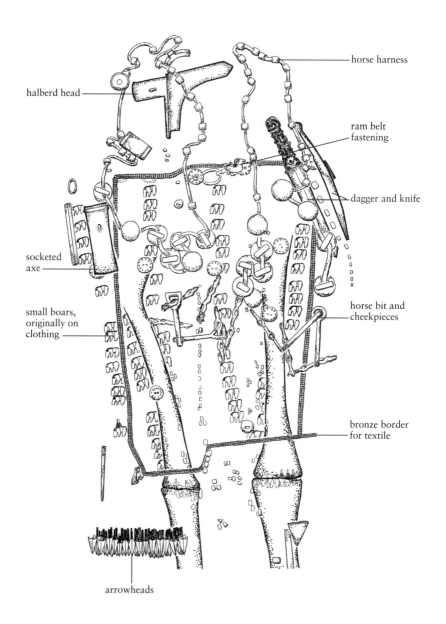

halberd head

horse harness

ram belt
fastening

dagger and knife

socketed
axe

small boars,
originally on
clothing

horse bit and
cheekpieces

bronze border
for textile

arrowheads

Interior of the coffin showing the weapons, harness equipment and ornaments.

stockbreeding; too many people, too much rain, too marshy a terrain and too few nutrients in the soil – the dearth of selenium meant that horses bred on the plains continued to lack strength. While the pastoralists did not often establish permanent holdings of land among the growing dynastic states, there was much to gain through exchanges, barter and raiding their supplies of grain and metal. Recognisable political or economic groups were only formed when the newcomers established themselves as equals with their settled neighbours. Over time, their neighbouring Zhou polities and allies found that the Rong had much to offer with their horses, gold, belt-fastenings, knives, swords, mirrors and stone tombs. Such exchanges could, but did not always, lead to cultural assimilation.[12]

A layer of stone over the earth in the Mountain Rong leader's tomb, level with the animal heads, belongs to the steppe tradition. Stone, used as fences around and within tombs, and in mounds over them, was the preferred material for monuments across present-day Mongolia and Siberia. The most prominent are the khirigsuurs and kurgans.[13] The Mountain Rong in the Yuhuangmiao cemtery must have come from this steppe community scattered across distant grasslands. Others will have stayed behind. In moving south, the tomb owner and his companions had not implemented even a modified form of a Zhou tomb; they had not taken up the full Zhou banqueting ritual; they did not own or treasure jade, nor had they sought a position within the Zhou nobility. There are no inscribed objects in their tombs. The people at Yuhuangmiao did not adopt any of the strategies we saw at Baoji or on the Fen River. Were the Mountain Rong indifferent to the power of the Zhou king, or did they not even know of its existence? They certainly held fast to their own traditions. This cemetery is a snapshot of the lives and identities of people from the steppe, who are otherwise very difficult to rescue from the past.

In addition to the stone layer, the horse heads and harnesses placed directly over the man's body centre horses in his life and afterlife. Two long sequences of bronze ornaments, with traces of leather indicating that they were threaded through the loops on their back, and other, smaller round bronze ornaments added along thongs were an ostentatious display. In many areas of the steppe, wood and bone were widely used for ornaments and tools. These have not survived, though later tombs in the Russian Altai and Kazakhstan offer examples.[14] This is why the bronze ornaments are so valuable, a rare glimpse of a society too readily eroded by and returned to the environment. The bronze was also a sign of newly acquired wealth. Two bronze horse bits, one with slightly angular ends, sometimes called stirrup-shaped bits, and eight bronze cheekpieces, partly threaded through the bits, emphasise the man's close relationship with his horses. Are other bits missing, or was rope or leather used instead? Each bronze cheekpiece has three holes, implying that, unlike the harness at Liangdaicun, these may have been tied to the bits with leather thongs, a trait of a new and popular form of steppe harness.[15] The man was completely up to date with changes on the steppe, where bronze or iron began to replace antler cheekpieces in the ninth century BC. Two further sets of harness and bronze bits suggest that two horses were used to pull a cart or a chariot, although there are no surviving chariot fittings at Yuhuangmiao. Steppe drivers did not have the wealth or the inclination to decorate their vehicles with bronze. The shape of the tomb and the horse heads at one end may have been intended to show that the tomb was a vehicle which would be drawn by horses into the afterlife.[16] With several horse heads and cheekpieces, we cannot rule out the possibility that the man and his comrades also rode. Riding for herding, raiding and warfare had now been taken up by pastoral groups in the eastern steppe, making them more threatening to the Zhou.[17] Horses were the defining element of life on the steppe and, therefore, for all those who intruded southwards; as a consequence, horses were now part of the landscape of the Central Plains. Yet little attention has been given to them by the historians and archaeologists of China. This may simply be because at most times in China's past, highly educated scholars and officials, who compiled the records on which modern scholarship depends, did not ride: they were driven in chariots and carriages and had servants and attendants to look after the horses.

Much has been made of the supposed contrast between the steppe and the sown. This is a great oversimplification, especially across much of northern China, with the Loess Plateau and its mixed life-style of agriculture and pasture. More fundamental was the enormity of the two territories either side of the Jundu Mountains and the depth and breadth of their resources. Both sides probably regarded the loess areas around the Yan Mountains as theirs. The conflicts were not between cultural and military unequals, but they were not well matched and ways had to be devised to manage the encounters. Each arrival from the north, each conflict, failed to resolve the dilemma. There were always more people moving south and there were always more armies and more cities to meet the intruders from the north.

The Mountain Rong were one such newcomer. They probably occupied the Yan slopes for a couple of centuries and were then per-haps integrated into the wider population. They had much to gain, as we have just seen in the bronze ornaments, but they could not take their mobile stockbreeding existence much further south. If they went south, they would have gradually had to change their lifestyles. Neither could the lords of the plains, not only for environmental rea-sons, but also because of the demands of their settled customs, move north to beyond the Yan Mountains. They were tied to their land by ritual loyalty to their ancestors. Moreover, they had not developed the stockbreeding needed to support lives on the steppe. Instead, forg-ing alliances and allowing, even encouraging, the Rong to settle on less fertile land in between their polities were deliberate strategies to lessen the impact of the northerners.[18] The ability to absorb new-comers into their culture, and even their political framework, was the ultimate strength of the Zhou and the lords of the polities.

In this context, we should not be misled by the four bronze vessels in the Mountain Rong leader's tomb. Though they appear to be a sign of assimilation into the practices of the Central Plains, the vessels do not even begin to form a viable banqueting set, a way to commune with ancestors. One of them is a roughly cast, rounded basin with looped handles on the lip, imitating cord or rope. Traces of soot indi-cate that it had been used in life. The cauldron, as we could call it, with its rope-like handles, also belonged with similar cooking or serving pots in the steppe, such as one that has been unearthed in one of the

A neatly cast small cup with a round handle,
height 6.9 cm, with a roughly cast cauldron, height 20.9 cm.

major kurgans in the Valley of the Kings in the Tuva Republic, which
is nearly half a metre in height. A smaller cauldron in the same kurgan
is only about 30 centimetres in height.[19] Was this vessel type invented
in the steppe, or was it developed within a local Loess Plateau tradition
that then travelled north? This reminds us that there is so much we do
not know about the constant but almost invisible interaction between
the northern pastoralists, who have left few traces, and the people in
the Loess Plateau, whose aspirations seem to have been to abandon
their origins and join the prosperous agricultural plains. Some scholars
have suggested that people with abundant bronze to hand produced
vessels and later belts and harness ornaments to exchange with steppe
groups further north.[20] The small cauldron in the Rong leader's tomb
may have been specifically made by Zhou casters for northerners.[21]

With it is a small, smoother oval cup with a ring handle and a design
of sunken triangles. These two types also appeared among the small
set of the spouse of the Lord of Rui.[22] While both were products of
Zhou casting traditions, they had become especially popular in the
Loess Plateau. It is worth thinking further about this cup. Among the
twenty-two vessels found in the 400 tombs at Yuhuangmiao, a cup
with one or two ring handles dominates.[23] Perhaps the Rong used it
to replace the wooden cups of the steppe. We know that it did not get
drawn in as a member of a standard ritual set, because similar cups
found in tombs to the south-east, in Shandong, were sometimes placed
among weapons and chariot fittings, not among the banqueting sets.[24]

A lidded cooking vessel, height 14.2 cm, and a decorated flask, height 26.6 cm.

The two others in the Rong leader's tomb were a covered cooking pot, of a type also found at Liangdaicun, and a more rounded flask for liquids that had parallels much further south. The covered cooking pot was a new addition and more popular in the Loess Plateau and Shandong, rather than in the south. The flask, a beautifully cast piece, has several abstract design patterns, which can be compared with the possessions of leaders occupying tombs on the Central Plains.[25] How the flask had come north we do not know, but it was not alone. One of the other tombs at Yuhuangmiao held two water vessels, a basin and a ewer, neither of which fitted life on the Jundu Mountains.[26] They illustrate a tendency among northerners to collect fine bronzes cast elsewhere. The vessels reveal that one of the major resources, prized above all by the new arrivals, was metalwork.

Here lies one of the differences between the northerners and the people on the Central Plains. In the north, horses were the source and emblem of wealth; on the Central Plains, wealth was expressed in bronze ritual vessels and banquets for ancestors with a generous array of food.[27] The horses flourished in the wide, dry grasslands. The banqueting vessels were the outcome of a much more humid, agricultural environment. Bronze vessels were always on the move, as the Zhou gave them to their allies and clients at Baoji or used them to cement ties among the polities along the Fen River. But the Mountain Rong at Yuhuangmiao were not following the Yu lineage in amassing them in sets – their vessels were not gifts. They were not looking for a guarantee of a good life by offering nourishment to their ancestors. They were showcasing their wealth in a commodity that might, in due course, be re-melted for, in their view, better use as horse ornaments. Bronzes, even bronze vessels, had a different role in the eyes of the pastoralists: they were stores of wealth for the future. We know that, many centuries later, steppe people bartered for metalwork as well as grain at trading posts not far from the Yan Mountains.[28]

The geographical position of the landscape where Beijing was to be built, and its immediate history before the arrival of the Mountain Rong, explain the presence of bronze vessels in the leader's tomb. A challenging conjunction of the steppe, mountains and agriculture was the driving force that brought ritual vessels north in the hands of the Zhou leaders of the Yan polity. The polity was there to defend this meeting point from pastoralists and to obtain horses. From a substantial cemetery at Liulihe, dating to the early tenth century BC, we know that a diverse population was settled in the area, some from the Central Plains, others from the borderlands of the steppe. They had unusual tombs which often did not follow Zhou practices. Their northern connections are visible in numerous chariot and horse burials, with short willow-leaf swords, horse harnesses and fittings decorated with horse heads.[29] As the Zhou leaders sought to create new centres in remote regions far beyond the Wei Valley, they inevitably recruited people with different cultural and ethnic backgrounds. Those loyal to the Zhou also obtained and buried bronze ritual vessels. Some are inscribed and give us a glimpse of members of an elite who were rewarded with land and labourers for their military efforts. But the Yan polity did not flourish much beyond the tenth century BC. All traces of their activity just disappeared. What changed? Why was life disrupted? We can't be sure, but do know that this disturbance coincided with the moment when the Yu disappeared in the far west. Perhaps hordes of fine bronzes from Liulihe were buried at the same time at a number of sites across the Yan Mountains.[30] Were these buried by their Zhou owners? Or had they been taken by other new-comers and buried to store their capital for future occasions?

The vessels were even more valuable to those who happened upon them by chance, including arrivals from the grasslands, named today as people belonging to the Upper Xiajiadian culture (thought to be active possibly as early as the tenth century BC and occupying the area into the eighth century BC or later). Their cemeteries were north-east of the Yan Mountains. Again stone was incorporated into their tombs. They are the predecessors of the Mountain Rong buried at Yuhuang-miao. Their long bronze swords and multiple bronze horse bits and cheekpieces, even more experimental than those at Yuhuangmiao, are signs that they were newcomers, advancing from the north. They wore coiled gold wire ornaments and reused some of the vessels that they found, burying them in their tombs. They melted down others to make their own vessels and weapons. The bountiful supply of bronze also allowed them to cast bronze helmets and transform their more mundane leather headgear.[31] Perhaps word had spread that metal was easily sourced at the foot of the Yan Mountains and that the loom-ing peaks offered pasture and shelter. From the material record, it appears as if these alien forms of metalwork emerged suddenly, as if from nowhere. There must have been earlier weapons and fittings in the area of present-day Mongolia, which may simply have been recy-cled again and again over several generations. With new sources of bronze found in abandoned hoards, the newcomers must now have felt able to take them into the afterlife. The Mountain Rong leader, with his four precious vessels, evidently thought the same.

There is additional evidence to show that people of the Upper Xia-jiadian and at Yuhuangmiao took bronze vessels as sources of metal to cast their own weapons, horse tack and ornaments. A lead-rich alloy has been discovered in many of these bronzes.[32] Other northern weap-onry in the Loess Plateau also has this lead-rich alloy.[33] This points to the alloys employed on the Central Plains, which often included lead as well as tin and copper, but not to bronze from the steppe, where such additions of lead were not common; people there used a copper alloy with arsenic. It is likely that people entering the Yan Mountains had found Zhou bronze vessels and melted some of them down to make their own unorthodox vessels, harnesses and weapons.[34] Mining, smelting and alloying copper, tin and lead require knowledge, experience, opportunity and manpower. There are sources of ore in the lands to the north-west of Beijing, but the people lacked an experienced labour force. Those who reached the areas north and south of the Yan Mountains, however, suddenly gained a fortune that did not demand mining or smelting and could just be looted from tombs.

The Mountain Rong leader's five weapons are conspicuously arranged. An angular bronze halberd head lies over his chest. This is not a steppe-type weapon at all. The pointed blade is quite broad and extended down the staff, with a tang at the back, which would have gone through the wooden staff to hold it in position. Such halberds abound in tombs of the late eighth and seventh centuries BC in the Central Plains. He may have gained the halberd in raids or combat. It had a hacking or chopping impact, as with the early axes of the Shang and Western Zhou. On the man's right side is a socketed axe, with a chisel lower down, near his right calf. These we recognise as steppe tools that were adopted by the Shang and Zhou chariot drivers for repairing their vehicles. Next to the axe is another intriguing object, a long, thin decorated bronze box. This was for holding needles or a spike, useful for piercing leather, or perhaps removing stones from the hoofs of his animals. Such narrow bronze boxes are found in several other tombs at Yuhuangmiao, each one slightly differently decorated, reflecting individual choice and also the plentiful bronze to hand. Their steppe peers did not use their scarce metal resources in this way, instead placing pins and sharp tools in leather scabbards.

A substantial dagger and a long knife to the left at the man's waist are the most lethal weapons, both thrusting instruments for close combat and for killing and skinning animals. In this instance, the dagger's grip carries an elaborate relief, which might have held tiny fragments of turquoise. The knife is slightly bowed with a loop at the top by which it could be attached to a thong. Almost all the occupants of the Yuhuangmiao tombs had this combination of dagger and knife, with personalised decoration.[35] Exactly the same pairing of a decorated dagger with a narrow single-edged knife is found in many steppe tombs in South Siberia. The most impressive have come from the later of the two Arzhan tombs.[36] Although no traces of a bow have been found, sixty arrowheads with sockets lie near the lower right leg of the leader, with the remains of a quiver. The distinction between steppe warfare and that of the Central Plains is embedded in these arrowheads, which were widely used across northern Eurasia. This tiny but essential feature definitively places the man's origins within a broader steppe culture.

A puzzling feature, an almost rectangular shape, is outlined across the middle of the man's body by 416 tiny, decorated bronzes pushed up against each other. They must have been attached to a spreading textile. We certainly have not come across anything like this before, although we can speculate that it formed something like a tunic, extending from his waist down to his boots. Or it may have been wound around his body. Individually, the bronzes, decorated with small S-shaped spirals, are almost inconsequential, but the fact that so

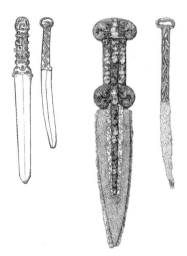

A dagger, length 28.6 cm, and a knife, length 23.1 cm, from the Mountain Rong leader's tomb and (*right*) an iron dagger with gold decoration, length 38.8 cm, and an iron knife also decorated in gold, length 28.8 cm, from Arzhan II.

many pieces were attached to a textile is proof that bronze added to his grandeur. And this instance is not alone. Other tombs at Yuhuang-miao show an identical practice. Although the leader may not have worn trousers, he will have had some form of leggings wrapped around his thighs and calves and tucked into his boots. His knees are marked by small bronze ornaments, and six vertical rows of small bronze boar-shaped plaques were almost certainly attached to vertical thongs or directly to his clothes. Fourteen in each of the four central rows and twelve in each of the two single outer ones have been thoughtfully arranged. A little bronze ram in relief, carrying a hook for attaching a loop, would have fastened the man's belt. Belts were essential for all riders, and probably for most chariot drivers, to hold scabbards for weapons and tools, including whips, which they might need at a moment's notice.[37] Hooks for fastening belts intrigued the southern neighbours, and it is from the horse managers that belt-hooks, with a range of different imagery and detail, were taken up by elites on the Central Plains for decorative purposes. Other belt ornaments found in the tombs at Yuhuangmiao are decorated with interlaced scrolls at the front and with a wide loop behind, through which a leather or hemp belt could be threaded. As with the ornaments in a rectangle on the textile, many were threaded on a single belt, producing a sparkling and jangling effect not adopted by people on the Central Plains. The exact same belts were used in South Siberia and eastern Kazakhstan, with the most elegant examples in gold buried in Arzhan II.[38]

Across the steppe, gold was the most valued way to show off status and wealth. The Rong leader had a gold tiger hung below his neck

A ram belt fastening, length *c.*5 cm.

with two loops on its back, to thread on a thong. This tiger is a visible marker of a new taste brought to China, which we shall meet again in the tomb of Lord Bai. Others at Yuhuangmiao also had an animal in profile around their neck, often a horse or a tiger, but in bronze. All seem to have been a highly valued and intimate way of reinforcing themselves to themselves. At the man's ears were fine spirals wound as rings from a long thread of gold, accompanied by a turquoise bead. Such spirals in gold or, as in the lesser tombs at Yuhuangmiao, in bronze, were, at all periods, markers of northerners. Long ornaments threaded with 175 turquoise beads were also part of the decoration of the man's clothes. Other men in the Yuhuangmiao tombs wore gold arcs or pectorals around their necks. This was not a primitive society, but one with distinct customs in the way clothes were worn, how they were decorated and the privileged use of gold for select individuals that mirrored the lifestyle of the greatest steppe lords of the day. The scale of the three largest tombs at Yuhuangmiao and their distribution of ornaments, belts, animal motifs and spiral earrings show that this was a prosperous, hierarchical society, with close ties with even more wealthy stockbreeders.

Belt ornaments, 3–4 cm in length, in gold from Arzhan II (*left*) and in bronze from Yuhuangmiao (*right*).

A gold tiger to be worn at the neck, *c.*4 cm in length.

★

A powerful group of steppe pastoralists, signalled by their gold ornaments, had found their way on to the southern slopes of the Jundu
Mountains. Both the great lords, far to the north in present-day Mongolia and the Tuva Republic, and the Mountain Rong shared a common
culture, the same inventory of daggers, knives, horse tack and animal
ornaments, traces of which reappear again and again in tombs, dating
from the ninth to the fourth to third century BC, from the eastern
steppe all the way to the Black Sea, with tombs found in Crimea and
present-day Ukraine.[39] The first tombs were discovered at the western
end of the steppe and are generally attributed to the Scythians, well
known from Herodotus' *Histories* of the fifth century BC.[40] These early
discoveries skewed a general emphasis towards the west. However,
exquisite gold belt fittings, again with animals in profile, were found
in Siberia in the eighteenth century and presented to Peter the Great
in the first stages of Russia's conquest of this huge territory. The eastern steppe and the kurgans in the Russian Federation were, it turned
out, at the heart of power, the origins of a movement westwards that
only later embraced the Scythians. The earliest kurgans were built in
the ninth century BC and the only intact, excavated kurgan belongs to
the mid-seventh century BC: Arzhan II, which revealed the sophistication of the steppe, as well as the long-established contacts with China.[41]

Of course, as we stand on the Jundu Mountains looking north, we
cannot see these communities far across the steppe, but their presence is felt as much as the agricultural settlements of the Zhou behind
us. If we recognise that the distant power of the Zhou court could

A bronze horse ornament to be worn at the neck, *c*.5 cm in length.

guide – even determine – the lives of Yu Bo and the Lord of Rui, we must equally acknowledge the lords at Arzhan, who were also riders accompanied by a consort and guards, in the story of the Mountain Rong leader. For the later Scythians, Herodotus listed the companions buried with their leaders as 'the king's concubines, his wine server, cook, groom, steward, messenger, some horses, a choice selection of his other possessions and some gold cups'.[42] This description reflects the author's familiarity with the royal Mediterranean courts rather than the steppe. Nonetheless, Herodotus was correct to recognise that attendants were buried with their lords, alongside horses and gold. At Arzhan, the lord's clothes glittered with 2,300 cast-gold panthers, many tiny gold boars were attached to his quiver and bow and he and his spouse had elegant horses on their hats (plate 7). The might and wealth of the leader of the Mountain Rong echoed those of the Arzhan lords.

For the steppe riders, animals were the defining elements of their culture and beliefs. It has often been called an 'animal style'.[43] Yet these creatures cast in gold or bronze, carved in wood, bone or ivory, or embroidered on textiles are not simply an artistic style – they are fundamental to the universe or cosmology of those who made and wore them. The boars on the Mountain Rong leader's clothes and boots belong to the same world as the stags on the deer stones of the steppe. We can now see that the people of the Jundu Mountains participated in a specific language of objects, widespread in many forms across the whole of Inner Asia. Their proud owners did not write, so we do not know how they described themselves or what the animals meant to them. They could be single species or compositions of several creatures, generally as a silhouette in profile. Most creatures were from the natural world but a few were imaginary. One ever-recurrent theme was of a predator, a tiger, an eagle or even a griffin attacking and capturing prey, a deer or a horse or a ram.

While it is tempting to guess at their meanings, it is more likely that the motifs carried multiple associations, varying across time and place. There is no single place of origin, and differences abound as much as similarities.[44] It is also misleading to see them as symbolic. They carried a certain reality and we should probably view them as auspicious or apotropaic. At a distance, we see a widely shared way of life and afterlife. Then, if we look closely, we discern idiosyncrasies and local preferences. However, the ram on the belt and the boars on the leader's clothes are easily recognisable as belonging to this steppe language. They do not reflect the beliefs and motifs that we find on the vessels in the agricultural lands. Remarkably, this cultural division held fast over many centuries. The rams, stags, tigers and eagles of the steppe are a vibrant tradition divided from, but adjacent to, the *taotie* faces, dragons and long-plumed birds of the Central Plains. Both distinctive visual languages were equally influential in uniting people across vast territories and reinforcing their sense of belonging.

We do not have a continuous picture, neither geographically nor chronologically, for this kaleidoscope of animal imagery. The sudden appearance of the leader and his comrades at Yuhuangmiao is part of this disconnection. Discovery of elaborate tombs of the steppe pastoralists has been uneven, and has often occurred by chance. And many of the kurgans have been robbed. Chiefly, the rather sporadic appearance of material evidence is because the steppe offered very little wealth.[45] The people across the often arid grasslands had little that they were willing to bury and valuable materials, such as bronze, were often recycled. Bronze vessels of the Central Plains and gold and iron from the Sayan and Altai Mountains stood alongside trees for fuel for metalworking and winter shelter. The pastoralist stockbreeders of the Loess Plateau and the Yan Mountains could thereby achieve a fuller material life, alongside the pastoralists in South Siberia, in the Tuva, wealthy enough to bury their possessions. But in between, across the Gobi Desert and the Mongolian Plateau, an enormous sweep of highland sometimes 2,000 metres in height, we have little information. Numerous engravings of animals survive on petroglyphs, but the bleak winds blowing throughout the winter repeatedly dispersed settlements or remains of settlements. While it is, therefore, not very likely that future archaeologists will find many more rich tombs there, the forgotten stockbreeders of the Plateau still belong to the interconnected steppe culture. They were more powerful, sophisticated and resourceful than the peoples in central China could ever imagine. And they were in constant communication with each other through competition, combat, exchange and cooperation.

We, like the people on the agricultural plains, only become aware of the stockbreeding pastoralists when they arrive on the northern borders of China.[46] Polities who managed successful agriculture and had the capacity to create valuable vessels and weapons were always going to be in the sights of those who lived in leaner territories. The Mountain Rong were probably not the first people with horses to be attracted to these hills. We are fortunate that the cemetery has illumined a new stage in relations between the planted fields and the steppe. Many others had already moved, including those who brought chariots to Anyang. Geography and climate also encouraged sporadic migration.[47] Rare moments of opportunity, such as more rainfall that could ease the crossing the Gobi, may explain some of the incursions. The foothills of the Yan Mountains were particularly appealing as, although there were deserts close by, these were less extensive than the Gobi. And the agricultural and metal resources of the plains around Beijing were much closer to the grasslands in today's Inner Mongolia than the fertile valleys of the Wei and the Fen Rivers. Movement over the Yan Mountains would continue. Indeed, we should see such movement south as a steady feature in the lives of both the pastoralists and the settled farmers.[48]

The Mountain Rong brought not only their possessions, but also their customs and beliefs. We recognise that the leader and his comrades had a clear conception of an afterlife that embraced their lives among animals, wild and domesticated. The interactions of the people at Yuhuangmiao with those on the Central Plains were very different from the alliances set up by the early Zhou. This leader of the Mountain Rong belonged to a new generation, a new kind of cultural encounter and a new form of mutual exploitation. As people began to routinely ride, heightened competition brought new challenges within the eastern steppe. A brief visit to the Arzhan kurgans is a salutary reminder of where power really lay. Less wealthy pastoralists on the Mongolian Plateau were clearly conscious of this swelling force to the north. As new centres of power were growing in the

Altai-Sayan region, other herders and stockbreeders, among them the Mountain Rong, may have wanted to move out of the way and find greener pastures; so they ended up on the borders of the Loess Plateau and the Yan Mountains.[49] Tombs at Yuhuangmiao represent the growing wealth and authority of the steppe lords. It is too easy to think of the Chinese rulers and polities as advancing towards a united Qin Empire. At this moment, in the late eighth and seventh centuries BC, the gold-adorned lords of the steppe may have been even more powerful.

Concurrently, polities, led by the Zhou, had spread across the agricultural lands, with tensions developing among them. This period is known as the Eastern Zhou (*c.*750–221 BC), and the first phases of what is termed the Spring and Autumn period (*c.*750–*c.* 475 BC). The rulers of the settled areas no longer saw the northerners as peaceful neighbours. It is from this time that we can explicitly chart the hostility that grew out of their meeting. Repeated asides in speeches recorded in the *Zuo Tradition* vilified the Rong:

> The Rong are lax and disorganized; they are greedy and know nothing of kith and kin. In victory, they will not defer to one another; and in defeat, they will not save one another.[50]

When we look at the histories of the Scythians as told by Herodotus, or the later accounts of the Xiongnu by Sima Qian, we recognise similar fear, contempt and xenophobia, and a deliberate lack of understanding.[51] In the modern world we are also familiar with disparaging accounts of the 'other'. When beliefs and customs are so different, as those were between the steppe riders and drivers from the north and the settled Zhou lineages of the Central Plains, there was always going to be friction. Inevitably, negative stereotypes in the ancient texts became a trope reiterated over many centuries. As a result, the officials and leaders of the states of the eighth and seventh centuries BC, and later historians, did not recognise what a meeting of the steppe and the settled states might foretell. To a degree, we can read the hostile words as a deliberate veil drawn over events in which some newcomers had been successful.

The lords of the polities inevitably had to deal with the people from the steppe as well as engage with more familiar Rong. Despite occasional clashes, some more positive, or rather productive, relationships continued, as a need for horses always dominated contact between agriculturalists and pastoralists. The same paradox persisted, as the horses needed in battle and as a display of power were provided by the very enemies themselves. As a result, the herders continued to be drawn towards the agricultural plains and, in due course, many were absorbed into settled societies and adopted Zhou practices, at least as a formality, amassing beautiful pieces for ceremonial banquets and accepting the strong social hierarchy, reinforced by a shared writing system. At the same time, close relationships between stockbreeders flourished on the steppe. Two worlds and two universes were growing alongside one another.

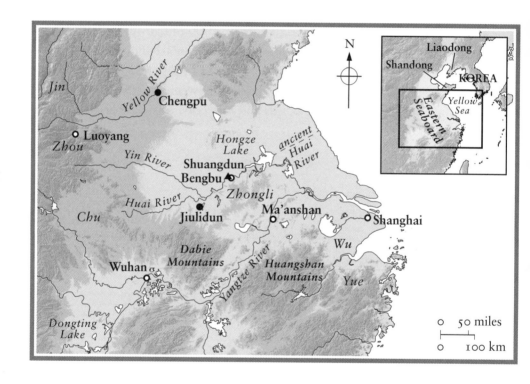

Bengbu on the Huai River

8

Circling South

Even as Zhou military and political domination dwindled from the eighth century BC, their cultural framework remained persuasive and spread in different degrees within a mosaic of prosperous southern states, adding to the colourful complexity of what is today recognised as China.[1] One of China's most remarkable achievements was to draw together disparate local southern traditions over 1,000 years so that, over time, the basins along the Yangtze complemented the settlements on the middle and lower Yellow River. In the centuries after the Zhou moved to Luoyang, the south was drawn into their conflicts, often in unexpected ways. The Qin took over much of the region as they unified the states in the third century BC, with their forces of soldiers from many regions and convict labourers.[2] And a further expansion followed the fall of the Han dynasty in the third century AD. Over several turbulent centuries, with changing rulers in the north, highly educated officials and scholars fled south. When, in the twelfth century AD, the Song were forced to transfer their capital to Hangzhou, beyond the Yangtze, the south had already become favoured by poets and artists. Li Bai, who composed verses on the planked road to Sichuan, spent his last years at Ma'anshan in Anhui province and his tomb is there. Further south are high mountains, among them Huangshan (the Yellow Mountain), inspiring many of the ink paintings by the four masters of which Hongren (1610–63) is the most famous.[3] When the Ming dynasty fell in 1644 Hongren became a Buddhist, another place of refuge, to evade a political forum now ruled by the Qing, the dynasty of Manchu rulers from the north. However, when the tomb of Lord Bai, the leader of the state of Zhongli, was dug near the town of Bengbu in Anhui around 600

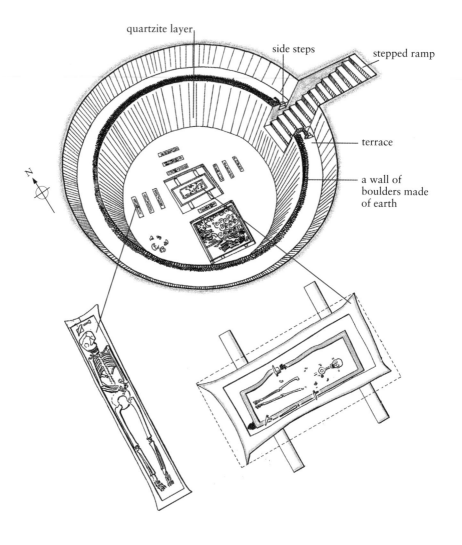

quartzite layer

side steps

stepped ramp

N

terrace

a wall of boulders made of earth

The tomb of Lord Bai of Zhongli at Shuangdun, Bengbu, Anhui province.

BC, his small state was only just beginning to participate in the world of competing polities that now dominated central China.

Nothing had prepared archaeologists for their discovery of Lord Bai's tomb, next to that of his spouse, at the site named today in Chinese as Shuangdun, that is, the Pair of Mounds. How they came to be at Bengbu remains unsettling. Bengbu lies along the massive Huai, the principal river between the Yellow River to the north and the Yangtze to the south, in lowlands, far from the mountains dominated by the Huangshan. It is also a long way from Luoyang and the northern Jundu Mountains. The name, Bengbu, which translates as Oyster Wharf, refers to its role as a centre for fishery and freshwater pearls. Today the city is known for food and textile industries and has all the features of a modern Chinese metropolis: factories, skyscrapers, repetitious apartment blocks and roads sometimes six lanes wide. A high-speed railway station has been built south of Bengbu and a new museum is our first source of information on this tomb.

The museum has a square entrance to pair with a second museum, nearby, for urban planning, which has a circular hall. Together they symbolise the square earth with a circular heaven above, echoing the trope developed in the fourth to third centuries BC and explored in the Han period to explain the shape of the *cong*, first known several millennia earlier at Liangzhu. Outside, high walls are marked with repeated lines in blocks. They replicate the horizontal sections of the *cong* and the layers of sediment and rock over deep geological time. Visitors walk through these concrete, rocky façades to a glass 'porch' leading to an enormous hall towering several storeys above, glazed on all sides and shielding the galleries. Escalators take visitors up to the main gallery and they can come down on long bridges, painted red on the underside, creating a three-dimensional work of art in themselves.

The museum has very early, beautiful ceramics for food and drink and, as the region later became a significant bridge between the Shang dynasty bronze workshops on the Central Plains and the copper mines along both banks of the lower Yangtze, it also holds some arresting bronze vessels. Most striking, however, is the model of Lord Bai's tomb. It is immediately obvious that the tomb is unique: it is circular.

And in the gallery, the model cuts down below the floor. The original tomb was impressive, 20 metres in diameter at the surface, more than 7 metres deep, with the chamber at the foot over 14 metres in diameter.[4] This dramatic form is an epic claim to wealth and power. Of the tombs we have encountered so far, only that of the Lord of Rui might be grudgingly considered to be of similar grandeur. But the Lord of Rui constructed a tomb within the mainstream Zhou tradition. This circular tomb lies far outside the culture of the Central Plains.[5] Its size, shape and location at Bengbu are all a surprise, and completely unlike the tombs of the major states of Rui and Jin, or of the neighbouring Chu state.

At the base of the tomb were the inner and outer coffins of the lord, orientated east–west. He did not enter the afterlife alone, another highly unusual decision within the Zhou sphere of influence. He was surrounded on three sides by three sets of carefully sited coffins for his attendants, and on the southern side there was just one. His skeleton is not well preserved, but some teeth tell us that he was forty years old when he died. The circular tomb and arrangement of coffins for his attendants indicate that this is a tomb of a powerful individual from a singular cultural background. Next to the southern coffin, an almost square wooden chest contained grave goods, including bronze vessels, ceramic jars, sets of bells and a set of chime stones, weapons and chariot fittings. This is also not at all typical of Zhou tombs, where such a wealth of possessions would have been installed on a ledge around the coffin; if they were personal items – weapons or ornaments – they were laid directly on the body. Lord Bai's chest does not appear to have had a lid. One part was for animal remains, another unusual feature. The steep, inwardly sloping sides of the pit had been covered with a layer of white quartzite, also unique. Above these sides, two metres below the surface, a terrace cut out of the side, about 1.8 metres wide, encircled the pit, again unknown elsewhere.

The terrace was accessed by a ramp and lined with imitations of stone boulders made of clay. On the fill above the terrace, a flat surface was levelled off and small half-mounds were set around what is now left of the wall of the pit. Oddly, small stones, also imitated in

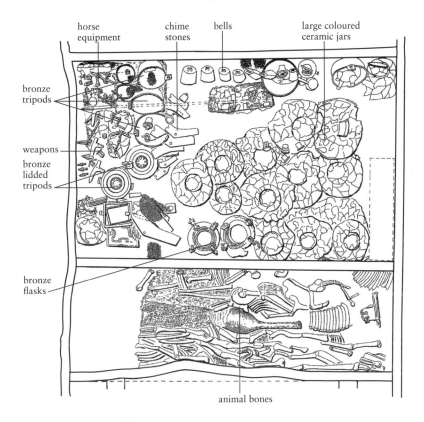

horse equipment   chime stones   bells   large coloured ceramic jars

bronze tripods

weapons
bronze lidded tripods

bronze flasks

animal bones

The contents of the wooden chest. Length 3.8 m, width 3.6 m.

clay, were scattered across the centre. To complete the tomb, a layer of earth filled the pit and a massive disc of quartzite was laid over it before the mound was built. The obsession with stone is startling, especially as the tomb builders decided to use earth to make replicas. The ramp has fourteen steps but it does not reach the base, where the coffins were placed. How such a ramp was devised and what its purpose was are pressing questions. The only two other circular tombs known in central China were for members of Lord Bai's immediate family, for his spouse and for his son. His son's was unfortunately found severely looted and his spouse's has not been excavated.[6] What were the origins of the man who commissioned and inhabited this unique afterlife palace?

While we have seen that unusual tombs can turn up in the Loess Plateau, to find one in the south – a region of wetlands and rice cultivation – is a different challenge. While Lord Bai's tomb may have been an innovation, it was clearly thoroughly planned and is likely to have been built by advisers with experience of customs and designs from elsewhere. There are many paths along which he or his advisers could have come to Bengbu. When looking east, Lord Bai had uninterrupted routes across low-lying land into the present-day provinces of Jiangsu and Shandong. Here China reaches out into the East China Sea, with huge cities now strung along the coast. As we saw at Liangzhu, there was an array of communication down the eastern seaboard, from far north to the Yangtze delta and present-day Zhejiang province, embracing regions occupied by people from the steppe.

In the opposite direction, the influence and importance of the south were growing, as the state of Chu, occupying land to the west of Zhongli, beyond present-day Wuhan, took over more territory.[7] Many polities across the Yellow River basin and well into the south had by now asserted themselves, taking advantage of the waning Zhou authority, during the eighth to sixth centuries BC, the Spring and Autumn Period. In these centuries the area embracing today's Dongting Lake was part of the vast Yunmeng Marsh, blocking easy expansion southwards. Thus the great state of Chu, with its early cities to the north of the Yangtze, well away from the Marsh, threatened the northern states, especially the state of Jin on the Fen River. Chu was climbing in power and absorbing competing polities. Yet although Chu's major role in the period is well recorded, the state's arrival on the political stage remains obscure.[8] We know that Chu was, at times, not fully accepted as a member of the central states and in due course, in the writings that have passed down to us, came to be described as a group with alliances with non-Zhou clans, or other local peoples, as in a comment in the *Annals*.[9] Another commentary, of 656 BC, bemoans the Chu as causing trouble for the Zhou:

> Only now when there was someone playing the part of the king had Chu yielded. With no one playing the part of the king, Chu had

taken the lead in rebellion – consider how the barbarous Di followed
Chu's example – and the Central States were greatly vexed. With
the southern barbarians [Chu] and the Di of the north in league, the
threat posed to the Central States was unremitting. Duke Huan [of
Qi] saved the Central States, brought the barbarous Di to heel and
finally pacified Jing [Chu].[10]

In this account, we see that Chu was appraised alongside other non-
Zhou clans. Chu posed a challenge to the internal struggles for
domination on the Central Plains. Meanwhile, the state was keeping
a watchful eye on its eastern flank and cultivating connections with
Zhongli. This tussle is one explanation of how Lord Bai came to build
his tomb. For to the south-east was another challenge, the state of
Wu, later famous for its weaponry decorated with skilled geometric patterns over their blades.[11] Though Zhongli is little known in the
records, the massive tomb tells us that Lord Bai was a wealthy player
in the political competition of his day.

He and his advisers at Zhongli must have had connections with both
Chu and other, smaller polities to the north-east, as his bells and vessels in his tomb are the essential equipment of the ancestral cult.
Inscriptions on the set of nine bells in his wooden chest announce
him as their owner. These are written in fine Chinese characters, a
southern version of the same script that we saw further north and
a visible sign of the penetration of Zhou culture. This is, however,
a different world. How did familiar bronzes emerge more than 500
kilometres south of Luoyang? The political and military upheavals
fostered conflict, of course, but also accommodation and imitation.
For Lord Bai, bell music was accompanied by chime stones. Both
would have hung from wooden frames. These have now disappeared,
leaving only a few traces of lacquer. The bells were sounded by striking them on the outside: the music was shared not just with the living
but also with the ancestors and other spirits in attendance at the banquets.[12] Two other instruments were also in the chest. One, a small
bell, had an internal clanger and thus possibly a military purpose, in

keeping with the conflicts of the day. More enigmatic is a small ring joined by a knob, with four faces, the heads of kneeling captives, to a 9-centimetres-square bronze plate.[13] With four sunken grooves on the underside, the plate must have been intended to hold up something

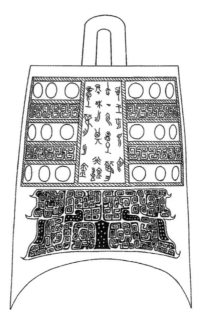

The third bronze bell in a set of nine, height 24.8 cm.
The inscription is cut into the bell, not cast, showing
that the set was acquired by Lord Bai and then inscribed.

This small bronze, 8 by 9 cm, is to hold a drum.
On the underside of the four heads are abbreviated kneeling legs.

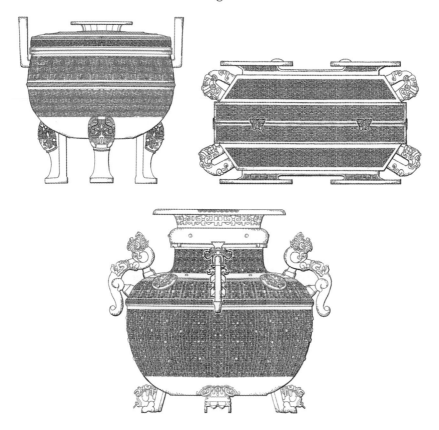

Lord Bai had a set of five tripods, *ding*, two with lids, height 37.1 cm; four *fu*, height 20.8 cm, length 36.8 cm; and a pair of impressive *lei*, height 45.9 cm.

substantial, perhaps a drum. Drums were a major instrument in the ancestral banquets of the south. And a descendant of Lord Bai, buried at Jiulidun, took with him an elaborate base for such a drum.[14]

By comparison with the spectacular scale of the tomb, the bronze vessels in the chest make up a fairly modest set. They were gathered from different sources: five tripods, *ding*, in two new updated forms, four rectangular serving basins known as *fu* replaced the earlier circular lidded basins, *gui*, and two impressive flasks for liquids, *lei*, probably alcohol, are the principal vessels. The flasks have rounded bodies covered in tiny raised circles and curved handles bearing dragon heads tossing their manes. Smaller dragons with unruly horns act as feet. An openwork band of decoration enhances the flask, which otherwise illustrates a clear understanding of the basic forms needed for the ceremonial banquets, perhaps as a result of contact with other leaders both north and south. Lord Bai had reasons to conform with a shared offering ritual. But this does not look like his top priority. He was more preoccupied with signalling his alliances with his powerful neighbours. All the calligraphy on the vessels and the bells emulates that of the leaders of the states around Zhongli. Some pieces may even have come from Chu foundries, or Chu casters now working at Zhongli.[15]

With its centre at Bengbu, Zhongli lay between the two formidable states of Wu and Chu. The politics of Wu and Chu appear in the *Spring and Autumn Annals* and the *Zuo Zhuan*, but references to the cultural environment of Zhongli are very sparse. The state passes swiftly across the stage and disappears. The *Zuo Zhuan* records a meeting held at Zhongli in 576 BC, which was the beginning of relations with the south-eastern state of Wu.[16] At that moment Wu (in present-day Zhejiang) was regarded as a distant southern power. States in the middle and lower Yellow River basin sought to mitigate the growing power of Chu in the south by drawing Wu into the struggle. Until the sixth century BC, Zhongli was probably also seen as an outsider. The *Zuo Zhuan* reports that in 538 BC Qian Yijiu, an official in the state of Chu, fortified Zhongli to guard against the Wu state.[17] But the text also reveals that this was all in vain as, twenty years later, in 518 BC, Zhongli was conquered by King Liao of Wu.[18] Perhaps Zhongli only survived for just over a century because it was a pawn in a political game. The brevity of the state is certainly an example of the fierce rivalries of the day. Its rapid decline may also have been a sign of the short period over which Zhongli took on the ritual apparatus of a state.

The *Zuo Zhuan* supplements the earlier *Annals* with vivid accounts of battles, debates about statehood and tactical agreements between states that had grown in number and strength from the ninth century BC onwards. The role of ritual in the management of conflict was as significant as warfare itself and is still a feature of China's geopolitics, as indeed of the politics and geopolitics of all nations. The inscribed vessels and bells are material evidence that Lord Bai too recognised the political value of joining, at least superficially, the ancestral cult. Its binding impact on China as a whole, especially in the conflicts and treaties of Lord Bai's time, was to be later expressed in words attributed to Confucius: 'A man who respects his parents and elders would hardly be inclined to defy his superiors. A man who is not inclined to defy his superiors will never foment a rebellion . . . To respect parents and elders is the root of humanity.'[19] Seniority was dominant in all social relations. The interplay between the ancestral cult and the organisation of inter-state relations is set out in a speech attributed to the Lord of the Zheng state in an entry of the *Zuo Zhuan* for 713 BC, when taking over a small southern state, not far from Zhongli:

> Ritual is that which regulates the domain and its patrimonies, stabilises the altars of the domain, gives order to the people, and benefits inheritors.[20]

The Zheng lord's conquest is framed as the proper outcome of the ritual regulation of states. Even though the direct jurisdiction and military prowess of the Zhou kings had diminished by the eighth century BC, they still commanded profound ritual respect and determined the hierarchy of states.[21] To gain traction among the lineages of the Central Plains the Chu, like the Zhongli, had nominally accepted the foundations of Zhou ritual culture. This was formally demonstrated after the major battle at Chengpu in 632 BC. The victor, the state of Jin, made a public display of Chu prisoners, the losers.[22] This triumph was underlined by reference to the ritual of an earlier Zhou king, Ping, who had rewarded an ancestor of the Jin lord for assisting the restoration of the Zhou in the eighth century BC with the move to Luoyang. Now the current Zhou king, Xiang (651–619 BC), demonstrated that the achievements of the current Jin lord were comparable. This emphasis on the accomplishments of and alliances between their predecessors was then reiterated by the same presentation of gifts in a manner typical of the Western Zhou period. As before, in the time of Yu Bo, despite the rituals of seniority, gifts also had a military purpose:

On the *dingwei* [day 10], Jin presented the Chu prisoners and booty to the Zhou king: one hundred chariot units with teams of four horses covered with armour and one thousand infantrymen. The Lord of Zheng acted as aide to the king and used the ritual of King Ping. On the *jiyou* [day 12], the king offered ceremonial toasts and presented sweet wine, commanding the Lord of Jin to offer toasts. The king commanded the Yin lineage head, Wangzi Hu, and the court scribe Shuxing to draw up a document on bamboo strips commanding the Lord of Jin to act as overlord of the lords. The king bestowed on him a grand ceremonial chariot and a war chariot with appropriate regalia, a red bow and one hundred red arrows, ebony bows, and one thousand ebony arrows, a pot of black millet wine perfumed with herbs, and three hundred 'tiger runner' guards, and said 'the king tells his paternal uncle, "respectfully obey the king's command and thereby pacify the domains in all directions. Discipline and banish all who would do ill to the king." '[23]

One might imagine that a major victory was enough. We see here instead that ritual was an essential tool to endorse authority; as the Jin ruler's position was confirmed, the Zhou king's was reaffirmed. The battle at Chengpu would have been reported across much of the territory that the Zhou nominally claimed, and the presentation of prisoners would have attracted widespread attention. Despite the growing power of Chu, Zhongli and Zheng, the notion of a single supreme leader prevailed.[24] Zhou ritual structure also informed the contemporary view of the cosmos. Natural phenomena – such as eclipses and earthquakes – now required a ritual and political response:

In the summer, in the sixth month, on the *jiaxu* day, the first day of the month, there was an eclipse of the sun. The invocators and scribes asked what sacrificial goods should be used. Shusun Chuo said, 'When there is an eclipse of the sun, the Son of Heaven does not dine with full ceremony, and he has drums struck at the altar of the earth. The lords offer sacrificial goods at their altars of the earth, and they have drums struck in court. That is in accordance with ritual propriety.'[25]

The inclusion of the forces of the skies in this ritual system signalled the ruler's standing as the Son of Heaven alongside the heavenly bodies and natural forces, all accumulating to form a complex correlative system.[26]

States living beneath this ritual shadow nonetheless continually challenged the Zhou. The rulers of Chu defied the due respect required for the Zhou, and even courted conflict as they expanded northwards into territory in the Yellow River basin. The same paradox is embodied in the objects of the tombs, as ritual vessels were combined with local practices in structure, burial position and weaponry.[27] Two strands of beliefs were in effect woven together – allowing the tomb owners to adopt a dual identity. The Zhou ritual and written system survived, even flourished, alongside local customs and no doubt local languages. As a result, cultural diversity, only revealed by extensive archaeological work, was one of the defining features of this period of political upheaval. The wider community likely took it for granted that some local customs would accompany the political and ritual rhetoric of the Zhou. An over-reliance on records written in characters has blotted out local dialects, songs and rituals, which we no longer know anything about. Where words do not give us the full story, his tomb opens up Lord Bai's background and the initiation of Zhongli into the inter-state rivalries in the seventh and sixth centuries BC.

Swords and single-edged knives are examples of local practices that were now spreading widely. They were the weapons of the northern stockbreeders and the steppe lords at Arzhan.[28] The grip and blade of Lord Bai's sword, placed on the edge of his inner coffin, were cast together in bronze. The cross-section shows that this is a complex weapon, designed by craftsmen with experience. Down the centre, on both sides, is a thickened rib between narrow cutting edges.[29] Like the lords of the steppe, Lord Bai also had two curved knives with rings on the grips, practical tools which had become common in central China from the eighth century BC, also found in the Rui state and

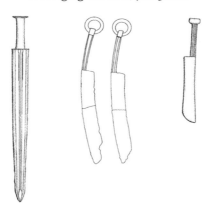

Lord Bai's sword, 47 cm in length, and two knives, 28.8 cm in length, in steppe style. The small knife, 13.5 cm in length, is one of eight allocated to his attendants.

at Yuhuangmiao. A persistent presence of one or more knives with rings or small rectangles on the grip was a major feature across the Eurasian steppe. The penchant for these indicates that steppe practices had spread through the whole of central and southern China. A much smaller local knife, with a sharper angle between the blade and the grip, was developed and one was placed with eight of the ten accompanying attendants. Four of these tombs have an unusual small oval section of a vessel with impressed patterns, presumably a sharpener. This piece, cut from high-fired ceramic, also occurs in a tomb in Shandong province, showing a route from Anhui that leads through Shandong to Liaodong in the north-east.[30] As the knives are small they may have been symbolic, and some have been found in tombs of women, the spouses of local rulers.[31] Lord Bai's companions may have included some women.[32]

The majority of Lord Bai's arrowheads lay in the chest with his ritual vessels, but some were in his coffin. Those closest to him are socketed, a steppe type. Not only the swords, knives and arrowheads, but probably also the northern warriors themselves had been absorbed into the military bands at Bengbu. A thick jade ring, extending in a scoop on one side, was also in the lord's coffin. This is a thumb ring for an archer. Jade suggests that it was to combat spirits in the afterlife. As with other lords of his neighbouring polities, Lord Bai had indications of a chariot force in his chest: numerous axle caps, sets of horse bits and cheekpieces. If the chariots and horses were buried, they were elsewhere. The region of dense rivers and lakes was of course not really suitable for raising horses, so the fittings may have just suggested horses and chariots as military status symbols.

Several thin bronze fragments decorated with gold foil are the remains of his armour. None of the pieces appear strong enough to fend off bronze weapons. They are more a display of might or defence against spirits rather than protection against living enemies. A plaque with contorted dragons or snakes, with raptor heads, is an example of Chu taste. This watery duel replaced the predators attacking deer or rams typical of steppe belt plaques, from which they were distantly derived. Decoration of this sort must have been recognised as auspicious. Armour originally taken over from the steppe is another clear sign of northern customs adopted not just by Zhongli, but by other allies of the Chu.[33] If Lord Bai had even worn a small assembly of golden armour – the rarest of materials, as we know – the sight would have been startling.

A fragment of bronze armour overlaid with gold foil, length 15.5 cm.

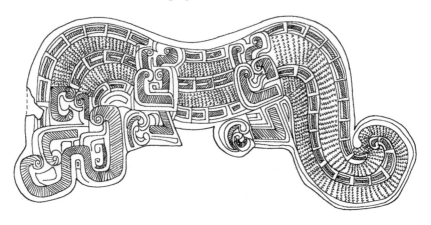

A fragment of bronze armour overlaid with
gold foil in the shape of a tiger, length 15 cm.

His armour also contained fragments shaped like tigers, with glowing gold surfaces. This is a powerful interpretation of the gold tiger at
Yuhuangmiao. Other gold tigers were also produced locally and have
been found among other tombs within the Chu orbit.[34] Tigers, known
for their ferocity in seizing and devouring their prey, must also have
been recognised as auspicious and included on the bronze armour to
ensure good outcomes with such imagery. The tiger, in Chinese the
hu, looks to be an introduction of a foreign fashion. It did not last. As
gold was less attractive to the lords in the Central Plains than jade,
the tiger subsequently gained a whole new life in jade, often recut
from discs, which today distracts attention away from tiger jades'
northern roots. So widespread was their popularity that the tiger was
included in the list of jades in China's ritual texts. The golden tiger of
the steppe, as it was transformed into jade, is a clear example of the
symbiosis that was under way as northerners, with their steppe connections, moved from the Loess Plateau into the settled states.[35] Such
fundamental elements of the steppe were taken over by the cultures
of the agricultural river basins. The tiger is a key as we decipher the
background behind Lord Bai's circular tomb.

A small double box or cup with its flat lid is similar to the cup with
a single ring handle in the leader's tomb at Yuhuangmiao. The animal

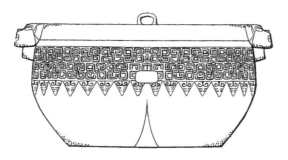

A small bronze box, height 8.3 cm and length 15.8 cm,
from a foundry in Shandong province.

bones in Lord Bai's chest are also a clear reference to his northern contacts. Burial of animal heads at the Yuhuangmiao tomb was an essential
part of a pastoral afterlife. The late Shang and early Zhou elites had
completely different attitudes to animals. They were pragmatic. Animals were for immediate use, for ritual offerings and for food, not for
stockbreeding, and not (apart from dogs) companions for the afterlife. Sometimes animal legs were allocated to tombs of individuals,
but these were to provide nourishment in the afterlife. At Zhongli, the
burial of not only pig bones, but also those typical of northern herds –
namely cattle and sheep – is almost certainly a custom brought from
elsewhere. The tomb was also well equipped with painted jars not
found anywhere else in China at this time (plate 24). They too were
part of a long north-eastern tradition of boldly painted ceramics.[36]
Presumably such jars held food provisions for the afterlife.

Lord Bai thus had a double allegiance: his Zhou ritual vessels on the
one hand and his northern, steppe weaponry and armour on the other.
He had adopted the ceremonial banquets of the ancestral cult as part
of a strategy to gain military support from Chu in life. The rituals
would also extend this support to his descendants as he entered the
afterlife. At the same time, his arsenal was essential in that afterlife to
deflect evil spirits. Northerners could and did move far south-east of
the main central states, so in warfare and in death Lord Bai kept hold of
these customs and materials. His possessions were not just functional;

lined up in his chest they are a convenient inventory of his dual identity. They are also a route for us to circumvent the simple comments on the 'barbarians' railed against in the commentary on Chu.

Lord Bai's tomb is the prime example of his conscious exploitation of the rituals of his neighbours. Its size and depth are competitive statements of his rank among them. Yet its strange circular shape reflects a different personal heritage. It is a vital statement of who he was and where he came from. The circular pit has nothing in common with Zhou, Jin or Chu burials, with their rectangular graves, vertical or stepped sides, secondary ledges, wooden chambers and one or two coffins inside. As far as we know, Zhou tombs did not, at this date, accommodate attendants or offer monuments above ground. They had no mounds.[37] The name Shuangdun, tells us, however, that two tombs, one for Lord Bai and the other for his consort, were capped by piled-up earth. The remains of the mound over the Lord Bai's tomb were 9 metres in height and about 60 metres in diameter, with a diameter of 20 metres for the pit below ground. Such a size is deliberately impressive, especially for a lord of a minor, almost unknown, polity and a minor ally of the Chu. At Stonehenge, the outer circle is 110 metres in diameter, and the famous inner stone Sarsen circle 33 metres. The Shuangdun mound was also calculated, made up of five colours of earth: yellow, grey, black, red and white. While the red, yellow and grey earths were sourced locally, the black and white earths came from elsewhere, the result of planning and an organised labour force. The tomb builders did not just use the earth that came from digging the pit.[38]

The tomb was built in stages, and its impressive diameter means it was planned from the very start. We can imagine that the first step must have been to lay out the circular outline and then to dig eight metres or so below ground level. From the surface, the sides slope sharply inwards. The slope may have been required to prevent the shaft from caving in.[39] Further north, with the deep layers of loess, vertical sides were much more stable. In southern central China, deposits of silt were heavily waterlogged and tomb walls were more likely to collapse. Layers of quartzite under the mound must have come from the mountains to the south-east, perhaps intended to seal and stabilise the sides.[40] This in itself was an elaborate operation. Quartzite rocks had to be mined, transported and ground. Somebody had decided that bright white layers were essential.

All eleven coffins were made in a particular form, with drawn-out corners, creating slightly bowed sides. This may have been intended to recall a tomb type, known in the north, from the Loess Plateau or even further north in Mongolia.[41] But how were the coffins and Lord Bai's chest brought down into such a deep chamber? It is likely that, as the tomb builders dug, they retained ramps used to remove the earth. Once they had placed the chest and coffins of Lord Bai and his attendants (almost certainly killed to join him), the ramps were discarded. What remains are the steps cut into the tomb wall from the top, crossing the terrace, but going no further than the edge of the tomb shaft. The steps look like a feature left behind in the construction process. We need, however, to examine the terrace and the strange wall around its inner side to see why the stepped ramp was needed.[42] The terrace is quite spacious, a step back to widen the shaft. It is bounded by a wall, giving us the most important clue as to the origin of the tomb plan and its principal occupant. The wall is composed of conical boulders of clay, bound together by cords to ensure

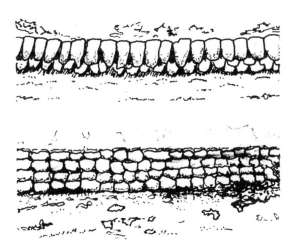

Views of the wall of earthen boulders, each between 15 cm and 20 cm in length, from inside the terrace (*top*) and from inside the burial pit (*bottom*)

they did not fall apart, with the pointed ends facing the terrace and a flat face looking into the tomb. The excavators call them models or replicas. But such terms do not explain what they mean. These teeth-like lumps must be imitations of stone boulders. Seen from within the tomb, the boulders replicate a stone wall. This marks out an inner boundary of the tomb and would have prevented people on the terrace from falling into the shaft. Additional steps either side of the ramp allowed people walking down towards the shaft to step on to the terrace. The small return of the wall also prevented them from slipping into the void below. Even if the shaft had already been filled, this terrace gave those attending the burial a position nearby. We are witnessing the careful preparation for the participation in rituals. People could walk down the steps on to the terrace and then find a space for themselves along it. Once this stage of the rites was over, the living could leave, and the rest of the shaft and the terrace were filled.

Over the course of the fill, two additional layers marked the next stages in the rituals. The first of these looks like a landscape. Once the terrace had been covered and a flat surface created, small mounds, or rather half-mounds, were arranged around the inner edge of the shaft. All were made of five careful layers of coloured earth, comparable with the main mound. On this level, small stones again were replicated out of earth. They are extraordinarily realistic. Like the mounds, they appear to be a scattering of stones left over from building a stone tomb in a stone environment. But this part of Anhui did not have much access to stone, so copies in earth were used instead. The mounds and the scattering of earthen stones all conjure up a different but remembered world. The second layer was a lid, so to speak, of quartzite, to match the sides of the shaft and to seal the tomb below the mound. The lid was made from an enormous quantity of ground-up rock. In the centre was another circle, in yellow earth, with a small rectangle on the eastern side, as if mirroring the diameter of the tomb base and its ramp. Now somewhat displaced, there is a sequence of radiating and alternating triangles in dark and yellow earth, somewhat like a dartboard. This is an unprecedented and puzzling emblem, one that must have conveyed something about the purpose of the tomb which the makers understood and we do not. Was this circle something the spirits could recognise and interpret? Or was the inner section over the tomb a recreation of the radiant patterns used among steppe people, including at Arzhan I in the Tuva, on the Liaodong Peninsula and in parts of present-day Korea?[43]

A circular tomb is more than an oddity in ancient China. Even disparate clans and polities, such as at Baoji, who may not have originally favoured formal rectangular tombs, usually adopted them. Lord Bai's tomb is the outcome of an administrative, ritual and religious programme that is now hidden from us, a revelation of an exceptional moment in history. Someone or several people had an absolute notion of the requirements of the tomb owner. Indeed, as in previous times, overseers with concern for ritual propriety must have had a particular vision and method in mind. They were able to give clear commands. Many groups of retainers would have had to work at the site. This was a significant engineering enterprise. As so few early monuments have survived above ground, and those that have are of rammed earth that is easily returned to the surrounding ground, the construction skills of ancient China have been widely ignored. The installation of the dead followed a funeral with mourners and their rituals that were not recorded in the transmitted texts. The tomb shows us that it is extremely unlikely that Lord Bai's ancestors originally belonged to the societies of the Yellow River basin or those of their competitors in the Yangtze basin. Wherever Lord Bai and his companions came from, their culture was powerfully understood within their community. The tomb was not a sudden improvisation, it was a remarkable recreation of a stone landscape of major burials.

Lord Bai had distant connections with the same shared steppe culture of Arzhan, the Jundu Mountains, Mongolia and South Siberia. At the centre of Arzhan I was a neat arrangement of a log coffin surrounded by attendants in their own log coffins.[44] Other attendants were buried separately in the tomb within its radiating pattern. This offers a prototype, not only for the Zhongli tomb but also for those on the Liaodong Peninsula, in Shandong province and even in tombs of the Rong near Luoyang. Yet there has been a tendency to associate joint burials with attendants with Shang practices.[45] However, the Zhou did not follow these. Attendant burial is a completely new development, introduced by newcomers and then spreading further into southern China in the sixth and fifth centuries BC.[46]

Arzhan I and II and other major kurgans in the Sayan Mountains are circular.[47] These extend into the Altai Mountains and present-day Xinjiang province.[48] At Arzhan II, the circular form is reiterated by three fences of stone, one around the centre, which includes the principal burial chamber. Within the outer boundary were additional tombs and a burial of horses.[49] We can now recognise Lord Bai's chest as recreating these separate burials.[50] The boulders of earth forming an inner boundary on the terrace in Lord Bai's tomb reproduce one of the stone fences, such as the one around the centre of Arzhan II. At Zhongli, this fence of boulders was carefully joined to the stepped ramp, with additional small steps and recesses in the wall on both sides. This organisation is an alternative to the access road into the centre of Arzhan II, laid down in clay. When the mourners there crossed the outer boundary along this clay path, they could stand on two curved bands of clay, looking towards the stone fence around

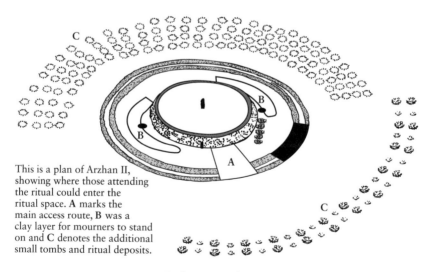

This is a plan of Arzhan II, showing where those attending the ritual could enter the ritual space. A marks the main access route, B was a clay layer for mourners to stand on and C denotes the additional small tombs and ritual deposits.

Arzhan II in Siberia.

the centre of the kurgan, and take part in the ceremony. The Zhongli tomb matched these with the circular terrace. The small mounds on the first layer of Lord Bai's tomb also mirror practices at Arzhan, where deposits or offerings were placed over time outside the outer stone fences. Some other kurgans in the same valley had quartz stones scattered over them, reminding us too of the quartzite in the Zhongli tomb and the clay copies of stones.

Anhui might seem a long leap from Arzhan. But we should instead see the leap as a form of cultural contagion, spreading gradually from the north since at least the eighth century BC. The *Zuo Zhuan* reports that the Rong sought a formal agreement with the Shandong state of Lu in 721 BC. In 666 BC, Lord Xian of Jin took two Rong women as wives, probably bringing more contact with northern customs.[51] A vivid account of negotiations between the Rong and the state of Jin (which we know was exposed to the north) about the value of an accord is set out in the year 569 BC:

> Through Wei Jiang of Jin, Meng Yue [an agent of the Rong] presented furs of tigers and leopards, requesting with these gifts that the Jin should reach a peace agreement with various Rong tribes.

At first, the rulers of Jin were reluctant to consider this route, but they were persuaded after a long discussion, leading to the following conclusion:

> Peace with the Rong has five advantages. First: the Rong and Di live off grasslands, they value goods and disdain land, and so land can be purchased from them. Second: if those at the frontiers are not fearful, the people will feel close to their fields, and the harvesters will achieve success. Third: if the Rong and Di serve Jin, our neighbours on four sides will be shaken and the lords will be awed into submission. Fourth: if we use our virtue to pacify the Rong, the soldiers and officers will not toil, and armour and weapons will not be ruined. Fifth: if we regard Archer Yi [a mythical figure] as our

cautionary mirror and employ the standards of virtue, those from afar will come to us and those close by will be at ease.[52]

Other peoples named by the chroniclers as the Yi, who undoubtedly were made up of several distinct groups, often allied with the Rong. The Eastern Yi are identified by today's historians and archaeologists as occupying parts of the eastern seaboard, with the Huai Yi thought to be situated in the Huai region, where Zhongli was located. Among the extensive compendia of inscriptions gathered over the last hundred or so years just fifty describe early Zhou military activity, and many refer to the Yi and the Huai Yi as well as the Rong. In the later tenth century BC, for example, the Huai Yi had launched a major attack from the south towards Luoyang and advanced to about 150 kilometres from the Zhou capital. The triumphs of a general in pushing back local people called the Hu are recorded in a vessel cast by him to honour his dead mother:

> [I] took one hundred heads, shackled two chiefs, and captured the belligerents' weapons, shields and spears, halberds, bows, quivers, arrows, uniforms and helmets, in all 135 pieces. [I] captured 114 belligerent captives and clothed [them].[53]

Even though, as usual, such texts relate Zhou success, this does not mean that they were always victorious. It also is worth looking hard

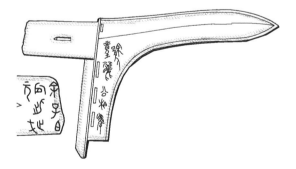

Lord Bai's bronze halberd from the Xu state,
showing two inscriptions, 20 cm in length.

at these few words. The event brought weapons and prisoners into the exchanges between hostile forces. We have an excavated axe with a bronze shaft found in a Yi tomb to the north-east of Zhongli, a version of axes found far away on the steppe lands.[54] And more directly a halberd of the Xu state, north of Zhongli, came into the hands of and was reinscribed by Lord Bai before being buried in his tomb. We know that Xu was still in existence at a meeting recorded by the *Annals* in 541 BC.[55] Combat thus spread objects and ideas: weapons, bronze vessels and burial practices. Weapons seized and prisoners detained gave precious materials and information to powerful states, including Lord Bai's at Zhongli. And perhaps, as a consequence of the constant conflict, Lord Bai had moved southwards, taking on halberds and chariots: forms of warfare now characteristic of the Zhou that they had brought from the Loess Plateau in the eleventh century BC. It seems likely that military successes underpinned Lord Bai's presence at Bengbu and equipped him with a large workforce, most probably of prisoners. The circular shape shows that he and his contemporaries wanted, and now were able, to celebrate their victories within the political and ritual norms of the day, with a monument that recalled the great stone tombs of much further north, from where they must have come.

Some of the Eastern Yi lords buried to the east in Shandong province, with many ordered coffined attendants under similarly impressive mounds, also replicated parts of the Zhou apparatus by adopting bronze vessels, bells and weapons.[56] Other southern clans advertised their new status, giving themselves lineage names in Chinese characters on their vessels. Thus the easterners, including the Yi, had taken advantage of the decline in central power to create small polities that implicitly challenged the leadership of the Zhou.[57] And it looks likely that Lord Bai belonged to this mixed group. We can now see his tomb as part of much more extensive developments in northern and eastern China.[58] While the ancient writers mention skirmishes and denigrate peoples with a pastoral way of life, extensive integration was afoot, which was an essential stage in the history of ancient China. The circular tomb of Lord Bai was part of a broader phenomenon with its roots in the steppe. Repeated skirmishes were catalysts in bringing more northerners south, in search of wealth and opportunities for pasture. In these engagements local leaders accumulated power and wealth, and were able to prepare for the afterlife in ways that combined their northern traditions with Zhou rituals.

We may never know where Lord Bai came from. But we know that he must have been very influential. Hundreds, if not thousands, of men were commanded to dig his tomb and to create its huge mound of five colours. As Lord Bai almost certainly oversaw the building of his spouse's tomb too, this doubled the manpower required. These were major engineering projects, rigorously planned and perfectly executed. Large-scale rice-farming was required to feed these bands. We find, therefore, a man with a hefty following. The tomb was well equipped, but not extravagantly. Although he had ritual vessels similar to those cast and employed by the Chu and other states, Lord Bai's suggest that he did not share their exact beliefs and practices. With the weapons, chariot fittings and armour, Lord Bai was certainly also a military leader among the clans of the east. Chu's decision to draw Zhongli into their alliances further suggests that the polity had powerful armies. At the same time, Lord Bai retained and indeed displayed his own inheritance. The lord claimed a very high status within the ritual framework of Zhou power, but at the same time was willing, even eager, to celebrate his own origins.

Lord Bai's tomb is spectacular, not just in its time but for its place in the tides of history. Circular tombs only survived for two generations of Zhongli rulers before they were replaced by a more conforming rectangular tomb in the third generation. In the following centuries, the Qi state took control of eastern areas thought to have been occupied by the Eastern Yi. Tombs of the Qi lords – among neat arrangements of their attendants in their own coffins – were given prominent mounds above deep, stepped rectangular pits, elaborating the terrace around the shaft of Lord Bai's burial chamber.[59] And the Qi lords were subsequently placed in tombs surrounded by stone. Northern practices had been endorsed by the Qi, now one of the most powerful central states.

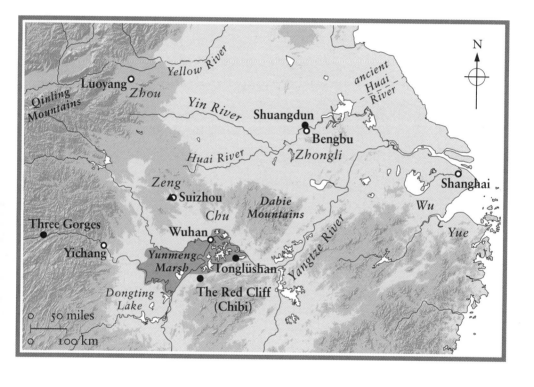

The Zeng and the Chu states

9

The Orchestra of Zeng

Before the Qin and the Han dynasties, the whole area south of present-day Wuhan was covered by a massive marsh, between 150 and 200 kilometres wide, known as the Yunmengze or Yunmeng Marsh. It joined the Dongting Lake and together they formed the floodplain for the Yangtze River. Although much of the Marsh has now been drained, spring brings huge deluges from the river and the Dongting Lake floods over the summer months, often spreading to ten times its winter size.[1] There remains a profound chasm between the Yellow River and the Loess Plateau and southern China of the Yangtze. Here the climate is humid and the air softer, without the dust storms and winter frosts of the north.

The state of Chu first emerged on lands to the north of the Marsh in the tenth century BC. The state grew to become one of the most threatening contenders for the domination of a unified China, before its conquest by the Qin in 223 BC. Tombs of wealthy landowners, filled with fine dishes, from the sixth to third centuries BC have left us a vivid picture of Chu prosperity. More textiles, wooden furniture and lacquered cups have been preserved in their landscape of bamboo groves, winding rivers and rising mists than in the much drier north. We can glimpse much more of the lives of southern lords and landowners, but our understanding is still often reduced to conjecture, as we have no detailed accounts of what the tomb owners thought. The poetry of the south was inspired by the hazy boundaries of rivers with the sky, with strange creatures taking spiritual journeys across the cosmos, as in a poem to summon the soul of a dying man, similar to the one which we met at Taosi. It is worth quoting in full, as it captures the wild environmental variance of China:

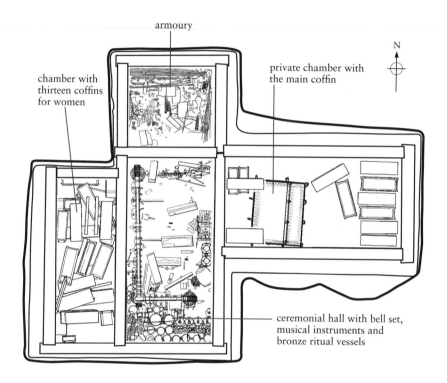

armoury

private chamber with
the main coffin

N

chamber with
thirteen coffins
for women

ceremonial hall with bell set,
musical instruments and
bronze ritual vessels

The Marquis Yi of Zeng's tomb. The eastern chamber is the marquis's
private room, length 9.5 m, with his outer and inner coffins and the coffins
of his eight attendants and dog. At the centre is a ceremonial chamber,
length 9.75 m. In the west is a room with coffins for thirteen women,
length 8.65 m. In the north is the armoury, length 4.25 m.

The Orchestra of Zeng

O soul, go not to the east!
In the east is the great sea, where the swelling waters billow
    endlessly,
And the water-dragons swim side by side, swiftly darting above
    and below.
It is clammy with rain and fog, that glisters white and heavy.
O soul, go not to the east, to the desolate Valley of Morning!

O soul, go not to the south! In the south is burning fire (for a
    hundred leagues), and coiling cobras;
The mountains rise sheer and steep; tigers and leopards slink;
The cow-fish is there, and the spit-sand, and the rearing python:
O soul, go not to the south! There are monsters there that will
    harm you.

Oh soul, go not to the west! In the west are the Moving Sands
    stretching endlessly on and on,
And beasts with heads like swine, slanting eyes and shaggy hair,
Long claws and serrated teeth, and wild, mad laughter.
O soul, go not to the west! In the west are many dangers.

O soul, go not to the north! In the north is the Frozen Mountain,
    and the Torch Dragon, glaring red;
And the Tai River than cannot be crossed, whose depths are
    unfathomable;
And the sky is white and glittering, and all is congealed with cold.
O soul, go not to the north! There is no bourn there to your
    journeying.

O soul, come back to leisure and quietness!
Enjoy yourself in the land of Chu, tranquil and untroubled.
Indulge your fancies, fulfil your wishes, set your mind at rest.
Spend all your days in lasting pleasure and old age, full of years.
O soul, come back to pleasures that cannot be told![2]

Many strange creatures, as those imagined here, were carved in wood and lacquered, using the toxic sap of a tree that flourished in the sub-tropical south.[3] Later the literati flourished here in the Song, Ming and Qing dynasties, painting in tranquil scenes of boys riding on water buffalo, fishermen with arched nets hung over the many lakes, and mountains among the inevitable summer mists, rising in intense heat. Among the mountains just south of the Yangtze is the Red Cliff (in modern-day Chibi), where a famous naval battle took place in AD 208–9, near the end of the Han dynasty, when southern warlords defeated Cao Cao, a northern invader. In the face of continuous incursions from the north, the south became a refuge. The Red Cliff is perhaps even more renowned for one of China's greatest prose poems, composed in AD 1082 by Su Shi, which heralds serenity rather than fear:

> In the autumn of the year *renxu* [1082], on the sixteenth day of the seventh month, I took some guests on an excursion by boat under the Red Cliff. A cool wind blew gently, without starting a ripple. I raised my cup to pledge the guests; and we chanted the Full Moon ode . . . After a while, the moon came up above the hills to the east, and wandered between the Dipper and the Herdboy star; a dewy whiteness spanned the river, merging the light on the water into the sky. We let the tiny reed drift on its course, over ten thousand acres of dissolving surface which streamed to the horizon, as though we were leaning on the void with winds for a chariot, on a journey none knew where, hovering above as though we had left the world of men behind us and risen as immortals on newly sprouted wings.[4]

When a ruler of the small state of Zeng, a dependant of the state of Chu, was buried around 433 BC, these famous words still lay over a millennium in the future. But the Zeng had a long history, initially supporting the Zhou conquest in the eleventh century BC.[5] By the fifth century BC their capital was at Suizhou, today a city similar in size to Bengbu. The ruler of Zeng claimed the title of *hou*. This is tradition-ally translated as marquis, which we will use for expedience, despite its being an unsuitable Western translation. His name was Yi – one of the ten Heavenly Stems which defined the ten-day week and combined, in due course, with the twelve earthly branches to make a cycle of sixty, used to designate the years. Why this name was chosen we do not know. His tomb was discovered by chance on the crest of a small hill outside Suizhou. The pit had been dug down to about 13.5 metres from the original surface. It is an impressive 21 metres from east to west, and similar in proportions to the tomb of Lord Bai. But the form is completely different, made up of four rectangular boxes, or rather rooms, connected as a single dwelling for the afterlife. These rooms were built of 171 squared catalpa beams, which are still in place in this extraordinary monument.

The marquis, thought to have been forty-five when he died, lay in the eastern chamber; his inner coffin was placed within a private outer coffin. The eastern chamber held musical instruments for private performances and lacquered cups and basins for private feasting.[6] Alongside him were eight small coffins for women – his concubines and servants – and one for a dog. A spacious reception room was the central chamber, with a heavy L-shaped wooden stand from which hung a set of sixty-five bronze bells in three tiers (plate 25).[7] The tomb is famous for this set, accompanied by other musical instruments to form an orchestra. Inserted into the set, replacing one in the original sequence, was a magnificent bell as a funeral gift from King Hui of Chu, carrying a date equivalent to 433 BC. The Marquis of Zeng was at this moment bound in an alliance with Chu.

The bell is hung from a substantial loop decorated with a dragon mounted by a small tiger. As bells were the music of ceremonial banquets, its size and central position are a ritual expression of political relations. No spectator would have been in any doubt about the subordinate position of Zeng to Chu. The seniority of the King of Chu, the highest-ranking lord in the region, was sounded in life and the afterlife. The marquis also had a cornucopia of bronze ritual vessels, likely possible because of the major copper mine some 200 kilometres to the south at Tonglüshan.[8] But how did the marquis successfully extract wealth from this mine? Were ores or ingots carried upriver towards metal-hungry loess lands, with the marquis extracting some sort of

Detail of one of a pair of dragons, with a tiger standing on its head, to bear the bell given by the King of Chu. An example of the dense luxury and perpetual movement created by southern casters.

toll? We do not know, but the mine must account for at least part of his wealth, which also lay in rice-farming south of the Qinling and Dabei Mountains. A smaller chamber to the west housed a further thirteen coffins for women, perhaps musicians and dancers, all aged between thirteen and twenty-five. To the north of the ceremonial chamber was the armoury, with leather armour for men and horses, weapons and chariot fittings, enumerated in a list on bamboo slips as gifts from the marquis's peers and dependants. Around the tomb were 60,000 kilos of charcoal covered with rammed earth and a layer of stones.

The splendour of this tomb is unparalleled, not only within China but also by comparison with tombs in other parts of the ancient world. No expense was spared and it held over 15,000 artefacts. The great tombs of Ur in Mesopotamia had very different expressions of power – gold drinking vessels, sharp weapons, agricultural images of rams, donkeys and oxen and harps, not bells and mystical monsters and spirits among the mists of Chu.[9] Even in the south, the marquis's tomb is unique with its orchestra and dancers. Around the world, the tombs of famous individuals have always been the most exposed and have often been looted. In China there is a further barrier to the riches of the most magnificent tombs. Under current laws and regulations, tombs of kings and emperors listed in the classical histories, including the kings of Chu, which have almost certainly been robbed, cannot be excavated.

The Zeng had been awarded land and bronzes in the early Zhou period, but their power had waned. The marquis was the last Zeng ruler with great wealth. Meanwhile Chu had continuously expanded its territory. The bronze bell donated by the Chu king was a sign of the diminished power of Zeng in the face of Chu's domination.[10] We know from the archaeological record and the history of Zhongli that Chu had become embroiled in conflicts with the state of Wu.[11] The burial of the spouse of the Crown Prince of Wu, built while on a campaign against Chu in present-day Henan in 504 BC, is below a huge mound and, although rectangular, it reproduced the style of the tomb at Zhongli, with a central coffin surrounded by attendants.[12] The marquis elaborated this northern practice by arranging for twenty-one women to be buried with him.

Brilliant painted lacquer emphasised the wooden columns and panels of his outer coffin, in effect a small building. Columns, four on the long sides and three on the short ones, frame panels with rope borders overlaid with abstract S-shaped dragons. These dizzying designs hide something more significant. The structure – the fourteen columns, with frames for the base and the roof – is made of bronze and is thus extremely heavy, perhaps several tons. No other bronze frame for a wooden coffin has been found anywhere else.[13] All ceremonial buildings above ground were traditionally built of wood, although some were decorated with bronze.[14] Bronze was not a fortuitous choice. As with all tombs, ritual specialists in charge of creating the pit and designing the tomb, as well as commissioning everything in it, must have had specific objectives. Someone decided to requisition bronze for the structure. Choosing this valuable metal was a search for permanence, for eternity, a quest often realised in jade.

The short end of the outer coffin, with a small door on
the right-hand side, length 3.2 m, width 2.1 m and height 2.19 m.

Creating an inner frame for the structure in bronze was probably
an innovation. Methods to fit together columns with I-shaped sections had to be devised, so that they would sit on small feet, with
beams of bronze joined to the tops to support a roof. The corners
are complex, as two columns had to be set at right angles against
each other, facing in two directions. There is a degree of experimentation in this, not entirely comfortable, solution. The extra weight of
bronze was a disadvantage and must have been difficult to manage
and install, especially if the building was moved as a single unit and
not assembled from parts. Lowering it down some 13 metres must
have been arduous. The small building is balanced at an awkward
angle, with one long lower edge dug into the base of the chamber
and the other tipped up into the air. Whether it was built within or

outside the tomb, something went wrong when it was manoeuvred into position.

As much in the tomb was displaced, it is likely that it was flooded after it was sealed. Deposits of sand were found, a sign of water damage. In a dry tomb, with sufficient oxygen, the coffin would have fallen to pieces, with the wood consumed by bacteria, leaving only shreds of lacquer behind. In the waterlogged south, when tombs were sealed, with, for example, charcoal and clay, water often seeped in, excluding any oxygen. Bacteria, which normally devour all organic materials, could not survive in such conditions. Thus wood, bamboo, lacquer and even silk were preserved, as in the marquis's tomb, where so much remains. He appears richer than his northern contemporaries, but this may be misleading as much less could survive there.

Flooding may also have affected the position of the outer coffin. As the eastern chamber is built in an east–west orientation inherited from the steppe and Loess Plateau, the outer coffin should have been set in this direction too, with the eight coffins of the women and that of the dog arranged around it. Many later tombs of the Chu state show the same orientation.[15] The Wu state tomb in Henan also has an east–west orientation, with attendants within the coffin chamber and guards around it. A burial pattern taken from the north had reached the Yangtze basin. It was here interpreted by the marquis in an entirely new manner, as the women were placed in different rooms.

The inner coffin, built of planks with a curved lid and sides, as if it had been carved out of a tree trunk, is brightly painted in orange lacquer (plate 26). A panelled door was painted on both sides and a window was painted at one end.[16] In the afterlife, the marquis was thus able to leave the inner coffin, his private bedchamber, and move around his entire palace. Square openings, like that in the outer coffin, also joined all four chambers. The eight women in the eastern chamber with the marquis and the thirteen in the western chamber would also have used these doorways to take part in the life of the palace: in the banquets, ceremonies and musical performances. Eleven of the coffins for women also had either a window or a door painted on them. A way to realise the afterlife had been extended. The analogies that governed the afterlife had grown. We need to adjust our use and understanding of words such as replica and copy in an ancient Chinese context. An instruction to put a door in the side of the coffin would have led an overseer and his artisans to either cut a door into the side or paint one on. To their minds, both would have been equally effective, at a time when analogies underpinned their understanding of the universe, namely that the afterlife provided by its own means for all aspects of life. This conception of the afterlife allowed the painted door, which we see as a representation, to function as an actual physical entrance for the marquis in his future existence.[17] We have seen this happen in all the tombs we have visited. Early jades and ceramic or bronze banqueting vessels functioned in both life and the afterlife. Doors could, therefore, serve their purpose if they were painted in the correct position.

On the long sides of the inner coffin figures wielding staffs, with two halberd blades each, guard the doors. These guards are creatures

Guardians of the marquis.

with wings and claws; two rising on cloud-like legs and two with human legs defy interpretation. All have strange faces and ears, some heads bristle with hair, others sprout horns. Four auspicious birds with open wings hover above one of the sets of figures.[18] These are guards to defend the marquis in the afterlife. They promise security and good fortune. Evils had to be avoided, so nothing that could possibly bring harm would be included or depicted in the tomb. If emblems of creatures could ensure good outcomes, those of harmful monsters could likewise act against the tomb owner. Such customs are still prevalent in China today – pictures of disasters and negative news are always avoided.

There are few other places to look for creatures like those on the coffin, but one is the 'Chu manuscript' painted on silk, now in the Arthur M. Sackler Museum in Washington. It is said to have come from a third-century BC Chu state tomb.[19] Twelve strange figures stand facing the viewer, with horns or antennae on their heads. They represent the months and are organised along the four sides, making up the seasons, and surround the text at the centre, which describes the creation of the world:

Long, long ago, Bao Xi . . . married Zuwei [. . .]'s granddaughter, named Nü Tian. She gave birth to four . . . [children] who then helped put things in motion making the transformations arrive according [to Heaven's plan]. Relinquishing [this] duty, they then rested and acted [in turn] controlling the sidewalls [of the calendrical plan]; they helped calculate time by steps. They separated [heaven] above and [earth] below. Since the mountains were out of order, they then named the mountains, rivers and four seas. They arranged [themselves] by [. . .] hot and cold *qi*. In order to cross mountains, rivers and streams [of various types] when there was as yet no sun or moon [for a guide], when the people travelled across mountains and rivers, the four gods stepped in succession to indicate the year; these are the four seasons.[20]

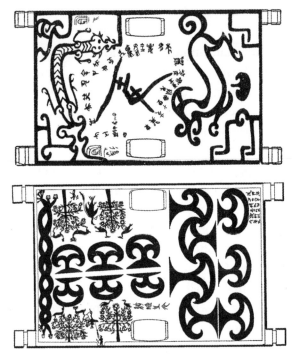

The lids of two wooden, lacquered clothes boxes, *c*.82 cm in length.

The text also describes customs and beliefs in language typical of the Yellow River basin and enduring Zhou court culture. Yet the depictions of the months and seasons are southern creations.

On the black domed lid of the marquis's clothes chest are brushstrokes of red lacquer that resemble a dragon and a tiger, later symbolic of the east and west. Here the creatures are joined by the twenty-eight lunar mansions, named in characters, through which the moon passes – the southerners' understanding of the passing of time. Another box of the same shape has four trees painted in red on the lid, blooming with what appear to be sunflowers, birds and indistinguishable creatures with human heads, another Chu origin story. They stand either side of a double row of what are often, and perhaps conveniently, identified as red mushrooms, which, from the Han period onwards, were regarded as medicinal and a route to immortality.[21]

More painted figures on the marquis's inner coffin carry us deeper

244

A bird atop a dragon surrounded by snakes on either
side of the window of the inner coffin.

into the southern marshes, the habitat of snakes. An array of strange creatures interlaced with snakes are threaded over its surface.[22] Dwarfing the intricate convulsions of heads and snakes, a bird stands still on the back of a dragon on either side of the window. Size alone indicates that we are meant to notice it. The same bird, often with wings made of antlers, clutching captive snakes or other fierce animals in its claws, has been found carved in wood, nearly a metre high, in several later Chu tombs.[23] Both on the coffin and when placed in a tomb, the mounted bird must have been a form of protection.

As stones placed over the tomb recalled a northern practice, so too a bird holding down a snake or a tiger probably originated in the steppe borderlands. It is a diluted version of the 'animal style', the visual language favoured in Inner Asia. The image of the bird and snake also appears in hunting scenes on bronze flasks cast on the Central Plains.[24] Other features from the north, such as the rope pattern on the outer coffin, slide into the world of Zeng and Chu. Despite their northern origins, the bird and rope pattern will have been recognised by members of the marquis's court as powerful, up-to-date forms of protection.

Antlers crown the head of a mystical long-necked bronze crane found among the eight coffins in the private chamber. Overpowering

The bronze antlered crane, height 1.43 m.

yet graceful, the antlers almost form a circle, which may have held a drum. Or a drum may have hung from the crane's beak. The crane has a relatively small, rounded body, of which every scrap is covered in fine sunken lines, and deep scrolls rise out of its short wings. Among the intense activity of the creatures on the marquis's coffin, its stillness is almost icy. The antlered crane was placed to the east of the main coffin and faces south. Was it intended to bear the marquis on journeys to the heavens? How far could it travel? Did drumming summon the spirits? Also puzzling are the rings around the edge of the stand,

The deer in lacquered wood, height 77 cm, length 45 cm.

apparently to carry the bird from one position to another. Where should it have been placed? Was it transported to other parts of the marquis's afterlife palace during ceremonies? Equally enigmatic is a wooden sculpture of a deer, its head raised to display its horns.[25] Painted in black and red lacquer, this creature is much more realistic than the crane. The deer here and another in the ceremonial hall must have delivered good fortune and were perhaps intended to accompany the marquis on visits to other parts of his universe. Antlers reflect the infiltration of creatures and ideas from the north as the marquis realised his own aspirations in a southern society.[26]

His myths and beliefs also jump out of framed scenes on an exquisite lacquered box shaped like a duck. In a small panel, a drum stands

The lacquered duck box, length 20.1 cm.

247

on an animal with figures wearing strange headdresses on either side. On the other side, two bells are held up by creatures with huge claws; next to them a masked figure, perhaps a performer, dances to draw beings from other worlds. Perhaps appropriately, this box was found in the coffin of one of the female attendants in the western chamber of the marquis's afterlife palace. It leads us to the swelling music in the central, ceremonial hall.

A philosophical text of the third century BC presents a sombre account of the role of music in maintaining the hierarchy within a family, in contrast to the commotion we can imagine in the marquis's tomb, with the antlered crane, drums, bells and masked dancers:

> When music is in the temple of the royal ancestors, and ruler and subject, superior and inferior, listen to it together, all of them are attuned in reverence; when it is in the household, father and son, elder and younger brother listen to it together, all are attuned in kinship; when it is in the neighbourhood, and elder and younger listen to it together, all are attuned in obedience.[27]

The long-standing bronze-casting tradition of the Yellow River basin had been exploited, honed and transformed here into one of the world's great works of art: three rows of sixty-five bronze bells hanging from a massive L-shaped wooden frame (plate 25).[28] As early as the thirteenth century BC, people in China had discovered that striking bronze produced a full, clear and powerful sound, and they had responded creatively by casting bells with an almond-shaped cross-section. That these bells should be the prized possession of the Marquis Yi of Zeng is a remarkable sign of his wealth and status. The Chu kings certainly must have had similar sets.[29] We see people playing bell sets with great vigour, along with chime stones and drums, while preparations for a banquet are in hand, on ritual vessels from further north from the same period. The sounds from such bells would have been awe-inspiring. For the marquis, five people played the bells, two at the front with long rods to strike the largest ones, and three behind with mallets for the top and middle rows.[30] These

Musical scenes of bells, chime stones and drums at a banquet,
from an inlaid bronze, fifth century BC.

tools have been found. Were these musicians drawn from the group
of thirteen women buried in the western chamber? Or were others
summoned in the afterlife? Yet more musicians must have played the
massive drum standing on a pile of writhing bronze dragons at the
shorter corner of the bell stand, and the stone chimes arranged in
two levels on a stand suspended by strange creatures with long necks.
There were two other drums in the reception chamber and musicians were also dedicated to the seven zithers (stringed instruments)
laid out with the bells, accompanied by flutes and pipes in wood and
bamboo. This music was enlivened by dance, captured in the *Summons of the Soul*:

> Before the dainties have left the tables, girl musicians take up their
>   places.
> They set up the bells and fasten the drums and sing the latest
>   songs:
> 'Crossing the River', 'Gathering Caltrops', and 'The Sunny Bank'.
> The lovely girls are drunk with wine, their faces flushed and red.
> With amorous glances and flirting looks, their eyes like wavelets
>   sparkle;

Dressed in embroideries, clad in finest silks, splendid but not
   showy;
Their long hair, falling from high chignons, hangs low in lovely
   tresses.
Two rows of eight, in perfect time, perform a dance of Zheng;
Their *xibi* buckles of Qin workmanship glitter like bright suns.
Bells clash in their swaying frames; the catalpa zither's strings are
   swept.
Their sleeves rise like crossed bamboo stems, then they bring
   them shimmering downwards.
Pipes and zithers rise in wild harmonies; the sounding drums
   thunderously roll;
And the courts of the palace quake and tremble as they throw
   themselves into the Whirling Chu.[31]

The instruments are a route into a world of unmatched musical and
technological prowess. The marquis's enormous bell set, with row
upon row of bells with almond-shaped mouths, was much more
melodious than those with a circular cross-section used later in the
West, whose tones are not as clear, and linger, as with the refrain of
distant church bells.

People in ancient China had discovered that their bells could give
them two notes, one by striking at the centre and another at the
corner, which were sometimes indicated with a sunken sign of a bird.
At first their bells stood on a vertical shaft, with the mouth upwards.
By the time of the Lord of Rui bells were hung at a slant, from a
loop on the shaft, as those of the marquis do too. While changes and
improvements must have been shared with the northern polities, the
most striking musical innovations were at a local level, where there
had been gradual changes to the pitch of bells over several centuries.[32]
The marquis's bells had been cast to almost exactly the correct size,
shape and weight to produce a full chromatic scale, the twelve notes
we know today for an octave, an astonishing feat. In some instances,
their weight and tone were improved by shaving part of the bronze
within the bell. We have no means of knowing how the bronze casters

reached this level of skill. It has been suggested that they relied on existing bells and previous models, worked out over centuries. This is a very different history from Europe, where the first bells were cast in the fifth century AD in Campagna in Italy, and used for funerals by the Reverend Bede in Jarrow in the eighth century AD. In Europe, bells were only turned into musical instruments from the seventeenth century, more than 2,000 years after the death of the Marquis Yi.

Although the marquis's set had all the bells for chromatic scales over three and a half octaves, this was not how music was played. The chime stones in the ceremonial hall in fact relied on pentatonic scales, the equivalent of the five black keys in the piano octave. The chimes fitted into three boxes, which still survive.[33] Two of the boxes contained the stones for a pentatonic scale each, but for two distinct scales, as the first notes produced were different. The third box added extra stones to create the full chromatic range. This allowed the pentatonic music to start on other notes, thus creating further pentatonic scales. In the musical vocabulary of the day, the various pentatonic scales starting on different pitches were given individual names. Ten notes were spaced at intervals of two semitones over an octave and a half, with names such as *muyin*, *yingyin* and *yingzi*. While the chime stones could be rearranged in different combinations for performances, the bells could not be moved so easily. Nonetheless, the pentatonic scale, with different starting notes, must have been applied to them too. We know about the musical structure both from the arrangement of the bells and from the inscriptions inlaid in gold on the bells themselves, a triumph of calligraphy as much as of musical technology. These inscriptions were cast with the bells, so the notes and their significance were determined *as* the moulds were made, not subsequently.

The small plain bells in three sets along the top beam carry the names of the notes in three standard pitches. The principal bells for playing the melodies were the three sets on the middle row, struck by three musicians from behind the rack. The first group of eleven are on the shorter arm, with two further sets, the first of twelve and the second of ten, on the longer arm. On each, the positions of the two notes are marked with single characters. The longer inscriptions

One of the bells from the central row of the set,
height 61.3 cm, weight 22.4 kg.

down the centre of these bells give the names of the note, following
those on the small bells above. They also give the name of the notes
at the corner. These inscriptions then become more complex, giving
the alternative names for the two notes that are used when starting at
a different place in the pentatonic scale. The sounds did not change,
but their position in the sequence did, depending on which note you
started on. We see a similar change in the *do re mi* system used in the
West. The *re* in the sequence switches note depending on the scale
that is played, or in the key, as we call it.

Surprisingly, two sets of bells in the middle row are given the
names of standard pitches in the Chu state, which have different
intervals from those of Zeng. Only one set along the middle row has
Zeng pitches, though many of the substantial bells along the bottom
also belong to the Zeng programme. On the bells in Zeng pitch, the
inscription also gives the name of the note in the Chu standard. Were
the sets of bells using the Chu standards cast in Chu, but with inscriptions explaining their notation when used in Zeng? Was this an early
form of musical transposition? What we do know for certain is that

the gold inscriptions suggest an intimate connection between Zeng and Chu bell-casting and performance, almost certainly invented in the musical world of Chu and then taken over and elaborated in Zeng.

The bell set is one of the wonders of the world. It was accompanied by a full orchestra of twelve zithers and ten wind instruments divided between the eastern chamber and the ceremonial hall, including transverse flutes, pan pipes and four mouth organs – made of gourds with pipes inserted into rings of holes in the body – which have survived better than in other tombs.[34] The zithers are formidable. They are more than one and a half metres in length, with a curved upper sounding board and holes in the underside, acting like those on a violin to release the sound. This upper sounding board is so long that it was made of several sections of wood. Twenty-five strings were stretched across it, which were sounded by plucking, with small movable bridges to create various notes. These were arranged to suit the different starting points of the scales performed on the bells and chime stones. The zithers were not the only plucked instrument. Among those owned by the marquis was one of the predecessors of the *qin*, the instrument known from later novels and poems that was favoured by the educated elite and is still played today. While the bells give the impression of a ritual performance, the string and wind instruments were part of an ensemble for dancing, in which some of the twenty-one women were no doubt expected to participate.

Above the almond-shaped opening of the bells are interlaced dragons, enhanced from their earlier iterations on the bells of Lord Bai, but now so heavily encrusted that they are hard to disentangle. Tiny scrolls even cover the shanks of the bells and the bosses. Small feline dragons clutching hooks hang the bells on the stand. And small bracing pillars between the upper and middle and the middle and lower rows are mounted on other coiled creatures, as if poised to drop their load.[35] Layers of small dragons mingling among flower heads decorate the ends of the beams. Multiple entwined creatures also form circular pods to support the stands, as if scrambling up towards the bells and drums above. This constant reiteration of reptile forms has a pervasive sense of unease. The same struggling rhythm is on the stand for the chime stones. Two creatures with rising horns, grinning heads, undulating necks and stunted wings and splayed feet hold the lower bar of the chime stones; their heads then advance another neck to a second head with an open mouth, fangs and vicious horns for the second row of stones. A far cry from soothing music, this is a vision of fearful anxiety in an unseen world of spirits and these creatures, as ever, were needed to deter evil. On the zithers too, strange faces and dragons call up protection from the spirit world. The unnerving – for us – cosmos of Chu and Zeng stands contrary to the staid ritual ceremonies of Zhou.

In the *Heavenly Question*, a later Chu document perhaps of the fourth or third century BC, we get a hint of the genesis of these visions:

Where is the Kunlun with its Hanging Gardens? How many miles high are its ninefold walls? Who goes through its gates in its four sides? When the northeast one opens, what wind is it that passes

The chime set suspended by two-headed monsters, height 1.09 m, width 2.15 m.

through? What land does the sun not reach to? How does the Torch Dragon light it? Why are the Jo flowers bright before Xihe is stirring? What place is warm in the winter? What place is cold in the summer? Where is the stone forest? What beast can talk? Where are the hornless dragons which carry bears on their backs for sport? Where is the great serpent with nine heads and where is the Shuhu? Where is it that people do not age? Where do giants live? Where is the nine-branched weed? Where is the flower of the Great Hemp? How does the snake that can swallow an elephant devour its bones? Where is the Black Water that dyes the feet and the mountain of Three Perils? The folk there put off death for many years. What is the limit of their age? Where does the man-fish live? Where is the Monster Bird?[36]

While these questions were compiled after the death of the marquis, his orchestra accessed this dynamic world through lacquer and bronze. Yet the physical creatures, and no doubt the music that accompanied it, were far more evocative and disturbing than words could ever be. The experience of seeing and hearing is always more visceral than reading. The stories of the south were dramatic interventions into a world view better known from the traditions of the Yellow River basin and its allies.

Yet, among this tumult of scrambling creatures, we find six men calmly supporting the bell stand, two sets, one of a tall figure and a shorter one above, at the two ends, and a further one where the short section of the L-shape meets the longer one at a right angle. Slim individuals with plain clothes, decorated only where their robes cross and pleat, buttress the beams with their hands. They all wear swords at their belts. Their immobility, enforced by the burden of their loads, offers a remarkable contrast: the human among the unhuman, the everyday alongside the unknown. Why this sudden switch of mode? The bell stand may have been made for the daily court life of the marquis, and then added to the tomb with his death. At that moment they joined the creatures there to defend the marquis. Of course, the men too must have been recognised as auspicious and protective.

Two bronze figures fitted to hold the central joint of the frame of the bell set.
The lower stand is 126 cm high, and the weight of the lower support 359 kg.

Human figures or indeed realistic animals were not a common device
in ancient China. The bronzes of the Loess Plateau had extended the
fashion for dragons as handles or feet on vessels. But humans bearing
loads were very rare. Small kneeling men raised up a miniature ritual
vessel in the tomb of the spouse of the Lord of Rui. But here at Zeng
is the first time that humans have a technical as well as decorative role.

A series of locking bronze parts, with plugs on the figures to secure
them in place, strengthen the wooden frame to hold the heavy bells.
With so much value at stake, no risks were taken. The metal expended
was huge. The three lower standing figures and their bases each weigh
over 350 kg, while the three upper figures each weigh just under 40 kg.
Was this construction a development that came with new interactions
with the lands westwards to Central Asia? These vigilant figures are so
out of kilter with the whirl of strange and, to us, fantastical creatures.

And they are not the only part of the marquis's lavish tomb that indicate his far-reaching contacts.

Among his possessions, we also find a flask standing in a basin magnificently encrusted with convoluted beasts and tentacled dragons, who are spitting out their long tongues (plate 27). An inscription tells us that it was owned by one of the marquis's predecessors.[37] This challenging yet fearsome piece may have been realised with the help of lost-wax casting.[38] Up to this point, we have not come across anything made by the lost-wax process, a technique favoured in Western Asia and the Mediterranean. This system allowed for a model to be made of wax on the structure of some other material. When the clay mould had been wrapped around it and heated, the wax would run out and bronze could be poured into the space left behind. The shells of the basin and of the flask were probably made by the traditional ceramic piece-mould casting developed under the Shang; the creatures and the filigree around the mouth of the flask may have been cast separately and attached. Thus the bronzes are visually arresting, first made with several smaller subunits of coiling dragons and frilly edges before putting the whole piece together. If they were not produced with the lost-wax technique, but with many separate cast pieces, it still tells us that openwork, most easily produced by lost-wax, had been observed or reported.[39] We also know that similar effects were achieved in carved bone and horn.[40] The marquis's flask in its basin is the climax of a taste for flamboyant detail.[41]

The flask, basin and six figures supporting the bell stand point to new encounters, perhaps as far as the oases of Central Asia, as well as further north. While the battles continued across the Central Plains and into the south, weaponry, horse equipment and gold were spreading from the north.[42] The Rong and many other groups from the borderlands were among the sources of new materials and technologies. Like Lord Bai at Bengbu, gold foils were used in Zeng and Chu tombs for decorative armour. But the marquis went one step further. He had two gold vessels for personal use in his private chamber, a lidded basin and a lidded cup. Both were traditional shapes for bronzes, and the gold too was cast, inevitably, at great

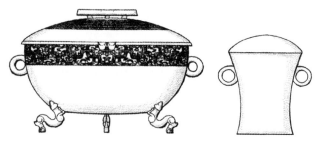

Cast-gold basin, diameter 15.1 cm, and cast-gold cup, height 10.65 cm.

expense. Supplies of gold were never abundant and casting, in place of hammering, required large quantities of metal. For this reason, the technique did not catch on for gold. Yet, this appearance of two elegant cast-gold vessels suggests some new impetus. What might have caused this sudden demand for gold drinking cups? Within a society bent towards the afterlife, the marquis would have followed any suggestions of new materials that might ensure his perpetuity. He made his choices and acquisitions not through markets but through craftsmen, servants and soldiers. Even today, the top craft items in China cannot be bought. Instead they are acquired in large numbers by official institutions and then given to distinguished guests.

Gold also appears in puzzling wire spirals. These spirals, threaded on silk and wound around wooden plugs, were arranged on one of the lacquered tables in the marquis's chamber.[43] Wire-making is not a skill that had been developed in China. The nearest examples we have seen are the spirals of gold at Yuhuangmiao, but these were made by twisting narrow sheets of gold. The most striking parallels are instead found in the western province of Xinjiang, at sites with connections with South Siberia (where more have been found), and further west in northern Iran. The balls of silken threads with tiny spirals of gold and tin are recognised by us, and of course by the spirits, as being of considerable value. While we can see that the technology and skill in making spirals had come from Western Asia by way of the steppe, it is impossible to decide what they were for. Archaeologists working at Arzhan in South Siberia and at Marlik in Iran have treated them as parts of personal ornaments.[44] But there are far too many on the table in the marquis's tomb for this to have been their primary use. The same threading of the spirals on cords has been found in tombs at Danyang, also in the Chu state.[45] The answer evades us, but the marquis, as a powerful landowner in his day, was abreast of new fashions that conferred on him status in life and the afterlife.

The marquis gained strength from his ancestors through offerings in his ritual vessels. In the ceremonial hall, 117 bronzes were carefully assembled in rows to the south of the bell stand, an explicit sign of the high rank he aspired to and claimed. They were, of course, the indispensable route to the blessings of his ancestors, but no doubt were also employed in extravagant feasts for other, living guests.[46] Over centuries, the Zeng lineage had followed the changes in vessel styles and shapes. Those of the marquis exceeded the bronzes of all his known predecessors in their imposing presence and extravagant decoration. Some were embellished with lively dragon patterns inlaid in a turquoise paste. He also had two sets of nine cauldrons, *ding*, a set of eight basins, *gui*, two immense cooking pots and two tall wine vessels. The cooking pots and wine vessels were traditional in shape, if deliberately ostentatious in size and casting skill. Features from the surfaces of these bronzes, including scrolls and dragons, were reproduced in some of the furniture in the chamber as part of a continuing exchange: bronze decoration incorporated the free composition that carving in wood and painting in lacquer encouraged.[47]

The main ritual set followed the vessels now typical of the Yellow River basin. Additions included an openwork shovel, rather like one we would use for a coal fire, and a copy of a traditional one in bamboo perhaps to accompany a brazier held up on long chains. A squat container with a thin chimney extension and a circular tube narrowing to the foot composed of elaborate openwork dragons and other creatures were probably for incense.[48] Intoxicating fumes may have facilitated the expeditions to the spirit world described a century later in Chu poetry and on bamboo slips, which tell of interactions between officials of the afterlife.[49] Patterning in relief or inlay gave all the marquis's possessions an intense luxury and, to our eyes, an impenetrable mystery.

A pair of immense square basins for ice or hot water to cool or heat alcoholic drinks had three hooks on the base to secure the rounded flasks. While the surface was emphasised by scrolls typical of the marquis's bronze works, the profiles of both the outer basins and the inner flasks were gracefully curved, with small dragon feet and eight arched dragon handles. The marquis's bronze casters were so preoccupied with flamboyance that they had to develop ways to stabilise their designs. Here the hooks were to fix the flask firmly in the basin. And the six bronze men were not merely artistic devices, they were actually bearing the load of the bells. In fact, they withstood their weight and pressure for more than two millennia. They again offer us evidence of the intricate expertise of Chu casters, an expertise that was never written down as it apparently did not interest the officials of the day.

Without excavation we would never have learned of the extraordinary artistic and technical skills of Chu, revealed in a yet more surprising form in bronze fittings in one of the five pits around the main tomb. They were spread over an area 3.7 metres long and 2.6 metres wide. Over 300 fittings were recovered, clearly intended to

A rounded basin – height 61.5 cm – square in cross-section, with a separate flask at the centre, just visible above the rim, together weighing 168.8 kg. Filled with either hot water or ice, the basin would have kept the contents of the flask at the optimum temperature.

create a portable structure built of wooden poles. Senior archaeologist at Wuhan University, Professor Zhang Changping, has shown that the most complicated fittings, many with two- or three-way joints, were destined for the ridge of a tent-like lodge. Some bronze fittings were equipped with a locking device to increase the stability of the structure. The wooden poles were of various thicknesses, depending on their position. In addition, some of the poles could be joined with bronze fittings to make subunits. When these were put together they constructed a rectangular tent. This clever system was the product of well-established methods of subdivision of labour, probably allowing several groups of assistants to work simultaneously so that the tent could be erected very quickly.[50] Parallel teams working concurrently are still one of China's industrial strengths, in everything down to its computer manufacture.[51] This is the first time we have come across the remnants of a tent in China. Although the people buried at Yuhuangmiao may have lived in tents like those of other mobile pastoralists, traces are not likely to be found, as they did not use metal fittings. But with the tomb of the Marquis Yi of Zeng we are not looking at a mobile, or so-called nomadic, lifestyle, but at a comfortable lodging for travel, hunting and war. That the marquis intended to travel in the afterlife is made plain by boxed sets of drinking and food vessels in lacquered wood. The drinking vessels are oval cups with two side handles, generally known as ear-cups. There were sixteen of these, accompanied by long instruments perhaps for stirring alcohol in deep vats.[52]

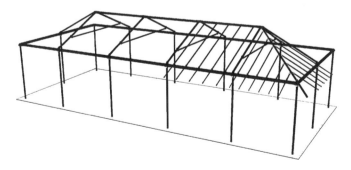

A partial reconstruction of the marquis's tent.

A tent and travelling trunks were essential preparations for an after-life trip. And further provisions were placed in the smaller, fourth chamber to the north of the ceremonial hall. This was clearly an arsenal, holding sixty-six standard halberd blades and thirty of the less common, but more lethal, halberds topped by spearheads. The standard halberds probably had a shaft of 1.3 metres in length, but the full weapon, when mounted on a staff, was over 3.25 metres long and had to be managed by two fighters. There were also forty-nine spears. The weapons suggest a small protective force rather than a full army. Although they were real, were they in fact just representative, to create a much greater fighting force in the afterlife? We can see something similar if we look at the provision for chariots, the main fighting vehicle for the elite during the Warring States. Parts for a single chariot were placed in the armoury, along with the structure for an umbrella to stand over it. This protected the driver and above all the marquis, perhaps being driven to meet with his peers or to embark on a hunting trip. With seventy-six axle caps in the store, a fleet of thirty-eight vehicles was imagined. However, the number of horse bits and cheekpieces was not adequate to supply bridles for seventy-six horses, which was the minimum needed to pull thirty-eight chariots. It was clearly not necessary to provide all the vehicles, the horses and their bridles; instead a selection of axle caps, bits and cheekpieces would conjure up the rest in the afterlife. Among the axle caps, several were cast with long, spear-like extensions, which would have cut through the spokes of enemy chariot wheels coming too close on the battlefield. The northern enemies might ride, but the wars on the Central Plains and in the south were still being fought in chariots. From the sixth century BC foot soldiers were also rapidly increasing.[53] As further protection, the marquis also had fifty-five bows, more than 4,000 arrowheads (including some socketed steppe types) and fifty-three shields.

As the damp conditions in the tomb preserved the bell stand, wooden furniture and lacquered drinking cups, it is not surprising that chariot parts and sections of lances, staffs, bows and shields also survived. Along with these was a pile of lacquered leather armour

A piece of leather horse armour, approximately 50 cm long.

sections for thirteen men and two horses. The sections were grouped together for the men to make helmets, collars, arm guards and tunics. For the horses, the most complex and highly decorated pieces were for their heads. Extensive sections of leather covered their bodies. Among the carefully painted designs are dragons with stag antlers and a bird standing on the body of a dragon, echoing the marquis's coffin and repeating the northern animal style. The horse head armour also has fine stippled surfaces, almost like silverwork. We know from Lord Bai's tomb that gold foil on bronze was favoured, and armour embellished with silver or tin was found elsewhere in the Chu state.[54] Armour was another arena through which to assert and gain status, now enhanced by the northerners' love of gold and silver or tin foil. Zeng antler cheekpieces for horse harnesses were possibly chosen by their Rong horse managers, recruited for their skill in driving horses or even as agents for acquiring them. The spread of newcomers among the principal states is almost never recorded in the transmitted writings. The authors avoided such an admission, as these mobile pastoralists were not accepted as major players in society, despite their talents. In China, as in all other countries, the past is remembered and reinterpreted to serve the present. Today a unified territory and a relatively homogeneous population are now celebrated. With the almost universal belief that settled societies with cities were the desired objective, mobile people who did not write were inevitably left out of the history and can only be found in the archaeology archives. Antler cheekpieces have been discovered in tombs across most of the central Chinese states of the fifth to third centuries BC. As elsewhere, northern horse managers and mercenaries had been accepted into Zeng military forces.[55]

A sword, which at first sight the marquis seemed to lack, is highly significant, albeit hard to identify. A composition of four carved jades devises the sword. Four, almost flat plaques, joined together by small vertical links, also in jade, seem unlikely candidates. Yet, this concoction of pieces creates the outline of a sword in a scabbard. We have what appears to be a jade shadow of a bronze weapon. An intricate carving is the pommel of the sword. It is attached to a short, plain section which produces the grip and then widens to form the outline of the upper part of a blade. Below this, at the centre, is a further joint, horizontally decorated to suggest the top of a scabbard. At the foot is another piece, this time, trapezoidal, proposing a chape. This jade sword was not for warfare in life; it is likely that it was a weapon to overcome spirits. To match it, a curved bronze steppe-type knife was supplied with a jade ring on the grip. Swords and daggers were

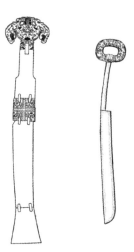

A jade sword, length 33.6 cm, and a bronze knife
with a jade ring on the grip, length 28.6 cm.

by now well known. The six figures holding up the stand all wore swords at their belts. And by the fifth century BC, splendidly decorated blades were made in the southern Wu and Yue states and acquired by Chu lords.[56] A sword in jade was not a replica, but a weapon of some special power, part of a culture in which the permanence and translucency of jade were analogous to the supernatural.

Although the marquis was buried far to the south of the Central Plains and west of the Jade Corridor, he had a considerable number of other jades, exhibiting an awareness of contemporary styles. The most spectacular is a combination of separate pieces making up the decoration for a belt, again reworking a steppe tradition in a central or southern mode. Each piece is a complete carving of a coiled snake, quintessential of the Yunmeng Marsh. Other, more conventional pieces followed the traditional shapes of the *bi*, *huang* (arc) and *cong*. One *cong* is cut from a fine white stone, unknown among its Neolithic ancestors, with a renovated version of the ancient *taotie* cut across its four flat surfaces.

The marquis and his retinue had married the technical musicality of the bell set and enthralling performances with the unparalleled exoticism of gold vessels, armour with gold foil, antlers and birds commanding felines. This contact with and even influence by people far from Zeng may simply show the marquis's fondness for novelty. More unusual are the complex structures engineered in bronze: the outer coffin, the bell stand and the tent. Such engineering ambition may have been the contribution of particular advisers. All the tombs we have visited reveal the presence of ritual specialists, foremen and horse managers. In looking at several regions over several centuries, it has become clear that these monuments of the afterlife were realised by advisers and organisers with a myriad of different customs, beliefs and skills. Similarities within the polities in the Yellow River basin – such as ritual vessel sets, certain weapon types, chariots, and even some features of tomb structure – imply a widely recognised cultural landscape. These shared practices were always blended, as at Zeng, with both local preferences and idiosyncrasies and outside, northern influences.

★

Everything the marquis owned was extraordinary, from his double coffin to his bell set and its stand, and of course the whole arrangement of his four-roomed palace with its twenty-one female attendants, protected by spirits. The swirling decoration in bronze and lacquer presented visually, not verbally, the hidden universe of Chu, Zeng and other southern neighbours. In the West, we too have ways to visualise a spiritual universe – a golden Heaven in the mosaics of the Virgin at Hagia Sophia, a torturous hell in Dante Alighieri's poetry and in the Last Judgment painting by Jan van Eyck. In southern China we find an afterlife of strange creatures, with incense, dance and music evoking the journeys subsequently recounted in the famous poetry of Chu. We should not interpret the whirling creatures as threatening. The complex artistry and the mass of different media and imagery that the casters and carvers employed offer us one of the most intriguing languages of objects of ancient China. Yet the objectives and ambitions were narrow: the huge investment in this grand tomb, drawing on all available powers and resources, was to ensure a fruitful afterlife for the marquis.

Although the Qin defeated the state of Chu in 223 BC, the visions of the southern poets were recaptured in the court poetry of the Han dynasty, this time giving almost divine status to Emperor Cheng in a poem of 10 BC celebrating a great hunt. 'When the Son of Heaven on a sunny morn first comes forth from the Dark Palace':

> They strike the great bells,
> Raise the nine-paneled flags,
> Yoke six white tigers,
> To carry Him in the divine chaise,
> With Chiyou flanking the wheels,
> And the Shaggy Lord racing to the fore.
>
> Raised standards cleave the heavens,
> Trailing flags brush the stars,
> Pealing thunder and fiery fissures,
> Spewing flames, ply their whips.

The Orchestra of Zeng

Grouped and gathered, in steady stream,
Continuously coursing, vast and wide,
They signal the eight outposts to open the gates.
Feilian and Cloud Master
Sniff and snort, huff and puff,
And in scalelike array, ranged in rows,
They mass as thick as dragon plumes.[57]

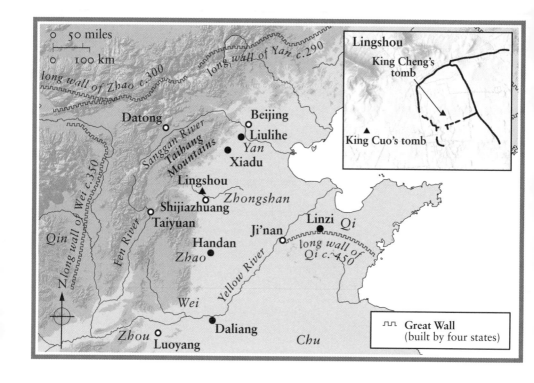

Lingshou and the Kingdom of Zhongshan

10.

A Kingdom by Design

Hidden by sprawling motorways, factories and suburbs is the Kingdom of Zhongshan.[1] It is tucked into a small enclave on the edge of the Taihang Mountains (plate 19). Looking east, its kings of the fourth century BC must have surveyed the rich lands that stretched before them. Behind, long roads come from the north through the sharp peaks of the Taihang into the lands of Zhongshan and their capital at Lingshou. One from Datong, just south of the modern province of Inner Mongolia, emerges here. The basin occupied by Zhongshan was, therefore, a pivot on the journeys from the grasslands, the Loess Plateau and the mountains to several states on the Central Plains.

The kingdom was founded in the fifth century BC by people we call the Di, drawn from historical writings. They were pastoralists with some settled farming occupying, with the Rong and no doubt many others, much of the northern area of the Loess Plateau. They received little attention from early historians and often, confusingly, the terms Rong and Di were used interchangeably. And, like the term Rong, the term the Di embraced several different groups, who from the seventh century BC were spreading southwards. We can track their movements through their tombs, filled with the typical inventory of the north – daggers, horse harnesses, animal heads and animal ornaments on belts and clothes.[2] As the Rong and the Di took over land, they became embroiled in the persistent conflicts between the central states, in particular with the Yan and the Zhao, who were using their improved iron tools for agriculture to press northwards into the Yan Mountains. One consequence of this pincer movement was that the Rong and the Di accepted at least some part of the culture of the Central Plains. While this suggests a powerful centre, a tradition

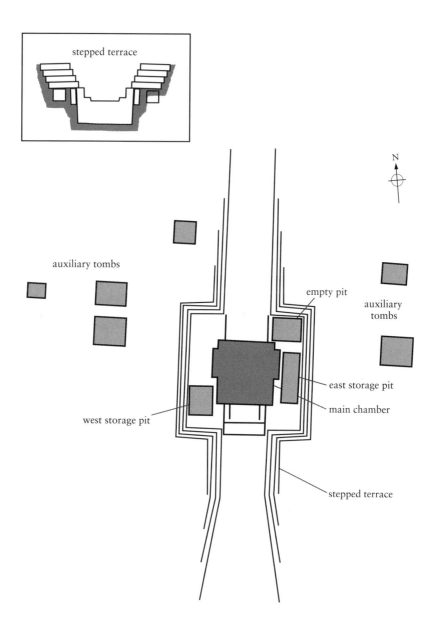

stepped terrace

N

auxiliary tombs

empty pit

auxiliary tombs

east storage pit

main chamber

west storage pit

stepped terrace

The tomb of King Cuo of Zhongshan. The western storage pit contained
ritual vessels and the eastern small animal sculptures. The burial chamber
c. 3 metres in height was placed in the burial pit 8.2 metres in depth. The four
steps around the platform on both sides of the burial chamber are
1.5 m high. The remaining length of the southern ramp is 40 m; the northern
ramp is 45 m. The base of the mound is 100 m by 90 m, remaining height 15 m.

originating with the Zhou, it also led the central states to have more direct contact with the inhabitants of the Loess Plateau. To protect the new land that they occupied, and to face people who often rode, the Yan and the Zhao began building defensive walls. And, conscious of the need for cavalry, in 304 BC King Wuling of Zhao ordered his army to adopt suitable dress for riding, namely, to abandon long robes in favour of trousers.[3] The state of Qi was also a dominant force in the east, with its own wall south of its capital at Linzi. Jin, a formidable presence on the Fen River in the time of the Lord of Rui, was no longer a major state. Ambitious ministers led to its division into three new states, Wei, Han and Zhao, with a protracted period of upheaval that began in 453 BC.[4] Lu and Song were to the south, with Chu much further south and Qin well to the west. The Warring States, as these centuries are named, were blighted not only by military campaigns but also by the endless political realignment of states. The Zhongshan kingdom took advantage of this disequilibrium.

These developments are also evident in several provinces: Shaanxi, Shanxi and Hebei.[5] Excavated tombs show that newcomers were now a dogged and increasingly prosperous presence, aspiring to political and economic standing within the existing communities across both the Loess Plateau and the agricultural plains.[6] Their burials were often impressive and formal: covered in stone, the main occupant was endowed with gold ornaments and accompanied by neatly arranged attendants and animal heads. Those around Lingshou show that the Di, or related peoples, settled there in the sixth to fifth centuries BC.[7] Initially, when the royal Zhongshan tombs were discovered, as some of the grandest in China, they seemed to fit nicely into the written history of the Warring States. However, the Zhongshan tombs express change and a mixed culture of people living in the area.[8] With the establishment of the kingdom, the ancestral cult and written documents became entwined with burials including stone, animal heads and gold.[9] The tomb of King Cuo, who reigned from about 327 to 313 BC, illustrates this combination of two different traditions, presenting us with a physical record of the geopolitics of the fourth century BC, as prevailing states swallowed up smaller ones.[10]

It was discovered 40 kilometres north-west of present-day Shijiazhuang, to the west of Lingshou.[11] As stone was only used in burial,
rather than for day-to-day construction, defensive walls of rammed
earth marked the city's boundary. They still survive in part at between
18 and 34 metres wide. The walls also took advantage of deep natural
landfalls and waterways. While the city looks out over agricultural
land, in danger its residents could retreat into the Taihang Mountains.
Additional fortified land was enclosed further east towards the Yellow
River.[12] Raids and warfare were clearly on everyone's mind. Lingshou
was considerable in size, about 4,500 metres north to south. An inner
wall divided the city into eastern and western districts. In the eastern
district, several rammed-earth foundations were found, probably for a
palace or administrative offices. To the west, the district was divided
into two halves. In the northern section, tombs had been installed for
two earlier kings, King Huan and King Cheng, with their spouses and
their attendants. King Cheng's tomb provides useful comparisons with
the tomb of our subject, his son King Cuo. To the south, residential
areas for commoners and workshops for ceramic manufacture and metalwork were uncovered, primarily by drilling cores at careful distances.[13]

Among the workshops lay a surprising discovery: moulds for coun-
terfeit coins fashioned in the shape of northern knife blades. Early
Chinese coins, known from the sixth century BC, were cast in bronze
and imitated curved knives and small spades – although often associated with agriculture, these were woodworking tools, buried with
earlier chariot drivers. At Zhongshan, the coins shaped like blades
and tools were probably to attract the northerners, such as the Di,
and their horses. As people on the northern borders were short of
bronze, raids on and trade with settled farming communities were
irresistible sources of metal, which could be melted down to make
weapons. We do not know how or when barter took place, but the
moulds carried the names of the more powerful states of Zhao and
Yan, and the analogous coins they produced would facilitate transactions.[14] Circular coins with a central square hole, for threading them
together, were in use in Qi from the fourth century BC. At a similar
time, the round coin of the Qin, the *banliang*, was introduced.[15] As the

individual states were conquered by Qin, this coin was authorised as the only standard currency. All such coins were cast in bronze, with characters indicating their place of origin, a technique completely unlike that of the ancient Greek world, where the early coins in gold and silver were minted, using dies to stamp a small lump of metal, thereby creating an approximately circular piece.

About 1,500 metres to the west of the walls of Lingshou, on a vast man-made terrace – a deliberate move away from the earlier royal cemetery – is the tomb of King Cuo. He was one of many local rulers who followed a new tradition of creating tombs outside the city. His tomb had its own walled enclosures, a new city for the after-life and an enormous investment and allocation of precious resources. The mound over his tomb stood at more than 15 metres, with a cen-tral raised area over a wider base and four sides about 100 metres in length. Mounds did not develop out of the ancient burial rituals of the states of the Central Plains; their origins were at Zhongli and among the Eastern Yi. For each king or lord, a high mound was now essential to declare his authority over his erstwhile subjects. At the same time, these mounds proclaimed to ancestors the achievements of their descendants. Mounds are also indicative of a pool of labour forces available to rulers. In place of one Zhou leader, there were now seven or eight kings who could command armies of thousands. They could also mobilise men to build and man the walls of their cities and to create impressive pyramid-like tombs.

With the division of Jin, Zhao now held land south of Zhongshan, and extended to the north on Zhongshan's western flank, taking over land previously occupied by the Di. Another competitor further south, the state of Wei, attacked Zhongshan in 407 BC, but the kingdom was restored in 381 BC by King Huan. The highest-ranking ministers, termed the *Shi*, often exploited this turbulence. Zhongshan also com-peted with the state of Yan and sought allies among the states of Qi and Lu, to the east in present-day Shandong. King Cuo was drawn into warfare with Yan as an ally of Qi.[16] We can trace the politics of the day by the sequence in which his tomb was created and installed. A deep rectangular burial pit was dug down to about 8 metres, reaching the bedrock below the platform. Two small rectangular extensions were made east and west. A massive wooden chamber was then built within the main pit. This was some 3 metres in height, and probably about 13 metres long and 12 metres wide. It had been completely looted and the inner coffins and wooden chamber were destroyed. Only some small bronze relics remained, among them hinges for wooden doors. Actual doors, which could open, must have been placed in the walls of the chamber, allowing the king to leave his tomb in the afterlife and travel elsewhere. To our eyes these seem more realistic than the painted doors in the Marquis Yi's coffin. But to the people of ancient China, both were equally convincing analogues. The whole of the burial chamber was encased in stone, again following the example of steppe customs; it lay on rock and all four sides were lined with roughly shaped stones between the wooden walls of the chamber and the earthen sides of the pit.[17] The top too was covered with thick layers of stones and the gaps filled with charcoal.[18]

Above the coffin chamber, stepped walls in four tiers effectively created the grave shaft above ground.[19] This device may have been chosen as, in this region, the loess is not thick over the rock below, and a deep tomb could not be dug there.[20] These walls were painted white and defined a space approximately 30 metres square, creating a room on the platform above the pit, which was, in due course, subsumed within the mound.[21] We can compare this arrangement with the earlier royal tomb of King Cheng. His coffin chamber was similarly positioned, with a stone surround, at the centre of a square space, but with outwardly sloping walls, not steps. In both tombs mourners at the funeral would have had access to these rooms, probably open to the sky, by walking along the north or south ramps. Just as the ceremonial banquets for the ancestors were restricted to members of the wider family, the mourners are likely to have been drawn from the same clan, those connected by marriage and members of the court, although a few valued dependants may have been welcomed as guests.[22] They entered the rooms where the ramps had cut through the walls. The ramps were as much part of the funeral space as the platforms. The sloping sides in King Cheng's tomb were plastered white and divided along the east and west walls by columns made of mud bricks covered in a green paint. These even had copies of the small shafts cut into the floor. In life, this would have given stability to the wooden columns in a hall above ground. Inside King Cheng's tomb, the mourners would have stood in a painted hall, divided into bays by the columns.

In Cuo's tomb they would have walked along a ramp, possibly painted to look like the corridor of a palace, to gather in a tiered space, with the rising steps allowing room for people or objects. A great deal of effort had gone into both tombs to create a very special environment for the funeral ritual. In effect, King Cuo's tomb, and that of his father King Cheng, took up several features of Lord Bai's circular tomb. A terrace, effectively a step above the burial pit, sheltered behind a row of replica boulders, was replaced here by platforms on the east and west sides of a square room above the grave, clearly implying an audience for participants in the rites. The walls in both Zhongshan tombs were also a version of the white quartzite at Zhongli. In all, access inside was by ramps. And again, only once the funeral rites were completed would the hall and ramps be filled in, and the mound was completed. The architecture respected and accommodated the inauguration of the afterlife.

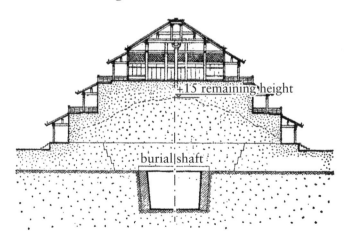

Reconstruction of the buildings on the tomb mound,
and the stepped terrace now buried within it.

The mound over the tomb was part of the ritual space. Three distinct tiers on the sides of the mound were used for wooden buildings with tiled roofs, stepping up to the top. The remains of buildings have survived on these tiers: decorated fragments of ceramic tiles, tile ends and ridge tiles.[23] Suggestions for the form that these buildings took have come by comparing them with buildings engraved or cast on fifth- and fourth-century BC bronzes. One telling example, recovered from an earlier tomb in the Lingshou region, shows a two-storey building.[24] Bronzes with cast or incised imagery depicting activity – banqueting and even performances of bell music – coincided with the widespread depiction in lacquer painting.[25] In the West we are biased in our views of the value of representation. Over millennia, we have prized images of deities as the primary route to reach them. This tradition has given representation a high status. In central China there was no equivalent search for a transcendent realm through representation. Instead, banqueting vessels have always offered a route to engage with the ancestors. As with images of the Virgin Mary, the artistic qualities of such vessels were of the highest importance. They presented the status of their owners and their families to themselves, and above all to their ancestors. Bronze, jade and later lacquer were works of art in their own time.

Small loggias around the two lower tiers on the mound led up to a ceremonial hall at the summit. Rituals for the dead king would have

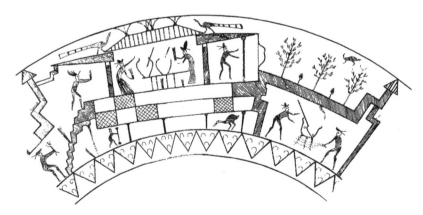

A similar building is engraved on a bronze basin in an earlier tomb at Lingshou.

been carried out regularly within this hall. Such halls may have been built over earlier tombs. Traces of the foundations for one were even found over the tomb of Fu Hao at Anyang. With a hall erected directly over King Cuo's coffin, the ceremonial offerings would have been carried out at close quarters. We do not know how such banquets hosted by the living were thought to chime with the bronze vessels buried with the king. But their presence in all high-ranking tombs suggests that they remained essential to nourish the dead in their afterlives.[26]

While personal items, which may have been in the main chamber or inner coffins, are now gone, the plunderers did not find all of King Cuo's ritual vessels. We are fortunate that they did not discover chests below the platform in the west and east storage pits. These chests follow the model we saw at Zhongli, also shared by eastern lords in Shandong, Cuo's neighbours in the Qi State.[27] His possessions were not placed on a secondary ledge, as in earlier times, but stored in separate wooden compartments. The tomb robbers were presumably unaware of this practice to enrich the afterlife. People outside immediate families and the closest retainers would have had no access to the rites of another clan, let alone those of the highest elite. The smaller, west chest held the king's ritual vessels. On the east side were two chests. One was empty and the other held more bronzes.[28] These exemplify the dual identity of Zhongshan, as a state led by descendants of the Di in which their king also took part in the political and ritual enterprises of his rivals in the central states.

One item left behind in the central chamber by the looters is a plan on a bronze plaque. This is an architectural edict for the proposed burial. No other such ground plan has ever been found. Inscriptions in gold and silver tell us what was intended and an admonishment is inscribed:

> The King ordered Zhou [the Chancellor] to set up standards [on this panel] of tomb sizes to be followed by those who will build them. Those who violate this edict will be executed without mercy, and their sons and grandsons will also be punished. One [plan] is to be buried [with the King] and the other to be stored in the archive.[29]

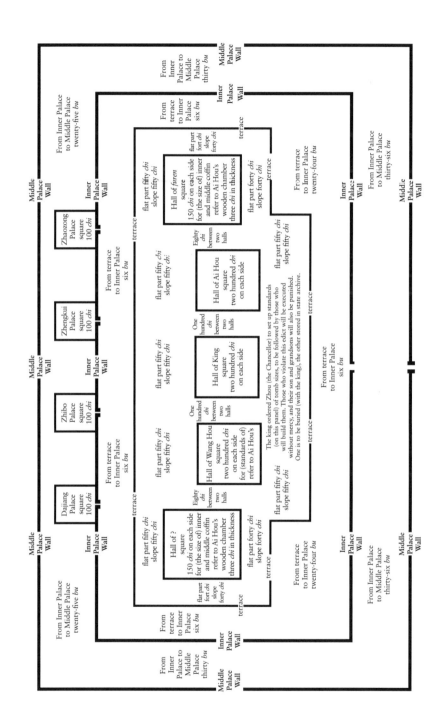

The bronze blueprint of King Cuo's afterlife palace, length 87.4 cm.

A square at the centre marks the king's tomb on the terrace. To the east is the tomb of his consort Ai Hou. To the west should have been the tomb of a second consort, Wang Hou (simply meaning the king's consort). All three tombs are the same size, with the king's mound, at about 44 metres along each side. Tomb measurements are included in the plan, with two additional small mounds and tombs next to the consorts' tombs. Five were planned for this terrace. On the north side, away from the terrace, between the middle and inner palace walls were four small pavilions with doorways into the Inner Palace for the king and his consorts to move around during the afterlife. The named consort, Ai Hou, had died before the king, and he had supervised her burial. The others may have died after him and possibly after Zhongshan ceased to exist in the third century BC. The plan was never fully realised. We can suppose that what remains was a different scheme devised by the king's successors.

We also know from an inscription on one of the bronze vessels in the tomb commissioned by the son of King Cuo that he, the successor, was not the son of one of the main consorts, but of a lesser concubine.[30] After a ruler's death, the positions of all consorts were in jeopardy. A woman who had not given birth to an heir, indeed to the most favoured heir, would have been in danger when her husband died, as was the case in many other societies. The plan may have been cast in bronze to protect both consorts after the king died, but also to give them status in the afterlife. More is known about a specific competition between royal consorts at Zhongshan, although it is not clear whether these were the consorts of King Cuo or another king. It is recorded in the *Stories of the Warring States (Zhangguo Ce)*, a collection of accounts compiled in the Western Han period (second to first century BC). Zhongshan is the only smaller state to have a section in this volume, alongside those of the larger states Qi, Zhao, Wei, Han, Yan, Chu and Qin and the Zhou themselves.[31] A struggle is noted between two concubines of a King of Zhongshan aspiring to become queen, a position that would determine the future of their children. It drew in court officials, among whom was Sima Xi (also known as Sima Zhou), who became chancellor during the reign of King Cuo. A chancellor was the most senior of all the executive officials. As Sima Zhou had also served other Zhongshan kings, we cannot be certain whether this story relates to King Cuo. Nonetheless, the plaque and its instructions to court officials demonstrate the force of King Cuo's intention to cement his power in the future. The location of afterlife palaces for his consorts and concubines close by was one of his central, and unfulfilled, demands. Many rulers may have had similar worries, but King Cuo's bronze plan is the only known attempt to categorically forecast his objectives.

Women were clearly important members of high-ranking society in ancient China, primarily as pawns in the alliances built between political competitors.[32] Many were accorded grand tombs with their own ritual vessels and other possessions, as rulers strove to protect their favoured spouses and concubines. Inscriptions on such bronzes also record their roles as ancestors alongside their spouses. Probably the most prominent engagement of women concerned their efforts to ensure that it was their son who would inherit the title and the position. The trials and tribulations of such ambitions enlivened the lives of many over millennia around the world. The women here and in the tomb of the Marquis Yi illustrate the service and support they offered to the male ruler.

Before we turn to the contents of the king's tomb, we must consider the wider context of the burial ground, which does not appear in the plan, with its hidden message of the king's personal-political ambitions. First of all, it is possible that some concubines or servants were also with the king in his burial chamber. Like the marquis, he may have taken his most intimate attendants into the afterlife with him. Six auxiliary pits were also placed around the main tomb, four to the west and two to the east. Perhaps they were for lesser concubines or for armed guards. These tombs were all dug deep into the rock so that they resembled stone chambers, showing us that their occupants, as with the king and his lineage, were newcomers from the northwest. This is confirmed by cattle bones found in three of the pits. As all the tombs had been disturbed, we do not know whether the other three also held such bones.[33]

If we look a little further afield to the south, we find two long char-iot and horse pits, a pit with tents and hunting equipment and an unusual pit for boats. Only the second chariot pit is still intact. It is in effect a stable for the afterlife, with walls supported by wooden col-umns and a ceiling held up with cross-beams. The inner walls were covered with mud and plaster. The space, 33 metres in length, was div-ided into two sections, one for four chariots and the other for twelve horses. From their assemblage and decoration, we see that the four chariots had different functions; some were for war, others were for hunting or travel. Similar numbers of horses were buried in the pits alongside King Cheng's tomb in the royal cemetery within Lingshou city. Some horse skeletons had split skulls and broken legs, showing that they had been killed before burial. These were not sacrifices; as with all horses buried with or near their owners, they were valued as live horses, intended to serve the king in the afterlife. Stables of good horses were now growing in value as mounted warriors approached the Central Plains.

While steppe lords and their followers had been riding for many centuries, the lords of the central polities did not ride, nor did the larger part of their armies. We even have very little evidence that Chinese rulers from the fourth century BC onwards started riding for war, or even for pleasure. Yet we know that the state of Zhao was creating a cavalry, and no doubt Zhongshan was too. Building up an effective mounted force took decades and northerners had to be employed to manage the horses. Rulers and high-ranking officials valued education and literary composition; they avoided physical labour and engagement with animals. The exceptions were of course the later emperors with a northern background; the most renowned are the Tang dynasty Emperor Taizong (AD 624–49) and the Qing emperors of the Kangxi (AD 1661–1722) and Qianlong (AD 1735–95) eras.

Familiarity with breeding, raising, driving and riding horses may have given the Rong and the Di significant advantages in warfare, as both enemies and allies in the ninth to fourth centuries BC.[34] The demand for horses is dramatically displayed in cemeteries in the neighbouring Qi state. In the most remarkable, attributed to the

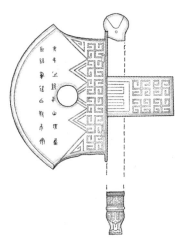

A bronze axe, height 29.4 cm.

sixth century BC, but possibly later, archaeologists, having excavated approximately 250 horses, estimate that 600 horses were buried encircling a central tomb (plate 29).[35] Later tombs of the Qi lords and their families were accompanied by lesser rows of horses, as such extravagance could only be realised through contact with northern horsemen. Horse-drawn chariots ceased to be as prominent and swathes of infantry were mobilised in the ever-growing battles.[36] Cavalry was directed at northern invaders, but chariots were still buried to confer status in the afterlife.[37]

The ceremonial bronze fittings of King Cuo's chariots, for instance the axle caps, are embellished by fine inlays of silver and gold. His weapons also had ornaments for the staff, decorated with birds, again with a patterned inlay, this time of feathers. The northerners' fondness for gold was now coupled with a growing interest in inlay for weaponry, chariots and horse tack. Gold was, after all, rare. Among more obviously ceremonial preparations are two rather puzzling objects. The first is a weapon, a wide axe with a curved sharp edge, a later copy of the axes used by the Shang and early Zhou. It carries the inscription:

The Son of Heaven [the Zhou king] established [my] state,

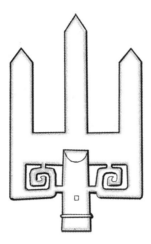

A bronze standard, height 1.19 m. With a staff it would have stood at about 7 m.

[I], Wen, the Marquis of Zhongshan,
Made this military axe,
To admonish the myriad people.[38]

It is not clear when the axe was made, but possibly before the time of King Cuo, and he inherited it. We do not know whether or not the Zhou king was involved in the establishment of the Zhongshan state. The axe may simply have been buried here so that King Cuo's legitimacy resonated in the afterlife. The other mystery is a group of five bronze symbolic standards, each with three points, shaped like three early jade halberd blades and linked together to form an impressive silhouette. It is estimated that, on their poles, they would have stood at about seven metres. They were previously thought to be travelling equipment, perhaps to stand next to a tent. However, like the axe, they are in fact references to past rituals. They are fourth-century BC versions of the thin bronze standards placed on coffins in the eighth century BC. It is possible that they stood on the chariot carrying the king's coffin or on another vehicle in the cortège. These special bronzes echo ancient ritual power. Their rather unlikely presence in this fourth-century BC tomb implies that the king had advisers familiar with early practices among the polities of the Wei Valley.

A hunting scene on the outside of a bronze basin of the
fifth century BC. The chariot drivers are wearing long robes,
while the huntsmen are dressed in leggings.

It is difficult to know how the third pit fitted into the ritual programme. Perhaps it did not. It may have been one of the many
innovations now chosen to enhance the afterlife. Two chariots and
six horses were found, alongside a tent, thought to have been circular.
It is possible that this was hunting equipment.[39] Two skeletons buried
beside the chariots were probably of hunting dogs. Much prized, we
assume by the king himself, they wore sumptuous collars of alternating gold and silver tubular bands. More unusual was the burial of
ten whole goats. This deviated from standard customs for tombs of
pastoralists in the north-west, where only the head and hoofs were
buried. The goats were possibly meant to be sacrificial offerings, not
at the time of the funeral but in the future. This would have allowed
for sacrifices in pursuit of victory and good fortune in the afterlife,
before hunting expeditions or even battles.[40]

To the west of the chariot pits was a long pit for boats, 30 metres in
length, divided into two parts. No other lord or local king we know
about had such a luxury. In the southern section were three wooden
boats joined by iron fixings.[41] Fragments of musical instruments and
remains of a canopy suggest that they were for pleasure cruising. In
the northern section was a longer boat, which may have been used
for expeditions along the local Hutuo River, or even for naval skirmishes. River battles sometimes appear on bronze vessels of the fifth
to fourth centuries BC. The Zhao king Wuling also mentioned that

Warfare on boats, with rowers in the galleys and armed soldiers
with flags on the decks, from a bronze vessel, fifth century BC.

his state lacked boats to defend the borders against Zhongshan and
Qi. He may even have known of the boats in Zhongshan's arsenal.
King Cuo needed and valued all this equipment, as he himself was
a key player in the military adventures of the late fourth century BC.

Iron nails in the pits evoke the strength of Zhongshan on the battlefield. They were the product of large-scale manufacture at Lingshou.
Iron weapons, agricultural tools, cauldrons and armour were probably all cast there and traded widely among neighbouring states,
especially Yan and Qi. Iron-casting is one of ancient China's most
famous technological developments, almost 2,000 years before a similar advance in Europe in the fourteenth century AD. Iron had already
been used in the steppe for many centuries, where it was generally
produced in bloomer furnaces at around 1,000 degrees Celsius and
then forged. Once iron had become better known to the south of
the Loess Plateau, the settled states developed their existing skills in
high temperatures for ceramic- and bronze-casting to handle iron.
They took ironwork to a completely new level by creating small blast
furnaces, fuelled by charcoal, that could melt iron at temperatures
approaching 1,500 degrees Celsius.[42] At this temperature, with the iron

in a semi-liquid state, a great range of casting was possible. Cast iron is very hard but brittle and heat treatment (annealing) was developed by heating the iron either in lumps or, once the actual implements had been cast, at a relatively low temperature to reduce the carbon content. Both technologies had developed and spread among the states of the Central Plains during the fifth century BC.

While iron advanced the development of weapons and armour, the transformation came when cast iron was used for tools. Iron tools allowed farming communities to move into less favourable regions to clear scrub and trees. Searches for more agricultural land northwards were one of the activities that had provoked encounters and combat with the Rong and the Di. Zhongshan is a clear example of two trends that prevailed over the period down to the Qin unification in 221 BC. As pastoralists were drawn south into farming regions and state geopolitics, the lands of the Loess Plateau no longer offered a buffer. Moreover, when the central states moved to farm further north, they encountered resistance not only from pastoralists moving south but, more critically, from the riders of the steppe.[43]

The Kingdom of Zhongshan reflects the great skill with which the newcomers had accommodated themselves within the wider Zhou community. But such assimilation had an unexpected consequence as, in the third century BC, the First Emperor began to join up existing sections of wall into a continuous defence of the territory he claimed: the Great Wall. Even without the threats from the north, the states generated unceasing conflict among themselves, in which iron was also widely exploited.

We know about King Cuo's military campaign from beautifully engraved inscriptions on several of his ritual vessels. Over thirty different vessels were divided between the west and the east chambers. Nine tripods, or *ding*, suggest that those in the west were used as primary vessels in offerings to the ancestors. These were sober bronzes with little or no decoration. Two long inscriptions of more than 400 characters each were engraved on the outside of two vessels, on the largest tripod, and on a square flask, *hu*. A shorter one appears on another circular *hu* placed in the eastern chamber, with an inscription added by King Cuo's son, Ci.[44]

Cuo's set of nine tripods was an indication of his royal status. Initially it is possible that, following the ritual reform, the tripod set of nine was reserved for the Zhou king; but from at least the fifth century BC onwards, rulers of the individual states started to claim sets of nine for themselves. Much the largest of the king's tripods, over 60 kilos in weight, has rare iron legs, emphasising its importance. It carries the inscription across both the body and lid.[45] On all earlier tripods, long inscriptions were cast on the inside. Engraving, not casting, the inscription on the outside was a major departure that implied that the ceremonies included the living, who could read the words, as well as the ancestors. Inscriptions inside a vessel suggested that they were transmitted to the ancestors with the aroma of food. Cuo's flask had an especially smooth surface for the viewer to read its long inscription. Four enormous cast dragons on its corners near the top draw attention to its message in graceful calligraphy. It also carries a note, stating that it was made from metal (seized) from Yan, presumably on a campaign in 314 BC and cast shortly before King Cuo died.

The subject of the long inscriptions on the square *hu* was the successful attack in 314 BC by the allied armies of Qi and Zhongshan on the state of Yan.[46] And they reveal the reason for this invasion, namely the decision by the chancellor, Zi Zhi, to force the abdication of the ruler of Yan, so he could take over. All three inscriptions condemn this event, rather than focusing on the details of the subsequent battle, and express that

'I, Zhou [the Chancellor of Zhongshan under King Cuo] desired attendant knights and grandees in order to pacify the borders of the State of Yan.' Because of this, I [Zhou] took on a tiger-skin buff-coat and helmet to punish the disobedient. Since Yan's old ruler, Zi Kuai, and the new ruler, Zi Zhi, did not employ the proper rites and decorum and went heedlessly against the proper order, therefore the state was ruined and they [themselves] died. There was not even a single man who [tried] to save them.[47]

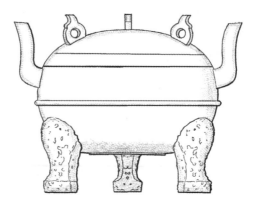

The largest of the king's bronze tripods, or *ding*,
with iron legs, standing at 51.5 cm.

Zhongshan claimed that they were reacting to unrighteous behaviour, a breach of conduct by which a minister should offer respect to his superior.[48] The perils of such disregard for hierarchy also advance King Cuo's own objectives. The inscriptions pair the criticism of Zi Zhi at Yan with praise for the chancellor of Zhongshan, Sima Zhou. Inscriptions that celebrated the virtue of the king would have been more typical. The inscription on the tripod tells us that the Sima Zhou had served two other kings as well as King Cuo. In addition, he controlled the army as the highest-ranking general:

> Now my elder [minister] Zhou has recently led three army troops to punish the unethical state. Brandishing drumsticks and tolling bells, he broke through and opened up the [walled] frontiers, several hundred *li* in every direction, and the outlying cities amounting to ten. He overcame and destroyed that great state. I, the unworthy, built upon his virtue and congratulate his strength.[49]

With this military success, Sima Zhou was obviously a threat to the authority of King Cuo. Would Sima Zhou oust his ruler? To ensure that he did not follow Zi Zhi's example, King Cuo includes Sima Zhou's own voice in the inscription. The king had an agenda. His followers, and indeed the world of the ancestors, should take care not

Square flask, *hu*, with inscriptions on all four sides and
four dragons on the corners, height 63 cm.

to be misled by ambitious chancellors and generals. And with this
comes a second warning, namely that the proper organisation of the
state must be observed if people are to prosper. Hierarchies of authority, modelled on seniority in a lineage, which had been entrenched
by the early Zhou, were fundamental to the legitimacy of a ruler.
The generations of the family were an enduring model; one could
not (and should not) replace one's father or grandfather in the generational sequence. The importance of a regulated family in the local
community and in the court remained a shared norm, even if it was
sometimes more of an ideal than a reality. To drive home not just the
words but the ancient culture of the Zhou, the Zhongshan inscriptions made use of phrases that would have been recognised by all from
poems in *The Book of Poetry*, collected several hundred years earlier.[50]

At the end of the inscription, the king punctuates his fears and
urges his successors to avoid the calamities that befell Yan. Moral

and political catastrophe could be brought on by the reckless impropriety of chancellors. This is a caution to his successors, but also to Sima Zhou:

> With full respect and deep reverence! Clearly proclaim to future generations: it is disobedience that gives rise to disaster and it is obedience that gives rise to blessing.
>
> Record it in the bamboo annals to warn succeeding kings: it is virtue that will keep the people attached [to the ruler]; it is by righteousness that one may last long.
>
> May the sons of sons and the grandsons of grandsons forever treasure and use [this] without limit.[51]

King Cuo's engraved inscriptions could immediately be read, perhaps out loud, by the ritual specialists, as part of the ceremony attended by his lineage. All would have quickly recognised his anxiety. Many of the longer Western Zhou inscriptions had similar but far less explicit intentions; for example, grants of land seem at first reading to proclaim the might of the king and the rewards lords could reap for loyalty. But underlying these inscriptions also lay threats of military uprising and disloyalty – the gifts, recorded for posterity, were an insurance policy to secure devotion in unsettled times. As the Zhou had avoided publishing their difficulties, in most cases problems were not spelled out. The opposite is true at Zhongshan, where the risks are crystal clear. Including Sima Zhou's name had another clear purpose: to engrave for eternity the king's direct exhortation for filial behaviour and loyalty. This change may, in part, reflect the threat of the growing power of educated officials, *Shi*, who had already ousted other rulers.[52] In addition, the Zhongshan rulers had only recently been drawn into the circle of the major states. Their links were tenuous. This may have prompted the quotations from *The Book of Poetry* to claim that Zhongshan shared a Zhou heritage. The inscriptions were a convenient way to support the political strategies of the king. This was especially needed because of the king's northern background.

The ritual set does, at first glance, suggest that King Cuo wanted to present himself as a full member of the central states. Yet they are austere. We recognise the forms, but there is no attempt to engage us. They do not have the lavish ornament that we have already seen on the inlaid chariot fittings and weapon ferrules. The straightforward forms show us that they were not intended to achieve a particularly strong visual impact. The two most imposing vessels, the tripod and the square flask, were first and foremost vehicles for inscriptions. The vessels had been adjusted to a new political purpose. We also know from traces found inside the tripods that Zhongshan did not follow the typical offerings of cattle, sheep and pigs, as seen in the tomb of the Marquis of Zeng.[53] The remains have been identified as those of horse meat in the biggest tripod and of dog meat in one of the smaller ones.[54] These foods were much more characteristic of people in the north.

More elaborate vessels in black burnished ceramic were in the west chamber. The solemn colour suggests that these too belong to the ritual offerings. But the decoration is curvilinear. The ceramics appear to be in perfect condition, so may have been made for the burial only. As similar ceramics have been found in Yan state, the Zhongshan officials may have borrowed the practice from there.[55] Such inconsistences suggest that there was a modicum of uncertainty about the exact designations and practices of the ceremonial banquets.

Objects offer subtle hints at the ways in which new ideas and artistic styles infiltrated and travelled between states. Small carvings with stripes along their backs are jade versions of the earlier golden tigers from the steppe. No text will tell us about these revered and feared beasts. Yet they show us two things: the borrowing of animal subjects from the northerners and the preference the central states gave to jade

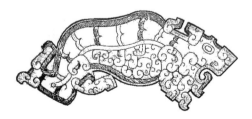

A jade tiger, length 10.9 cm.

over gold. Other jades are shaped as dragons or discs. Dense scrolls on all of them are reinterpretations of bronze decoration.[56] All the jades were in the west chamber with the primary ritual vessels, which may not have fitted with the northern taste of the king, represented in the eastern chamber, where gold was more valued than jade.

Finds in tombs accompanying King Cheng's burial reveal that jade had a different role at Zhongshan. Intriguing jades were found in the subordinate tombs, including a stone gaming board with intertwined snakes. Nine separate sections, of which four are carved with interlacing snakes, and four with dragons and animal heads, some combined together, are a spectacle. The ninth, central square has more heads within triangles. Looking closely among the dizzying motifs, we can see angular L-shaped markings. This is a board game known as *liubo*.

Board for the game of *liubo* made of several
pieces of carved stone, 45 by 40.2 cm.

The markings alone, irrespective of the splendid imagery, provided the roads that determined the course of play. The two players each needed six pieces, rectangular blocks, to move around the board and six rods or dice. The twelve pieces in total matched the twelve divisions of the year, which may have connected the game to predictions for the prosperity of the players.[57] The throwing of the rods or dice introduced the matter of fate, which played a significant role in divination. The Zhou and their successors were always anxious to obtain evidence of what might happen on particular days, which led in due course to the creation of auspicious calendars, still widely used in China. Images of the spirits playing *liubo* appear on bricks of Han tombs. And these geometric marks on the board continued to appear on Han mirrors cast in the later centuries; the game and its beliefs certainly lasted down to third century AD. From this board, we see a local interest in the wider cosmos beyond the ancestral cult. Despite the growing communication between distant regions, local beliefs rose in prominence as societies became more diverse and more complex.

If we turn to the extraordinary contents of the eastern chamber, we find more about King Cuo's world of spirits. A pair of flasks, with

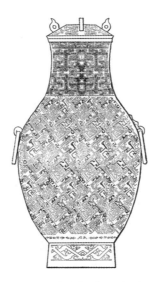

One of a pair of alcohol flasks, inlaid with copper,
turquoise and lacquer, from the east chamber, height 45 cm.

A bronze basin with a raptor at the centre, height 47.5 cm.

square sections, inlaid with copper, turquoise and lacquer and an inscription naming a leading craftsman, Bo Geng, as overseer, quite closely resemble a pair from the state of Yan.[58] They may have been brought back to Lingshou after the invasion of Yan and their glittering surfaces diverge from the plain set for the ancestral cult. They introduce another universe, as does a strange basin on a stand with a raptor flying across it. Its purpose and its associations are just as unknown. But the inlay and the raptor belong to a different and surprising language of objects. We are also confronted by a new spirit or being in the form of two winged creatures in the eastern chest, one of two pairs cast in bronze, their vicious jaws open in their broad heads, scanning the landscape. They have four sturdy legs, each with four threatening claws, and their bodies and wings are covered in silver spirals. Impressively long, they each weigh around 10 to 11.5 kilos. Wings allowed them to soar above the human world. We are used to wings in a biblical context, but wings rarely appeared in China – even most dragons did not have them. As wings were not then, nor later, a feature of the spirit world and immortals in this part of East Asia, it is likely that the

A bronze winged creature, inlaid with silver, length 40.1 cm,
and an ox inlaid with silver and gold, length 55.5 cm.

ideas which lay behind the creation of these beasts must have come
from elsewhere, perhaps Central Asia.[59] We sense their tension, as if
they are ready to spring into action. They are part of a stage setting,
with five other animals cast in bronze, in the eastern chamber. Two
other bronze animals, an ox and a rhinoceros, probably carried the two
ends of a rectangular screen. And at the central joint, the screen was
supported by a most inventive sculpture: a tiger with a strong, slinking
body holding a deer in its jaws (plate 28). The tiger swerves as it attacks
and devours the deer. Here we recognise a subject brought from the
steppe, of a predator seizing its prey.[60] Steppe tigers and raptors clutching deer or rams, almost invariably shown in silhouette, were here

brokered with the three-dimensional moving beasts in the king's tomb. On several earlier fifth- and fourth-century BC bronzes, including some found at Lingshou, are dense scenes of strange creatures, some with wings (below) – local interpretations of northern myths, perhaps ultimately sourced in Iran.[61] This may be what brought wings to the attention of the Zhongshan craftsmen.

Dramatic lifelike creatures are not a simple translation of the steppe subject. Some brilliant craftsmen moved away from the silhouette to satisfy new belief systems, bringing them into a physical existence. Bright copper, silver or gold inlay was used to emphasise their realistic bodies. Perhaps the carved lacquered wooden sculpture of the south offered beguiling models.[62] This stimulus is seen most clearly in similar deer in bronze, with inlaid droplets in gold to indicate their coats, recalling the red drops on the lacquered coats of the deer in the tomb of the Marquis of Zeng. They support another extraordinary object in this eastern chamber, a bronze frame for a table. A square frame, perhaps to hold a wooden sheet in place, is supported by four dragons at the corners with four peacocks and four deer between them. This group facilitated an interaction with invisible spirits. These beasts contrast with other whirling creatures in the tomb of the Marquis Yi; two different craft traditions and two separate world-views coexisted. As at Zeng, the great artisanal workshops here offered remarkable aesthetic drama. In other areas of the Central Plains a few three-dimensional bronze figures were made, but none with the skill and expressiveness of the tiger and winged beasts

A mythical hunting scene, a detail from a large
flask from the fifth century BC, height 46.4 cm.

owned by King Cuo. Sculptures in inlaid bronze are distinct from the traditional bronze-casting of the day. The King of Zhongshan and his court had harnessed skills from the central states to express their own beliefs and desires. As we cannot meet and talk with the many people who made use of the objects, we will never discover the numerous associations that they may have carried.

The eastern chamber has sometimes been described as providing for King Cuo's everyday life – for eating, drinking and relaxing. The vessels in the western chamber are then seen as being for special occasions, for ritual ceremonies. Yet the exquisite animal bronzes in the eastern chamber are anything but ordinary. They must have been for display and engagement. Or perhaps they were, in our language, representative of spirits. A separation between representation and our notions of reality did not exist at Zhongshan, so by making winged creatures in bronze, these spirits were present in the afterlife. The same is true of an extraordinary lamp in the shape of a tree. Its branches each bear a tray for oil and a wick. Hanging from these

Inlaid bronze table frame, width 47.5 cm.

are monkeys who seem to be tossing fruit to small figures standing below. Lamps first appeared in the Warring States period, but we do not know what inspired their use – perhaps interaction again with Central Asia.[63] Buildings were probably lit earlier by torches of wood.

The material in the eastern chest gathered ideas from different directions, part of the ever-growing contacts between the Central Plains and societies in the steppe and Central Asia. Although King Cuo's lineage had earlier belonged to the Di, with a background among peoples on the Loess Plateau, he was also eager to join the

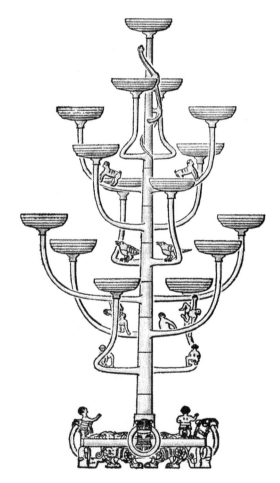

A bronze lamp, height 82.9 cm.

society of the organised states in the fourth century BC. There was a blending process under way, with beliefs of the northern, western and even southern regions being melded with the ritual vessels and the ceremonial banquets for the ancestors. King Cuo bridged two worlds, even for a time bringing them together, symbolised by the western and eastern chests of his coffin chamber. He celebrated his virtues and pursued his objectives after death. With his plan for the afterlife, he hoped and expected that his tombs would be built as he demanded. The inscribed bronzes announced his wish that his kingdom would not be overturned by grasping ministers. His offerings to his ancestors, which were followed by his descendants, were intended to secure his future. At the same time, in the same tomb and in the same afterlife, the king enjoyed another part of his universe, a world of spirits, which was presented with great confidence. And in the king's eyes, these existed side by side.

We have so far visited ten different regions, with different landfall and climates, different customs, different ways of life and afterlife and very different cosmoses, at Liangzhu, Taosi, Anyang, Sanxingdui, Baoji, Rui, Yuhuangmiao, Zhongli, Zeng and now Zhongshan. As the customs and social hierarchies of the ancestral cult were gradually adopted, often far from the Yellow River basin, they were overlaid with alternative beliefs about the seen and unseen. For all rulers who aspired to control their territories, ancestors, deities, spirits and local legends were crucial aspects of their present and their future.

PART IV

Conquest on Horseback, 300–221 BC

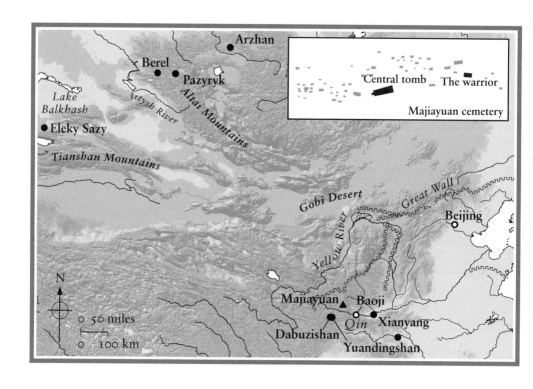

Majiayuan and the western edge of the Qin state

II.

Catacombs and Chariots

Five men with pointed hats tied under their chins, with a horse, walk calmly among a procession on the eastern staircase of the Apadana at Persepolis, the great audience hall of the kings of the Persian Achaemenid Empire (550–330 BC).[1] These carved figures are the Saka from the steppe north of Iran, offering 'tribute' or gifts as one of multiple delegations from all regions drawn under Achaemenid rule – Syria, Lydia, Armenia, Bactria and Egypt. Founded by Darius the Great in 518 BC, the Apadana, with its towering columns, shows the Saka with their long beards wearing short tunics, leggings and boots, with shethed daggers (*akinkai*) hanging from their belts (plate 30). They carry torcs or armbands, perhaps in gold, and three with heavy woollen or felt textiles, perhaps cloaks and leggings – the essential luxuries for life on the steppe. The horse is a sign of their formidable power. As in so many statements of authority by rulers across Eurasia, the procession and variety of the people in it, the notion of tribute even, conceal the reality, that the Achaemenids had repeatedly to subdue the steppe peoples to the north to safeguard their empire. There is no suggestion that their King Cyrus II had been killed in a battle on the steppe, nor that his campaign against the Massagetai on the lower Oxus in 530 BC had failed.

The founders of the Achaemenids were originally also pastoralists who had settled in the ninth century BC around Pasargadae on the south-eastern Iranian Plateau. From there, they built up one of the world's most powerful empires. Undoubted parallels emerge between how the Achaemenids interacted with their steppe neighbours and how the Zhou and the Qin dealt with the eastern steppe. The herders and stockbreeders brought important materials and horses to the

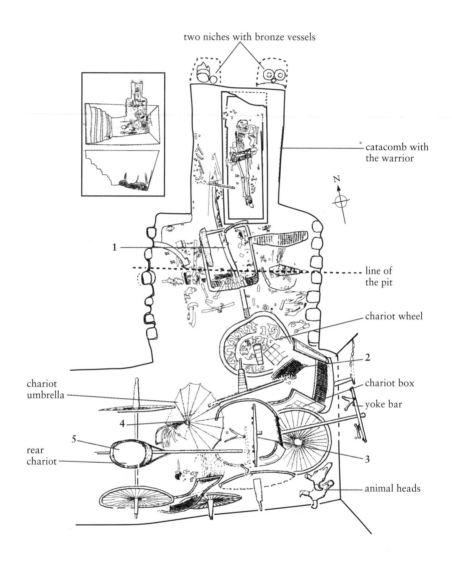

two niches with bronze vessels

catacomb with
the warrior

1

line of
the pit

chariot wheel

2

chariot
umbrella

chariot box

yoke bar

4

rear
chariot

5

3

animal heads

N

The tomb of the warrior at Majiayuan.

settled states in both Iran and China, while the people of the steppe imported their bronze metalwork and fine patterned textiles. Tombs below large mounds have revealed the wealth of the pastoralists in gold-embellished weapons, belts and ornaments. And from the ninth to the third century BC, a shared material culture spread the whole length of the steppe.

Belts, torcs, earrings and bracelets reside with warriors buried in the fourth to the third century BC in a cemetery at Majiayuan on the hills of southern Gansu province, pressed up against the regions where the Qin had earlier established their own burial grounds (in the seventh to the sixth century BC). The Qin had moved east by the time these stockbreeders sheltered beneath the Liupan range and assumed a high vantage point across undulating hills. Small towns, villages and carefully tended terraces planted with maize and vegetables fill the modern landscape, but in the fourth and third centuries BC it would have been covered in woodland. Today the tombs look down on the small town of Zhangjiachuan, one of several Muslim enclaves in Gansu province where minarets thread the sky. Sogdians, merchants from present-day Uzbekistan, set up trading posts from the fifth century AD, reaching from Central Asia to Xi'an, and built temples for their Zoroastrian faith.[2] Sogdians were followed from the late seventh century AD by merchants and officials from the newly established Islamic lands further west.[3]

The Majiayuan cemetery is a rich repository of the steppe stockbreeding culture that stretched from the Saka in the west to the northern Loess Plateau in the east. There were between sixty and seventy tombs in its two parts. The more substantial tombs in the eastern section form an arc around a central tomb, which was unfortunately destroyed.[4] The mouth of this tomb, clearly for the leader, is 10 metres wide at the entrance and has a ramp 30 metres long, with steps down either side. These descend into the coffin chamber at an immense depth of 14 metres. Such an extravagant ramp and tomb depth could only be achieved in loess. The steps along the ramp were a northern choice. They would have allowed many to accompany their leader, carrying and displaying his coffin. Among the surviving finds are fragments of glass beads and a few small gold discs, with faces, whose conspicuous moustaches are in the style of the steppe rather than of the central states (page 313). Full sets of horse skeletons have also been recovered.

The central tomb and the surrounding arc of subordinate tombs resemble the arrangement of the contemporary great steppe kurgans.[5] To replicate a kurgan, the leader at Majiayuan must have been a venerated lord from the steppe, with his entourage of warriors and attendants. We only have this cemetery to measure his status. And too often he and his clan are subsumed under the name Rong. The tombs at Majiayuan are dated to the late fourth or third centuries BC. However, we have no sense as to whether or not the occupants were buried together with their leader. But the similar belts, weapons and chariots distributed across the tombs do suggest that they were all created over a relatively short time.

The careful arrangement of the Majiayuan cemetery, the exquisite gold and silver now displayed in a museum in Zhangjiachuan, and the many iron weapons, chariots and animal heads are indicative of an intimidating group. One almost square pit holds over 100 heads and hoofs of sheep and an unrecorded number of horse heads.[6] Even if the people had small settlements for the winter, none of which have been found, in the summer months they had to pasture their herds on the wide summits, such as the hill where this cemetery lies. As they travelled with animals, they must have lived in tents or simple shelters. Thus the killing of so many animals from precious herds, on which they depended for their livelihoods, implies some major tragedy or political catastrophe. We do not know why these people gathered in the Liupan foothills to create a great cemetery, but clearly something important lay behind this moment in their history.

Just as we only have unreliable narratives about the death of Cyrus at the hands of the Massagetai, we also have rather biased descriptions of the mobile pastoralists on the borders of the settled agricultural plains. This almost deliberate ignorance – seen among other settled civilisations – was a feature throughout much of Chinese history, arising out of disdain for 'the other'. Sima Qian in his description of the Xiongnu, who were in his time a major power to the north, paints a picture of the gulf between those who wrote in Chinese characters and those who 'have no writing':

> As early as the time of Emperors Yao and Shun [the legendary early rulers] and before, we hear of these people, known as the Mountain Barbarians, Xianyun or Hunzhu, living in the region of the northern barbarians and wandering from place to place pasturing their animals. The animals they raise consist mainly of horses, cows and sheep, but include such rare beasts as camels, asses, mules and the wild horses known as *taotu* and *tuoqi*. They move about in search of water and pasture and have no walled cities or fixed dwellings, nor do they engage in any kind of agriculture. Their lands, however, are divided into regions under the control of various leaders. They have no writing and even promises and agreements are only verbal. The little boys start out learning to ride sheep and shoot rats and birds with a bow and arrow, and when they get a little older they shoot foxes and hares, which are used for food. Thus all young men are able to use a bow and act as armed cavalry in time of war.[7]

This same tone is repeated in Caesar's comments on the Germans across the Rhine.[8] Modern historians have also taken a rather dismissive approach to ancient peoples who did not record their lives. Majiayuan shows that literacy is not essential for a rich and successful cultural life. Its tombs reflect an affluent society living a rewarding life, occasionally turning to disrupt and destroy the lives of settled farmers but, arguably more importantly, spending their time enriching their own lives and commemorating their achievements. We would be echoing the condescension of our predecessors if we only concentrated on combat and ignored the deep sophistication of mobile cultures. Buried at Majiayuan are early fragments of a people who continually matched and often challenged the settled societies not only in China, but in Iran, Anatolia and Europe for many centuries to come.[9]

Some of the subordinate tombs in the arc are L-shaped, with steep steps on one side leading down to the base. The tomb owner on which we shall concentrate was a warrior. He was placed in a coffin at a right angle to the floor, in a small cavity or room, a catacomb (plate 32). The catacomb was another afterlife dwelling, reproducing tents and shelters, with the chariots and animal heads in the open shaft of the tomb representing the animal pens. Catacomb tombs were important among the Scythians.[10] Seen much less frequently in the eastern steppe, they are even more rare in China. When they do occur they were for fighters, above all chariot drivers and horse managers.[11] Three other cemeteries with catacomb tombs have also been found in Gansu province.[12]

Two tiny niches behind the head of our warrior held bronze vessels. These are often taken as confirmation that he and his comrades were members of tribes called the Western Rong by Sima Qian and vassals of the Qin. This was a typical way of interpreting the warriors' lives within the context of the central states.[13] Their culture and their wealth would not have been recognised or understood. Two tall bronze flasks were traditional alcohol vessels but, tucked in the small crevices of a catacomb, they must have had a different purpose. They were precious and prestigious possessions, but not part of any ritual set. The same is true of a bronze steamer, a tripod to be filled with water over a fire and beneath a basin to steam grain or vegetables. As we saw with relative newcomers, such as Ya Chang or Yu Bo, their allegiance to the ancestral cult was exhibited in their complete sets of bronze vessels in canonical shapes. Here the flasks were probably acquired as gifts or spoils rather than made locally. As with the vessels at Yuhuangmiao, these objects were valued for their bronze, not for their role in the ancestral cult.

In the spirit of the carvings of the Saka on the Apadana, it has been attractive for some scholars to overlook the dates and to think of the people at Majiayuan as lower-ranking subjects, with the Qin, and their early tombs about 150 kilometres to the south-west, as their overlords.[14] As the Zhou left the Wei Valley in the eighth century BC, they encouraged the Qin to take over their land. This is set out by Sima Qian, and, in explaining their genealogy, he offers a brief note about one earlier local leader, Feizi, living at the time of the Zhou king Xiao (872–866 BC):

> Feizi lived at Quanqiu or Dog Hill. He loved horses and domestic animals and was skilled at raising and breeding them. The people of Dog Hill mentioned him to King Xiao of the Zhou dynasty, and King Xiao summoned him and ordered him to pasture the royal horses in the area between the Qian and the Wei Rivers [north-west of Baoji]. The horses greatly increased in number.[15]

Sima Qian then links the success of the Qin with their supposed supremacy over Western Rong pastoralists:

> In his thirty-seventh year [619 BC] Duke Mu [the Qin state ruler] employed Yong Yu's advice [a member of the Rong] to carry out an attack on the Rong ruler, acquiring twelve new states, extending his territory 1,000 *li*, and making himself overlord of the Western Rong. The Son of Heaven despatched Guo, the Duke of Shao, to congratulate Duke Mu and present him with a golden drum.[16]

We have no sense of what Sima Qian meant by the Rong states, as the Rong did not create polities that resembled those of central China. Sima Qian's history describes the seventh century BC, three or four centuries before the construction of the Majiayuan cemetery. He was interpreting past events through his own unfavourable lens, and also knew that his Han rulers were confronted in the north by the Xiongnu pastoralists. He undoubtedly wanted to demonstrate that rulers of Chinese states could subdue borderland clans. And had Sima Qian known of the people of Majiayuan, we can be sure that he would have regarded them as insignificant newcomers and called them the Rong.

Today, the people at Majiayuan are still often named as the Western Rong, following Sima Qian, a way to fit them neatly into the history of the Qin. However, they were not settled agriculturalists. They had probably only recently arrived in the basin. Before them, the area had been occupied by others, perhaps including Feizi and his horses, with their own local customs, such as east–west burials.[17] Flexed body positions of those earlier tomb occupants also tell us that many had contact with the north-west.[18] We know that, over several centuries, the Qin moved eastwards and by the time the cemetery was installed at Majiayuan, they had already established substantial cities and cemeteries further east along the Wei Valley.[19] In the late fourth to third centuries BC, the Qin were well on the way to realising their ambitions of conquest. Their interests were to the east; the people at Majiayuan, if the Qin – from kings to peasants – knew of them at all, were probably simply regarded as a useful source of horses.

Majiayuan wealth is displayed in one of the accompanying intact tombs, with the bronze vessels we have already seen; it is among the most lavish.[20] The entrance of the shaft is 12.6 metres east–west and 6.7 metres north–south. It is precipitously deep at 7 metres, which is still much shallower than the leader's central tomb at 14 metres. A small opening at one corner, on the north side, is the entry to the catacomb. On the west are nine steps. They do not look as though they are intended to be used, as they are relatively narrow. Some have suggested that the steps signify rank, since the numbers vary among the Majiayuan tombs. However, to be a useful marker of status, they must also have had some purpose, or signalled a function. It is possible that the steps offered access to mourners during the ceremony, belonging to a wider tradition that we first saw at Zhongli.[21] Methods by which to place the coffin and arrange the chariots at the base of the main shaft have now been lost, but perhaps ramps were used that were later removed, although no traces have yet been found.

The wooden coffin in the catacomb was decorated with flat silhouettes of striding ibex with immense curved horns. These must have been cut out of sheets of silver or gold, with craftsmen treating the fine metal in effect as a textile. Repeated small holes in some of them suggest that the animals were sewn to cloth, perhaps draped over the coffin.[22] Around the warrior's neck was a gold pectoral, cut from sheet metal. He also had a similar one in silver, now shifted to one side. They are much less elaborate than the immense torc or pectoral in Arzhan II, with its procession of creatures, but they had the same

An ibex, with holes for stitching, length 7.5 cm.

purpose: to draw attention to the warrior's head.[23] We share this tradition in the West, with our sparkling jewels, necklaces, crowns and diadems. The Majiayuan warrior also wore earrings. These are complicated tiny layers of gold around turquoise beads hanging from a gold loop to be pierced through his lobes. On his right arm was a band of gold, its bulging layers alternating with inlaid fragments of glass and faience (glass stained blue-green to look like turquoise) among twisted wire. Armbands of this form have been found in Siberia and had a distant origin in Western Asia.[24] As an essential part of their culture, steppe leaders gained status by acquiring goods that they could distribute to their followers.[25] They displayed their gold and silver on their person, presenting themselves as charismatic leaders to attract clients, increase their herds and overcome enemies. This was very different from the tiered hierarchies that gave status to the rulers of the Central Plains.

In the same exhibition of status, the warrior also had three belts, following the inventory of steppe possessions of the Mountain Rong at Yuhuangmiao. Belts were a favourite item for those living on the grasslands with animals. Tools and weapons hung from them.[26] The most visible and presumably the most important belt has vertical gold plaques alternating between lines of turquoise and carnelian beads. Along the upper and lower edges of the belt were small gold bosses. The plaques are in openwork, each with two raptors hacking at two snakes with their beaks. On the tips of the raptors' tails are small circles, which may be eyes of miniature birds also grasping at the snakes. The two smaller belts also carry intertwined creatures. All are local

Raptors entwined with snakes and small bird heads on a belt, length 6.4 cm.

interpretations of the auspicious 'predator and prey' theme. There is also an enormous cast-gold plaque with a hook to join a ring at the other end of a belt. Remains of red stripes show two tigers. Each grips a stag by the neck, whose legs and hooves are bent in fear. Dazzling with colour inlays among the gold, the creatures reveal how unique the three-dimensional sculptures were at Zhongshan. King Cuo was recreating memories of the mobile world he had left behind that the warrior at Majiayuan was still living in full.

Herding, riding and travelling people attached their valuables to themselves. It was a steppe aesthetic to fasten them to clothes and hang tools from a belt. Here at Majiayuan, the iron weapons and tools are badly corroded. In the late fourth and third centuries BC, belts had not yet been taken up enthusiastically by the lords of the central states, perhaps because they did not themselves carry weapons; they had infantry armies to fight for them. In China the aura of power has generally been maintained not by such individual display but by highly organised retinues, with the ranks of officials and soldiers marked in different robes and the ruler almost out of sight, as seen in the seventeenth- and eighteenth-century paintings of court rituals and receptions. The allocations to Ya Chang, Yu Bo and the Lord of Rui of bronze ritual vessels are early evidence that numbers, size and uniformity were significant.[27]

In life, the Majiayuan warrior is not likely to have worn three belts with gold plaques. This was an extravagance reserved for the afterlife. He had been able to commission, or acquire, several belts of supreme quality. Where the gold was mined or sieved in rivers is another puzzle. The most likely sources are the famous gold seams of the Altai Mountains. The warrior and his comrades clearly belonged to a society where gold was readily available to those in power, perhaps by exchange. Such precious materials may also have come from the Tianshan range, where similar gold ornaments were owned by steppe lords, as on the clothes of a lord buried at Issyk near Almaty in Kazakhstan.[28] And yet at Majiayuan the warrior is only a first among equals. This was a whole clan of impressive individuals.

Boots were an essential part of the warrior's daily life on horseback. Silver soles have survived in his tomb, which were attached to boots for the afterlife.[29] The steppe people are embodied in a small lead figure from one of the other tombs in the Majiayuan cemetery. Boots and leggings distinguished the northern riders from the farmers of the agricultural basins. Occasionally, the silver soles were imitated in jade, reminding us that, if we move towards the Central Plains, the materials of value changed.[30] There is no jade in any of the tombs at Majiayuan, nor did the people compose the kinds of inscriptions we saw at Zhongshan. The small lead figure also wears a pointed cap with flaps, as on the reliefs at Persepolis.[31] Constant interactions between the Saka and their settled neighbours are displayed on the cliff at Bisitun, where an immense relief of 520–519 BC shows King Darius the Great (522–486 BC), standing much taller than his enemies,

The moustached face of a man in gold, retrieved from the robbed central tomb, height 1.6 cm, and a steppe rider in lead with a pointed cap, a belted tunic, leggings and boots, height 7.5 cm.

and confronting a line of defeated rebel kings, roped together, with the Saka king Skunkha at the rear wearing his tall pointed hat.[32] Darius addresses his subjects, proclaiming his success against conspirators in inscriptions in Old Persian, Elamite and Babylonian, a measure of the reach of his rule. King Skunkha was added after the inscriptions were completed, perhaps as an afterthought or a later conquest. While the Saka had been a persistent presence, the extent of the lands they occupied was unknown to the Achaemenids. Only with much more excavation in Kazakhstan has the might of the Saka come to light. The warrior and his comrades at Majiayuan were members of this network of interlinked societies which could confront powers as awesome as the Achaemenids.[33] The success of this extreme eastern tip of the steppe is further displayed in the Zhangjiachuan museum, with personal effects from other tombs in the cemetery: gold belt plaques made up of four wings of two raptors, plaques with tigers and their prey and belt-hooks of solid gold. A silver wolf presents the dangerous packs that attacked the stockbreeders' herds, particularly in the north and on the mountains. Sheep, mountain goats, tigers and above all wolves were as much part of an imagined landscape as of the natural world. They were repeatedly realised in multiple techniques: in casting, hammering, gold-pressing on a matrix, inlay and granulation, where tiny gold pearls are soldered to a gold sheet. Surprisingly, the technique of tinning bronze had also arrived here from the distant west. These processes alone are testimony to the sharing of ideas, materials and technologies over the steppe.[34] Excavation across South Siberia from Arzhan in the Sayan to the Altai and China's Xinjiang

A gold tiger, length 9.5 cm, and a silver wolf, length 7.7 cm.

province along the Tianshan range stretching more than 3,000 kilometres has revealed similar imagery, powered by similar beliefs and metalwork, as well as almost identical boots, weapons and horse tack.

The chains of Tianshan mountains were not barriers, but paths offering pasture, water and even shelter. People have always moved along them, first as hunters and then with their herds.[35] The formidable early tombs at Arzhan, where kurgans guarded men and their spouses, their possessions: gold pectorals or torcs, gold horses (plate 7), gold-decorated weapons and deer and crouching felines on their clothes – were the ancestors of the tigers and raptors at Majiayuan. Settled agriculturalists would have found it almost impossible to imagine, to reach or to control these communities across South Siberia, western Mongolia and Kazakhstan. It is not surprising that there are no reliable accounts of their activities, particularly as the Zhou had failed to control the neighbouring area around Baoji. We too should never underestimate the power and wealth that the steppe could bestow on its pastoralists in gold, pasture and horses, and via long-distance communication that fostered bands of mounted warriors in later empires.

The Majiayuan warrior echoed his predecessors and borrowed from his contemporaries. At Arzhan II, the leader and his spouse wore clothes with hundreds of small beads sewn on them. These were also found in the warrior's tomb in gold, carnelian, turquoise and faience. Faience originated in Egypt and Western Asia, and had reached central China, perhaps in the tenth century BC. It was especially popular on the north-western borders and trade in faience, sometimes as cups, enjoyed a strong revival in the fourth century BC, as seen in a beaker found at Majiayuan.[36] In some of the tombs the beads were so numerous – on clothes, hats and boots – that sections of the floors of the catacombs were cut out, framed, boxed and taken to the Institute of Archaeology at the provincial capital, Lanzhou, for full excavation in a laboratory there.[37]

The people at Majiayuan were not a negligible group existing on the borderlands of a greater power but essential figures in exchanges across vast regions.[38] If we want to imagine how exchange – the life-blood of the steppe – took place, we can look forward to the great kumis feasts of fermented mare's milk, hosted by the Mongols in the thirteenth and fourteenth centuries AD. As Friar William of Rubruck, sent on a mission to the Mongols by the French king Louis IX, reports in AD 1254:

> On the Feast of St John [24 June] he [the Great Khan Möngke] held a great drinking session, and I counted a hundred and five waggons loaded with mares' milk and ninety horses; and the same again on the feast of the Apostles Peter and Paul [29 June].[39]

As the friar describes, ambassadors from settled states also came to pay respects and give gifts to the Great Khan. We know that the Mongols certainly captured or simply attracted craftsmen from elsewhere to work for them. While delegates from distant settled states probably did not cluster around the tents of earlier pastoralists, their encampments must have drawn members of other steppe clans, and perhaps also craftsmen. In these earlier centuries, steppe lords certainly held large feasts. The Majiayuan warrior owned a small silver beaker for such drinking sessions. Cups in the steppe were often made of wood, sometimes with handles in the shape of a horse's leg and hoof, a reflection of the long-standing love of mare's milk.[40] Stock-breeding neighbours and contemporaries of Majiayuan have been found at a cemetery named Pazyryk in the Altai Mountains. This remote site was identified before the Second World War, but only excavated after it. Today we can see its hanging textiles and wooden tables in the State Hermitage Museum in St Petersburg. Extraordinarily, the tombs, covered by mounds, were kept frozen. And in the graves below, within their log coffins, the bodies of their occupants were still so well preserved by the permafrost that it was possible to see the detail of their tattoos – creatures mirroring the decoration on their saddles and bridles.[41] Unlike elsewhere, the Pazyryk world of wood, textiles and leather has survived. One large hanging carries repeated images in coloured felts of a horseman (plate 31). This gives us a rare picture of how people of the steppe rode and what they wore. We can clearly see his head in profile with a moustache and curled hair. He wears a neat jacket with tight-fitted sleeves over leggings or trousers and boots, rounded at the ends. A small cloak floats behind him. Below his waist is a large quiver and he clutches the reins in his left hand.[42] A rope or cord runs from the saddle under the tail of his horse, a feature also of horse harnesses found at a tomb in Berel, Kazakhstan and later in the cavalry of the First Emperor.[43]

Long-horned mountain sheep attacked by tigers and griffins – borrowed from Iran – are displayed in felt appliqués on Pazyryk saddle covers. We can find similar silhouettes along routes across Xinjiang province into the Altai and as far as Issyk at Almaty.[44] Predators – tigers, eagles and mythical winged beasts – were also prominent on the saddles. The openwork in gold belt plaques of the Majiayuan warrior was a rendition of the felt on these saddles. Another great advantage of Pazyryk is that wooden horse bridles have been preserved. Among the wooden ornaments were carvings of rams leaping on the local mountains, prominent across the steppe, where they were often enhanced with gold or silver foil, as at Berel.[45] They were joined by remarkable bridles with palmette patterns, famous in the architecture and painted ceramics of not only the ancient Assyrians and Greeks, but, above all, the Achaemenids. The horses were also transformed with fantastic headdresses of horns and masks, accompanied by stags' heads with antlers tipped by raptors.[46] The same horns with small raptor heads were taken by steppe pastoralists east, far into northern China, and displayed on a small golden deer, a sign of the deep contacts across the north (plate 9).

The Achaemenid archives tell us that delegations were gifted robes, arms, horse decoration and jewellery in return for their horses.[47] The third-century AD Greek author Aelianus recorded that ambassadors to the Persian king could expect to receive two silver cups weighing a talent each, bracelets, daggers (*akinkai*) and a necklace.[48] Over time, luxuries spread among the mobile groups, and we can see that they made a strong impact in the east at Pazyryk, with a tapestry carpet and saddle cloth in Iranian style accompanying steppe felt and leather.[49]

A bridle, with S-shaped cheekpieces in wood,
decorated with palmettes in Iranian style, from Pazyryk.

These are signs of the exchanges made possible by feasts and gatherings, which seem to have built strong contacts between Western Asia and the Persians with the Saka and the Pazyryk peoples, who in turn had relations further east. For other luxuries, including a fragment of bronze mirror and another saddle cover – a silk embroidery with phoenixes in a dark thread against a now pale-buff background – also came from further east. This saddle cover must have been woven and embroidered in China, the only source of silk at the time.[50] Moving in the opposite direction towards China were the horses, in exchange for both silk and especially metal, as had happened previously on the northern Loess Plateau. Here is one of the fuses that lit what we term the Silk Road. This, of course, was not a single route and was instead built by multiple exchanges across vast distances over centuries.[51] Long after the community had left Majiayuan, the Chinese continued to seek horses from the west to fend off other northern steppe people, especially the Xiongnu during the Han dynasty. And in due course, the Tang regularly sent bolts of silk into Xinjiang to purchase horses for their wars with the Turkic peoples.[52] We cannot identify the exchanges during the lifetime of the warrior at Majiayuan as Silk Road trade. Animals, metals and fine textiles will have been seized as booty as one group claimed victory over another.[53] Combats, but also marriages and

19. The precipitous and craggy Taihang Mountains border the eastern Loess Plateau.

20. The inner coffin of the Lord of Rui, eighth century BC. His gold belt lies across the centre, with a jade arc and rows of beads to the right and a jade halberd blade on the left. On the far left are four small *cong*, evidence of the enthusiasm for jade as many such pieces were made, admired and buried over millennia.

21. & 22. A heavy stone 'pig dragon' belonging to Zhong Jiang, the spouse of the Lord of Rui. It is either an original or a copy of jades from Hongshan in the distant northwest, such as this translucent green jade 'pig dragon' (*right*) from a tomb at Niuheliang, *c.* 3500 BC.

23. Zhong Jiang's carnelian, turquoise and stone beads strung from a trapezoidal plaque, length *c.* 97 cm.

24. A colourful ceramic jar from the tomb of Lord Bai of Zhongli at Bengbu on the Huai River, Anhui Province, *c.* 600 BC.

25. The majestic set of 65 bells belonging to the Marquis Yi of Zeng. The central bell on the long side was a gift from the King of Chu, *c.* 433 BC.

26. The Marquis's inner coffin. The lacquered wood is embellished with a mass of writhing snakes. The double door is guarded by strange figures with antennae and the window is flanked by birds.

27. Dense dragons and intricate scrolls transform a flask standing in a basin from the Marquis Yi of Zeng's tomb into one of the rarest and most unusual ritual vessels in China.

28. A bronze tiger inlaid with gold slinks in a wide curve, with a deer seized in its jaws. It was the central support for a screen in the tomb of the King of Zhongshan, fourth century BC.

29. One section of a burial of up to 600 horses for the afterlife which encircles a Qi state tomb at Linzi, Shandong Province, sixth–fifth century BC.

30. A delegation of Sakas bear gifts of textiles, gold treasures and a horse to the King of the Persians in a stone frieze on the Apadana at Persepolis, sixth century BC.

31. A steppe rider, one of many horsemen on a magnificent felt textile from Pazyryk, fourth–third century BC, now in the State Hermitage Museum, St Petersburg.

32. The tomb of the warrior at Majiayuan, fourth–third century BC.

33. A fragment of stone relief from the Apadana showing a chariot, with a geometric pattern across the centre of the box and a procession of lions in the outer border, sixth century BC.

34. A reconstruction of the warrior's principal chariot. The height of the box and the combination of a central geometric design surrounded by a procession of animals shows that vehicles employed in Persia were known to his chariot-builders at Majiayuan.

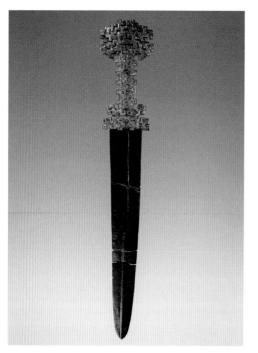

35. One of the iron daggers with an elaborate gold grip and pommel inlaid with turquoise, length 37.8cm, from a Qin state tomb at Yimencun, Shaanxi province, sixth–fifth century BC.

36. Attention was paid to every aspect of the warriors' faces, dress and caps, to create a formidable army of lifelike soldiers, numbering over 7000 people, 100 chariots and 600 horses.

37. The afterlife army in the tomb of the First Emperor is one of the world's greatest achievements. It was created by thousands of craftsmen, organized in teams, who were clearly following the ambitions and instructions of a powerful ruler.

festivals, brought people together, spreading belts, the antlers tipped with raptors, burial patterns and technologies, especially chariots.

Despite the many aspects of the warrior's lifestyle and ornaments that he shared with hundreds, if not thousands, of groups, his chariots made him an outlier. They place him and his comrades in Gansu, in their own league. We discover the chariots by looking down into the precipitous shaft of the tomb. We can make out six or seven discs, two at the western end. Rectangular sections, originally of wood, join the two discs to a point below a small oval seat hiding the centre of the axle below it. This is the last chariot in a convoy of five, neatly ordered within the tomb (plates 32, 34). These are far more complex than those of the Zhou and their allies, with brilliantly decorated wheels of up to forty spokes, decidedly more than the thirty or less in central China. And the draught pole, to which the horses would have been harnessed, was also attached differently to the axle. Several other forms of joint were used, including mortise and tenons, sockets for the sections of the decorated iron gates at the chariots' rear, inlaid with gold and silver, and multiple forms of cord-tying for the yoke bar and the yoke saddles for the horses.[54] There also seems to have been serious stress on the draught pole, and additional struts were inserted alongside it to distribute the pressure from either side on to the two halves of the axle.[55] No other steppe groups we know buried such magnificent and colourful vehicles, nor did the Qin lords own anything so grand. In interring these chariots, the warriors may have been emulating the settled leaders in the central states, even intending to outdo them. The forms of display that they chose, however, are their own local interpretation of the traditions of the Achaemenid Empire, translated and transformed at Pazyryk, where a chariot, also with forty spokes to its wheels, has been excavated.[56]

The most important chariot had a prime position within the warrior's catacomb, directly outside the coffin.[57] This half of the long catacomb had been widened, and the chariot protected by a wooden structure. The remains of columns, up to three metres high, lined the two sides and must have supported a roof. The other four chariots were installed in the main area, at the bottom of the shaft. Detailed

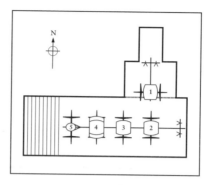

The five chariots in the tomb of the warrior at Majiayuan.

excavation of all the chariots discovered at Majiayuan has led archaeologists to distinguish at least five different types, which presumably
had different functions.[58] Both the shapes of the chariot boxes and
their decoration are distinct from the Zhou tradition.

The chariot boxes, in which the driver and the fighter would have
sat or stood, give us the best indication of the different structures.
The three most extravagant ones, recognised by their design and position, had slightly curved, high sides. These were deliberate additions,
rising well above the lower lattice sides. The two higher sides were
not joined as a single structure in a circle or rectangle, but had been
made separately, with the rather shallower, lattice sections joining
them front and back. The lattice was made by passing narrow vertical sections through holes in the horizontal ones. To demonstrate the
warrior's eminent status, a further iron frame of three rows of five
squares was attached to the trellis, with golden bosses at the joints of
the squares enclosing a sumptuous scroll pattern in silver in each. This
highly decorated panel was surrounded by ibex and tigers, alternating in silver and gold (plate 34). The wheels were decorated with two
borders of silver or tin cut-outs, producing a glimmering pattern as
they turned. The extended axles, projecting beyond the wheels, were
intricately painted, adding to the striking revolving patterns. The next
two chariots, lower in status, had equally high, solid sides which were
planked, one with painted designs on a bright-red surface. Wheels
were also decorated, again with cut-out metal patterns. The next step

down offered a chariot with lower sides, extended outwards, regarded as a more comfortable vehicle and provided with an umbrella.[59]

The fourth tier is made up of several smaller, plain chariots with shallow boxes of wood and leather, more like Zhou chariots. The final type, not owned by the warrior, held just a single, undecorated chariot with a wide box, perhaps for transporting women and children or equipment such as tents. In each category there are several variations, but in all the eminent ones the high sides are a distinctive feature. These repeated categories across several tombs tell us that they must have been made over a fairly short period of time: either over a few years for a single burial ceremony or, at most, over a decade. Some tombs may have been added to the cemetery much later, but all those with chariots appear to belong to a particular moment.

Attached to the grid on the rear of the pre-eminent chariots were decorated vertical iron straps topped by L-shaped sockets, accentuated by gold and silver patterns, stepping down in the middle as if to form a gate into the box. However strengthened the wheels and the draught pole might have been, the weight on the rear of the box would have distorted the balance of the vehicle, dragging it down from the back and obstructing the movement. This would have impeded the practical use of all the most valuable chariots in processions as well as in war. The heavy iron frame on the sides would also have been a serious burden. And two of these attached to the box would have reduced its speed and stability. It looks extremely unlikely that they were used in life. Simple chariot boxes of wood and leather, as well as ridden horses, would have been more viable options for the people of Majiayuan.

How did the chariots come to be constructed and then installed? It is probable that parts of each vehicle were built first, carried down into the tombs and assembled there. This further suggests that the chariots were made for a funeral or for the afterlife. While we see only a limited number of burials, the chariots, their decoration and the ornaments required significant groups of artisans. A whole community must have been dedicated to creating them. Materials had to be sourced and hundreds of skilled craftsmen will have worked on them. The makers are lost in history, but their talent is their legacy, embedded in what we still admire. This community was also fully alive to practices at Pazyryk and elsewhere across the steppe. They must have moved to Majiayuan with their leaders. Among them would have been craftsmen familiar with both the form and structure of chariots further west. In later periods, we know that the Mongols took craftsmen as captives and encouraged others to move to work for them in their large satellite cities.[60] It is likely that many of the steppe groups had attracted craftsmen, as well as training up their own. The warrior and his comrades were certainly keen to exploit fine metal-work and skilled artisans.

The chariots, with their detailed ornament, were for display.[61] With iron frames and planked panels they offered drama in processions, festivals and even in battle. More pertinent, though, is the forum of this performance: the gold ornaments and decorated chariots were not in dialogue with the Qin, or the ritualised cosmos of ancestors, but aimed at the people of the wider steppe. The relief at Apadana offers further evidence of this network. A section of stone from the eastern staircase shows a chariot with decorated sides, similar to those we see at Majiayuan (plate 33). Across the panel of the chariot on the stone is a criss-cross pattern held in place by small round bosses. Around the sides are prowling lions, which were replaced at Majiayuan by ibex and tigers. This close reproduction of the decoration of an Apadana chariot is an important sign of the bridges between Majiayuan and the Achaemenids.[62]

The famous tapestry carpet from Pazyryk shows us the route by which contact was made. This textile is much more elaborate than the chariot panel, with a central section decorated with stars, with two processions around it, one of animals and the other of riders.[63] It takes its composition from carvings in Mesopotamia, such as the door sills at Nineveh in Iraq, one of which is in the British Museum.[64] The iron chariot frames with gold bosses and a silver-star pattern of scrolls are recreations of this motif. A saddle from Pazyryk also has the diamond pattern from the Persepolis chariot, with round bosses at each junction of the lines.[65] Craftsmen familiar with the motifs at Pazyryk and the high-sided Achaemenid chariots must have contributed to the fleet of exotic vehicles at Majiayuan. This is one of the most revealing examples of the close bonds between the people of the steppe and their western neighbours, bonds which, within only a generation, underpinned the First Emperor's claims over his whole world.

An elegant S-shaped iron band decorated at both ends with bird heads and appliqué of silver and gold is a direct copy of a cheekpiece in wood for a bridle buried at Pazyryk.[66] And the S-shaped form was well established in the steppe, as in wooden examples with griffin heads found further west at Berel.[67] This form was taken over by the Qin and their successors the Han.[68] We know from excavations of horses in a stable pit adjacent to a tomb of a sixth-century BC ruler of Qin that he had acquired horses from as far away as 300 kilometres to the north-west.[69] The meetings across the steppe certainly involved exchanges of horses. Throughout this book, horses have joined several diverse societies and cultures together. They were one of the currencies with which the steppe peoples gained the luxuries that they coveted. To maintain their status within and between clans, the steppe leaders needed metals – bronze, silver and gold – to distribute as gifts to their subordinates. They turned west for gold and silver, and east for bronze.

Climate change, with increased moisture in the air, may have stimulated the search for good pasture that generated these interactions.[70] Concurrently, the Majiayuan cemetery was made when movements of steppe peoples from present-day Mongolia towards northern China and into the Loess Plateau were driving retaliations and walled resistance, and possibly limiting exchanges. The warrior and his comrades were part of a complex history in which the advances of powerful pastoralists, completely unaware of the political and military structures of the central states, played a pivotal role in intensifying conflicts among those states, which culminated in the conquests of the First Emperor. On the western reaches of the Qin state, some of these northerners may well have been gathered as mercenaries on defensive walls, as well as providing cavalry and archers. Horses, however, were the main attraction.

While we can locate the lives of the Majiayuan warrior and his

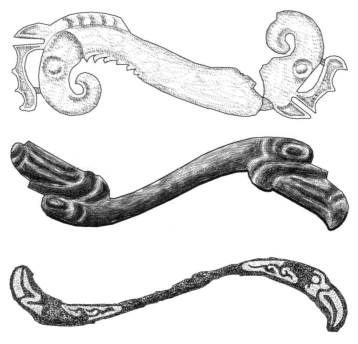

Three S-shaped cheekpieces, fourth to third centuries BC. The top one, from Berel, is made from horn, the middle, from Pazyryk, wood, and the bottom one from Majiayuan, of iron and gold, length 25.3 cm.

comrades within a larger geopolitical transformation, breeding and raising herds consumed their daily lives. A dramatic event must have led them to choose the site in eastern Gansu, with its immense and auspicious views into the distance. The size of the central burial suggests that the leader was recognised, not just at Majiayuan but across the wider steppe, for his wealth. And the splendid chariots bound him and his followers not merely to neighbouring pastoralists but to the faraway riders among the Saka. The chariots and the mass of gold in the warrior's tomb far exceed the material in other local catacombs. But how did steppe peoples with such long-distance contacts travel so far east? What drew them here? Was the cemetery part of an invasion or attack that never happened, or was the Qin's need for horses the impetus? This juncture of two of the world's most powerful cultural groups, the steppe riders and the settled dynasties, lies at the beginning of a long and stirring dialogue. The catacomb tombs at Majiayuan illuminate one of the most extensive and persistent ways of life in all Eurasia. We should never underestimate these mobile peoples' ingenuity and engagement with nature. The interlinked steppe culture was one of the most significant developments in the world, the consequences of which included the invasions of the Huns, the fall of Rome, the Avars and the Golden Horde in the west, or the Tuoba Wei (AD 386–535), the Liao (AD 907–1125), the Jin (AD 1115–1234), and the sophisticated organisation of the Mongols and their dynasty, the Yuan (AD 1271–1368), in the east. The Majiayuan pastoralists belonged to communities that were to overturn the great settled states again and again, injecting new ideas and new materials into their histories.

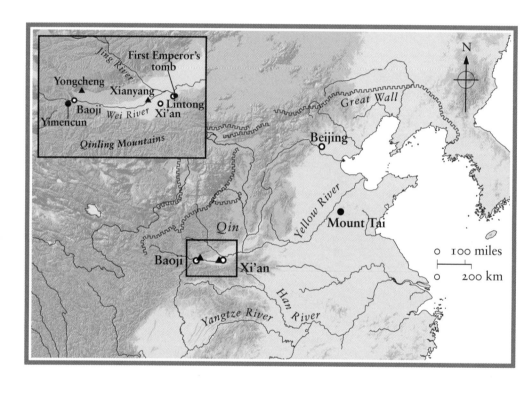

Xianyang and Xi'an

12.

The Everlasting Army

Swells of eager tourists now shuffle along galleries looking down at the columns of the terracotta warriors (plate 37). The crush of visitors, each trying to catch their own glimpse and preserve it on their phone or camera, moves and stretches and regroups again, a new kind of army, with a restless energy that emphasises the motionless, eternal figures below. No guidebook nor postcard can truly recreate this strange phenomenon: a complete army, but one in clay. The grey soldiers, the brilliant colours of their uniforms now lost, belong to another world, beyond death.

As the Zhou lost control of the Wei Valley in the ninth and eighth centuries BC, the early rulers of what was to become the Qin state were encouraged to move east in Gansu, into the western Wei Valley.[1] The Zhou may have been hoping that the Qin would block the back door, so to speak, from the west. The army of clay soldiers appears at first glance to be part of this anticipated defence. But they face east. They are not blocking advances from where the Qin came from, and it seems that, by the third century BC, the First Emperor had turned his back on danger from the west. Is the army a potent demonstration of these new military ambitions? What is the purpose of these immovable regiments?

The early power and wealth of the Qin lords, preserved in their seventh- and sixth-century BC tombs, had been founded south of Majiayuan.[2] From the ninth to the eighth century BC onwards, when the Qin lords first emerge into written history, we know that their enemies lay to the east. Then, the Qin appeared almost peripheral to competitions between the central states – instead they had strong contacts with populations to the west. By the sixth century BC, the Qin dynasty had

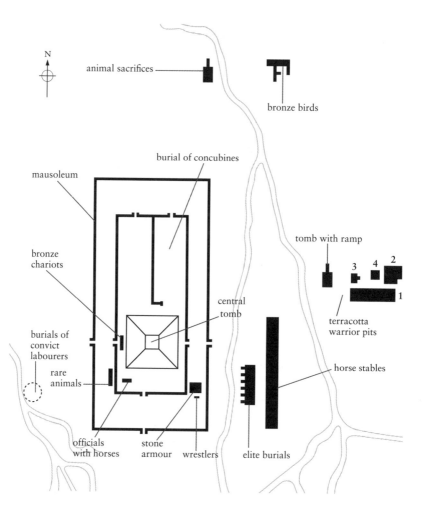

N

animal sacrifices

bronze birds

burial of concubines

mausoleum

tomb with ramp

bronze
chariots

3 4 2

1

central
tomb

terracotta
warrior pits

burials of
convict
labourers

rare
animals

horse stables

officials
with horses

stone
armour

wrestlers

elite burials

The First Emperor's tomb mound, his walled mausoleum
and the funerary park with the terracotta warriors.

Tomb of Lord Jing of Qin

built a new capital and cemetery at Yongcheng in today's Fengxiang county. The First Emperor's astonishing tomb is the culmination of at least five centuries of steady and strategic advance.[3]

At a gigantic tomb at Yongcheng, built over 300 years before the First Emperor's reign, we feel, even dread, the awe of Qin power. It would be fatal to fall in. This rectangular pit is a dizzying 24 metres below present ground level. It is thought to have been the tomb of the Qin ruler Lord Jing (r. 576–537 BC). The exaggerated size of the ramps – 156 metres in the east and 84.5 metres in the west – is a statement of Lord Jing's lofty status in the afterlife.[4] The excavation of Lord Jing's tomb had been a mammoth task. And when the archaeologists finally reached the coffins, they found that the tomb had been ransacked but its structure was undisturbed.[5] The sides were stepped and the lord had a huge double coffin chamber, built of cedar beams, each more than 7 metres long and with a cross-section of about 21 centimetres. An extensive labour force must have sought out and cut down many trees. As at the tomb of the Marquis Yi of Zeng, the central coffin had several separate rooms with doors within the chamber, through which Lord Jing could move. He was not alone. There are several estimates of how many individuals accompanied the lord, but certainly more than 100, some in coffins and some not, depending on their status. According to Sima Qian, one of Lord Jing's predecessors, Lord Wu had been buried in 678 BC with sixty-six companions. Then, in 621 BC, Lord Mu had been buried with 177. The practice had simply expanded on an ever-increasing scale.[6]

Almost everything had been looted from the coffins, and the beams lay smashed. Only a few small gold animals and a section of a belt fastening remained.[7] This tiny gold fitting would have had a leather or textile belt pushed into the open slit beneath the duck's head, which acted as a hook for a ring at the other end of the belt. It is possible that some of the loot, including lavish iron daggers with gold hilts, which resemble the weapons of Arzhan II, was buried in a small tomb at Yimencun near Baoji, an extravagance not in keeping with the size of the tomb (plate 35).[8] Yimencun also housed a belt of jade-like stone, a close replica of steppe belts. The steppe recurs again with a crouching boar, also found in Lord Jing's tomb, but in the lacquered wood of Central Plains workmanship.[9] We can now see Lord Jing's tomb as a bridge between the steppe kurgans and the afterlife residences eventually adopted at the court of the First Emperor, an important stage in the evolution of Qin monuments.[10]

Life in the Qin state was heterogeneous, shown above all by how its population constructed their afterlives, with a mixture of standard Zhou rituals accompanied by northern or even steppe burial practices.

A gold belt fixing, length 1.9 cm.

The burials of attendants, a practice often ascribed to the First Emperor's disregard for human life, should in fact be placed within this Qin ceremonial tradition, where loyal retainers and guards were interred to defend their lords in the afterlife.[11] Other Qin tombs also included people buried with their legs bent, another indication of northerners living within Qin-controlled lands.[12]

Qin cooperation with its northern neighbours was its great strength, underlying the state's growing power in the political and military melees of the sixth century BC and beyond. Long before the people moved to Majiayuan, the Qin in southern Gansu were living among the agro-pastoralists, as Sima Qian notes, and making use of their horse-managing skills.[13] Lord Jing displayed the benefits of his relationship with northerners by burying his horses in a pit adjacent to his mound. An assessment of the horses' DNA shows that they came from a number of different regions in the north-west.[14] The power of the Qin may have lain in their ability to acquire horses and to ranch them on the hills of Gansu. Their cavalry was probably superior to that of other states, because of their interaction with horse breeders. In this spirit, the Qin continued the tactics of the Zhou in making allies and clients of their neighbours. The forebears of the First Emperor also successfully moved their cities east in stages, gradually taking control of new territories.

It was hard to imagine when the First Emperor was born that he would eventually triumph over all other competitors. Ying Zheng, where Ying is his lineage name, did not enter the world in auspicious circumstances. He was born not at the Qin palaces at Xianyang, but in what is now the city of Handan, then the capital of the Zhao state. His father, the future King Zhuangxiang, was living effectively as a hostage in Zhao as a guarantor of peace between Qin and Zhao. Zhuangxiang had taken as his consort a woman who had originally been a concubine of a powerful merchant at Handan, Lü Buwei. Their son moved to Xianyang when Zhuangxiang took up the throne in 249 BC and Lü Buwei became his chancellor. He is portrayed by Sima Qian as a skilful manoeuvrer. He was also to be a major contributor to the court of the First Emperor, when Ying Zheng took over the state on his father's death in 246 BC. Many of the achievements we now recognise as those of the First Emperor were built on the advice of Lü Buwei. After 238 BC, when Lü was accused of plotting against Ying Zheng and took his own life, Li Si assumed his position.[15]

From the moment the First Emperor's tomb was created it was legendary. Work began when King Zheng, aged only thirteen, succeeded to the throne of the state of Qin in 246 BC, accelerated when the unification was complete and when, in 221 BC, he changed his title to the Great August Thearch, with its spiritual overtones. We translate the characters Huangdi as the August Thearch, as the word *di* signifies a supernatural power. For the following millennia, Huangdi is the title we translate as emperor. We have an account of the supposed interior of the tomb, written more than 100 years later by Sima Qian, whose chapter on the First Emperor is our major source on his life and his ambitions:

> In the ninth month the First Emperor was interred at Mt Li. When the emperor first came to the throne he began digging and shaping Mt Li. Later, when he unified the empire, he had over 700,000 men from all over the empire transported to the spot. They dug down to the third layer of the underground springs and poured in bronze to make the outer coffin. Palaces, scenic towers and the hundred officials, as well as rare utensils and wonderful objects, were brought to fill up the tomb. Craftsmen were ordered to set up crossbows and arrows, rigged so they would immediately shoot down anyone attempting to break in. Mercury was used to fashion the hundred rivers and the Yellow River and the Yangtze, and the seas, constructed in such a way that they seemed to flow. Above were all the heavenly bodies, below, the features of the earth. 'Man-fish' oil was used for lamps, which were calculated to burn for a long time without going out.[16]

This is immediately followed by a comment about a decision to send those women who had not borne sons to accompany the emperor. And then:

After the interment had been completed, someone pointed out that the artisans and craftsmen who had built the tomb knew what was buried there and, if they should leak word of the treasures, it would be a serious affair. Therefore, after the articles had been placed in the tomb, the inner gate was closed off and the outer gate lowered, so that all the artisans and craftsmen were shut in the tomb and unable to get out. Trees and bushes were planted to make an analogue of a mountain.[17]

We have no way to verify this description. Given, however, the efforts to create lifelike interiors, the tomb did probably provide the emperor with a fully mapped, realistic landscape of his world, the heavens above and the earth below, in which he could live and rule.[18]

While the burial chamber has not yet been excavated, the mound has been examined with coring – a standard system using a tool known as the Luoyang spade employed across the whole of China – to reveal two different types of rammed earth. And an unexpected internal form has been discovered by remote sensing, described in detail by the excavator, Duan Qingbo.[19]

The mound that we see today is made of layers of coarse earth over the structure of much finer rammed loess. It stands at about 55 metres above the so-called palace, an enormous rectangular pit perhaps nearly 170 metres east to west and about 140 metres north to south and thought to be more than 30 metres deep – an underground vault equivalent to ten storeys. The palace is orientated east–west, following the orientation of the First Emperor's ancestors in the Qin state, which had long overtaken the traditional Shang-Zhou north–south orientation. Digging this out will have been a major feat, going beyond even the tomb of Lord Jing. From Sima Qian's account, we know that labourers working on this large pit had encountered underground springs or streams that they had to divert; he then says that the outer coffin or burial chamber, we do not know which, was cast in bronze. Duan Qingbo identifies parts of a stone structure around the burial chamber, a more elaborate version of the stones encircling King Cuo's chamber at Zhongshan. This wall is 14 metres high and 8 metres

First Qin Emperor's Tomb

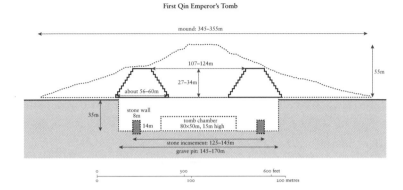

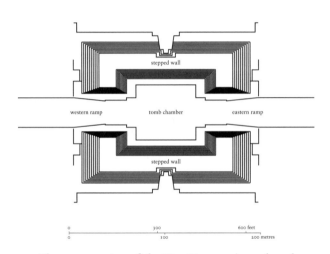

The cross-section of the First Emperor's tomb and
plan of the stepped grave shaft.

thick, probably made by skilled masonrywork rather than by piling
rocks or roughly shaped stones in a trench. By this date, stone encase-
ments, which were widespread in the steppe, had become popular in
northern China, as at Zhongshan, and especially in the Qi state, but
the massive wall which erupted in the burial chamber of the First
Emperor is a surprise.[20]

The most extraordinary engineering achievement is the grave shaft
of rammed loess, 30 metres or so above ground. In the reconstruction based on Duan's work it seems more like an embankment, but

if viewed from above it forms a rectangle, stepped on its two external faces, around and above the chamber. In section, the wall looks like two turrets but is a complete shaft, interrupted by two ramps, one from the west and the other from the east, giving access into the centre. The shaft was probably in position as the coffin was lowered in and the most prized possessions in lacquer, bronze, gold and jade were installed around it. Not only were nine large steps cut on the inside of the wall, more steps were made on the outside. We do not know how these steps were used; perhaps they were simply part of the engineering of this immense structure, making it taper towards the top. Traces of buildings, perhaps with column bases and tiles, have been identified on the steps, probably positioned for the funeral rites, but we cannot rule out the possibility that they made some sort of terrace or afterlife garden for the First Emperor. In any event, the whole composition on the steps was crushed and flattened as it was covered by the mound.[21] This magnificent dwelling lies securely within the tradition of deep tombs in loess, the culmination of many other innovations gathered over several hundred years: mounds and a terrace at Lord Bai's tomb; steps on the burial shaft at Lord Jing's; stone surrounds in the Qi state; and steps on the outside of the mound at the tomb at Zhongshan. The First Emperor's tomb and intimidating ritual space are, however, of unparalleled grandeur.

The wider landscape around the tomb may cover as much as 50 square kilometres.[22] Coring has given the archaeologists a sense of the multitude of deposits around the mound. The First Emperor's agents extended the existing practice – at Zeng and Zhongshan, and with the horse burials of Lord Jing – of accompanying pits. As a complete palace, it was encircled above ground by inner and outer rectangular city walls, with major gates in the east and west, complete with watchtowers. This is the mausoleum, with a wider funerary park beyond.

The emperor was accompanied by chief officials and military leaders, buried in tombs some 1.5 kilometres to the east of the outer walls. Inside the walls were underground buildings, some of wood, to house his court, including an armoury, stables and coffins for rare animals – all essential for a prosperous afterlife. Some of these buildings were manned by clay figures. The area north of the mound is dedicated to halls for ritual offerings in the afterlife. The different buildings and institutions, people and animals, officials and subordinates, and the palace and its environs were all known to the emperor in life. Officials who prepared the daily rituals were accommodated to the west, between the inner and outer walls. Another section within the inner wall, also north of the mound, may have been for the women accompanying the emperor, mentioned by Sima Qian. Miniature bronze chariots were found just west of the mound within the inner wall, as was a building housing more terracotta functionaries who were in charge of horses. Horses were also buried at several points, some of the most valued in their own coffins. Outside the walls was the renowned army in several underground wooden structures and, further north, an underground waterway enlivened with bronze birds. There may have been more than fifty buildings and smaller pits, of which only a selection has been excavated. It is therefore not possible to capture the full diversity of the mausoleum and the funerary park, the culmination of 3,000 years of leaders creating their own afterlives, but driven above all by the First Emperor's determination to rule for eternity.

A small kneeling boy was the first clay figure to be excavated. He had a thick scarf around his neck, like many of the soldiers, with a simple

A clay stable-hand, height 68 cm.

robe, loose at the arms, showing his hands peeping out at the ends. This was a stable-hand, an attendant of animals or horses. He and others like him are about 68 centimetres tall, much smaller than the emperor's army.[23] In 1974, more fragments of heads and limbs emerging from the loess were discovered by farmers digging a well during a period of drought. They called in archaeologists, and the first soldiers were gradually assembled from these finds.[24] In excavations from 1978 to 1981, four structures for the army were discovered, one of which was empty. Archaeologists calculate that the other three were filled with between 6,000 and 8,000 infantrymen, archers, cavalry and generals.

It will help us understand the purpose of the army and the objectives of the First Emperor if we accept that we are not looking at a replica, as we would understand it. This was not a memorial. The figures were the emperor's actual army for the afterlife. Such a concept is hard to comprehend using our English language and our intellectual framework, in which images, such as models or pictures, are less valued than what we might call the 'real' things. In written classical Chinese, there is often no distinction between a soldier and a model of a soldier. Even today, reconstructions of pavilions are named and treated as the ancient pavilions they replace. Sima Qian in his description of the towers and palaces does not use the words replica or representation. Instead he states that the tomb contains palaces and towers. For the mound covered with trees, Sima Qian said it was a mountain, using the word *xiang*, which I translate as analogue. That is to say, the tree-covered tomb was an analogue, a *xiang*, of a mountain. In the same sense, we can see the soldiers as analogues of living soldiers. The care and detail with which they were made were essential, for without this accuracy they could not serve as an army.[25]

To the east of the tomb, the main pit, pit 1, 230 metres long and 62 metres wide, with nine principal columns of armoured figures, has not been completely excavated. Around the outer edges are archers, crouching on one knee. Their slightly twisted bodies make them some of the most attractive of the figures. In the main lines are members of the First Emperor's huge infantry. In among them are chariots with their drivers. Many more chariots and cavalry are in pit 2, while pit 3 is the command station for military leaders. A general at the highest level may have been buried in his own tomb or even with the emperor.

Attention was paid to every aspect of dress, from hair ties down to shoes: knotted soles with upturned toes for archers and infantry, but soft sewn pumps for the cavalry. The armour differs depending on status: generals have long armour, lesser officers shorter armour, as do chariot drivers, cavalry riders, archers and foot soldiers. Some foot soldiers and standing archers have no armour at all, and instead wear a heavy double coat.[26] The caps or hats were also indicative of status, as among the non-military population. The generals had elaborate caps, with hollow, wing-like extensions, that were more decorative than helmets. In contrast the cavalry riders had neat caps drawn under their chins. Great care was also taken to show different hairstyles.[27]

Simple methods were used to create different populations; there are eight face shapes, some rounded and broad, others narrow with

Two archers from pit 1, (*left*) in armour, height 1.22 m,
and (*right*) with a thick coat, height 1.78 m.

pointed chins, perhaps intended to indicate the various regions from which such an army would have been drawn.[28] There are also careful choices between the lengths and shapes of beards and moustaches. Although we can see regional variations in the faces, we do not have any information about how the army was recruited in real life.[29] The soldiers were all painted with a layer of lacquer. Careful scientific examination, often in cooperation with the Bavarian Research Institute for Heritage Monuments in Munich, has revealed a spectrum of colours for their faces, hair, caps and armour to accentuate their dress and dynamic appearance. The (re)creation of specific ranks was crucial. A palette of dark blue, rust-red and pale green was used for clothing, with woven bands and ribbons in rust-red bordering armour and tying it front and back.[30]

The army stands to the east of the central tomb, as well as facing east. This was not a formation to defend the empire from warriors from the steppe, riding from the west, but to defend the emperor against forces coming through the Pass from the wide agricultural plains.[31] The generals appointed by the First Emperor had fought many

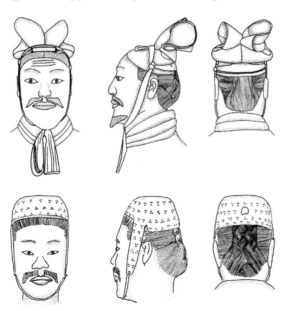

The caps of a general (*above*) and a cavalry rider (*below*).

battles in the long wars that drove the unification of the states into a single empire. We know that the Qin generals were efficient and relentless leaders of a feared army. In later texts, the Qin were condemned for their lack of humanity and described as building an aggressive state, awash with atrocities, massacres of captives and the forced movement of populations from one region to another, involving the destruction of the gates, granaries and water supplies of settlements in their path.[32] Many soldiers of the opposing armies had been slaughtered. After death, these rivals and their leaders would face the emperor again, assembled as ghost regiments.[33] To defend himself and his afterlife palace, the First Emperor needed his own army. Just as a living army had to be summoned and was composed of many units of trained men who needed to be equipped and fed as they advanced, so too similar preparation had to be made for the army of clay.

The Qin had embarked step by step on their mission to conquer and then dominate the ancient Zhou lands. At first the Qin had moved only slowly, creating a capital and a cemetery at Yongcheng. Then they moved towards Xi'an, culminating in a successful campaign in the Sichuan basin in 316 BC. From this pivotal spot, the Qin gathered the momentum to capture Chu. Advances to the south established a fruitful network which gave not only the Qin, but also later rulers, access to the rich resources of rice, metals and animals.[34] Command of the south was the foundation of the final campaigns to the east. Zhao, the major successor of the Jin state, was defeated in 259 BC at a ferocious battle at Changping.[35] But the final unification campaign only started in 230 BC. Its stages are not fully recorded, but by 221 BC the last state, Qi, in the north-east, had fallen.[36] Despite this success, the emperor had reason to fear insurgency. Even after the unification had been declared, rebellions continued, particularly in the eastern territories.[37]

While we can recognise the clay warriors in the context of the Qin military, we have not encountered such realism before, and won't do so again for several centuries. A narrow but long building 40 metres east–west, between the inner and outer walls of the mausoleum on the east side, may help us discover its origin. Many fragments, perhaps of over thirty figures, were discovered here. They were originally identified as entertainers or acrobats as they are dressed only in loin-cloths, whose flecks of colour hint at fine patterned silks. But from their position near an armoury it is more likely that these individuals had something to do with protecting the emperor. Some figures have an arm raised above their heads or lift a foot, as though in movement. Others stand waiting with heavy, rounded weights in their hands. Some are thin and agile, others have clasped hands, strong arm muscles and spreading bellies over their belts. Managing the dynamic group, it seems, is a man seated on a couch. In these bodies we see a much closer interest in the human form, very different from the rendering of the still soldiers, wrapped in scarves, coats and armour and booted.

In a recent paper, Armin Selbitschka has convincingly proposed that they are not acrobats but elite members of the army, wrestlers trained by exercise drills. Their loincloths and those with slender bodies reproduce wrestlers painted on a wooden comb of a similar date found in the south. A further example is on a bronze belt plaque worn and owned by the Xiongnu.[38] Stone weights, a strange bronze and a massive tripod were probably all for weightlifting. Although the tripod is just like the bronzes used for the ancestral offerings, its extreme weight, 212 kilos, and its position, possibly atop a beam or furnishing, suggest that it could have been held aloft to demonstrate the strength of a trainee, as emphasised in an earlier military treatise by Master Wu (d. 381 BC):

> Thus an army needs to comprise soldiers who are as agile as tigers, who are so strong that they can easily lift a tripod, whose feet are so light as the horses of the Rong people, and who can seize the enemies' banners and decapitate their generals. Those are the skills [soldiers] need to have.[39]

A reference to horses may in part explain a set of miniature hoofs found in the building. Are they remains of a sculpture of a running horse, a metaphor to encourage the trainees to move swiftly? This agility training is similar to the wrestling and weightlifting popular in

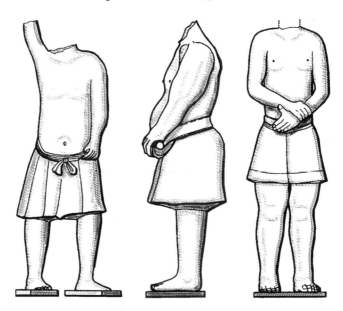

Three wrestlers with different physiognomies,
(*left*) 1.62 m, (*middle*) 1.68 m, (*right*) 1.52 m.

the Olympic Games of the ancient Greek world. In the culture of the central states, figurative sculpture was typically avoided. Nudes, so famous in ancient Greece, were not favoured in China. The only nude figures we know were employed to demonstrate acupuncture points.[40]

Duan Qingbo has suggested that extensive contacts with the Iranian world across Central Asia were the driving force for the First Emperor's spectacular tomb.[41] As the Qin were building their state, Alexander the Great established his principalities in what is present-day Afghanistan, bringing the Hellenistic world to Central Asia. Dozens of fragmentary sculptures and architectural decorations have been found at Ai-Khanoum in Afghanistan, on the south bank of the Oxus, facing another city at Takht-i-Sangin on the north bank, in today's Tajikistan.[42] Lukas Nickel of Vienna University has pointed to a few sentences in Sima Qian's chapter on the First Emperor to propose that some distant news of sculpture similar to those at Ai-Khanoum had been conveyed to the First Emperor, encouraging him to create his own:

Bronze tripod of 212 kg for weightlifting.

Weapons from all over the Empire were confiscated and brought to Xianyang, and melted down to be used in casting bells, bell stands, and twelve men made of metal. These last weighed 1,000 piculs each and were set up in the palace.[43]

Nickel argues that the castings of the twelve figures at Xianyang were prompted by information about strange giants reported to be in the Gansu Corridor. It is likely that information on such sculpture had been moving east, at least as far as present-day Xinjiang, as we can see in a small kneeling warrior. He wears a loincloth and is bare above the waist, rather like the wrestlers, with marks of a collar below his neck. His massive hat or helmet also recalls the Hellenistic world.

The rare stone and bronze sculptures in Afghanistan and the multiple figures around the Mediterranean, and even the reported giants, were for specific religious or political purposes. The First Emperor and his advisers, perhaps knowing that strong competitors to the west were building tombs and creating life-size figures, had been inspired to (re) create an army, wrestlers and officials. These too, we could argue, had a spiritual purpose, as they were to defend and support the emperor in the afterlife. The figures are the remarkable achievement of an organised mass of craftsmen and administrators. A blueprint must have been drawn up, ordered by the generals and military planners and delivered to the First Emperor.[44] To model row upon row of soldiers of similar heights, correctly dressed, armoured and armed, craftsmen must have been carefully instructed and overseen, and they must have all worked to a shared plan in which the different components of the soldiers, their heads, arms, hands, armour, legs and feet, were made to agreed and precise forms. Decisions were taken to use moulds for the heads and hands, which were then cleverly modified to create a sense of individuality, dependent on a comprehensive understanding of the living army itself. Then the figures had to be fired in kilns. And all these steps must have been discussed and carried out alongside the tomb-building process. It is quite unnerving to look at the different faces, hair arrangements, caps, clothes and shoes and realise that these must all have been worked out in advance (plate 36).[45]

Direct knowledge of Western metallurgy and expertise could also have inspired the endeavour, as we know that the graceful bronze cranes, their long necks and heads curved down to catch fish, were made by a new technology. These were lined up with bronze geese and swans along a waterway, attended by pottery figures, sometimes described as musicians, to the north of the tomb of the First Emperor.[46]

A warrior with a Phrygian-style helmet, height 40 cm.

As with the army in clay, exquisite birds along a river were something entirely new. In earlier centuries, birds attacking snakes and felines (and the three-dimensional animals in the King of Zhongshan's tomb) followed the subjects of the steppe, but in local materials. Here the birds do not make any visual references to the predators and prey of the north; such accomplished, naturalistic forms had come from elsewhere.

Metallurgists have come to the conclusion that the birds were likely cast using the lost-wax technique. Armatures in the long necks of some birds reinforce this suggestion. Some were made in several parts and joined in the same way that bronze figures in the Hellenistic world were built of discrete sections.[47] Repairs to these bronze birds were also probably made by craftsmen familiar with techniques in other parts of Asia.[48] Expertise in lost-wax casting is also evident in sections welded together on two miniature chariots. These complicated bronze vehicles, with gold horse ornaments, are at half the size of wooden chariots. Planners and artisans with Central Asian skills and experience had clearly been at work at Majiayuan.[49] It is very likely that some members of the emperor's court knew about these distant, well-established projects and may even have taken part in them.

Far-reaching contacts may also explain the sudden burst of talent in the third century BC. Hellenistic and other Western techniques and horses indicate that technologies were introduced under the guidance of a range of advisers in the First Emperor's court. Just as we

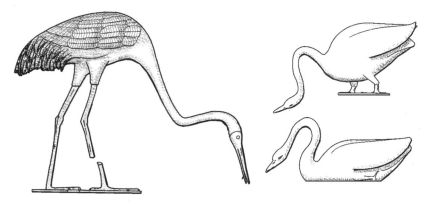

A crane, height 77.5 cm, and two geese, height 57.5 cm and 39.5 cm, in bronze.

have only patchy details on the movements of his army, so we do not have records of those who worked on this great enterprise; we do not know who the planners and the overseers were. But, as the Qing-period scholar Hong Liangji (1746–1809) pointed out, the Qin did not have a well-educated base and had to draw in people from elsewhere, so that many of the highest-ranking Qin officials came from other states.[50] Some may have come from the states of Qi or Chu, both with rich histories of figures in tombs. People from Gansu with contacts in present-day Xinjiang and Kazakhstan will certainly have been involved. Others may have come from much further away, perhaps from the oases of Central Asia.

The blossoming of three-dimensional figurative sculpture for the First Emperor's mausoleum subsided after his death – perhaps because the craftsmen and overseers died or were even buried with him, or perhaps because they were not taken into the succeeding Han court.[51] Small figurines of soldiers continued to be placed in or along-side important Han dynasty tombs, but nothing life-size.[52] The huge tomb, a masonry structure around the deep grave, the army, the birds and the bronze chariots all speak of the emperor's ambition. Through contact with the western regions, he and his court had received news of strange wonders that fuelled their desire to create something com-pletely unprecedented.[53]

Carefully fashioned heads of ceramic cavalry horses in pit 2, restrained by S-shaped cheekpieces, tell us how contact with the west may have been reinforced. The cheekpieces indicate that the intended riders were familiar with harnesses used at Majiayuan and further west along the Tianshan Mountains into Kazakhstan. A neatly crafted saddle carved on the horse's body is also revealing. The clay (re)pro-duced a soft leather or textile saddle, with extended triangle straps, perhaps originally of leather, to join a cord around the horse's tail. The same arrangement is found on the horse with the steppe rider on the Pazyryk felt (plate 31). Hanging from some of these straps are decorative threads, identical to those found among the horses buried at Berel. This saddle must ultimately have been devised there and introduced to the First Emperor's cavalry by steppe groups such as those at Majiayuan.[54] The *Zuo Zhuan*, edited in the fourth to third centuries BC, mentions that the northern state of Jin had access to horses of the Rong.[55] And it is clear that the horses of the First Emperor were provided by similar northerners.

A large stable building on the western side of the mausoleum between the inner and outer walls, with two narrow structures at right angles, one 117 metres in length and the other 84.3 metres, housed several hundred horses, buried kneeling in groups of three with knives (presumably those used to kill them) in their mouths.[56] Just as actual people were buried with the emperor in adjacent tombs, so too the cavalry in clay was supplemented by real horses. In another wooden stable, significantly positioned within the inner wall, near the south-west corner of the mound, twenty-four horses were overseen by more figures in clay. A line of twelve men in the usual long coats each had a knife and grinding stone.[57] These tools were for scraping off any incorrect characters as they wrote instructions on bamboo strips, effectively erasers for spelling mistakes. The individuals have been called officials as they wore distinctive caps, and the variety between them indicates a hierarchy of ranks. One possibility is that they may have been in charge of organising horses, including for sending messages.[58] The horses were exceptional and, from their tall stature, we suppose probably came from elsewhere. The courier service of the late Warring States and Qin periods, with messengers on horseback, in chariots or on foot, may have been adopted from the earlier system developed by the Achaemenids.[59]

Understanding the role of horses in the success of the First Emperor is inevitably dependent on archaeological research, as the usual bias towards state organisation and political ambition in the histories ignores the practicalities of rebuffing incursions from the north. Yet the Qin and their successors, the Han, were duly conscious of the equine gift from the west, which they celebrated in a massive sacrificial ground around a mound at Yongcheng, with the evocative name of the Pool of Blood, the Xue Chi.[60] Hundreds, if not thousands, of horses were sacrificed there as offerings over several centuries, which

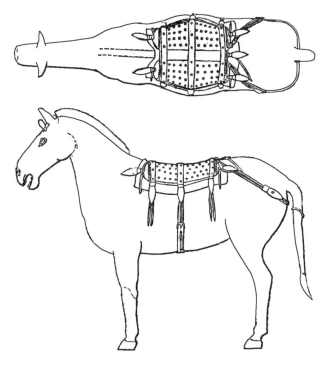

A cavalry horse, saddled in the same way as steppe horses
from Pazyryk and Berel. Height 1.75 m, length 2 m.

jolts our understanding of early China. There is no evidence of other
major horse sacrifices in the central states. While we know from the
inventory of the tombs of Majiayuan and of the Mountain Rong that
animals had an essential role in their understanding of the universe,
this was not the case among the Zhou and their immediate associ-
ates. Yet at Yongcheng, horses had a ritual role in mediating between
their owners and the spirits.

While horses had built the First Emperor's relations with pastoralists in the north-west, incursions from the north, through the centre
of the Loess Plateau, clearly continued. Sima Qian knew that the state
of Zhao had been successful in gaining territory and pushing back
incursions from the north. With the conquest of Zhao, leaving a gap
in the defences, the First Emperor and his military advisers decided
to take action:

A horse official, height 1.87 m.

Finally Qin overthrew the other six states, and the First Emperor of the Qin despatched Meng Tian to lead a force of a hundred thousand men north to attack the barbarians. He seized control of all the lands south of the Yellow River and established border defences along the river, constructing forty-four walled district cities overlooking the river and manning them with convict labourers transported to the border for garrison duty.[61]

In taking the land south of the Great Bend of the Yellow River, the emperor had gained control of much of the Loess Plateau. This appeared to be a great military triumph. However, the emperor's lands were now much closer to the steppe and the Xiongnu. And the Han were to feel the full brute of their force in the following century. The management of the borderlands and the extraction of its labour forces are signs of the organisation of the Qin state, which matched and even underpinned its visionary building projects, from the mausoleum to the Great Wall.

Writing as a tool in administration is everywhere in the tomb of the First Emperor. Abundant traces of inscriptions flow from traditions

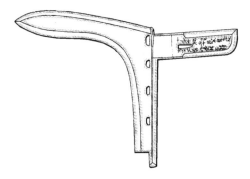

Bronze halberd inscribed with the name of the chancellor Lü Buwei.

that we have already met on the Central Plains. The First Emperor and his court were intent on combining these with new designs from his multiple advisers. Some weapons, especially lances and halberds, date from the period 244–228 BC, that is, before the unification, and carry long inscriptions from which we learn more about the hierarchy of the workers. The chancellor Lü Buwei is named as the supervisor of halberd production, though it seems unlikely that he was involved day to day. His position certainly indicates the central administration's concern with preparations for war. Listed in the inscriptions, Lü had command over three levels of organisation, the *sigong*, or officials, the *cheng*, craftsmen, and the *gong*, workers. It was common practice to treat those at the top as officials, with a public duty to the emperor. After Lü was dismissed from his post in 238 BC, perhaps for his overbearing ambitions as much as for the accusation of plotting a rebellion, no further weapons name a supervisor. And there are none naming his successor, Li Si. The formality of the inscriptions reflects a strictly ordered society. The government of the First Emperor was certainly a forerunner in modern Chinese social organisation.

An equally intense preoccupation with organisation in the service of war appeared in piles of stone plaques, each drilled with twelve tiny holes when found by the excavators. These have been reassembled into sections of armour. Reconstructing them was a challenging jigsaw puzzle. An arsenal of stone suits of armour lies in a vast underground building that has not been fully excavated, but eighty-seven

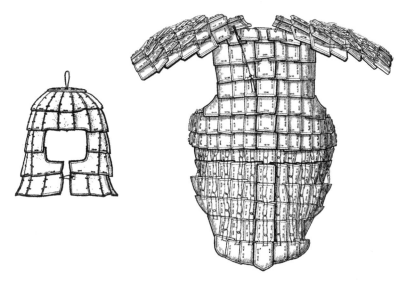

A helmet, height 38 cm, and armour, height c.75 cm,
of small limestone plaques joined with narrow threads of bronze.

suits, forty-three helmets and four sets of horse armour were retrieved from the trenches that were opened.[62] They were not, of course, intended for the terracotta warriors, who had their own armour on them already. These stone suits must have been for the senior officials and leaders buried in a row of tombs outside the eastern wall of the city, where human skeletons have been recovered. Others may have been buried within the tomb itself. Presumably, junior members of the army would have brought the suits to the leaders to put on when a major crisis loomed. In life, in warfare with bronze and iron weapons, the stone armour would have offered no protection. One hard blow and the plaques would have shattered. Yet we have found jade weapons in much earlier tombs, presumably for defence against the spirits.[63] Stone armour was a part of a parallel scheme to defend leaders from the ghost armies in the afterlife.

As the buildings were razed after the fall of the Qin, the soldiers' weapons were forgotten. In the hands of the clay figures these were actual weapons, the majority in bronze. So far, among the clay soldiers, 40,000 arrowheads have been recovered, as well as bronze swords, lances, spears and halberds, and most importantly triggers for crossbows. This was a fighting force, ready for every eventuality. By looking at the alloy composition of the arrows, which have been found in groups of 100 – the number in the quiver of a single archer – the scientists found that they were made in batches, in a careful manufacturing system, with the heads, the tangs and the bamboo shafts produced separately and then assembled. Several subdivided groups worked in parallel, in an efficient production line. The triggers too were made in batches by different cells of workers. They had three parts to be fitted together, requiring fiddly casting and careful grinding and polishing to enable their seamless function. This was a level of organisation of labourers, artisans and craftsmen rooted in China's ancient subdivision of labour.[64]

Inscriptions and stamped seals also appear on the soldiers. One seal impression gives the name of a foreman, Jiang, from the palace workshop. The place of work and personal name determined who was responsible if the work was found to be faulty. These records to ensure accountability were indicative of a well-established administration. Other overseers marshalled crowds of men to dig out the pits in order to create the many underground buildings and city walls.[65] While Sima Qian gives the overall number of workers building the mausoleum as 700,000, he makes no mention of the planning that underpinned their labour. As an educated official working in the archives, this part of the process was of no interest to him. At all times, the scholarly elites were not exercised by details of technical and physical work. Moreover, Sima Qian's motive was to paint the First Emperor as cruelly exploiting his subjects.

Traces of the emperor's administration can also be found on pottery fragments faintly scratched with sad messages. The fragments were found in the small makeshift graves to the west of the tomb mound in which labourers were buried, worn out, underfed and punished by their workloads.[66] This was a workforce of prisoners. Some characters say where the labourer came from, his name and what kind of sentence he had been given. The fragment above states: 'Ju, from Dongxian Village, Dongwu county [in modern Shandong in the east],

A craftsman's seal from the palace workshop (*left*) and a rubbing
of a fragment of pottery tile to accompany a convict in his grave (*right*).

is here working for the government to pay his debt.'[67] The convicts
had generally been recruited by commuting their debts to labour.
Cumulatively, hundreds of fragments tell us that the convicts came
from all across the emperor's new lands. The efficiency of the state
had transported them all here, just as the state had recruited soldiers
from many different parts of the empire. Convict labour was widespread and was an essential instrument in the expansion of the Qin to
the south.[68] We do not know whether the gangs of men building earlier dams, walls or temple platforms were also prisoners, convicted of
crimes or with accumulated debts and hauled into working for local
lords in lieu of a prison sentence.

The administrative success of the First Emperor was nothing new.[69]
An efficient bureaucratic organisation was achieved more than a century earlier by a formidable government minister, Lord Shang, or
Shang Yang (d. 338 BC), who himself adapted existing traditions from
the ninth or eighth centuries BC onwards.[70] He had moved from the
state of Wei, where he had been in the employment of the king, to
seek influence in Qin, which was gaining power in the fourth century BC. Lord Shang set out his plan to enhance the authority of the
state and its economy in writing, today given the title *The Book of
Lord Shang (Shang Jun Shu)*.[71] In it he combined an assessment of the
need to grow agricultural output with his view that an effective state
warranted a highly centralised government, maintained by a policy
of punishments and rewards. The hereditary lords were replaced by a

new system in which status was dependent on individual merit. The lowest ranks were allocated to individuals based on their military success, for example on the number of enemies they had killed, assessed by counting heads. Lord Shang divided achievement in society into approximately twenty ranks, with people granted a variety of legal and economic privileges.[72] The entire population was registered and restrained from moving between districts, a sign of their importance as a major resource. Members of a family were obliged to report on one another. Everything was recorded in writing. Laws were severe; procedure was followed precisely and punishment was brutal, most visibly with mutilation, execution and an established custom of putting to death three sets of a criminal's relatives.[73] These elaborate regulations were discovered on bamboo slips, excavated from tombs or deposits, mainly in southern China, where the waterlogged ground has preserved them for us. As well as ordering the lives of the people, horses and manufacture, markets were controlled as well.[74]

The chancellor, Li Si, is credited by Sima Qian with reforming the characters, unifying them by eliminating regional variants, as we see on the fragment with Ju's sentence.[75] This was a significant step towards creating a workforce bound by a given code; although oversight was tight and punishment fierce, it followed a given legal system. Small bronze weights inscribed with edicts were widely distributed across the empire. These were also repeated on rectangular bronze plaques. The penetration of the Qin was made visible to all who were literate.[76] One reads:

> The Emperor united All-Under-Heaven. All lords and the black-headed ones were appeased. [He] established the title 'Emperor' [*huangdi*] and issued this [edict] to Chancellors Zhuang and Wan: 'Order the Measuring System! If inconsistencies and doubts arise, resolve and standardise everything'.[77]

With control down to even weights and measures, every detail of daily life was drawn into official oversight. Everything in the mausoleum must have been requisitioned and delivered through the official systems of the state.

Nothing was beyond the emperor's gaze. In his lifetime, he claimed the whole world and gathered all he could together around him in his mausoleum. We will never hear the discussions and commands, nor observe the grind of the huge workforce. As we absorb the emperor's afterlife army and his figural experimentation, we can lose ourselves in this welter of output from thousands upon thousands of craftsmen. We can sense the movement of many hands under firm orders. Yet the emperor had inherited much more than a commitment to create the greatest afterlife palace of all time. He and his Qin ancestors were seeking not just domination of the other states, but also eternal rule. And in the tradition of the Zhou, the welfare of the people would only be possible under a single benevolent ruler. This was the project that had occupied the thinkers, whom we today call philosophers, for several hundred years. Unification after so many centuries of competition was the undisputed aim.

In the sixth century BC, Confucius had been at the forefront in urging a return to the rituals and practices of the Zhou. The supremacy of the Zhou model had remained in both early writing and later revisions of what were thought to be accounts of Zhou achievements. The shadow of the Zhou was remarkably long and was continually reviewed and expanded. There was widespread recognition that a single, supreme monarch was vital. A rival philosopher, Mozi (460–390 BC), looked back even further than the Zhou and urged the appointment of a worthy, virtuous man to rule All-Under-Heaven. Virtue and unity were joined in one prevailing message in the decades surrounding the First Emperor as he ascended the throne:

> The True Monarch upholds oneness and becomes the rectifier of the myriad things. The army needs a general: thereby it is unified. The state needs a ruler: thereby it is unified. All under Heaven needs the Son of Heaven: thereby it is unified. The Son of Heaven upholds

oneness, thereby unifying it [the realm]. Oneness brings orderly rule; doubleness brings chaos.[78]

The First Emperor's tomb, with its high mound, was the ultimate expression of oneness, to stand at the centre of the whole world for all time. And in changing his title to that of the Great August Thearch, the First Emperor had assumed a supernatural sovereignty. He had boosted his claims from the very beginning by placing his dynasty within the now well-established framework of the correlations that held the world together: the forces of *Yin* and *Yang* and the powers of the Five Phases, the cardinal directions, colours, musical notation and many other essential features of the universe. The emperor declared that he was taking the colour black as the symbol of the force of water that could overcome fire and the colour red of the Zhou. Yet despite this alignment with the cosmos and its spirits, the emperor presented his ambitions in a pragmatic manner. To create unity out of conquest, he is said to have had models of the palaces and temples of the states that he had annihilated built around his own palaces. In them he installed beautiful women and bells and drums that he had seized from other states.[79] These buildings captured the early polities physically and re-established them within the Qin capital. A similar capture of the terrestrial world was, according to Sima Qian, placed inside the tomb. And the emperor went one step further to draw down the heavens into the physical geography of his capital and his tomb. He used astral terms to name the buildings and palaces in and around Xianyang. As he built the Epang Palace south of the Wei River, he named it Jimiao, as the celestial pole, the counterpart of his own position in the world. Sima Qian writes,

> An elevated walk extended from Epang north across the Wei River to connect the palace with Xianyang as an analogue of the way in which in the heavens a corridor leads from the Heavenly Pole star across the Milky Way to the Royal Chamber Star.[80]

Here we recognise the Epang Palace as the Pole Star on the south side of the Wei River, which is the Milky Way, and the capital, Xianyang, on the north side, as the Royal Chamber Star, the name of a star in the Pegasus constellation.[81]

The emperor's authority was spread to distant areas, such as the west, the Sichuan basin and south into present-day Hunan by despatching both officials and exiles to organise and develop these regions.[82] He had roads built of packed earth, which he could use to visit and survey his empire, for he, of course, did not know of any world that he could not reach.[83] And to make these journeys in the future, he had the two bronze chariots placed alongside the main tomb mound, on the west. When unearthed they were flattened into fragments. With enormous care they have been reconstructed. They were made of more than 3,000 separate pieces and together the two weigh over 2,000 kilos. Careful examination by research scientists has

Chariot with an umbrella and standing driver, length 2.25 m, and a private carriage for the First Emperor, length 3.17 m.

established that the intricate bronze creations were based on new technologies derived from lost-wax casting.[84] The emperor's advisers must have recognised the innovation and believed it to be the best method to achieve vehicles for eternity. The first chariot has an open box with a single standing chariot driver, under a wide umbrella, holding the reins of four horses. The wheels are large with nearly thirty spokes, a hint that we are looking at a vehicle that owes some of its design to the chariots we saw at Majiayuan.[85] The second vehicle is much more unusual, as a travelling carriage, probably for the First Emperor to visit his domains. It is a private vehicle, with solid sides which would have concealed the emperor from view, though he could have looked out from the windows. A curved roof, perhaps of textile or leather, was held in position by a fan of rods, rather like the rodded structure of the tents we know from later mobile pastoralists.[86] The driver at the front was seated under an overhanging roof, and he too had command of four elaborately harnessed horses. Their straps were threaded through tubes alternating in gold and silver, as we have seen for the collars of the hounds at Zhongshan.[87] And a glowing plaque with gold foil was placed on the horses' heads just below their ears. As with the harnesses and saddles of the cavalry horses, the chariots are direct evidence of the skills from Central Asia and the steppe.

It is likely that in life the First Emperor had similar chariots for journeys to the very corners of his territory, often as much as 800 or 1,000 kilometres away. Soon after the unification, between 219 and his death in 210 BC, the emperor travelled to the eastern edge, where he and his court ascended the mountains to make offerings that took him closer to the spirits. Mount Tai was his target, with an immense height of 1,533 metres, which is still the most famous of today's five sacred mountains. While we may be familiar with later landscape paintings, few who visit the terracotta warriors have any idea of the existence, let alone significance, of mountains in the First Emperor's cosmology. Mountains in China have a spiritual power, as pilgrimage sites, and literally carry the weight of history, with long carved inscriptions on their rocks to be read and meditated upon by those who climb their thousands of stone steps to the summits. Offerings were made at Mount Tai by later rulers and at the imperial tombs down to the end of the Qing dynasty in 1911. The grave-sweeping ceremony, still observed in early spring by many families in China, perpetuates these ritual practices.

With his inspection tours, the First Emperor had, in fact, reinforced the literal and cosmological position of great mountains, incorporated thereafter by subsequent dynasties into their ceremonies and views of the universe. His visit to the sacred mountain in present-day Shandong province took the emperor to the heart of the original state of Qi – marking this, his final conquest. Stelae – stone slabs – were set up and inscribed with eulogies of his achievements. As the First Emperor was accompanied by his advisers and scholars, these inscriptions set out events in traditional Zhou style, describing the six kingdoms he conquered as 'the restive and perverse'; his concern for the multitudes, called the 'black-haired people'; and his administration's objective to 'promulgate the shining laws' to give 'warp and weft to all under heaven – forever to serve as ritual norm and guideline'.[88] At the same time as the emperor installed himself within the

Rubbing of a Song dynasty copy of the original inscription on
Mount Yi, 219 BC, in the small seal script favoured by the First Emperor.

geographical and cosmological universes, he followed the Zhou in recruiting history to seal the legitimacy of his conquest and his government. He acknowledged and admired the legendary ruler Shun, who had made a similar inspection tour and offerings to Heaven on Mount Tai. Shun also regulated the months and the seasons. When visiting Mount Kuaiji, far to the south, where the emperor Yu had died and been buried, the First Emperor made offerings to this mythic hero, thus bringing the ritual acknowledgement of his august predecessors within his own self-presentation. Yu was of special significance in these tours, as he was famed for defining the land and organising the waters.[89] Sima Qian includes in his narrative of these journeys a description of the emperor's commands to his officials to send out searches for herbs that would confer immortality, not just on the land on which he stood, but out in the eastern sea, on the magical islands of Penglai, which disappeared as boats approached them. As Wu Hung of the University of Chicago writes, notions of immortality and access to paradises were developing in parallel with the ancestral cult and its preparation of tombs for the afterlife.[90] In all his deeds, the First Emperor gave himself supremacy over all past rulers and elevated himself to stand alongside the legendary Sage Kings as a new Sage King.

Of course, the First Emperor anticipated that similar rituals of the ancestral cult would be performed regularly, even daily, at his tomb by the officials stationed there. He would also have anticipated that his supreme success would spread far into the future, with later rulers making offerings at his tomb. The mausoleum had even given the emperor his own sacred mountain. His enormous precinct is not the work of a violent military leader, solely embodying the punishment of hundreds of thousands of convicts. It was and is a unique creation stimulated by the emperor's far-reaching contacts, including the borderlands and the Hellenistic regions beyond, while exploiting the skills and labour of all those around him. As in all the tombs we have visited, the construction of the emperor's view of the universe was supported by the management of the state, with its history and its regulations inherited from his ancestors.

Epilogue: Lives Long Buried

The great tombs of China allow us to enter a deep past that is otherwise difficult to penetrate – an era in which written evidence is often fragmentary or expounds a political agenda – and to discover the universes which dominated life and afterlife of this ancient civilisation. All were built with varied ambitions, plans and profiles, and their contents reveal distinct biographies of unique individuals, from singular jades to whole symphonies of ceramics and bronzes. Their design and furnishings offer an alternative history to the early texts. In place of disparities between one ruling dynasty and the next, a record of the decline of the Zhou, or contempt for the stockbreeders from the steppe, we find in the tombs a much more nuanced, heterogeneous world. They grant us access to a vibrant constellation of ideas about life after death, all sustained by one central belief that the dead would continue to follow the life they had lived. The universe of ancestors is without doubt one of the world's most powerful religious practices, joining generations over deep time through performance rather than a shared creed, continually underpinning family ties and providing the ethical foundation of an entire society. And tombs narrate the stories of the historical, cultural and ritual contexts in which the people of ancient China moved.

Landfall and climate governed all life and afterlife. Farmers on the Central Plains and along the Yangtze certainly recognised the geographical phenomenon of the Pacific Monsoon and the prosperous grains that these summer rains provided as the humid south's rice-growing potential, with terraced fields and irrigation channels. But the people living between 3000 BC and 221 BC did not, and could not, know about the Tibetan Plateau that separated them from other civilisations in Western Asia. The ritualised rule of the Shang and the Zhou differed profoundly from the military and legal powers on the other side of the Plateau. Large earthen platforms for wooden buildings and rammed loess walls created an urban environment very different from the stone temples of Egypt and the layers of mud-brick structures that dominated Western Asia. The tombs and their objects in jade, bronze, lacquer, ceramics and silk reflect the impact of this division and the spectacular creativity that grew from such independence. Ancient China was not, however, cut off. Others circumnavigated the highland, along routes forced north by the Tibetan Plateau; they traversed mountain ranges and the steppe, bringing wheat and barley grains, herded animals, materials such as bronze and iron and new technologies to create chariots and to work gold. Ultimately they passed through the Loess Plateau, one of the most remarkable regions of China. Its malleable soil meant that high city walls and large platforms with wooden structures could be built without stone. China thus set out in a direction quite different from the stone castles, forts and churches in the West.

Loess also stimulated the creation of the tombs as builders descended to baffling depths, from the vandalised tomb of the leader at Taosi to the First Emperor's cavernous array of palaces, pavilions and towers. Underground chambers, some with ramps, as first built for the kings at Anyang, must have stood open before they were refilled. Those dug in the south could not rely on the strength of loess, of course, and were therefore likely to be shallow or have sloping sides, as in the tomb of Lord Bai. The tombs were the stage settings for grand funerals with colourful processions and music. And, in an unending feedback loop, magnitude also encouraged an increasingly lavish display of possessions, facilitated by a dense and sophisticated workforce. The Zhou kings' tombs have not yet been discovered, but the afterlife dwellings of numerous Zhou lords have been excavated, including the simple tomb of a northern ally, Yu Bo, the sumptuous mansion of the Lord of Rui, the four-roomed palace for the Marquis Yi of Zeng and the tiered chamber for the King of Zhongshan. The demand for impressive tombs for rulers and their officials never ceased, but burials were increasingly created away from the loess, as for the imperial princes of the Han in the second century BC, when horizontal tombs were dug into small, rocky mountains. And the epic tombs of the Qin lords are the precursors of the mounded tombs of the Tang emperors (AD 618–906), the tomb of the Wanli Emperor, the fourteenth emperor of the Ming dynasty (AD 1562–1620), outside Beijing or that of Sun Yat-sen (1866–1925), the first provisional leader of the Republic of China.

The majority of the tombs are manifestations of the beliefs and architecture of two key tenets of the ancestral cult: firstly, the need to provide suitable dwellings and ritual spaces, and secondly, the regular offering of nourishment that increased in complexity and presentation through subsequent dynasties, from the leader at Taosi to the Lord of Rui's participation in the ritual revolution. Only in tombs do we witness an engagement with the rituals of the Zhou accompanied by localised and idiosyncratic preferences, as Ya Chang, Yu Bo, the Marquis of Zeng and the King of Zhongshan expressed multiple identities and allegiances. Carefully curated textual history rarely offers such complexity. We can trace how the languages of objects expanded from a few bells in the tombs of Ya Chang to a larger set for the Lord of Rui and then, explosively, to a whole orchestra in Zeng. We can discover far-reaching contacts through materials such as jade from the enigmatic forms at Liangzhu to sceptres in Sichuan, in steppe arrowheads in the southern tomb of Lord Bai and animal motifs across the grasslands from gold-rich kurgans at Arzhan in South Siberia to Majiayuan in Gansu province. But we are also struck by how distinctive many societies and their universes were – the forests of Sanxingdui, the whirling spirits at Hubei and the slinking beasts at Zhongshan. And our Western dichotomy between real and replica is challenged by the vocabulary and philosophy of China, most especially by the Marquis of Zeng's inner coffin and the clay figures populating the mausoleum of the First Emperor.

A mobile livelihood among animals took steppe warriors with their distinctive inventory of belts, horse tack, animal ornaments, daggers and knives to Yuhuangmiao and Majiayuan. The pastoralists had no vessel sets and no jades or inscribed bronzes, yet they offered valuable materials, technologies and, most significantly, horses to the dynasties on the Central Plains. While the continual need to seek horses could be interpreted as a burden, we can also look at it another way. Horses and their riders brought the settled states – from the Zhou to the Qin, to their successors – into contact with the people and skills of Inner Asia. Eventually, horses led them into present-day Xinjiang, a preliminary move to begin exporting silk and building settlements and trade across its oases, what we now call the Silk Roads.[1] These dialogues with horse breeders, silk merchants and later Buddhist monks opened the Indo-Iranian world to China in the second century BC, and brought China closer to the rest of Eurasia, an early form of globalisation.[2] Today Siberian gas and Mongolian copper have taken the place of armies of horses.

No approach to understanding China is free from one's geographical and cultural position, for we are all the product of our histories, languages and traditions, and tied to the universes that we believe in. However, rather than fostering mutual miscomprehension, or a distrust of 'the other' we should recognise the majesty of Chinese civilisation and the imperatives of its ancient culture, formed by its continental scale. Differences in material life and belief do not have to be, and should not be, boundaries. If our planet is to remain safely shared, we must see them as invitations to interact, learn and prosper.

List of Tombs

1. The tomb of the leader with the king-*cong*, at Fanshan, M12, at Liangzhu, Zhejiang province. Length 3.1 m, width 1.65 m, depth 1.1 m. Zhejiangsheng Wenwu Kaogu Yanjiusuo, *Liangzhu Yizhiqun Kaogu Baogao 2: Fanshan* (*Report of the Group of Sites at Liangzhu 2: Fanshan*), 2 vols. (Wenwu Chubanshe, 2005), vol. 1, p. 29, fig. 11.

2. The vandalised tomb, M22, at Taosi, Linfen, Shanxi province. Length 5–5.3 m, width 3.7 m, area 19.34 sqm, depth between 7 and 8 m. He Nu, Yan Zhibin and Song Jianzhong, 'Taosi Chengzhi Faxian Taosi Wenhua Zhongqi Muzang' ('The Middle-period Tombs of the Taosi Culture at Taosi'), *Kaogu* 9 (2003), pp. 3–6, fig. 1.

3. Ya Chang's tomb, M54, at Huayuanzhuang, Anyang, Henan province. Length 6.03 m, width 4.4 m, area 24 sqm, depth between 5 and 6 m. Zhongguo Shehui Kexueyuan Kaogu Yanjiusuo, *Anyang Yinxu Huayuanzhuang Dongdi Shangdai Muzang* (*Report on the Excavations of Huayuanzhuang Locus East in Anyang*) (Kexue Chubanshe, 2007), figs. 62, 64, for objects fig. 77.

4. Sacrificial Pit 2 at Sanxingdui, Guanghan City, Sichuan province. Approx. 5 by 2 m, area 10 sqm, depth *c.*1.5 m. Sichuansheng Wenwu Kaogu Yanjiusuo (ed.), *Sanxingdui Jisikeng* (*The Sacrificial Pits at Sanxingdui*) (Wenwu Chubanshe, 1999), p.160.

5. Yu Bo's double tomb, M13, at Zhuyuangou, Baoji, Shaanxi province. Length 3.75 m, width 4.4 m, area 16.5 sqm, depth 2.8 m. Lu Liancheng and Hu Zhisheng, *Baoji Yuguo Mudi* (*Yu State Cemeteries in Baoji*), 2 vols. (Wenwu Chubanshe, 1988), vol. 1, p. 48, fig. 34.

6. The Lord of Rui's tomb, M27, with those of his main consort, M26, his secondary consort, M19, and a man, perhaps his son, M28, at Liangdaicun, Hancheng, Shaanxi province. M27: length 7.5 m, width 4.98 m, area 37.35 sqm, depth 13.2 m, southern ramp *c.*34 m, northern ramp 18 m. Sun Bingjun et al., 'Shaanxi Hancheng Liangdaicun Yizhi M27 Fajue Jianbao' ('The Excavation of Tomb M27 at Liangdaicun, Hancheng County'), *Kaogu yu Wenwu* 6 (2007), pp. 3–22, p. 3, fig. 1. M26: length 5.6 m, width 4.5 m, area 25.2 sqm, depth 12.1 m, southern ramp 26 m. Sun Bingjun et al., 'Shaanxi Hancheng Liangdaicun Yizhi M26 Fajue Jianbao' ('The Excavation of Tomb M26 at Liangdaicun, Hancheng County'), *Wenwu* 1 (2008), pp. 4–21, p. 5, fig. 2. M19: length 5.73 m, width 4.7 m,

area 26.9 sqm, depth 11.98 m, southern ramp 26 m. Sun Bingjun et al., 'Shaanxi Hancheng Liangdaicun Yizhi M19 Fajue Jianbao' ('The Excavation of Tomb M19 at Liangdaicun, Hancheng County'), *Kaogu yu Wenwu* 2 (2007), pp. 3–14, p. 5, fig. 5. M28: length 5 m, width 3.5 m, area 17.5 sqm, southern ramp 19 m. Shaanxisheng Kaogu Yanjiuyuan, Weinanshi Wenwu Baohu Kaogu Yanjiusuo and Hanchengshi Jingqu Guanli Weiyuanhui, *Liangdaicun Ruiguo Mudi: 2007 Nian Fajue Baogao* (*Cemetery of Rui State at Liangdaicun: An Excavation Report of 2007*) (Wenwu Chubanshe, 2010), p. 104, figs. 105, 106.

7. Plan and section of the tomb of the Mountain Rong leader, M18, at Yuhuangmiao, Jundushan, Hebei province. Length at the mouth 3.6 m, width at the western end 3.23 m, width at the eastern end 1.6 m, depth 2.66 m. Beijingshi Wenwu Yanjiusuo, *Jundushan Mudi: Yuhuangmiao* (*Yuhuangmiao at the Jundushan Cemeteries*), 4 vols. (Wenwu Chubanshe, 2010), vol. 1, pp. 287–91.

8. The tomb of Lord Bai of Zhongli at Shuangdun, Bengbu, Anhui province. Diameter at the top 20 m, diameter at the base 14 m, depth 7.5 m. Mound height 9 m, base 70 m by 56 m remaining. Anhuisheng Wenwu Kaogu Yanjiusuo and Bengbushi Bowuguan, *Zhonglijun Bai Mu* (*The Tomb of Lord Bai of the Zhongli State*), 3 vols. (Wenwu Chubanshe, 2013), vol. 1, p. 37, fig. 6.

9. The tomb of the Marquis Yi of Zeng, Suizhou, Hubei province. The pit is 13 m deep and in it at the base is a tomb of four rooms built of wood, all between 3.3 m and 3.5 m in height. The private room in the east is 9.5 m long and 4.75 m wide, the central ceremonial room is 9.75 m long and 4.75 m wide, the west room for the female attendants is 8.65 m long and 3.25 m wide, and the northern room, the armoury, is 4.25 m long and 4.75 m wide. Hubeisheng Bowuguan, *Zenghou Yi Mu* (*Tomb of Marquis Yi of State Zeng*), 2 vols. (Wenwu Chubanshe, 1989), vol. 1, pp. 7–19.

10. The tomb of King Cuo of Zhongshan at Lingshou, near Shijiazhuang, Hebei province. The burial pit is 8.2 m deep, length 13.7 m and width 12.6 m, with the outer wooden coffin *c.* 3 m in height. The four steps around the platform on both sides of the burial chamber were 1.5 m high. Southern ramp height is 40 m remaining; northern ramp 45 m remaining. Mound base 100 m by 90 m, height 15 m remaining. Hebeisheng Wenwu Yanjiusuo, *Cuo Mu: Zhanguo Zhongshanguo Guowang Zhi Mu* (*Tomb of Cuo, the King of the Zhongshan State in the Warring States Period*), 2 vols. (Wenwu Chubanshe, 1995), vol. 1, pp. 27–38.

11. The tomb of the warrior, M16, at Majiayuan, Zhangjiachuan, Gansu province. Length east–west at the mouth 12.6 m, and north to south 6.7 m, depth 7 m. Wang Hui et al., 'Zhangjiachuan Majiayuan Zhanguo Mudi 2008–2009 Nian Fajue Jianbao' ('Brief Report on the 2008–2009 Excavation of the Majiayuan Cemetery in Zhangjiachuan, of the Warring States Period'), *Wenwu* 10 (2010), pp. 4–26, p. 20, fig. 49.

12. The mound of the First Emperor's tomb, 355 m by 345 m (almost a square), 55 m high. Stepped walls starting at ground level base: 170 m east–west, 145 m north–south; top: 124 m east–west, 107 m north-south; 30 m high, openings for the ramps through the walls to the coffin chamber 52–57 m in width. Pit: 170 m east–west, 145 m north–south, around 30 m deep. The tomb chamber: 80 m by 50 m by 15 m. The stone wall surrounding the tomb chamber: 145 m east–west, 125 m north–south, 14 m high, 8 m thick. Walls of the mausoleum: outer wall: 2,188 m by 971 m; inner wall: 1,355 m by 580 m. Duan Qingbo, 'Qinshihuangdi Ling de Wutan Kaogu Diaocha: "863" Jihua Qinshihuang Ling Wutan Kaogu Jinzhan Qingkuang de Baogao' ('The Geophysical Exploration of the Mausoleum of Emperor Qin Shihuang: The New Archaeological Discovery of the National 863 Project'), *Xibei Daxue Xuebao* 1 (2005), pp. 80–86; Duan Qingbo, 'Qinshihuang Ling Fengtu Jianzhu Tantao: Jianshi "Zhongcheng Guanyou"' ('On the Mound of the First Emperor's Tomb'), *Kaogu* 5 (2006), pp. 70–76.

List of Illustrations

Chapter 1

Chapter 2

Chapter 3

Chapter 4

List of Illustrations

Chapter 5

Chapter 6

Chapter 7

Chapter 8

Chapter 9

Chapter 10

Chapter 11

List of Illustrations

Colour Photographs

List of Illustrations

Notes

Introduction: The World of the Afterlife

1 https://www.theguardian.com/politics/2022/mar/31/teach-uk-students-about-china-to-tackle-knowledge-deficit-say-experts.

2 The Loess Plateau is used as a convenient shorthand for the much larger area covered in loess. The fine dust is often called rockflour.

3 By the fifteenth century AD wheat had generally replaced millet, but was prepared and presented in a Chinese rather than in a Western style.

4 Rammed earth is a specific building technique in which earth is pounded or tamped within a form by a tool, see Xie Liye et al., 'Architectural Energetics for Rammed-earth Compaction in the Context of Neolithic to Early Bronze Age Sites in the Middle Yellow River Valley, China', *Journal of Archaeological Science* 126 (2021), pp. 1–14.

5 As illustrated as early as the construction of the ancient city at Liangzhu (Chapter 1), large tasks were divided between smaller groups, Wang Ningyuan, Dong Chuanwan, Xu Honggen and Zhuang Yijie, 'Letting the Stones Speak: An Interdisciplinary Survey of Stone Collection and Construction at Liangzhu City, Prehistoric Lower Yangtze River', *Geoarchaeology* 35 (2020), pp. 625–43.

6 Sima Qian's history, the *Shi Ji*, will be mentioned many times as an important source. Major parts are translated and published in English in Burton Watson, *Records of the Grand Historian of China. Translated from the Shih Chi of Ssu-Ma Ch'ien*, 2 vols. (Columbia University Press, 1961). See also William H. Nienhauser (ed.), *The Grand Scribe's Records*, 10 vols. (Indiana University Press, 1994).

7 Loess is a wind-blown deposit covering large areas of northern China. Near Lanzhou it can be as much as 300 metres deep, while further east it may be 40–80 metres. The loess is highly relevant to China's northern ceramic tradition, described in Chapter 2; see also Rose Kerr and Nigel Wood, *Science and Civilisation in China*, vol. 5, *Chemistry and Chemical Technology*, part 12: *Ceramic Technology* (Cambridge University Press, 2004), pp. 90–112. Also, in both the wind-blown and water-deposited forms, loess offers very stable cliff faces. These enabled the construction of the deep tombs described in Chapters 3, 5 and 6. The stability of loess is fundamental to the discussion of large tombs in these chapters. For stability see Li Yanrong, Zhang Tao, Zhang Yongbo and

Xu Qiang, 'Geometrical Appearance and Spatial Arrangement of Structural Blocks of the Malan Loess in NW China: Implications for the Formation of Loess Columns', *Journal of Asian Earth Sciences* 158 (2018), pp. 18–28; Ruth Mostern, *The Yellow River: A Natural and Unnatural History* (Yale University Press, 2021).

8 The term civilisation is often used rather loosely to refer to the complex societies in Western Asia and ancient Egypt, as in David Wengrow, *What Makes Civilization? The Ancient Near East and the Future of the West* (Oxford University Press, 2010). In this book the cultures of the Mediterranean and Europe are treated as descendants of those earlier societies. This has given so-called 'Western civilisation' prominence, which it might not have had if, for example, the cultures of the Aztecs or the indigenous peoples of North America had effectively withstood the diseases which accompanied Western colonisation. The geography of Eurasia has allowed both China and the steppe to develop what we should recognise as, at least, two further and different advanced civilisations.

9 In the past there were rather simplistic notions that civilisation developed in stages adopted almost independently by peoples across the Western world, known as Neo-evolutionism. Today the role of contact between peoples, spreading what we call civilisation, is much more clearly recognised and is discussed in depth in Mark D. Pagel, *Wired for Culture: The Natural History of Human Cooperation* (Allen Lane, 2012).

10 Norman Yoffee's definitions and comparisons of cities and states based on those in Western Asia and Egypt have been especially compelling, as in *Myths of the Archaic State: Evolution of the Earliest Cities, States, and Civilizations* (Cambridge University Press, 2005). As much has been revealed by excavation in China since Yoffee's work was published, it is likely that he and others would now have a different perspective on developments in China and would limit direct comparisons with regions to the west of Tibet.

11 People in many early societies around the world prepared elaborate tombs to the degree that their beliefs and possessions permitted. All of them allow us some understanding of their societies. If the burials are restricted in size or content, we will be able to explore the social conditions of relative wealth, status, the position of the society as a whole and the interest or otherwise in puritanism. Larger tombs offer different degrees of information. In all cases, this burial information must be meshed with evidence from other sources, including not only texts but the landfall and climate also. The beliefs of the peoples across China, and their skills in manufacture, with the spaces offered by large tombs, led to elaborate depositions of exceptional quantities of artefacts. In the case of China, the role of the ancestral cult was another

contributing factor to the social importance of the tombs. While in many parts of Eurasia, Christianity, Islam and Buddhism inhibited later use of such complex burials, these beliefs did not have the same impact in China.

12 Anthony Barbieri-Low makes a revealing comparison between ancient Egypt and early China in *Ancient Egypt and Early China: State, Society, and Culture* (University of Washington Press, 2021).

13 The tombs number eleven, but the two pits in Chapter 4, with fine bronzes, jade and gold at Sanxingdui, were also ways of meeting the spirits and the supernatural in another part of the universe.

14 Neil MacGregor, *Living with the Gods: On Beliefs and Peoples* (Allen Lane, 2018), pp. xx–xxi.

15 It is probably not correct to see the choice of the language of objects as a paraphrase or watered-down version of Pierre Bourdieu's concept of Habitus, in *Outline of a Theory of Practice* (Cambridge University Press, 1977). Bourdieu's work is concerned with Western society and its class structures, whereas here the objects are taken as a means to enter into the lifestyles, customs and beliefs of societies difficult for us otherwise to reach. While there were undoubtedly several different strata in all Chinese societies, these are not readily examined in the framework chosen here.

16 Art is a slippery concept and its definition depends on the demands and beliefs of a society. Western preconceptions, emphasising representation, have put up barriers to recognising artistic achievement in early China; objects for the offerings to the ancestors were the centre of artistic activity.

17 Wu Hung, *Monumentality in Early Chinese Art and Architecture* (Stanford University Press, 1995), p. 71.

18 For the *Zuo Zhuan* see a translation that will be used throughout, Stephen W. Durrant, Wai-yee Li and David Schaberg, *Zuo Tradition/Zuozhuan: Commentary on the 'Spring and Autumn Annals'*, 3 vols. (University of Washington Press, 2016), vol. 1, p. 301.The translation used here is from Maria Khayutina, 'The Sacred Space of an Aristocratic Clan in Zhou China (11th–3rd Centuries BC) under Transformation: An Attempt at Interpretation', in Michael Dickhardt and Vera Dorofeeva-Lichtmann (eds.), *Creating and Representing Sacred Spaces*. Göttinger Studien Zur Asienforschung (Monograph Series), Heft 2–3 (Peust & Gutschmidt Verlag, 2003), pp. 113–44, where she makes use of a translation by James Legge, *The Ch'un Ts'ew with the Tso Chuen. The Chinese Classics: With a Translation, Critical and Exegetical Notes, Prolegomena, and Copious Indexes* (1865, repr. Taipei: SMC Publishing, 1991), p. 157. The term is correctly referred to as 'sacrifice' in both translations, but as always describes offerings or ceremonial ritual banquets in which large numbers of vessels for food and alcohol were used. In this book the term sacrifice is replaced by ritual banquet or

offerings. A discussion of who might attend such family offerings is discussed in Maria Khayutina, 'Welcoming Guests – Constructing Corporate Privacy? An Attempt at a Socio-anthropological Interpretation of Ancestral Rituals Evolution in Ancient China (ca. XI–V cc. BC)', *Berliner China-Hefte* 24 (2003), pp. 35–50.

19 However, over time, long after the rule of the First Emperor, very large clans grew in southern China and overseas, with their own forms of large communities.

20 Li Feng, *Early China: A Social and Cultural History* (Cambridge University Press, 2013), pp. 144–6.

21 Organisations existed in China, but they took forms unlike those in Western Europe. The highly controlled and supervised organisation of artisans is described in Lothar von Falkenhausen, *Chinese Society in the Age of Confucius (1000–250 BC): The Archaeological Evidence* (Cotsen Institute of Archaeology, University of California, 2006), pp. 419–20. The priority given to the educated elite over such groups as merchants and even landowners, as late as the Song dynasty, is described in Yuri Pines, *The Everlasting Empire: The Political Culture of Ancient China and Its Imperial Legacy* (Princeton University Press, 2012), pp. 113–14.

22 Riccardo Fracasso, 'Holy Mothers of Ancient China: A New Approach to the "Hsi-Wang-Mu"', *T'oung Pao* 74 (1988), pp. 1–46; Elfriede R. Knauer, 'The Queen Mother of the West: A Study of the Influence of Western Prototypes on the Iconography of the Taoist Deity', in Victor H. Mair (ed.), *Contact and Exchange in the Ancient World* (University of Hawai'i Press, 2006), pp. 62–115. A large number of different legends have been assembled in volumes such as Anne Birrell, *Chinese Mythology: An Introduction* (Johns Hopkins University Press, 1993). They come from a multitude of sources and at the earliest usually date from the late Warring States (475–221 BC) and the Han Dynasty (206 BC–AD 220). Such groups also include a creation myth. However, these legends carry less weight than the complex correlations and divinations that describe a universe of multiple components without creation by gods or spirits.

23 Falkenhausen, *Chinese Society*, p. 287.

24 Angus Charles Graham, *Disputers of the Tao: Philosophical Argument in Ancient China* (Open Court, 1989), p. 320.

25 MacGregor, *Living with the Gods*, p. vii.

26 Lothar Ledderose, *China Schreibt Anders* (Alfred Kröner Verlag, 2021).

27 Extensive excavation of tombs, especially since the 1950s, has unearthed further documents which offer new information and also embellish the traditional story.

Chapter 1: The Mystery of Jade

1 While the Kunlun Mountains are the best-known source of jade in China, there are many potential seams in several areas. These have been exploited at different times. A full overview of sources is in Gina Lee Barnes, 'Understanding Chinese Jade in a World Context', *Journal of the British Academy* 6 (2018), pp. 1–63.

2 Sun E-tu Zen and Sun Shiou-chuan (trans.), *T'ien-Kung K'ai-Wu: Chinese Technology in the Seventeenth Century* (Pennsylvania State University, 1966), p. 300.

3 Zhuang Yijie and Du Shenglun, 'Holocene Sea-level Change and Evolution of Prehistoric Settlements Around the Yangtze Delta Region', in M. T. Carson (ed.), *Palaeolandscapes in Archaeology: Lessons for the Past and Future* (Routledge, 2021), pp. 192–214.

4 For a survey of the archaeology of the south-east see Liu Li and Chen Xing-can, *The Archaeology of China: From the Late Paleolithic to the Early Bronze Age* (Cambridge University Press, 2012), pp. 197–212.

5 The identification of a city is usually equated with urbanism, resting on a definition that applies above all to Mesopotamia. Yoffee, in *Myths of the Archaic State*, pp. 60–62, emphasises the revolutionary nature of the creation of cities and states as set out first by V. Gordon Childe. Liangzhu and Taosi were undoubtedly revolutionary within their own contexts. The large size of China and the scale of its populations across a range of diverse regions present us with a series of social developments very different from those in Mesopotamia or Egypt. Given the geographical separation of the core of China from the early developments in Mesopotamia, Iran and the Indus Valley, we cannot expect to see developments there mirrored in ancient China. The use and application of the term 'state' is likewise debated in the case of China. A single definition for a city or for a state implies a strong unity across the whole territory, which during the early centuries of ancient China does not fit with what we see across the vast area. A case-by-case examination for the arrival of statehood probably fits best with China's huge regional diversity. For an argument for the case-by-case approach with respect to the notion of state see Gideon Shelach and Yitzhak Jaffee, 'The Earliest States in China: A Long-term Trajectory Approach', *Journal of Archaeological Research* 22 (2014), pp. 327–64.

6 For an introduction on the position of Liangzhu among the many discoveries that have changed our view of early China see Jessica Rawson (ed.), *Mysteries of Ancient China: New Discoveries from the Early Dynasties* (British Museum Publications, 1996).

7 The history of the excavation of the sites in and around the Liangzhu city is fully described in Liu Bin, Qin Ling and Zhuang Yijie (eds.), *Liangzhu Culture:*

Society, Belief and Art in Neolithic China (Routledge, 2020). A full archaeological description is in Zhejiangsheng Wenwu Kaogu Yanjiusuo, *Liangzhu Gucheng Zonghe Yanjiu Baogao (A Comprehensive Study of Liangzhu Ancient City)* (Wenwu Chubanshe, 2019). All descriptions in this chapter of the cemeteries and their jades, and of the archaeological features of the ancient city, draw on these volumes.

8   A key paper that led to this assessment is Colin A. Renfrew and Liu Bin, 'The Emergence of Complex Society in China: The Case of Liangzhu', *Antiquity* 92 (2018), pp. 975–90.

9   This jade was excavated from Yaoshan tomb M2, Zhejiangsheng Wenwu Kaogu Yanjiusuo, *Liangzhu Yizhiqun Kaogu Baogao 1: Yaoshan (Reports of the Group Sites at Liangzhu 1: Yaoshan)* (Wenwu Chubanshe, 2003), p. 220, col. pl. 30. This was the upper section of a comb. For one with the tines still in place see Zhejiangsheng, *Liangzhu Gucheng*, pp. 20–33.

10 For the mineralogy of jade and nephrite in particular see Andrew Middleton and Ian Freestone, 'The Mineralogy and Occurrence of Jade', in Jessica Rawson, *Chinese Jade: From the Neolithic to the Qing* (British Museum Publications, 1995), pp. 413–23 and Katherine Eremin, Angela Chang and Ariel O'Conner, 'Jade in the Lab', in Jenny F. So, *Early Chinese Jades in the Harvard Art Museums* (Harvard Art Museums, 2019), pp. 29–47.

11 For technologies in working jade at Liangzhu see Fang Xiangming, 'A Controlled Fine Craft: Jade Production Techniques in the Liangzhu Culture', in Liu et al. (eds.), *Liangzhu Culture*, pp. 115–64.

12 For discussion of jade-working techniques see Margaret Sax, Nigel D. Meeks, Carol Michaelson and Andrew P. Middleton, 'The Identification of Carving Techniques on Chinese Jade', *Journal of Archaeological Science* 31 (2004), pp. 1413–28.

13 Qin Ling, 'The Liangzhu Culture', in Anne P. Underhill (ed.), *A Companion to Chinese Archaeology* (Wiley-Blackwell, 2013), pp. 574–96; pp. 589–90 mention the discoveries of workshops at Tangshan.

14 For the history of the Warring States see Mark Edward Lewis, 'Warring States: Political History', in Michael Loewe and Edward L. Shaughnessy (eds.), *The Cambridge History of Ancient China: From the Origins of Civilization to 221 BC* (Cambridge University Press, 1999), pp. 587–650.

15 For an account of the list of ritual jades from the *Rites of Zhou* in English, see Berthold Laufer, *Jade: A Study in Chinese Archaeology and Religion* (Field Museum of Natural History, 1912), pp. 120–21. For a summary of the early textual tradition on jade see Rawson, *Chinese Jade*, pp. 54–60.

16 Correlative thinking and concepts are discussed in Graham, *Disputers of the Tao*, pp. 315–18; Derk Bodde, *Chinese Thought, Society and Science: The Intellectual*

    and Social Background of Science and Technology in Pre-Modern China (University of Hawai'i Press, 1991), pp. 97–147; Roel Sterckx, *Chinese Thought from Confucius to Cook Ding* (Pelican, 2019), pp. 84–94.

17 Zhejiangsheng Wenwu Kaogu Yanjiusuo, *Liangzhu Yizhiqun Kaogu Baogao 2: Fanshan (Reports of the Group of Sites at Liangzhu 2: Fanshan)*, 2 vols. (Wenwu Chubanshe, 2005). The discussions of tomb M12 and its contents are drawn from these two volumes.

18 For the contrast between the use of jade versus gold for weapons of authority, personal ornaments and symbols, the discoveries at the Varna cemetery in Bulgaria are vital. See Vladimir Slavchev, 'The Varna Eneolithic Cemetery in the Context of the Late Copper Age in the East Balkans', in David W. Anthony and Jennifer Y. Chi (eds.), *The Lost World of Old Europe: The Danube Valley, 5000–3500 BC* (Institute for the Study of the Ancient World / Princeton University Press, 2010), pp. 193–210. These two different materials, jade and gold, were used in parallel ways as signs of authority in life and the afterlife, Svend Hansen, *Repräsentationen Der Macht* (Harrassowitz Verlag, 2020).

19 Liu et al. (eds.), *Liangzhu Culture*, pp. 49–114.

20 Very little is known or recognised about the views of the spirits in early China. They certainly differed from region to region, as we shall see in the next chapter when we compare the tomb contents at Liangzhu with those at Taosi. For a general introduction see Guo Jue, 'The Spirit World', in P. R. Goldin (ed.), *Routledge Handbook of Early Chinese History* (Routledge, 2018), pp. 229–60.

21 Rawson, *Chinese Jade*, pp. 32–348.

22 Liu et al. (eds.), *Liangzhu Culture*, p. 45; Yoffee, *Myths of the Archaic State*, p. 43, Liu et al. (eds.), *Liangzhu Culture*, pp. 13–6, 40–42.

23 For discussion of the domestication of rice see Dorian Q. Fuller, Emma Harvey and Qin Ling, 'Presumed Domestication? Evidence for Wild Rice Cultivation and Domestication in the Fifth Millennium BC of the Lower Yangtze Region', *Antiquity* 81 (2007), pp. 316–31; Dorian Q. Fuller and Qin Ling, 'Water Management and Labour in the Origins and Dispersal of Asian Rice', *World Archaeology* 41 (2009), pp. 88–111.

24 Zhuang Yijie, Ding Pin and Charles French, 'Water Management and Agricultural Intensification of Rice Farming at the Late-Neolithic Site of Maoshan, Lower Yangtze River, China', *The Holocene* 24 (2014), pp. 531–45.

25 Qin Ling and Dorian Q. Fuller, 'Why Rice Farmers Don't Sail: Coastal Subsistence Traditions and Maritime Trends in Early China', in Wu Chunming and Barry Vladimir Rolett (eds.), *Prehistoric Maritime Cultures and Seafaring in East Asia* (Springer, 2019), pp. 159–91.

26 Zhejiangsheng, *Liangzhu Gucheng*, pp. 195–6, figs. 7-64, 7-65.

27 Liu et al. (eds.), *Liangzhu Culture*, pp. 33–6.

28 Liu Bin et al., 'Earliest Hydraulic Enterprise in China, 5,100 Years Ago', *Proceedings of the National Academy of Sciences* 114 (2017), pp. 13637–42.

29 Liu et al. (eds.), *Liangzhu Culture*, p. 45.

30 For a plan of the mounds in the outer city see Zhejiangsheng, *Liangzhu Gucheng*, p. 201, fig. 8-1.

31 For the range of different forms of construction, including the dams, see Zhejiangsheng, *Liangzhu Gucheng*; for the consolidation of Mojiashan see Zhejiangsheng, *Liangzhu Gucheng*, pp. 138–9.

32 Paola Demattè, 'Longshan-Era Urbanism: The Role of Cities in Predynastic China', *Asian Perspectives* 38 (1999), pp. 119–53.

33 Zhejiangsheng, *Liangzhu Gucheng*, p. 139.

34 We can follow the introduction of jade as a valued material and its spread in stages by analogy with the discovery and spread of metallurgy, as proposed by Evgeny Chernykh, in the form of metallurgical provinces in Evgeny N. Chernykh, S. V. Kuz'minykh and L. B. Orlovskaya, 'Ancient Metallurgy of Northeast Asia: From the Urals to the Saiano-Altai', in Katheryn M. Linduff (ed.), *Metallurgy in Ancient Eastern Eurasia from the Urals to the Yellow River* (Edwin Mellen Press, 2004), pp. 15–36.

35 The earliest personal ornaments, widely used in the Palaeolithic period, were fine stones, animal teeth and bone ornaments. Jade appearing among these is illustrated in Ji Ping and Tang Chung (eds.), *Hamin Yuqi Yanjiu* (*Study of the Jades from Harmin*) (Zhonghua Shuju, 2018). A few examples are also mapped in Teng Shu-p'ing (ed.), *Select Jades in the National Palace Museum, Vol 1: The Spirit of Jade, 1* (National Palace Museum, 2019), p. 128.

36 This important site is reported in Li Yingkui and Gao Bo, 'Heilongjiang Raohexian Xiaonanshan Xinshiqi Shidai Muzang' ('Neolithic Tombs at Xiaonanshan, Raohe County, Heilongjiang'), *Kaogu* 2 (1996), pp. 1–8. For the site of Harmin see Ji Ping, 'The Excavation of the Neolithic Site at Hamin Mangha in Horqin Left Middle Banner, Inner Mongolia in 2011', *Chinese Archaeology* 14 (2014), pp. 10–17.

37 Archaeological work in the Hongshan area is discussed and described in Christian E. Peterson and Lu Xueming, 'Understanding Hongshan Period Social Dynamics', in Underhill (ed.), *A Companion to Chinese Archaeology*, pp. 55–80. For a full three-volume report on the excavations of tombs and their jades at the important site at Niuheliang in the Hongshan culture region see Liaoningsheng Wenwu Kaogu Yanjiusuo, *Niuheliang: Hongshan Wenhua Yizhi Fajue Baogao (1983–2003 Niandu)* (*Niuheliang: The Excavation Report of the Hongshan Culture Site*), 3 vols. (Wenwu Chubanshe, 2012). Comments on the Hongshan jades are also available in So, *Early Chinese Jades*, pp. 49–55.

38 Guo, 'The Spirit World', pp. 232–3.

39 Zhao Hui, 'From the "Songze Style" to the "Liangzhu Mode"', in Liu et al. (eds.), *Liangzhu Culture*, pp. 165–85.

40 This preponderance of early jade along the eastern seaboard was first discussed by Tang Chung, 'Dongya Jueshi de Qiyuan yu Kuosan' ('The Origin and the Spread of Slit Jade Rings in East Asia'), in Shandong Daxue Dongfang Kaogu Yanjiu Zhongxin (ed.), *Dongfang Kaogu 1* (Kexue Chubanshe, 2004), pp. 23–35. See also Tang Chung, Mana Hayashi Tang, Liu Guoxiang and Wen Yadi, 'The Neolithic Jade Revolution in Northeast China', in Elizabeth Childs-Johnson (ed.), *The Oxford Handbook of Early China* (Oxford University Press, 2020), pp. 73–100. See also Guo Dashun, 'Hongshan and Related Cultures', in Sarah Milledge Nelson (ed.), *The Archaeology of Northeast China: Beyond the Great Wall* (Routledge, 1995), pp. 21–64. The extraordinary abundance of jade has led to suggestions that we should place a Jade Age between the Stone Age and the Bronze Age, in the well-studied sequence proposed by V. Gordon Childe, 'Archaeological Ages as Technological Stages', *The Journal of the Royal Anthropological Institute of Great Britain and Ireland* 74 (1944), pp. 7–24. The existence of a Jade Age is argued most cogently in Paola Demattè, 'The Chinese Jade Age: Between Antiquarianism and Archaeology', *Journal of Social Archaeology* 6 (2006), pp. 202–26.

41 Comparison between the faces on the Hongshan jades and the Liangzhu *cong* has been made by Li Xueqin, 'Liangzhu Culture and the Shang Dynasty *Taotie* Motif', in Roderick Whitfield (ed.), *The Problem of Meaning in Early Chinese Ritual Bronzes* (Percival David Foundation of Chinese Art, 1992), pp. 56–66; Fang, 'A Controlled Fine Craft', p. 150, fig. 4.30. Hangzhou Liangzhu Yizhi Guanliqu Guanli Weiyuanhui and Zhejiangsheng Wenwu Kaogu Yanjiusuo, *Liangzhu Yuqi* (*Liangzhu Jades*) (Kexue Chubanshe, 2018), pl. III 1-20; Teng (ed.), *Selected Jades*, Map B, p. 138.

42 Rings with faces on them – in the first arrangement along the curve and then later at right angles to the curve – are found at Yaoshan; see Zhejiangsheng, *Yaoshan*, col. pls. 13, 313, 328. An important series of jades with such faces are illustrated in Fang, 'A Controlled Fine Craft', p. 151, fig. 4.31. These motifs were evidently highly dependent on the new technique of cutting the jade with small silica-like tools.

43 Fang, 'A Controlled Fine Craft', pp. 121–2.

44 Some of the cores have survived, showing us the stepped columns that came out of such a centre; see Qin Ling, 'Power and Belief: Reading the Liangzhu Jade and Society', in Liu et al. (eds.), *Liangzhu Culture*, p. 88, fig. 2.33c.

45 A variety of suggestions have been made by Elizabeth Childs-Johnson; see 'The Jade Age Revisited, ca. 3500–2000 BCE', in Childs-Johnson (ed.), *The Oxford Handbook of Early China*, pp. 101–17.

46 Similar motifs are incised on ceramics. They have not been so fully reconstructed, Liu et al. (eds.), *Liangzhu Culture*, p. 47, fig. 2.24.

47 For an illustration of a mass of jades in a tomb at Sidun see So, *Early Chinese Jades*, pp. 60–61; Chen Lihua, 'Jiangsu Wujin Sidun Yizhi de Xinshiqi Shidai Yiwu' ('The Neolithic Site of Sidun in Wujin, Jiangsu'), *Wenwu* 2 (1984), pp. 17–22. In this tomb, two rows of twenty-six *cong* and also many axes and *bi* covered the occupant's body.

48 James B. Innes and Zong Yongqiang, 'History of Mid- and Late Holocene Palaeofloods in the Yangtze Coastal Lowlands, East China: Evaluation of Non-Pollen Palynomorph Evidence, Review and Synthesis', *Quaternary* 4 (2021), p. 21.

49 Zhuang et al., 'Water Management and Agricultural Intensification'.

50 What happened along the eastern coast is much disputed. However, deposition of silt and small shells is taken to indicate sea rise and sea incursion. Liu Yan, Sun Qianli, Ian Thomas, Zhang Li, Brian Finlayson, Zhang Weiguo, Chen Jing and Chen Zhongyuan, 'Middle Holocene Coastal Environment and the Rise of the Liangzhu City Complex on the Yangtze Delta, China', *Quaternary Research* 84 (2015), pp. 326–34; He Keyang, Lu Houyuan, Sun Guoping, Ji Xiang, Wang Yonglei, Yan Kaikai, Zuo Xinxin, Zhang Jiangping et al., 'Multi-Proxy Evidence of Environmental Change Related to Collapse of the Liangzhu Culture in the Yangtze Delta, China', *Science China Earth Sciences* 64 (2021), pp. 890–905.

51 Wang Zhanghua et al., 'Middle Holocene Marine Flooding and Human Response in the South Yangtze Coastal Plain, East China', *Quaternary Science Reviews* 187 (2018), pp. 80–93. Zhang Haiwei et al., 'Collapse of the Liangzhu and Other Neolithic Cultures in the Lower Yangtze Region in Response to Climate Change', *Science Advances* 7 (2021), eabi9275.

52 For the spread of jade *cong* and the development of different types see Huang Tsui-mei, 'Zailun Zhongguo Xinshiqi Shidai Wanqi Yucong Xingzhi yu Juese Zhi Yanbian' ('The Evolution of Style and Role of Jade *Cong* in the Late Neolithic China: An In-depth Analysis'), *Nanyi Xuebao* 1 (2010), pp. 25–52. Huang offers a useful map of the distribution of *cong* across China.

53 Investigation of the Shijiahe site is reported in Hubeisheng Jingzhou Bowuguan Shijiahe Kaogudui, Hubeisheng Wenwu Kaogu Yanjiusuo Shijiahe Kaogudui and Beijing Daxue Kaogu Xuexi Shijiahe Kaogudui, *Tianmen Shijiahe Kaogu Fajue Baogao 1: Xiaojiawuji (Xiaojiawuji: Archaeological Excavations at Shijiahe, Tianmen)*, 2 vols. (Wenwu Chubanshe, 1999). See also Meng Huaping, Liu Hui, Xiang Qifang and Lu Chengqiu, 'Surveys and Excavations in 2014–2016 at Shijiahe Site in Tianmen City, Hubei', *Chinese Archaeology* 18 (2018), pp. 13–27.

54 Mark E. Lewis, *The Flood Myths of Early China* (SUNY, 2006).

55 Accounts of the work of Emperor Yu and other legendary emperors are set out in a late section of *The Book of Documents*, the *Shu Jing*; see James Legge, *The Chinese Classics*, vol. 3, part 1: *The First Parts of the Shoo-King* (Trübner & Co., 1865). They are also recounted by the great Han historian Sima Qian; see Nienhauser (ed.), *The Grand Scribe's Records*, vol. 1. The use of the flood control legends as foundations of Chinese myths of its past is described in Li Min, *Social Memory and State Formation in Early China* (Cambridge University Press, 2018).

56 As well as the *cong* and *bi*, many arcs, fewer creatures and of course beads and plaques were spread.

57 Wu Wenxiang and Liu Tungsheng, 'Possible Role of the "Holocene Event 3" on the Collapse of Neolithic Cultures around the Central Plain of China', *Quaternary International* 117 (2004), pp. 153–66; Zhuang Yijie and Tristram R. Kidder, 'Archaeology of the Anthropocene in the Yellow River Region, China, 8000–2000 Cal. BP', *The Holocene* 24 (2014), pp. 1602–23.

58 Teng (ed.), *Select Jades*, pp. 133–41. The very early use of jade among Yangshao societies in the Wei Valley and the western Loess Plateau down to and including Taosi and Shimao (see Chapter 2) is now coming to light. Teng Shu-p'ing, 'Shiqian Zhi Xiashiqi "Huaxi Xi Yuqi" Yanjiu' ('Research on the Jade Artifacts of the "Western China Archetype" from the Prehistoric Time to the Xia Period'), 1–3, *Zhongyuan Wenwu* (2021–2). As both *cong* and *bi* discs are found, some connection with the eastern seaboard must have been established. This connection is not yet understood.

59 For a brief comment on Confucius' view on the exemplary and references to different textual versions see So, *Early Chinese Jades*, p. 190.

60 Interesting finds of both bronze and ceramic versions are illustrated in Yang Wencheng et al., 'Sichuan Pengzhou Songdai Qingtongqi Jiaocang' ('Song Period Bronze Hoards from Pengzhou, Sichuan'), *Wenwu* 1 (2009), pp. 54–70.

61 For illustrations of jades of the Qianlong period see Evelyn S. Rawski and Jessica Rawson, *China: The Three Emperors, 1662–1795* (Royal Academy of Arts, 2005).

62 Cao Xueqin (trans. D. Hawkes and J. Minford.), *The Story of the Stone*, 5 vols. (Penguin, 2012).

Chapter 2: A Disrupted Banquet

1 This vast area, the Loess Plateau, our name for the loess region, is often overlooked, but its people have played important roles in the development of

China's history and civilisation. It was singled out by Professor Tong Enzheng for its distinctive material and social culture, with an emphasis on pastoralism, Tong Enzheng, 'Shilun Woguo Cong Dongbei Zhi Xinan de Biandi Ban-yuexing Wenhua Chuanbodai' ('On the Crescent-shaped Cultural-contact Belt from North-east to South-west China'), in Wenwu Chubanshe Bianjibu (ed.), *Wenwu yu Kaogu Lunji* (Wenwu Chubanshe, 1987), pp. 17–43. Tong extended this crescent into the very different regions along the eastern mountains of the Tibetan Plateau. In other chapters of this book the Loess Plateau is empha-sised for its role in the introduction of horses to the agricultural regions, as well as providing territory in which stockbreeders could build lives and from there move into more central regions, as described in Chapters, 5, 6, 7, 10 and 11. In many papers I have given the region selected by Tong the name 'the Arc', Jessica Rawson, 'China and the Steppe: Reception and Resistance', *Antiquity* 91 (2017), pp. 375–88. In his volume *Social Memory* Li Min calls the region the Highlands, but this obliterates one major characteristic, namely the loess, and suggests by implication that the whole region was already linked or joined in some way with what he calls the lowlands, to be claimed in due course by the Shang and Zhou dynasties. The loess region was to remain distinct down to the Tang period and later.

2 For a discussion of the geological qualities of loess see Yang Xiaoping, Liu Tao and Yuan Baoyin, 'The Loess Plateau of China: Aeolian Sedimentation and Fluvial Erosion, Both with Superlative Rates', in Piotr Migoń (ed.), *Geomorphological Landscapes of the World* (Springer Netherlands, 2010), pp. 275–82.

3 The dynamics of the massed loess is very unusual, Li Yanrong, 'A Review of Shear and Tensile Strengths of the Malan Loess in China', *Engineering Geology* 236 (2018), pp. 4–10.

4 For the transfer of grains across Eurasia see Liu Xinyi et al., 'From Ecological Opportunism to Multi-Cropping: Mapping Food Globalisation in Prehistory', *Quaternary Science Reviews* 206 (2019), pp. 21–8.

5 Harry Alverson Franck, *Wandering in Northern China* (The Century Co., 1923), p. 391.

6 Although there were certainly many settled communities from 7000 BC, the growth of the larger Yangshao group across much of the loess region dates from about 5000 BC. The Yangshao sites were among the earliest discoveries of China's Neolithic. For an overview of the settlements of this stage see Liu and Chen, *The Archaeology of China*, pp. 169–212.

7 Pablo Librado et al., 'The Origins and Spread of Domestic Horses from the Western Eurasian Steppes', *Nature* 598 (2021), pp. 634–40.

8 For overviews of these changes see Dominic Hosner et al., 'Spatiotemporal Distribution Patterns of Archaeological Sites in China During the Neolithic

and Bronze Age: An Overview', *The Holocene* 26 (2016), pp. 1576–93; Zhang Chi et al., 'China's Major Late Neolithic Centres and the Rise of Erlitou', *Antiquity* 93 (2019), pp. 588–603; Zhang Chi, 'Longshan-Erlitou: Zhongguo Shiqian Wenhua Geju de Gaibian yu Qingtong Shidai Quanqiuhua de Xingcheng' ('Longshan-Erlitou Cultures: Changing Cultural Patterns in Prehistoric China and the Emergence of the Globalization in the Bronze Age'), *Wenwu* 6 (2017), pp. 50–59.

9   For the major archaeological report see Zhongguo Shehui Kexueyuan Kaogu Yanjiusuo and Shanxisheng Linfenshi Wenwuju, *Xiangfen Taosi: 1978–1985 Nian Fajue Baogao (Taosi Site in Xiangfen: Report on Archaeological Excavations in 1978– 1985)*, 4 vols. (Wenwu Chubanshe, 2015).

10 The identification of sites associated with the Xia has preoccupied many archaeologists, Sun Qingwei, 'Toward an Archaeological Reconstruction of the Xia Dynasty as History: Delineations and Methods', *Journal of Chinese Humanities (Leiden)* 1 (2019), pp. 18–42.

11 For all early Chinese writings mentioned in this book valuable background information is to be found in Michael Loewe (ed.), *Early Chinese Texts: A Bibliographical Guide* (Society for the Study of Early China and the Institute of East Asian Studies, 1993). For *The Book of Documents* see Michael Nylan, *The Five "Confucian" Classics* (Yale University Press, 2001).

12 Translations of the sections of the *Shi Ji* on the Sage Kings can be found in Nienhauser (ed.), *The Grand Scribe's Records*, vol. 1, pp. 1–20.

13 He Nu, 'The Longshan Period Site of Taosi in Southern Shanxi Province', in Underhill (ed.), *A Companion to Chinese Archaeology*, pp. 255–77.

14 Another previously unknown city is described in Sun Zhouyong et al., 'The First Neolithic Urban Center on China's North Loess Plateau: The Rise and Fall of Shimao', *Archaeological Research in Asia* 14 (2018), pp. 33–45.

15 Another important city, Zhoujiazhuang, is to the south, Zhang et al., 'China's Major Neolithic Centres'.

16 The exceptionally stable construction possible with loess stimulated the use of large walls and platforms, Xie et al., 'Architectural Energetics', 105303.

17 Xie Liye, Zahid Daudjee, Liu Chunfu and Pauline Sebillaud, 'Settlement Relocation, Urban Construction, and Social Transformation in China's Central Plain, 2300–1500 B.C.', *Asian Perspectives* 59 (2020), pp. 299–329.

18 He Nu, 'Taosi: An Archaeological Example of Urbanization as a Political Center in Prehistoric China', *Archaeological Research in Asia* 14 (2018), pp. 20–32.

19 The structures and contents of these important tombs are described and illustrated in Zhongguo et al., *Xiangfen Taosi*, vol. 2.

20 We only have a brief report on this tomb, see He Nu, Yan Zhibin and Song Jianzhong, 'Taosi Chengzhi Faxian Taosi Wenhua Zhongqi Muzang' ('The

Middle-period Tombs of the Taosi Culture at Taosi'), *Kaogu* 9 (2003), pp. 3–6. Additional information for this chapter has been taken from the main four-volume report.

21 He Nu, 'Longshan Culture Issues: Taosi and Cosmology', in Childs-Johnson (ed.), *The Oxford Handbook of Early China*, pp. 139–57.

22 One issue is that the ground level at Taosi may have been shaved and the depth of the earlier tombs, which appear to be between one and three metres, may originally have been more considerable.

23 Such a niched tomb can be compared with later tombs to the east of the Loess Plateau at Dadianzi, Zhongguo Shehui Kexueyuan Kaogu Yanjiusuo, *Dadianzi: Xiajiadian Xiaceng Wenhua Yichi yu Mudi* (*Dadianzi: Excavations on the Residence and Cemetery of the Lower Xiajiadian Culture*) (Kexue Chubanshe, 1996); and at Zhukaigou, Neimenggu Zizhiqu Wenwu Kaogu Yanjiusuo and E'erduosi Bowuguan, *Zhukaigou: Qingtong Shidai Zaoqi Yizhi Fajue Baogao* (*Zhukaigou: Excavation Report on the Early Bronze Age Site*) (Wenwu Chubanshe, 2000). Niches are found in cave houses in the Loess Plateau, as at Xiaweiluo, Xibei Daxue et al., *Xunyi Xiaweiluo* (*Xiaweiluo Site, Xunyi County, Shaanxi*) (Kexue Chubanshe, 2006). A recent discussion is in Zhang Chi, 'Yaodong Zhengfu Shiqian Huangtu Gaoyuan' ('On the Prehistoric Occupation of the Loess Plateau in Cave Dwellings'), *Kaogu yu Wenwu* 2 (2022), pp. 102–18.

24 For the mining of the ore see Chen Kuang-yu, 'The Cinnabar and Mercury Industry of the Qin Empire', in Liu Yang (ed.), *Beyond the First Emperor's Mausoleum: New Perspectives on Qin Art* (Minneapolis Institute of Arts, 2014), pp. 139–58.

25 Reported and illustrated in Song Jianzhong and Xue Xinmin, 'Shanxi Linfen Xiajin Mudi Fajue Jianbao' ('The Preliminary Report of the Excavation of the Xiajin Cemetery, Linfen, Shanxi'), *Wenwu* 12 (1998), pp. 4–13.

26 Hong Shi, 'Xian Qin Liang Han Qian Lüsongshi Qiqi Yanjiu' ('Research on Turquoise-inlaid Lacquerware in the Pre-Qin and Han Periods'), *Kaogu yu Wenwu* 3 (2019), pp. 75–87.

27 A significant number of examples were found at Qingliangsi, Shanxisheng Kaogu Yanjiusuo, Yunchengshi Wenwu Gongzuozhan and Ruichengxian Lüyou Wenhuaju, *Qingliangsi Shiqian Mudi* (*The Prehistoric Cemetery of Qingliangsi*), 3 vols. (Wenwu Chubanshe, 2016).

28 For a similar jade face from Shijiahe see Meng et al., 'Surveys and Excavations', pp. 13–27, fig. 15. The widespread distribution of these Shijiahe-type faces is seen in the discovery of one in a Western Zhou tomb at Fengxi in Shaanxi, see Zhang Changshou, 'Ji Fengxi Xinfaxian de Shoumian Yushi' ('On the Newly Discovered Jade Ornament with Animal Face Patterns from Fengxi'), *Kaogu* 5 (1987), pp. 470–73.

29 Chen Guoke, Jiang Chaonian, Wang Hui and Yang Yueguang, 'The Excavation of the Mazongshan Jade Quarry Sites in Subei County, Gansu', *Chinese Archaeology* 16 (2016), pp. 1–12.

30 Domestication of pigs is described in Liu and Chen, *The Archaeology of China*, pp. 97–104. This emphasis reveals the importance of the arrival of sheep and cattle from further west, travelling across the steppe.

31 Thomas O. Höllmann, *The Land of the Five Flavors: A Cultural History of Chinese Cuisine* (Columbia University Press, 2013), p. 49.

32 The earlier graves are reported and illustrated in Zhongguo et al., *Xiangfen Taosi*, vol. 2.

33 Quoted from David Hawkes, *Ch'u Tz'u: The Songs of the South, an Ancient Chinese Anthology* (Clarendon Press, 1959), p. 107.

34 For some alternative accounts of feasting in different cultures see Kaori O'Connor, *The Never-Ending Feast: The Anthropology and Archaeology of Feasting* (Bloomsbury Academic, 2015).

35 Typical cooking basins had been adapted by cutting holes in their bases and inserting three conical legs, to hold them over a fire. These legs were often formed around inner models of the shape required by wrapping clay around them, described in Li Wenjie, *Zhongguo Gudai Zhitao Gongyi Yanjiu (A Study of Pottery Production in Ancient China)* (Kexue Chubnashe, 1996). This is an important development affecting a very large region, mainly in loess areas, occupied by several different groups often called cultures. The topic requires more analysis and research, see Han Jianye, 'Jinxinan Yuxi Xibu Miaodigou Erqi-Longshan Shidai Wenhua de Fenqi yu Puxi' ('The Chronological Study of the Miaodigou II–Longshan Periods in North-western Shanxi and Western Henan'), *Kaogu Xuebao* 3 (2006), pp. 179–204. For the small tools used for forming the legs over moulds see Zhongguo et al., *Xiangfen Taosi*, vol. 1, pp. 286–94.

36 Kerr and Wood, *Science and Civilisation in China*, pp. 87–120.

37 The *li* also had a long future ahead of it, not only as a cooking vessel in ceramic but as a standard member of later ritual banqueting sets in bronze (Chapter 3), where the large pouches were shrunk down to become small lobes.

38 David R. Knechtges, 'A Literary Feast: Food in Early Chinese Literature', *Journal of the American Oriental Society* 106 (1986), pp. 49–63.

39 Patrick E. McGovern et al., 'Chemical Identification and Cultural Implications of a Mixed Fermented Beverage from Late Prehistoric China', *Asian Perspectives* 44 (2005), pp. 249–75.

40 Arthur Waley, *The Book of Songs* (George Allen & Unwin, 1937), p. 161.

41 For a discussion of vessel sets in the Chinese Neolithic see Zhang Chi, 'Xinshiqi Shidai Zangyi Kongjian Suojian Yinju Sili' ('Four Case Studies on Drinking Vessels Used in Neolithic Funerals'), *Jianghan Kaogu* 1 (2019), pp. 62–70.

42 Illustrated and discussed as contributing to the growth of urban settlements in Anne P. Underhill, 'Urbanization and New Social Contexts for Consumption of Food and Drink in Northern China', *Archaeological Research in Asia* 14 (2018), pp. 7–19.

43 For the social role of feasting see Brian Hayden, 'Fabulous Feasts: A Prolegomenon to the Importance of Feasting', in Michael Dietler and Brian Hayden (eds.), *Feasts: Archaeological and Ethnographic Perspectives on Food, Politics, and Power* (Smithsonian Institution Press, 2001), pp. 23–64.

44 Peter N. Hommel, 'Hunter-Gatherer Pottery: An Emerging fourteenth-century Chronology', in Peter Jordan and M. Zvelebil (eds.), *Ceramics before Farming: The Dispersal of Pottery among Prehistoric Eurasian Hunter-Gatherers* (Left Coast Press, 2009), pp. 561–9; Wang Lixin and Pauline Sebillaud, 'The Emergence of Early Pottery in East Asia: New Discoveries and Perspectives', *Journal of World Prehistory* 32 (2019), pp. 73–110.

45 Ma Hongjiao, Anke Hein, Julian Henderson and Ma Qinglin, 'The Geology of Tianshui-Qin'an Area of the Western Loess Plateau and the Chemical Characteristics of Its Neolithic Pottery', *Geoarchaeology* 35 (2020), pp. 611–24.

46 Höllmann, *The Land of the Five Flavors*, pp. 73–4.

47 China's abundance of unglazed and later glazed bowls, saucers and cups also confirms the importance of a diversity of food and an elaborate cuisine, presented in a diversity of fine ceramic dishes and bowls.

48 Rowan K. Flad, 'Urbanism as Technology in Early China', *Archaeological Research in Asia* 14 (2018), pp. 121–34; He, 'Taosi: An Archaeological Example', pp. 20–32; Demattè, 'Longshan-era Urbanism', pp. 119–53.

49 Early drums are discussed in Bo Lawergren, 'Neolithic Drums in China', *Orient-Archaologie* 20 (2006), pp. 109–27. For alligators see Wu Xiaotong et al., 'Strontium Isotope Analysis of Yangtze Alligator Remains from Late Neolithic North China', *Archaeological and Anthropological Sciences* 11 (2017), pp. 1049–58.

50 The destruction is described in He, 'The Longshan Period Site of Taosi'.

51 For discussion of different archaeological aspects of the Shimao site see Shaanxisheng Kaogu Yanjiuyuan, Yulinshi Wenwu Kaogu Kantan Gongzuodui, Shenmuxian Wenti Guangdianju and Shenmuxian Shimao Yizhi Guanlichu, *Faxian Shimao Gucheng (The Discovery of Shimao Ancient City)* (Wenwu Chubanshe, 2016). For an overview in English see Sun et al., 'The First Neolithic Urban Center'; and an appraisal in a wider context is Jaang Li, Sun Zhouyong, Shao Jing and Li Min, 'When Peripheries Were Centres: A Preliminary Study of the Shimao-centred Polity in the Loess Highland, China', *Antiquity* 92 (2018), pp. 1008–22.

52 For an outline discussion of this movement see David W. Anthony, *The Horse, the Wheel, and Language: How Bronze Age Riders from the Eurasian Steppes Shaped*

the Modern World (Princeton University Press, 2007), pp. 307–18. This movement is now a topic of much debate with new research emerging based on DNA, see Librado et al., 'The Origins and Spread of Domestic Horses'; see also Lisa Janz et al., 'Expanding Frontier and Building the Sphere in Arid East Asia', *Quaternary International* 559 (2020), pp. 150–64; Alexei A. Kovalev and Diimaajav Erdenebaatar, 'Discovery of New Cultures of the Bronze Age in Mongolia According to the Data Obtained by the International Central Asian Archaeological Expedition', in Jan Bemmann, Hermann Parzinger, Ernst Pohl and Damsdüren Tseveendorj (eds.), *Current Archaeological Research in Mongolia: Papers from the First International Conference on 'Archaeological Research in Mongolia' Held in Ulaanbaatar, August 19–23, 2007* (Vor- und Frühgeschichtliche Archäologie, Rheinische Friedrich-Wilhelms-Universität, 2009), pp. 149–70; Alicia R. Ventresca Miller and Cheryl A. Makarewicz, 'Intensification in Pastoralist Cereal Use Coincides with the Expansion of Trans-Regional Networks in the Eurasian Steppe', *Scientific Reports* 9 (2019), 8363.

53 For the transition from hunting to herding see Choongwon Jeong et al., 'Bronze Age Population Dynamics and the Rise of Dairy Pastoralism on the Eastern Eurasian Steppe', *Proceedings of the National Academy of Sciences* 115 (2018), E11248–55; see also Jean-Luc Houle, 'Emergent Complexity on the Mongolian Steppe: Mobility, Territoriality, and the Development of Early Nomadic Polities', PhD dissertation (University of Pittsburgh, 2010); William T. T. Taylor et al., 'Radiocarbon Dating and Cultural Dynamics across Mongolia's Early Pastoral Transition', *PLoS ONE* 14 (2019), e0224241. For a recent discussion of the introduction of herding to the Altai and horses see Alicia R. Ventresca Miller et al., 'The Spread of Herds and Horses into the Altai: How Livestock and Dairying Drove Social Complexity in Mongolia', *PLoS ONE* 17 (2022), e0265775.

54 For a discussion of domesticated animals in China see Rowan K. Flad, Yuan Jing and Li Shuicheng, 'Zooarcheological Evidence for Animal Domestication in Northwest China', *Developments in Quaternary Science* 9 (2007), pp. 167–203; for animals at Taosi see Katherine R. Brunson, He Nu and Dai Xiangming, 'Sheep, Cattle, and Specialization: New Zooarchaeological Perspectives on the Taosi Longshan', *International Journal of Osteoarchaeology* 26 (2016), pp. 460–75.

55 Shimao's position above a high cliff resembles that of fortifications called *Sves* in the Minusinsk basin. A. I. Gotlib and M. L. Podol'skii, *Sve-gornye Sooruzheniia Minusinskoy Kotloviny (Sve-Mountain Constructions of the Minusinsk Valley)* (Elexis Print, 2008).

56 Sun Zhouyong et al., 'The Imperial City Terrace Locality of the Shimao City Site in Shenmu County, Shaanxi Province', *Chinese Archaeology* 18 (2018), pp. 28–37; Sun Zhouyong et al., 'Shaanxi Shenmushi Shimao Yizhi Huangchengtai

Dataiji Yizhi' ('The Grand Platform Foundation in the Huangchengtai Area at Shimao Site in Shenmu City, Shaanxi'), *Kaogu* 7 (2020), pp. 34–46.

57 Han Jianye, 'Laohushan Wenhua de Kuozhang yu Duiwai Yingxiang' ('The Expansion of the Laohushan Culture and its External Impact'), *Zhongyuan Wenwu* 1 (2007), pp. 20–26.

58 A detailed revealing comparison is made in Shao Jing, 'Shimao Yizhi yu Taosi Yizhi de Bijiao Yanjiu' (Shimao and Taosi: A Comparative Study), *Kaogu* 5 (2020), pp. 65–77.

59 For examples see Suo Xiufen et al., 'Neimenggu Yijinhuoyiqi Baiaobao Yizhi Fajue Baogao' ('The Excavation of the Baiaobao Site, Ejin Horo Banner, Inner Mongolia'), *Kaogu Xuebao* 2 (2021), pp. 233–60.

60 He presents his argument in 'The Longshan Period Site of Taosi', pp. 269–70.

61 For examples with double burials see Wei Huaiheng, 'Wuwei Huangniang-niangtai Yizhi Disici Fajue' ('The Fourth Excavation of the Huangniangniangtai Site, Wuwei'), *Kaogu Xuebao* 4 (1978), pp. 421–48; Suo et al., 'Neimenggu Yijin-huoyiqi Baiaobao' and for the cemetery at Zhukaigou see above, this chapter, note 23.

62 Ores were available in the Hexi Corridor and much further east in the Zhong-tiao Mountains, on the southern edge of the Taihang Mountains. But ores were inaccessible over most of the Loess Plateau. Thus, unlike many regions in Western Asia, Anatolia and the Balkans, people did not come across the coloured rocks that they might at first have used as personal ornaments. In due course the principal mines exploited were those in the Taihang on a small scale and on a much larger one in the Yangtze Valley, Shi Tao, 'Copper Mining and Metallurgy in the Zhongtiao Mountains and Yangzi River Valleys in Early China', *Asian Perspectives* 60 (2021), pp. 382–416.

63 Evgeny N. Chernykh, *Ancient Metallurgy in the USSR: The Early Metal Age* (Cambridge University Press, 1992); Chernykh et al., 'Ancient Metallurgy of Northeast Asia', pp. 15–36.

64 For the intense exploration of sites and analysis of early metalwork and its development see Chen Guoke et al., 'The Xichengyi Site in Zhangye City, Gansu', *Chinese Archaeology* 15 (2015), pp. 14–25; Chen Kunlong, Mei Jianjun and Wang Lu, 'Zhongguo Zaoqi Yejin de Bentuhua yu Quyu Hudong' ('The Localisation and Regional Interaction of Early Metallurgy in China'), *Kaogu yu Wenwu* 3 (2019), pp. 114–21; Mei Jianjun et al., 'Archaeometallurgical Stud-ies in China: Some Recent Developments and Challenging Issues', *Journal of Archaeological Science* 56 (2015), pp. 221–32; Huan Limin, 'Taming Metals: The Use of Leaded Bronze in Early China, 2000–1250 BC', DPhil thesis (University of Oxford, 2021).

65 Brunson et al., 'Sheep, Cattle, and Specialization'.

66 Gao Jiangtao and He Nu, 'Taosi Yizhi Chutu Tongqi Chutan' ('The Preliminary Study of the Bronze Objects from Taosi'), *Nanfang Wenwu* 1 (2014), pp. 91–5.

67 Chen Kunlong et al., 'Shaanxi Shenmu Shimao Yizhi Chutu Tongqi de Kexue Fenxi ji Xiangguan Wenti' ('On the Scientific Analysis of Bronze Objects from Shimao and the Related Questions'), *Kaogu* 7 (2022), pp. 127–39 argue that the early metallurgy at Taosi and Erlitou came from the north-west by way of the Wei River Valley. This claim elides the complexity of the multiple possible routes of contact between the Loess Plateau and the steppe. The proposal is as yet incomplete as the sources of the metal along the Wei Valley are not yet well established.

68 Traces of one or more characters have been found on ceramic sherds at Taosi. Their identity and significance are highly debated, for the early history of Chinese characters is contested. For different balances in their interpretations see Paola Demattè, 'The Origins of Chinese Writing: The Neolithic Evidence', *Cambridge Archaeological Journal* 20 (2010), pp. 211–28, with a wider study of the development in Adam Smith, 'Writing at Anyang: The Role of the Divination Record in the Emergence of Chinese Literacy', PhD dissertation (University of California, Los Angeles, 2008).

69 Armin Selbitschka, 'Sacrifice vs. Sustenance: Food as a Burial Good in Late Pre-imperial and Early Imperial Chinese Tombs and Its Relation to Funerary Rites', *Early China* 41 (2018), pp. 179–243; Rowan K. Flad, 'Divination and Power: A Multi-regional View of the Development of Oracle Bone Divination in Early China', *Current Anthropology* 49 (2008), pp. 403–37.

70 Moreover, as metal was now used for the presentation of the banquet, one of the most popular vessel types for heating alcohol to be made in bronze had three spear-like legs, borrowed from examples with conical legs from the Loess Plateau. A bronze version with four legs is illustrated in Chapter 3.

Chapter 3: The Warrior with the Bronze Hand

1 Over this long period of excavation very many archaeological reports, specialised papers and general surveys have been published. For an introduction to the initial excavations in English see Li Chi, *Anyang* (University of Washington Press, 1977). A full description of the site at the time of its publication is in Chang Kwang-chih, *Shang Civilization* (Yale University Press, 1980). For more recent analysis see Roderick B. Campbell, *Violence, Kinship and the Early Chinese State: The Shang and Their World* (Cambridge University Press, 2018).

2 Traces and examples of Shang ritual vessels both in the northern Loess Plateau and near the Yangtze have sometimes been taken as evidence of the supposed size of the Shang state. The notion of a state was developed with respect to Western Asia. The definition has puzzled many; see Shelach and Jaffee, 'The Earliest States in China'. However, a network approach is probably the best way forward on present evidence, as in Roderick Campbell, 'Toward a Networks and Boundaries Approach to Early Complex Polities: The Late Shang Case', *Current Anthropology* 50 (2009), pp. 821–48. Communication north and south is revealed by the wide geographical distribution of bronze vessels that had their origins in the conception of bronze ritual containers developed by the Shang, as shown in the map at fig. 2 in Jessica Rawson, 'Bronze Vessels in Early China', in Shing Müller and Armin Selbitschka (eds.), *Über den Alltag hinaus: Festschrift für Thomas O. Höllmann zum 65. Geburtstag* (Harrassowitz, 2017), pp. 3–17. These vessels illustrate different modes of communication and indicate that one binding force in some of the regions, but not all, was the ancestral cult. They do not, on the other hand, indicate close official control.

3 Maria Khayutina, 'Kinship, Marriage and Politics in Early China (13–8 c. BCE) in the Light of Ritual Bronze Inscriptions', Habilitation thesis (Ludwig Maximilian University of Munich, 2017), p. 89.

4 For the archaeological report, on which the description and discussion of the tomb depend, see Zhongguo Shehui Kexueyuan Kaogu Yanjiusuo, *Anyang Yinxu Huayuanzhuang Dongdi Shangdai Muzang (Report on the Excavations of Huayuanzhuang Locus East in Anyang)* (Kexue Chubanshe, 2007).

5 There is no separate contemporary Shang account of the cardinal directions. However, concern with the directions appears not only in the shape of the tombs but also in the concept of the *fang*; see David N. Keightley, *The Ancestral Landscape: Time, Space, and Community in Late Shang China (ca. 1200–1045 B.C.* (Institute of East Asian Studies, University of California, 2000), pp. 67–72.

6 The view was developed, we know, in later periods that the burial of people who had been injured in battle was met with dread and concern, Lai Guolong, *Excavating the Afterlife: The Archaeology of Early Chinese Religion* (University of Washington Press, 2015), pp. 48–9. The period the author describes is the devastating Warring States and attitudes were certainly different from those under the Shang. Nonetheless, efforts to restore a lost hand suggest a concern to present Ya Chang with a complete body.

7 For a discussion of burial patterns in the Shang period see Jessica Rawson, Konstantin V. Chugunov, Yegor Grebnev and Huan Limin, 'Chariotry and Prone Burials: Reassessing Late Shang China's Relationship with Its Northern Neighbours', *Journal of World Prehistory* 33 (2020), pp. 135–68.

8 Zhongguo, *Anyang Yinxu Huayuanzhuang*, pp. 232–52.

9 As noted in connection with the niched tomb at Taosi, burials with a female companion were found to the north, at both the Shimao area and Zhukaigou, see Neimenggu, *Zhukaigou*, pp. 180–84.

10 For the excavation report on Ya Zhi's tomb see Zhongguo Shehui Kexueyuan Kaogu Yanjiusuo, *Anyang Yinxu Guojiazhuang Shangdai Muzang: 1982 Nian–1992 Nian Kaogu Fajue Baogao (Guojiazhuang Cemetery of the Shang Period within the Yin Ruins, Anyang)* (Zhongguo Dabaike Quanshu Chubanshe, 1998). The title Ya is discussed in Khayutina, 'Kinship, Marriage and Politics', pp. 165–96, where she gives an alternative interpretation. As Ya Zhi and Ya Chang were both involved in warfare, the title Ya may have indicated this role among others.

11 The burial of attendants has been widely discussed and recorded; see Huang Zhanyue, *Gudai Rensheng Renxun Tonglun (On Ancient Chinese Human Immolation)* (Wenwu Chubanshe, 2004) for a full account. There was a clear distinction between those who accompanied the dead to assist them in the afterlife and those who were buried as sacrifices to attract support from the Shang kings' ancestors, Meng Xianwu, 'Tan Yinxu Fushenzang' ('On the Prone Burials in Yinxu'), *Zhongyuan Wenwu* 3 (1992), pp. 52–5; Roderick B. Campbell, 'On Sacrifice: An Archaeology of Shang Sacrifice', in Anne Porter and Glenn M. Schwartz (eds.), *Sacred Killing: The Archaeology of Sacrifice in the Ancient Near East* (Eisenbrauns, 2012), pp. 305–23.

12 Li Zhipeng and Roderick B. Campbell, 'Puppies for the Ancestors: The Many Roles of Shang Dogs', *Archaeological Research in Asia* 17 (2019), pp. 161–72.

13 David N. Keightley, *Working for His Majesty: Research Notes on Labor Mobilization in Late Shang China (ca. 1200–1045 B.C.), as Seen in the Oracle-Bone Inscriptions, with Particular Attention to Handicraft Industries, Agriculture, Warfare, Hunting, Construction, and the Shang's Legacies*, China Research Monograph 67 (Institute of East Asian Studies, University of California, Berkeley, 2012), p. 198. Such inscriptions noted a day in a sixty-day cycle. This cycle, the ten-day 'week' and the sequences of the moon are discussed in Keightley, *The Ancestral Landscape*, pp. 37–53.

14 The royal Shang tombs were deliberately looted, with deep pits cutting down into them. These may have been left exposed over a long period to display the achievements of the Zhou, Li Min, 'Ruins, Refugees, and Urban Abandonment in Bronze Age China', *Journal of Urban Archaeology* 4 (2021), pp. 99–117, fig. 5.5.

15 For translations of Sima Qian's history see Nienhauser (ed.), *The Grand Scribe's Records* and Watson, *Records*.

16 The early discovery of the oracle bones at Anyang and the first excavations are described in Li, *Anyang*.

17 For an overview of Shang history in the light of the oracle bone inscriptions see David N. Keightley, 'The Shang: China's First Historical Dynasty', in Loewe and Shaughnessy (eds.), *The Cambridge History of Ancient China*, pp. 232–91.

18 There is little certainty about the foundations of writing in China. Demattè, 'The Origins of Chinese Writing' and others argue for an early origin. See also, Smith, 'Writing at Anyang'.

19 For a discussion of Chinese writing see William G. Boltz, 'Language and Writing', in Loewe and Shaughnessy (eds.), *The Cambridge History of Ancient China*, pp. 74–123; Robert W. Bagley, 'Anyang Writing and the Origin of the Chinese Writing System', in Stephen D. Houston (ed.), *The First Writing: Script Invention as History and Process* (Cambridge University Press, 2004), pp. 190–249; Smith, 'Writing at Anyang'.

20 For the early history of divination with bones in China see Flad, 'Divination and Power'.

21 The divinations were not so much questions as wishes or propositions, see David Keightley, *Sources of Shang History: The Oracle Bones Inscriptions of Shang China* (University of California Press, 1978), p. 33.

22 Writing systems in a survey of the ancient world from the perspective of writing in China are discussed in Wang Haicheng, *Writing and the Ancient State: Early China in Comparative Perspective* (Cambridge University Press, 2014).

23 The clear control of activity at Anyang by rulers and their ritual specialists is outlined in Keightley, *Working for His Majesty*, p. 231.

24 The abundance of ceramics in most large tombs of the Neolithic can be read as the presentation of food both for the funeral and for the afterlife. As there were no written records we cannot know how these were interpreted in each case.

25 The leading excavator of Erlitou is Xu Hong of the Institute of Archaeology, Chinese Academy of Social Sciences, Xu Hong, 'The Erlitou Culture', in Underhill (ed.), *A Companion to Chinese Archaeology*, pp. 300–322.

26 For a discussion of Zhengzhou and its expansion to the south to Panlongcheng see Robert W. Bagley, 'Shang Archaeology', in Loewe and Shaughnessy (eds.), *The Cambridge History of Ancient China*, pp. 124–231; Kyle Steinke and Dora C. Y. Ching (eds.), *Art and Archaeology of the Erligang Civilization* (P. Y. and Kinmay W. Tang Center for East Asian Art, Department of Art and Archaeology, Princeton University, 2014).

27 The numbering of the kings follows their sequence in the king list; for the quotation see Keightley, *Working for His Majesty*, p. 107.

28 Ibid., p. 109.

29 The discovery of the cemetery is described by Li, *Anyang*. For a fuller account of the cemetery see Chang, *Shang Civilization*, pp. 110–24.

30 Campbell, 'On Sacrifice'.

31 Gideon Shelach-Lavi, 'The Qiang and the Question of Human Sacrifice in the Late Shang Period', *Asian Perspectives* 35 (1996), pp. 1–26.

32 After Li, *Early China*, p. 103.

33 For the concept of good and bad days see Keightley, *The Ancestral Landscape*, pp. 121–9. The wider topic of the early ideas of auspiciousness has not attracted much attention. But we know that the bronze used in Zhou ritual vessels was often described in inscriptions as auspicious.

34 The discovery of the tomb of Fu Hao was one of the major advances made in early Chinese history. The fact that it was intact gave the world a partial view of the magnificence of royal Shang tombs. The archaeological report is Zhongguo Shehui Kexueyuan Kaogu Yanjiusuo, *Yinxu Fuhao Mu* (*Tomb of Lady Fuhao in Anyang*) (Wenwu Chubanshe, 1980); an exceptional exhibition illustrates some of the finest bronzes and jades, Ts'ai Mei-fen, Zhu Naicheng and Chen Kwang-tzuu (eds.), *Shangwang Wuding yu Fuhao: Yinshang Shengshi Wenhua Yishu Tezhan* (*King Wu Ding and Lady Fuhao: Art and Culture of the Late Shang Dynasty*) (Guoli Gugong Bowuyuan, 2012). For oracle bone inscriptions that mention Fu Hao see Chang Ping-ch'üan, 'A Brief Description of the Fu Hao Oracle Bone Inscriptions', in Chang Kwang-chih (ed.), *Studies of Shang Archaeology: Selected Papers from the International Conference on Shang Civilization* (Yale University Press, 1986), pp. 121–40.

35 Campbell, *Violence, Kinship and the Early Chinese State*, p. 164.

36 Two lesser, but still rich tombs, M17 and M18, show up the wealth of Ya Chang and Fu Hao; see Zheng Zhenxiang, 'Anyang Xiaotuncun Bei de Liangzuo Yindaimu' ('Two Yin Period Tombs in the North of Xiaotun Village, Anyang'), *Kaogu Xuebao* 4 (1981), pp. 491–518.

37 For the contents of Ya Chang's tomb see Zhongguo, *Anyang Yinxu Huayuanzhuang*.

38 The possible meanings of the *taotie* have been widely debated. Important contributions by Robert Bagley and Sarah Allan are set out in Whitfield (ed.), *The Problem of Meaning*, pp. 9–33, 34–55. The difficulties of attributing meaning to motifs for which there is no written record are also mentioned above in Chapter 1, with the transfer of face designs from the Hongshan people to the Liangzhu people. As more archaeological work reveals faces across many different large and small local groups, it is clear that the face motifs were significant to those who made them, but in many cases we have no means to decipher them with certainty.

39 Maria Khayutina, 'Sacred Space of the Aristocratic Clan in Ancient China under Transformation', in Vera Michael Dickhardt and Dorofeeva-Lichtmann (eds.), *Creating and Representing Sacred Spaces*, p. 107.

40 This comparison is made by Nigel Wood in Kerr and Wood, *Science and Civilisation in China,* vol. 5:12, pp. 102–3.

41 For discussion of the role of ceramics as a prelude for casting ritual bronzes see Bagley, 'Shang Archaeology'; Robert W. Bagley, *Shang Ritual Bronzes in the Arthur M. Sackler Collections* (Arthur M. Sackler Foundation, 1987). The exact processes by which the moulds were decorated and the methods for creating the models and the core are still debated. Robert W. Bagley, 'Anyang Mould-making and the Decorated Model', *Artibus Asiae* 69 (2009), pp. 39–90; Lukas Nickel, 'Imperfect Symmetry: Re-thinking Bronze Casting Technology in Ancient China', *Artibus Asiae* 66 (2006), pp. 5–39. Workshops of different periods and places probably followed different customs. Yung-ti Li, *Kingly Crafts: The Archaeology of Craft Production in Late Shang China* (Columbia University Press, 2022).

42 Research by Matthew Chastain has changed and expanded our understanding of the extraordinary skill committed to making the moulds for the bronzes, especially in the early Zhou period, Matthew Chastain, 'The Ceramic Technology of Bronze-casting Molds in Ancient China: Production Practices at Three Western Zhou Foundry Sites in the Zhouyuan Area', PhD dissertation (Massachusetts Institute of Technology, 2019).

43 Nigel Wood was probably the first to recognise the very special character of the loess both for ceramics and for casting moulds, in Kerr and Wood, *Science and Civilisation in China,* vol. 5:12, pp. 102–3. For some early comments on the materials employed see Jessica Rawson, Ian Freestone and Nigel Wood, 'Chinese Bronze Casting Molds and Ceramic Figures', in Patrick E. McGovern and M. D. Notis (eds.), *Cross-Craft and Cross-Cultural Interactions in Ceramics* (American Ceramic Society, 1989), pp. 253–73.

44 Liu Li and Chen Xingcan, *State Formation in Early China* (Duckworth, 2003), pp. 37–43.

45 John Baines and Norman Yoffee, 'Order, Legitimacy and Wealth in Ancient Egypt and Mesopotamia', in Gary M. Feinman and Joyce Marcus (eds.), *Archaic States* (School of American Research Press, 1998), pp. 199–260, on p. 238, give a convincing account of the importance of great aesthetic achievement in fine materials that reinforced the legitimacy of ancient rulers and the elite.

46 For sets in Shang tombs see Jessica Rawson, 'Late Shang Bronze Design: Meaning and Purpose', in Whitfield (ed.), *The Problem of Meaning*, pp. 67–95.

47 It is often designated in English as an ox also.

48 The pouring jug, or *gong*, with a lid in Ya Chang's tomb was adapted to fit into a more traditional decorative scheme. On both sides of the body is a *taotie* face, divided down the centre. It shows the features of the face detached from one another and embedded in the angular scrolls of the background. This is an example of the kinds of variations that the casters and their patrons enjoyed, distinguishing this example from the more solid *taotie* face on the *fang jia*. The neck and lid, however, resort to the mixture of motifs seen on the buffalo, with small elephants and birds around the neck and the dragon head on the lid given a double body. Stunted triangular legs suggest that the caster was still working out the likeness as he went about making the model and the moulds. Compare Fong Wen (ed.), *The Great Bronze Age of China: An Exhibition from the People's Republic of China* (Metropolitan Museum of Art, 1980), p. 163, no. 29 and p. 163, no. 30.

49 A comparison with a *jia* in Fu Hao's tomb (illustrated in Rawson (ed.), *Mysteries*, p. 96, no. 42 and p. 97, fig. 42.2) shows up the remarkable quality of Ya Chang's vessel.

50 Katheryn M. Linduff, 'Why Have Siberian Artefacts Been Excavated Inside the Ancient Chinese Dynastic Borders?', in Laura. M. Popova, Adam T. Smith and David L. Peterson (eds.), *Beyond the Steppe and the Sown: Proceedings of the 2002 University of Chicago Conference on Eurasian Archaeology* (Brill, 2006), pp. 358–70.

51 Campbell, 'Toward a Networks and Boundaries Approach'; Roderick B. Campbell, Yitzchak Jaffe, Christopher Kim, Camilla Sturm and Jaang Li, 'Chinese Bronze Age Political Economies: A Complex Polity Provisioning Approach', *Journal of Archaeological Research* 30 (2021), pp. 69–116.

52 Robert W. Bagley, 'Percussion', in Jenny F. So (ed.), *Music in the Age of Confucius* (Freer Gallery of Art and Arthur M. Sackler Gallery, 2000), pp. 35–63.

53 High-fired ceramics, made south of the Yangtze, or copies from further north were much prized and were buried with bronze sets, Bagley, 'Shang Archaeology', p. 171.

54 For the axe see Rawson (ed.), *Mysteries*, no. 46, pp. 103–4.

55 Campbell, 'On Sacrifice' makes some interesting suggestions at the end of his paper, which conflate beheading in war with the multiple beheaded sacrifices in and around the tombs of the Shang kings, raising the possibility that these were captives and victims from the Qiang who may have been particularly threatening in Wu Ding's reign.

56 The jade axes are illustrated in Zhongguo, *Anyang Yinxu Huayuanzhuang*, pp. 185–6, figs. 136, 137.

57 For a description of Shang period jades see Rawson, *Chinese Jade*, pp. 39–44; So, *Early Chinese Jades*, pp. 101–44.

58 Quoted from Keightley, *Working for His Majesty*, p. 179.

59 Robin D. S. Yates, 'Early China', in Kurt A. Raaflaub and Nathan Stewart Rosenstein (eds.), *War and Society in the Ancient and Medieval Worlds: Asia, the Mediterranean, Europe, and Mesoamerica* (Center for Hellenic Studies, Harvard University Press, 1999), pp. 7–45.

60 Quoted from Keightley, *Working for His Majesty*, p. 182.

61 The tool has generated controversy. However, it now seems evident that it was some form of rein holder, derived ultimately from the hooks attached to belts illustrated on Mongolian deer stones, as in Vitali V. Volkov, *Olennyye Kamni Mongolii* (*Deer Stones from Mongolia*) (Nauchnyy Mir, 2002). Examples with a long bar are rare on the deer stones, but have been reported. Further, the highly decorated Shang examples may have been for display rather than everyday use.

62 For turquoise see Hong, 'Xian Qin Liang Han Qian Lüsongshi'.

63 This site is important for its relatively early date in the late Shang period and for its early discovery within the history of Anyang excavations, Li, *Anyang*, pp. 111–15, and above all for its location in the same general area as the tombs of Ya Chang and Fu Hao. The archaeological report is in Shih Chang-Ju, *Xiaotun 1: Yizhi de Faxian yu Fajue 3: Yinxu Muzang 1 (Beizu Muzang)* (*Hsiao-T'un, vol. 1: The Discovery and Excavations Fascicle 3: Burials of the Northern Section*), 2 vols. (Chungyang Yenchiuyuan Lishih Yuyen Yenchiuso, 1970).

64 For discussion of the chariot structure, its history and its publication see Wu Hsiao-yun, *Chariots in Early China: Origins, Cultural Interaction and Identity* (Archaeopress, 2013); an earlier discussion from a Eurasian perspective is in Stuart Piggott, 'Chariots in the Caucasus and in China', *Antiquity* 48 (1974), pp. 16–24; Viktor A. Novozhenov, *Communications and the Earliest Wheeled Transport of Eurasia* (TAUS Publishing, 2012); Igor V. Chechushkov and Andrey V. Epimakhov, 'Eurasian Steppe Chariots and Social Complexity During the Bronze Age', *Journal of World Prehistory* 31 (2018), pp. 435–83; Elena E. Kuzmina, *The Prehistory of the Silk Road* (University of Pennsylvania Press, 2008); Liu Yong-hua, *Zhongguo Gudai Che yu Maju* (*Chariots and Horse Fittings in Ancient China*) (Qinghua Daxue Chubanshe, 2013).

65 For a discussion of the term *fang* see Keightley, *Working for His Majesty*, pp. 293–4.

66 Roderick Campbell has kindly sent me an English translation of a well-known inscription about a chariot accident in which the graph is used: *Heji 10405 (obverse) 4)* 'Cracked on *Guisi* day, Ke tested: This coming week will have no difficulties. The king, prognosticating, said: "there will be trouble after all." It was as he said: On *jiawu* day the king pursued buffalo. Lesser retainer Ye's horse and chariot team collided with the king's chariot. Prince Yang also fell.'

67 Quoted from Keightley, *Working for His Majesty*, p. 180.

68 Ibid., pp. 187–8.

69 The best-known episode of a chariot battle in ancient Egypt is the Battle of Kadesh in 1275 BC against the Hittites from Anatolia in what is now Syria. For wide-ranging discussions of aspects of Egyptian and Western Asian chariots and horses see Mary A. Littauer and Joost H. Crouwel, *Selected Writings on Chariots and Other Early Vehicles, Riding and Harness* (Brill, 2002). For illustrations of a variety of Egyptian depictions of chariot warfare see A. J. Veldmeijer and Salima Ikram (eds.), *Chasing Chariots: Proceedings of the First International Chariot Conference (Cairo 2012)* (Sidestone Press, 2013). For photographic publication of the carved slabs from the Assyrian Palaces see Paul T. Collins, Lisa Baylis and Sandra L. Marshall, *Assyrian Palace Sculptures* (British Museum, 2008). For an outline of horse exploitation see Pita Kelekna, *The Horse in Human History* (Cambridge University Press, 2009).

70 The resolution of the question of which genera of horses were employed in Mongolia and China is a relatively new development, as is exploration of the ways by which horses travelled across Eurasia; for further research see Librado et al., 'The Origins and Spread of Domestic Horses'.

71 For an account of tracing this movement through dairy consumption see Ventresca Miller et al., 'The Spread of Herds and Horses into the Altai'.

72 Esther Jacobson-Tepfer, 'The Emergence of Cultures of Mobility in the Altai Mountains of Mongolia: Evidence from the Intersection of Rock Art and Paleoenvironment', in Hans Barnard and Willeke Wendrich (eds.), *The Archaeology of Mobility: Old World and New World Nomadism* (Cotsen Institute of Archaeology, University of California, 2008), pp. 200–29.

73 William W. Fitzhugh, 'The Mongolian Deer Stone-Khirigsuur Complex: Dating and Organisation of a Late Bronze Age Menagerie', in Bemmann et al. (eds.), *Current Archaeological Research in Mongolia*, pp. 183–99.

74 The knives are brought into the discussion of contact in Rawson et al., 'Chariotry and Prone Burials'; Lin Yun, 'A Reexamination of the Relationship between Bronzes of the Shang Culture and of the Northern Zone', in Chang (ed.), *Studies of Shang Archaeology*, pp. 237–73; Katheryn M. Linduff, Yan Sun, Cao Wei and Liu Yuanqing, *Ancient China and Its Eurasian Neighbors: Artifacts, Identity and Death in the Frontier, 3000–700 BCE* (Cambridge University Press, 2017). The wider context of steppe-type metalwork found on the northern borders of China is also discussed in Yang Jianhua, Shao Huiqiu and Pan Ling, *The Metal Road of the Eastern Eurasian Steppe: The Formation of the Xiongnu Confederation and the Silk Road* (Springer, 2020).

75 Francis Allard et al., 'Ritual and Horses in Bronze Age and Present-day Mongolia: Some Preliminary Observations from Khanuy Valley', in Laura M. Popova,

Charles W. Hartley and Adam T. Smith (eds.), *Social Orders and Social Land-scapes* (Cambridge Scholars, 2007), pp. 151–67; Stuart Piggott, 'Heads and Hoofs', *Antiquity* 36 (1962), pp. 110–18; William T. T. Taylor et al., 'Horse Demography and Use in Bronze Age Mongolia', *Quaternary International* 436 (2017), pp. 270–82; William T. T. Taylor et al., 'A Bayesian Chronology for Early Domestic Horse Use in the Eastern Steppe', *Journal of Archaeological Science* 81 (2017), pp. 49–58.

76 Lower temperatures, increases in moisture and an increase in the biomass have been cited as possible drivers for the expansion of activity by the horse owners on the Mongolian steppe, Julian Struck et al., 'Central Mongolian Lake Sedi-ments Reveal New Insights on Climate Change and Equestrian Empires in the Eastern Steppes', *Scientific Reports* 12 (2022), 2829.

77 Traces of the jointing of the felloes is revealed in excavation, see Zhang Chang-shou and Zhang Xiaoguang, 'Jingshu Mudi Suojian Xizhou Lunyu' ('Western Zhou Chariots from the Jingshu Family's Cemetery'), *Kaogu Xuebao* 2 (1994), pp. 155–72.

78 A famous text in cuneiform composed for the Hurrians, contemporary with the Hittites, by Kikkuli, a Mitannian, living probably in Syria *c*.1300 BC, gives extensive advice on how pairs of horses have to be trained together, see Kelekna, *The Horse in Human History*, pp. 98–9.

79 Prone burial has been identified in southern and eastern Mongolia and in Inner Mongolia, south of the Yin Mountains: Alexey A. Kovalev and Diimaajav Erdenebaatar, 'Pozdnii Bronzovyi Vek I Nachalo Rannego Zheleznogo Veka Mongolii V Svete Otkrytii Mezhdunarodnoi Tsentralno-Aziatskoi Arkheolog-icheskoi Ekspeditsii' ('The Late Bronze Age and Early Iron Age Discoveries in Mongolia by the International Central Asian Archaeological Expedition'), in A. D. Tsybiktarov (ed.), *Drevniye Kul'tury Mongolii I Baykal'skoy Sibiri. Materi-aly Mezhdunarodnoy Nauchnoy Konferentsii (Ulan-Ude, 20–24 Sentyabrya 2010 G.) (Ancient Cultures of Mongolia and Baikal Siberia. Materials of the International Scientific Conference (Ulan-Ude, September 20–24, 2010)* (Buryat State University, 2010), pp. 104–17; Dashtseveg Tumen, Dorjpurev Khatanbaatar and Myagmar Erdene, 'Bronze Age Graves in the Delgerkhaan Mountain Area of Eastern Mongolia', *Asian Archaeology* 2 (2013), pp. 40–49; Ma Jian, 'Neimenggu Yin-shan Diqu Zaoqi Shibanmu de Chubu Diaocha yu Yanjiu' ('Survey and Study of Slab Burials in Yinshan Mountains'), in Neimenggu Bowuyuan and Nei-menggu Zizhiqu Wenwu Kaogu Yanjiusuo (eds.), *Zhongguo Beifang ji Menggu, Beijiaer, Xiboliya Diqu Gudai Wenhua (Study of the Ancient Culture of Northern China, Mongolia and the Area of Siberia at Lake Baikal)*, 3 vols (Kexue Chubanshe, 2015), vol. 1, pp. 278–86; Kazuo Miyamoto and Hiroki Obata (eds.), *Excavations at Daram and Tevsh Sites: A Report on Joint Mongolian-Japanese Excavations in*

Outer Mongolia (Department of Archaeology, Faculty of Humanities, Kyushu University, 2016).

80 He Yuling, 'Yinxu Huayuanzhuang Dongdi M54 Muzhu Zaiyanjiu' ('Reconsidering the Tomb Owner of tomb M54, East of Huayuanzhuang, Yinxu'), in Zhongguo Shehui Kexueyuan Kaogu Yanjiusuo Xia Shang Zhou Kaogu Yanjiushi (ed.), *Sandai Kaogu*, vol. 5 (Kexue Chubanshe, 2013), pp. 110–17. Some scholars suggest that Ya Chang was a member of the royal clan and had southern connections, Khayutina, 'Kinship, Marriage and Politics', p. 172.

81 Rawson et al., 'Chariotry and Prone Burials'.

82 The problems posed by the demand for pasture are documented for a later period by Noa Grass, 'A Million Horses: Raising Government Horses in Early Ming China', in Rotem Kowner et al. (eds.), *Animals and Human Society in Asia: Historical, Cultural and Ethical Perspectives* (Springer, 2019), pp. 299–328.

83 William T. T. Taylor and Tumurbaatar Tuvshinjargal, 'Horseback Riding, Asymmetry, and Changes to the Equine Skull: Evidence for Mounted Riding in Mongolia's Late Bronze Age', in László Bartosiewicz and Erika Gál (eds.), *Care or Neglect? Evidence of Animal Disease in Archaeology: Proceedings of the 6th Meeting of the Animal Palaeopathology Working Group of the International Council for Archaeozoology (Icaz), Budapest, Hungary, 2016* (Oxbow Books, 2018), pp. 134–54. See also Jessica Rawson, Huan Limin and William T. T. Taylor, 'Seeking Horses: Allies, Clients and Exchanges in the Zhou Period (1045–221 BC)', *Journal of World Prehistory* 34 (2021), 489–530.

84 On close examination this has proved to be a very severe problem that affects humans as seriously as horses, Richard Stone, 'A Medical Mystery in Middle China', *Science* 324 (2009), pp. 1378–81. Several explanations have been given for the reasons why selenium was so deficient in the Central Plains, and also further south-west and north-east; see Sun Guoxin et al., 'Distribution of Soil Selenium in China Is Potentially Controlled by Deposition and Volatilization?', *Scientific Reports* 6 (2016), 20953. The underlying geology is of fundamental significance, with the prime deposits of selenium lying in the Yangtze area, Wen Hanjie and Qiu Yuzhuo, 'Geology and Geochemistry of Se-Bearing Formations in Central China', *International Geology Review* 44 (2002), pp. 164–78; Marek Kieliszek, 'Selenium–Fascinating Microelement, Properties and Sources in Food', *Molecules* 24 (2019), 1298. The loess also has a major role to play, providing enriching deposits in the north-western areas. See also the discussion in Rawson et al., 'Seeking Horses'.

85 Dazhi Cao, 'The Loess Highland in a Trading Network (1300–1050 BC)', PhD dissertation (Princeton University, 2014). The region includes the Loess Plateau, but is much larger and has been called the crescent-shaped region, translated as the Arc, Tong, 'Shilun Woguo Cong Dongbei Zhi Xinan'.

86 Susan Whitfield, 'Alfalfa, Pasture and the Horse in China: A Review', *Quaderni di Studi Indo-Mediterranei* 12 (2020), pp. 227–45.

87 Rawson, 'China and the Steppe'; Iver B. Neumann and Einar Wigen, *The Steppe Tradition in International Relations: Russians, Turks and European State-Building 4000 BCE–2018 CE* (Cambridge University Press, 2018).

88 The sets of *gu* and the sets of *jue* appear to come from different sources, Zhongguo, *Anyang Yinxu Huayuanzhuang*, pp. 105–14.

89 The sources of the multitude of cowries used to ornament people and their horses have provoked debate. Did they come from the South China Sea or from the Indian Ocean? See Peng Ke and Zhu Yanshi, 'New Research on the Origin of Cowries Used in Ancient China', *Sino-Platonic Papers* 68 (2010), pp. 1–21; Yung-ti Li, 'On the Function of Cowries in Shang and Western Zhou China', *Journal of East Asian Archaeology* 5 (2003), pp. 1–26.

Chapter 4: Sacrifices in a Hidden Land

1 John Minford and Joseph S. M. Lau (eds.), *An Anthology of Translations of Classical Chinese Literature*, Vol. 1: *From Antiquity to the Tang Dynasty* (Columbia University Press, 2000), p. 725.

2 Robert E. Harrist Jr, *The Landscape of Words: Stone Inscriptions from Early and Medieval China* (University of Washington Press, 2008), pp. 31–91.

3 Extensive efforts were made by the states of Qin and Chu, and later the Han, to extend control through population movement, effectively forms of colonisation, see Maxim Korolkov and Anke Hein, 'State-induced Migration and the Creation of State Spaces in Early Chinese Empires: Perspectives from History and Archaeology', *Journal of Chinese History* 5 (2021), pp. 203–25.

4 The importance of this project as one of the major state enterprises of the Qin is mentioned in Yuri Pines, Gideon Shelach-Lavi, Lothar von Falkenhausen and Robin D. S. Yates (eds.), *Birth of an Empire: The State of Qin Revisited* (University of California Press, 2014), p. 22. For a later survey of the Dujiangyan and comments on the iron statues see James Hutson, *Mythical and Practical in Szechwan* (The National Review Office, 1915), pp. 14–15.

5 For correlative philosophy and the role of iron as one of the Five Phases see Graham, *Disputers of the Tao*, pp. 340–56; Sterckx, *Chinese Thought*, p. 88. The choice of iron for sculptures, particularly along rivers, is illustrated by Ann Paludan, *Chinese Sculpture: A Great Tradition* (Serindia Publications, 2006). For famous iron figures and oxen holding a pontoon bridge across the Yellow River see Ann Paludan, 'The Tang Dynasty Iron Oxen at Pujin Bridge', *Orientations* 25 (1994), pp. 61–8.

6 Quoted from Minford and Lau (eds.), *An Anthology of Translations*, pp. 723–5.

7 The most famous painting illustrating the flight of Emperor Xuanzong (685–762) to Sichuan is in the National Palace Museum, Taiwan (plate 14), and though attributed to Li Zhaodao, is almost certainly by an unknown artist of the ninth to tenth century AD, see Harrist, *The Landscape of Words*, p. 37, fig. 1.4. The painting conveys the perilous mountains across which planked roads were the only means of access.

8 Quoted from Corey J. Byrnes, *Fixing Landscape: A Techno-Poetic History of China's Three Gorges* (Columbia University Press, 2018), p. 3. For other quotations from Li Daoyuan and travel writing in general see Richard E. Strassberg, *Inscribed Landscapes: Travel Writing from Imperial China* (University of California Press, 1994).

9 Isabella Lucy Bishop, *The Yangtze Valley and Beyond: An Account of Journeys in China, Chiefly in the Province of Sze Chuan and among the Man-Tze of the Somo Territory* (John Murray, 1899), p. 117.

10 For a description of the villages and landscape before and during the building of the dam see Deidre Chetham, *Before the Deluge: The Vanishing World of the Yangtze's Three Gorges* (Palgrave Macmillan, 2002).

11 For discussion of Baodun see Rowan K. Flad and Chen Pochan, *Ancient Central China: An Archaeological Study of Centers and Peripheries Along the Yangzi River* (Cambridge University Press, 2013); Jade A. d'Alpoim Guedes, Jiang Ming, He Kunyu, Wu Xiaohong and Jiang Zhanghua, 'Site of Baodun Yields Earliest Evidence for the Spread of Rice and Foxtail Millet Agriculture to South-West China', *Antiquity* 87 (2013), pp. 758–71.

12 Jay Xu, 'Lithic Artifacts from Yueliangwan: Research Notes on an Early Discovery at the Sanxingdui Site', in Jerome Silbergeld, Dora C. Y. Ching, Judith G. Smith and Alfreda Murck (eds.), *Bridges to Heaven: Essays on East Asian Art in Honor of Professor Wen C. Fong* (Princeton University Press, 2011), pp. 233–50.

13 Lothar von Falkenhausen, 'The External Connections of Sanxingdui', *Journal of East Asian Archaeology* 5 (2003), pp. 191–245.

14 For a full description of the site and also essays on individual topics see Robert W. Bagley (ed.), *Ancient Sichuan: Treasures from a Lost Civilization* (Seattle Art Museum/Princeton University Press, 2001). For archaeological reports see Sichuansheng Wenwu Kaogu Yanjiusuo (ed.), *Sanxingdui Jisikeng (The Sacrificial Pits at Sanxingdui)* (Wenwu Chubanshe, 1999); Sichuansheng Wenwu Kaogu Yanjiusuo, Sanxingdui Bowuguan and Sanxingdui Yanjiuyuan (eds.), *Sanxingdui Chutu Wenwu Quanjilu (The Complete Collection of the Relics from Sanxingdui)*, 3 vols. (Tiandi Chubanshe, 2009).

15 For a description of the pits and a summary of their contents see Jay Xu, 'Sichuan Before the Warring States Period', in Bagley (ed.), *Ancient Sichuan*,

pp. 21–38. A summary of the wealth in the pits is in Rowan K. Flad, 'Bronze, Jade, Gold, and Ivory: Valuable Objects in Ancient Sichuan', in John K. Papadopoulos and Gary Urton (eds.), *The Construction of Value in the Ancient World* (Cotsen Institute of Archaeology Press, 2012), pp. 306–35.

16 We now have news (2021–2), although few formal reports, that six further pits have been found nearby, making eight in all so far; see Jay Xu, 'Sanxingdui: New Wonders of a Lost Civilization', *China Pictorial*, no. 874 (2021), pp. 38–41; Lei Yu et al., 'Sanxingdui Yizhi Sihao Jisikeng Chutu Tong Niutou Guizuo Renxiang' ('Bronze Kneeling Statues with Turned Heads from Sanxingdui Sacrificial Pit No. 4'), *Sichuan Wenwu* 4 (2021), pp. 104–18. Ran Honglin et al., 'Sichuan Guanghanshi Sanxingdui Yizhi Jisiqu' ('The Sacrificial Place at Sanxingdui, Guanghan City in Sichuan Province'), *Kaogu* 7 (2022), pp. 15–33.

17 A full description of the figures is in Bagley (ed.), *Ancient Sichuan*, pp. 72–6.

18 Jay Xu, 'Bronze at Sanxingdui', in ibid., pp. 59–152; Jay Xu, 'Sanxingdui Wenming de Qingtong Zhuzao Jishu' ('On the Bronze Casting Technology of the Sanxingdui Civilization'), in Guojia Wenwu Churujing Jianding Sichuanzhan and Sichuan Daxue Bowuguan (eds.), *Sichuan Wenwu Jingpin: Qingtongqi (Selected Artefacts from Sichuan: Bronzes)* (Bashu Shushe, 2021), pp. 245–72. Other figures have now emerged in the six newly excavated pits, adding to the community represented in bronze, often in complex images of multiple individuals. Many are small figures and may have had connections with unseen spirits; some may have been dancers, actors or musicians.

19 Small-scale white stone or marble sculptures were found in the royal tombs at Anyang. For a few examples see Ts'ai et al., *Shangwang Wuding*, pp. 226–31. Carvings in wood or other organic materials may have existed but have disappeared.

20 This proposal is made by Sun Hua, 'The Sanxingdui Culture of the Sichuan Basin', in Underhill (ed.), *A Companion to Chinese Archaeology*, pp. 147–68.

21 Sources of gold have been identified in the mountains west and north-west of Chengdu, see Zhongguo Kuangchuang Faxianshi Bianweihui, *Zhongguo Kuangchuang Faxianshi: Sichuan Juan (The Discovery History of Mineral Deposits of China: Sichuan)* (Dizhi Chubanshe, 1996), pp. 118–30.

22 The possibility of prototypes in wood has been extensively discussed by Jay Xu, 'The Sanxingdui Site: Art and Archaeology', PhD dissertation (Princeton University, 2008). See also Jay Xu, 'Reconstructing Sanxingdui Imagery: Some Speculations', *Orientations* 32 (2001), pp. 32–44.

23 Wu Hung, 'All About the Eyes: Two Groups of Sculptures from the Sanxingdui Culture', *Orientations* 28 (1997), pp. 58–66.

24 For several examples with the flat head and sharply cut chin see Xu, 'Bronze at Sanxingdui', pp. 84–93.

25 One exception to this general formula is a head from pit 1 (which was once thought to be several decades earlier than pit 2), with much softer features; its rounded chin is more realistic than the angular chins on most of the bronze heads, see ibid., p. 79.

26 We should also consider whether working in wood could only be done when bronze was available and thus wood-carving may have been ancillary to the bronzes.

27 Jay Xu, 'Mysterious Creatures, Towering Trees and Lofty Figures in Sacrifice: The Lost Civilization at Sanxingdui, China', *The Oriental Ceramic Society of Hong Kong Bulletin* 15 (2012), pp. 57–67.

28 Xu, 'Bronze at Sanxingdui', pp. 77–8.

29 A section on the bronzes with strange faces created on U-shaped frames, here called masks, is in the report Sichuansheng, *Sanxingdui Jisikeng*, pp. 118–201.

30 Xu, 'Reconstructing Sanxingdui Imagery'.

31 Xu, 'Bronze at Sanxingdui', pp. 134–5.

32 Triangular designs are familiar from bronze vessels on the Central Plains, as on the flask, or *zun*, seen in Ya Chang's tomb (Chapter 3, p. 71), see Zhongguo, *Anyang Yinxu Huayuanzhuang*, p. 119, fig. 92.

33 The second wing has been repaired or replicated and can be seen in the display at the museum in Guanghan county.

34 This comparison is made in Xu, 'Bronze at Sanxingdui', p. 78.

35 Sichuansheng, *Sanxingdui Jisikeng*, p. 255, fig. 142.

36 For bronze-casting at Sanxingdui see Ma Jiangbo, Jin Zhengyao, Tian Jianhua and Chen De'an, 'Sanxingdui Tongqi de Heji Chengfen he Jinxiang Yanjiu' ('The Compositional and Metallographic Analyses of Sanxingdui Bronzes'), *Sichuan Wenwu* 2 (2012), pp. 90–96.

37 The study of bronze-casting in the Yangtze basin is a significant area of research, revealing both outposts of the bronze-casting activity from the Central Plains and also a number of independent centres developed in the basins of major tributaries; see Kyle Steinke, 'Erligang and the Southern Bronze Industries', in Steinke and Ching (eds.), *Art and Archaeology of the Erligang Civilization*, pp. 151–70; Robin McNeal, 'Erligang Contacts South of the Yangzi River: The Expansion of Interaction Networks in Early Bronze Age Hunan', in ibid., pp. 173–87. The site of Panlongcheng is particularly important, bringing bronze-casting south, Hubeisheng Wenwu Kaogu Yanjiusuo, *Panlongcheng: 1963–1994 Nian Kaogu Fajue Baogao (Panlongcheng: Report of Excavations in the 1963–1994 Seasons)*, 2 vols. (Wenwu Chubanshe, 2001). From this we can see bronze-casting spreading, Chen Jianming and Jay Xu, *Along the Yangzi River: Regional Culture of the Bronze Age from Hunan* (China Institute Gallery, 2011); He Xiaolin and Gong Xicheng, 'Anhui Funanxian Taijiasi Yizhi Fajue Jianbao'

('Preliminary Report on the Excavation of Taijiasi, Funan County, Anhui'), *Kaogu* 6 (2018), pp. 3–13; Robert W. Bagley, 'An Early Bronze Age Tomb in Jiangxi Province', *Orientations* 24 (1993), pp. 20–36; Jiangxisheng Wenwu Kaogu Yanjiusuo, *Xin'gan Shangdai Damu* (*The Large Shang Tomb in Xin'gan*) (Wenwu Chubanshe, 1997); Zhang Liangren, 'Wucheng and Shang: A New History of a Bronze Age Civilization', *Bulletin of the Museum of Far Eastern Antiquities* 78 (2006), pp. 53–78; Hunansheng Bowuguan (ed.), *Hunan Chutu Yinshang Xizhou Qingtongqi* (*Shang and Western Zhou Bronzes from Hunan*) (Yuelu Shushe, 2007).

38 An example of a bronze vessel found in Hunan province holding a number of jades is the Ge *you*, see Fong (ed.), *The Great Bronze Age of China*, no. 25, pp. 129–31, where other examples are mentioned.

39 Discussed in the 1970s by Robert W. Bagley, 'P'an-Lung-Ch'eng: A Shang City in Hupei', *Artibus Asiae* 39 (1977), pp. 165–219.

40 For a discussion of the mines along the lower Yangtze River see Liu Haifeng, Mei Haotian, Bai Guozhu and Chen Jianli, 'Zonglun Changjiang Zhongxiayou Tongkuangdai Xian Qin Kuangye Kaogu' ('A Review of Archaeometallurgical Research on the Copper Ore Belt of the Middle and Lower Reaches of the Yangtze River in the Pre-Qin Period'), *Zhongguo Guojia Bowuguan Guankan* 7 (2020), pp. 17–34; Pan Yuanming and Dong Ping, 'The Lower Changjiang (Yangzi/Yangtze River) Metallogenic Belt, East Central China: Intrusion- and Wall Rock-Hosted Cu–Fe–Au, Mo, Zn, Pb, Ag Deposits', *Ore Geology Reviews* 15 (1999), pp. 177–242.

41 A possible contact along the Yangtze is suggested in Falkenhausen, 'The External Connections of Sanxingdui'; for the bronzes found at Hanzhong on the upper Han River and implications of communication within a wider network see Cao Wei (ed.), *Hanzhong Chutu Shangdai Qingtongqi* (*Shang Dynasty Bronzes Found in the Han River Region*), 4 vols. (Bashu Shushe, 2006–11), vol. 1, no. 18:1 and Jessica Rawson, 'Ornament and Territory: The Case of the Bronzes from Hanzhong', in Cao (ed.), *Hanzhong*, vol. 4, pp. 341–77.

42 The jade culture at Sanxingdui is described in Jenny F. So, 'Jade and Stone at Sanxingdui', in Bagley (ed.), *Ancient Sichuan*, pp. 153–76; see also So, *Early Chinese Jades*, pp. 92–4, and Xu, 'Sichuan Guanghan Yueliangwan'.

43 Large numbers of this type of sceptre have been found at Shimao in Shaanxi province in a dark or even black jade, Dai Xiangming, 'Beifang Diqu Longshan Shidai de Juluo yu Shehui' ('Settlements and Societies of the Longshan Period in North China'), *Kaogu yu Wenwu* 4 (2016), pp. 60–69, fig. 9; Shao Jing, 'Lun Shimao Wenhua yu Hou Shijiahe Wenhua de Yuancheng Jiaoliu: Cong Yazhang, Yingji, Hutou Deng Yuqi Shuoqi' ('On the Long-distance Interaction Between the Shimao Culture and the Post-Shijiahe Culture: Jade Zhang, Eagle Hairpins, and Tiger-head Jade Artefacts'), *Zhongyuan Wenwu* 3 (2021), pp. 59–66;

connections with Erlitou are discussed in Tang Chung and Wang Fang, 'The Spread of Erlitou Yazhang to South China and the Origin and Dispersal of Early Political States', in Childs-Johnson (ed.), *The Oxford Handbook of Early China*, pp. 202–23. The type appears in the Warring States list of jades we saw in Chapter 1, 'The red *zhang* [sceptre] for offering ritual to the South'. But as with the *cong*, the *bi* and the arc called the *huang*, this jade too, the *zhang*, was much more ancient than anyone could have known when these lines were composed.

44 Possible sources of the stone are discussed in Flad, 'Bronze, Jade, Gold, and Ivory', p. 322.

45 For sceptres in the shape of fish see Sichuansheng (ed.), *Sanxingdui Jisikeng*, pls. 14–17.

46 For the full range of jades interred at Sanxingdui see ibid., pp. 354–413.

47 James I. Porter, 'The Value of Aesthetic Value', in Papadopoulos and Urton (eds.), *The Construction of Value*, pp. 336–53.

48 Zhu Zhangyi, Zhang Qing and Wang Fang, 'The Jinsha Site: An Introduction', *Journal of East Asian Archaeology* 5 (2003), 247–76. For the bronze alloys see Li Haichao, Cui Jianfeng, Zhou Zhiqing, Wang Yi and Wang Zhankui, 'Jinsha Yizhi "Jisiqu" Chutu Tongqi de Shengchan Wenti Yanjiu ('On the Provenance of the Bronzes from the Sacrificial Area of Jinsha'), in Jilin Daxue Bianjiang Kaogu Yanjiu Zhongxin and Bianjiang Kaogu Yu Zhongguo Wenhua Rentong Chuangxin Zhongxin (eds.), *Bianjiang Kaogu Yanjiu* 25 (Kexue Chubanshe, 2019), pp. 335–48.

49 With the discovery of the six new pits we have learned that two of those were dedicated to offerings that were consumed by fire while the other four, together with the two we have looked at here, were deposits of the destroyed riches of the society. An up-to-date partial report is in Ran et al., 'Sichuan Guanghanshi Sanxingdui'.

Chapter 5: The Gift Economy at Baoji

1 Franck, *Wandering in Northern China*, p. 371.

2 Two tiny bronze figures with huge hands, like those seen on the bronze man from Sanxingdui, are direct evidence of communication over this formidable mountain range, Lu Liancheng and Hu Zhisheng, *Baoji Yuguo Mudi* (*Yu State Cemeteries in Baoji*), 2 vols. (Wenwu Chubanshe, 1988), vol. 1, p. 315, fig. 221, p. 375, fig. 257.

3 Huang Chun et al., 'Climatic Aridity and the Relocations of the Zhou Culture in the Southern Loess Plateau of China', *Climatic Change* 61 (2003), pp. 361–78.

For the humid conditions that may have encouraged more activity in the steppe from the ninth century BC see Struck et al., 'Central Mongolian Lake Sediments'.

4 Waley, *The Book of Songs*, p. 242.

5 Ibid., p. 248.

6 The archaeological report for all the Yu tombs mentioned is in Lu and Hu, *Baoji Yuguo Mudi*, and will be referred to throughout the chapter.

7 Double burials to the north of Shimao, at Zhukaigou, have been mentioned in Chapter 2. Some burials of this type, often earlier in date, have been found in the north-west, Han Jianye, *Zhongguo Xibei Diqu Xian Qin Shiqi de Ziran Huanjing yu Wenhua Fazhan* (*The Environmental and Cultural Development in Pre-Qin North-western China*) (Wenwu Chubanshe, 2008), p. 259.

8 Of these, another two were similar and in both the lord was also buried with a woman.

9 There is to date no proper explanation as to why in both the late Shang and the early Zhou predator imagery appears on handles of bronze vessels and realistic tigers, oxen and stags are presented in jade. However, as these chime with the kinds of images shown on bronze, ivory and stone in Iran, it seems likely that some form of these motifs had reached northern China from that direction. This topic requires much future research.

10 Maria Khayutina (private communication) suggests that this character was not accepted as a standard form in the Zhou period and was likely a local concoction to render the name of the clan.

11 The divisions into separate branches are often termed as segmented lineages, see Khayutina, 'Kinship, Marriage and Politics', pp. 14–18.

12 Inscriptions produced locally show poor levels of character formation, and probably low levels of literacy, see Li Feng, 'Literacy Crossing Cultural Borders: Evidence from the Bronze Inscriptions of the Western Zhou Period (1045–771 BC)', *Bulletin of the Museum of Far Eastern Antiquities* 74 (2002), pp. 210–42. However, the inscriptions on the Yu bronzes at Zhuyuangou are well written and well cast. Some of those at Rujiazhuang, the last cemetery, are poorly written and must have been cast locally.

13 Additional sites are mapped in Yan Sun, *Many Worlds under One Heaven: Material Culture, Identity, and Power in the Northern Frontiers of the Western Zhou, 1045–771 BCE* (Columbia University Press, 2021), p. 22, map 11.

14 Lin, 'A Reexamination of the Relationship'. For discussion of these weapons also see Zhang Wenli and Lin Yun, 'Heidouzui Leixing Qingtongqi Zhong de Xilai Yinsu' ('The Western Cultural Elements in the Heidouzui Bronzes'), *Kaogu* 5 (2004), pp. 65–73. These northern weapons have attracted extensive work connecting them with the steppe, as in Yang et al., *The Metal Road*. An

alternative approach has been to consider the wide borderlands as a whole and illustrate extensive variations and hybridity, as in Linduff et al., *Ancient China and Its Eurasian Neighbors*.

15 The tombs and their contents with references to archaeological reports are surveyed in Rawson et al., 'Seeking Horses'.

16 For the alloy composition of the locally made bronzes found in the Yu tombs see Li Haichao et al., 'Production and Circulation of Bronzes among the Regional States in the Western Zhou Dynasty', *Journal of Archaeological Science* 121 (2020), 105191. However, in terms of casting, it is essential to distinguish these from the principal ritual vessels, often with inscriptions, made at metropolitan workshops. It has been suggested (Maria Khayutina personal correspondence) that the miniature vessels represented originals for cloth-dyeing.

17 When first discovered, the excavators suggested a relatively close connection with the south-west, the region of present-day Sichuan, Lu and Hu, *Baoji Yuguo Mudi*, pp. 431–62. Yan Sun has continued the discussion of a connection with the south-west, citing the appearance in that region of willow-leaf swords, as described in Yan Sun, 'A Divergent Life History of Bronze Willow-leaf-shaped Swords of Western Zhou China from the Eleventh to the Tenth Century BCE', in Francis Allard, Yan Sun and Kathryn M. Linduff (eds.), *Memory and Agency in Ancient China: Shaping the Life History of Objects* (Cambridge University Press, 2018), pp. 120–51. See also Sun, *Many Worlds under One Heaven*. The Yu may indeed have brought in some traits from the south-west, but clearly had connections with several other regions, most notably the north, as seen in the tomb construction, as noted above in note 7. In terms of the south as well as the north, it is likely that, as the swords are similar, there was one principal source. And as swords were used in the steppe, it is unlikely that this fashion for willow-leaf swords was separately invented in the Sichuan area. It may have been transmitted to Sichuan down the foothills of mountains along the west.

18 For discussion of carnelian beads see Jessica Rawson, 'Ordering the Exotic: Ritual Practices in the Late Western and Early Eastern Zhou', *Artibus Asiae* 73 (2013), pp. 5–76.

19 For the history of the Western Zhou see Edward L. Shaughnessy, 'Western Zhou History', in Loewe and Shaughnessy (eds.), *The Cambridge History of Ancient China*, pp. 293–351.

20 David Pankenier, 'The Cosmo-Political Background of Heaven's Mandate', *Early China* 20 (1995), pp. 121–76. Concern with auspicious signs was much more strongly expressed in the Eastern Zhou period than at the time of the conquest.

21 The text from which this quotation comes, *The Collection of Leftover Documents* (*Yi Zhou Shu*), is translated and discussed in Edward L. Shaughnessy, *Before Confucius: Studies in the Creation of the Chinese Classics* (State University of New York Press, 1997), see p. 32. For a discussion of this text and others see Yegor Grebnev, *Mediation of Legitimacy in Early China: A Study of the Neglected Zhou Scriptures and the Grand Duke Traditions* (Columbia University Press, 2022).

22 Shaughnessy, *Before Confucius*, p. 33.

23 An invaluable source for the contents and historical transmission of the major texts mentioned in this book is Loewe (ed.), *Early Chinese Texts*. For *The Book of Documents* see pp. 376–89. An important commentary on this text and its dating is in Nylan, *The Five 'Confucian' Classics*. For *The Book of Poetry*, see Loewe (ed.), *Early Chinese Texts*, pp. 415–23. The most widely used translation is Waley, *The Book of Songs*.

24 We can see parallels in the way in which the Zhou attracted many followers with their own customs and drew them in almost as satellites, interested in joining a successful enterprise, described as a wider phenomenon in general terms in David Graeber and Marshall Sahlins, *On Kings* (Hau Books, 2017).

25 Tombs with vessels, especially *gui*, with bells within their stands have been surveyed and listed in Chen Beichen, 'Cultural Interactions during the Zhou Period (c.a. 1000–350 B.C.): A Study of Networks from the Suizao Corridor', DPhil thesis (University of Oxford, 2016). An interesting example is in tomb M1 of the Ba polity at Dahekou, Xie Yaoting et al., 'Shanxi Yicheng Dahekou Xizhou Mudi Yihaomu Fajue' ('The Excavation of Tomb M1 at the Western Zhou Dahekou Cemetery in Yicheng County'), *Kaogu Xuebao* 2 (2020), pp. 177–290, fig. 42.

26 As suggested in Chapter 2, the niches in the vandalised tomb indicate contacts with areas in the north of the Loess Plateau; niches have also been found in cave houses in northern sites such as Xibei Daxue, *Xunyi Xiaweiluo*, also discussed in Chapter 2 above.

27 The vessels can be matched with casting moulds found at a workshop at Xiaomintun at Anyang, see Yue Zhanwei, '2000–2001 Nian Anyang Xiaomintun Dongnandi Yindai Zhutong Yizhi Fajue Baogao' ('Excavation of the Bronze Foundry Site in the South-east of Xiaomintun, Anyang, 2000–2001'), *Kaogu Xuebao* 2 (2006), pp. 351–81. This was a very surprising and important discovery, emphasising again the origin further east, in the hands of either the Shang or the Zhou kings, of the ritual vessels that ended up in the Shigushan tombs and also at Daijiawan, Liu Junshe et al., 'Shaanxi Baoji Shigushan Xizhou Muzang Fajue Jianbao' ('The Excavation of the Western Zhou Tombs at Shigushan in Baoji, Shaanxi'), *Wenwu* 2 (2013), pp. 4–54; Wang Zhankui et al., 'Shaanxi Baoji Shigushan Shang Zhou Mudi M4 Fajue Jianbao' ('The Excavation of Tomb

M4 at Shigushan, Baoji'), *Wenwu* 1 (2016), pp. 4–52. Another unexpected comparison could be made with vessels retrieved before the Second World War in the Baoji area, described and illustrated fully in Ch'en Chao-jung (ed.), *Baoji Daijiawan yu Shigushan Chutu Shang Zhou Qingtongqi (Shang and Zhou Bronzes from Daijiawan and Shigushan at Baoji)* (Chungyang Yenchiuyuan Lishih Yuyen Yenchiuso and Shaanxi Kaogu Yanjiuyuan, 2015). Also significant is that at least one inscribed name or sign found on the Shigushan and Daijiawan bronzes is also found in a Yu tomb at Zhifangtou, Liu Junshe et al., 'Shaanxi Baoji Zhifangtou Xizhou Zaoqi Muzang Qingli Jianbao' ('The Early Western Zhou Tombs at Zhifangtou, Baoji'), *Wenwu* 8 (2007), pp. 28–47, fig. 35.1.

28 For a detailed account of bronzes from earlier tombs or sites buried in Zhou times see Hwang Ming-chorng, 'Cong Kaogu Faxian Kan Xizhou Muzang de "Fenqi" Xianxiang yu Xizhou Shidai Liqi Zhidu de Leixing yu Jieduan' ('The "Fenqi" Phenomena in Western Zhou Tombs Observed in Archaeological Discoveries and Types and Stages of Ritual System During the Western Zhou Period') 1–2 (two parts published in vols. 83 and 84 of the journal *Chungyang Yenchiuyuan Lishih Yuyen Yenchiuso Chik'an* 83–4 (2012–13)).

29 Sun, *Many Worlds under One Heaven*, p. 64.

30 Legge, *The Chinese Classics*, vol. 3, part 1, pp. 300–301. This late section of *The Book of Documents* is discussed in Nylan, *The Five 'Confucian' Classics*, p. 135.

31 A different inscription, relating to Zhou activity in the north-east, also shows their use of many different peoples in their manoeuvres to gain and control land, Constance A. Cook and Paul R. Goldin (eds.), *A Source Book of Ancient Chinese Bronze Inscriptions* (Society for the Study of Early China, 2016), pp. 18–20.

32 The creation of polities, led by members of the Zhou royal family, the Ji clan, is outlined in Shaughnessy, 'Western Zhou History', p. 312.

33 Ibid., p. 305.

34 Edward L. Shaughnessy, *Sources of Western Zhou History: Inscribed Bronze Vessels* (University of California Press, 1991), pp. 87–105. There is considerable debate about the content of the second line of the inscription.

35 Fong (ed.), *The Great Bronze Age of China*, no. 41.

36 Ibid., no. 42; Maria Khayutina, 'The Story of the He *Zun*: From Political Intermediary to National Treasure', *Orientations* 50 (2019), pp. 54–60.

37 The dates of the reigns of the Zhou kings have been much discussed and debated. The dates given here are taken from Shaughnessy, *Sources of Western Zhou History*, p. xix.

38 An outstanding example is the series of inscriptions of the Wei lineage, on bronzes excavated at Zhuangbai in Shaanxi province, offering us a sequence of generations linked in the inscription on the Shi Qiang *pan* with a parallel sequence of Zhou kings, see ibid., pp. 3–4.

39 Jessica Rawson, 'Ancient Chinese Rituals as Seen in the Material Record', in J. P. McDermott (ed.), *State and Court Ritual in China* (Cambridge University Press, 1999), pp. 20–49.

40 Nylan, *The Five 'Confucian' Classics*, p. 5.

41 The concept of the 'Great Unity' as it developed is described by Pines, *The Everlasting Empire*, pp. 11–43.

42 David Keightley has argued that direct combat between high-ranking Shang and Western Zhou leaders and their enemies was not common, in 'Clean Hands and Shining Helmets: Heroic Action in early Chinese and Greek Culture', in David N. Keightley, *These Bones Shall Rise Again: Selected Writings on Early China* (SUNY Press, 2014), pp. 253–81.

43 For comparisons of the willow-leaf sword with blades further north and west see Li Gang, *Zhongguo Beifang Qingtongqi de Ouya Caoyuan Wenhua Yinsu (The Cultural Elements of Eurasian Steppes in the Bronzes of North China)* (Wenwu Chubanshe, 2011), pp. 57–8. See also Wu'en Yuesitu, *Beifang Caoyuan Kaoguxue Wenhua Bijiao Yanjiu: Qingtong Shidai Zhi Zaoqi Xiongnu Shiqi (A Comparative Study on Archaeological Cultures of the Northern Steppe: From the Bronze Age to the Early Xiongnu Period)* (Kexue Chubanshe, 2008), p. 18. It seems unlikely that the whole tradition of willow-leaf swords arose independently in Sichuan or in the north-west. They must be interconnected with each other and both are likely to have been stimulated by swords used further west, including in Xinjiang. Evidence of these western connections is provided by a greave in tomb M3 at Shigushan, Liu et al., 'Shaanxi Baoji Shigushan', p. 13, fig. 15. It appears to be a section of armour better recognised in Western Asia or even Western Europe, as suggested by Chen Kunlong et al., 'Shaanxi Baoji Shigushan Xinchu Xizhou Tongjia de Chubu Kexue Fenxi' ('The Scientific Analysis on the Western Zhou Armour from Shigushan, Baoji'), *Wenwu* 4 (2015), pp. 68–75. An interest in armour is another feature of warfare introduced from further west, V. I. Matyushchenko and G. V. Sinitsyna, *Mogil'nik u Derevni Rostovka Blizi Omska (The Burial Site Near the Village of Rostovka in Omsk Suburbs)* (Tomsk State University, 1988). Another western weapon is the axe with 'window' openings, see Zhang and Lin, 'Heidouzui Leixing'. See also note 48 below for an example where the willow-leaf sword appears among other northern weapons.

44 For mace distribution see Li Shuicheng, 'The Mace-Head: A Significant Evidence of the Early Cultural Interaction between West and East', *Social Evolution & History* 17 (2018), pp. 258–72.

45 Fully set out in Sun, 'A Divergent Life History'. For the willow-leaf swords in tomb M1 at Yejiashan see the report in Zeng Lingbin et al., 'Hubei Suizhou Yejiashan Xizhou Mudi Fajue Jianbao' ('Preliminary Report on the Western Zhou Cemetery of Yejiashan, Suizhou, Hubei'), *Wenwu* 11 (2011), pp. 4–60,

p. 53, fig. 81; for the bird-head staff in tomb MIII at Yejiashan see Huang Feng-chun et al., 'Hubei Suizhou Yejiashan MIII Fajue Jianbao' ('Preliminary Report on Yejiashan Tomb MIII, Suizhou, Hubei'), *Jianghan Kaogu* 2 (2020), pp. 3–86, p. 65, fig. 31.

46 The report on this tomb is at Xie et al., 'Shanxi Yicheng Dahekou'. For the marriage link see Sun, *Many Worlds under One Heaven*, pp. 136–9.

47 In making this proposal I am building on the work of Yan Sun on the willow-leaf swords in her discussion 'A Divergent Life History'.

48 The four-horse Zhou chariot is described in Wu, *Chariots in Early China*, pp. 63–6, where she also shows that a willow-leaf sword was part of the weaponry that has northern associations.

49 Jacobson-Tepfer, 'The Emergence of Cultures of Mobility'.

50 Waley, *The Book of Songs*, p. 123.

51 As described in Igor V. Chechushkov, Andrei V. Epimakhov and Andrei G. Bersenev, 'Early Horse Bridle with Cheekpieces as a Marker of Social Change: An Experimental and Statistical Study', *Journal of Archaeological Science* 97 (2018), pp. 125–36.

52 Shū Takahama, 'Two Technical Traditions of Casting Horse Bits in China and Their Relationships with the Steppe Area', *Asian Archaeology* 3 (2020), pp. 47–57.

53 Rawson et al., 'Seeking Horses'.

54 Durrant et al., *Zuo Tradition*, p. 1365. This sort of statement, valuing virtue and ritual above military defence, is uttered under many a later dynasty. It certainly reflects the claims of morality by the literati, but also illustrates a claim to be superior to the horse riders of the Loess Plateau and the steppe.

55 Rawson et al., 'Seeking Horses' describes the areas with adequate selenium.

56 Li Feng, *Landscape and Power in Early China: The Crisis and Fall of the Western Zhou, 1045–771 BC* (Cambridge University Press, 2006), pp. 141–92.

57 Such inscriptions are often termed investiture inscriptions, as the recipient of gifts was often awarded a position or land. The gifts, however, interest us here. Edward Shaughnessy gives an account of the long-term influence of this gifting system in his *Sources of Western Zhou History*, pp. 73–6, 85–7.

58 Cook and Goldin (eds.), *A Source Book*, pp. 204–9.

59 Li, *Landscape and Power*, pp. 180–87.

60 The dating of the bronze vessels relies on those inscriptions that include the names of the Zhou kings and the names of their patrons or owners. A particularly important hoard from Zhuangbai in Shaanxi province has enabled a secure sequence of vessel forms and decoration to be established, discussed in Jessica Rawson, 'Western Zhou Archaeology', in Loewe and Shaughnessy (eds.), *The Cambridge History of Ancient China*, pp. 352–449. For the principal inscription from the Zhuangbai hoard see Cook and Goldin (eds.), *A Source*

Book, pp. 93–101. For further discussion see Falkenhausen, *Chinese Society*, pp. 43–52.

61 Discussed in the light of the discovery of new documents, Chen Minzhen and Yuri Pines, 'Where Is King Ping? The History and Historiography of the Zhou Dynasty's Eastward Relocation', *Asia Major* 31 (2018), pp. 1–27.

62 The arrival of the Qin is described in Pines et al. (eds.), *Birth of an Empire*, p. 53.

Chapter 6: Innovations and Heirlooms

1 Shaughnessy, 'Western Zhou History'; Li, *Landscape and Power*, pp. 105–9.

2 The constant search for material to fill these gaps is illustrated by recent discoveries of bamboo documents that have changed the chronology traditionally followed for the move to Luoyang, Chen and Pines, 'Where Is King Ping?'.

3 The creation of polities, led by members of the Zhou royal family, the Ji clan, is mentioned in Chapter 5 and outlined in Shaughnessy, 'Western Zhou History', p. 312.

4 Li, *Landscape and Power*, pp. 84–8; Yitzchak Jaffe and Cao Bin, 'Communities of Mortuary Practice: A Renewed Study of the Tianma-Qucun Western Zhou Cemetery', *Cambridge Archaeological Journal* 28 (2018), pp. 23–44; Jay Xu, 'The Cemetery of the Western Zhou Lords of Jin', *Artibus Asiae* 56 (1996), pp. 193–231. See also Beijing Daxue Kaoguxuexi Shang Zhou Zu and Shanxisheng Kaogu Yanjiusuo, *Tianma-Qucun (1980–1989) (The Tianma-Qucun Site)*, 4 vols. (Kexue Chubanshe, 2000).

5 For the Ba see Xie et al., 'The Excavation of Tomb M1'; for the Peng see Xie Yaoting et al., 'Shanxi Jiangxian Hengshui Xizhou Mudi M2158 fajue jianbao' ('The Excavation of Tomb M2158 at the Hengshui Western Zhou Cemetery in Jiang County'), *Kaogu* 1 (2019), pp. 15–59 (further description is in Rawson et al., 'Seeking Horses'); for a discussion of the role of the Peng in the wider history of the Zhou see Maria Khayutina, 'The Tombs of the Rulers of Peng and Relationships between Zhou and Northern Non-Zhou Lineages (Until the Early Ninth Century BC)', in Edward L. Shaughnessy (ed.), *Imprints of Kinship: Studies of Recently Discovered Bronze Inscriptions from Ancient China* (CUHK Press, 2017), pp. 71–132.

6 We only have a short report on the Lord of Rui's tomb in Sun Bingjun et al., 'Shaanxi Hancheng Liangdaicun Yizhi M27 Fajue Jianbao' ('The Excavation of Tomb M27 at Liangdaicun, Hancheng County'), *Kaogu yu Wenwu* 6 (2007), pp. 3–22; that of his spouse is described in Sun Bingjun et al., 'Shaanxi Hancheng Liangdaicun Yizhi M26 Fajue Jianbao' ('The Excavation of Tomb M26 at Liangdaocun, Hancheng County'), *Wenwu* 1 (2008), pp. 4–21; a fuller

report of other tombs in the site is Shaanxisheng Kaogu Yanjiuyuan, Weinanshi Wenwu Baohu Kaogu Yanjiusuo and Hanchengshi Jingqu Guanli Weiyuan-hui, *Liangdaicun Ruiguo Mudi: 2007 Nian Fajue Baogao (Cemetery of Rui State at Liangdaicun: An Excavation Report of 2007)* (Wenwu Chubanshe, 2010).

7 Newcomers had also imitated the ramps and the deep tombs, as at Kongtou-gou at Qishan in the middle Western Zhou, Wang Yang, Zhong Jianrong, Lei Xingshan and Wang Zhankui, 'Shaanxi Qishanxian Kongtougou Yizhi Xizhou Muzang M10 de Fajue' ('The Excavation of the Western Zhou Tomb M10 at Kongtougou, Qishan County, Shaanxi'), *Kaogu* 9 (2021), pp. 24–42.

8 Keightley, *The Ancestral Landscape*, pp. 86–93 mentions the directions in Shang-period inscriptions on oracle bones. There is no account of Shang or Western Zhou understanding of the powers of the cardinal directions. Such descrip-tions only become more systematised in the correlative thinking of the late Zhou and Han periods.

9 This arrangement was displayed in an exhibition in Shanghai Museum and published in the catalogue in 2012, Shanghai Bowuguan and Shaanxisheng Kaogu Yanjiuyuan (eds.), *Jinyu Nianhua: Shaanxi Hancheng Chutu Zhoudai Ruiguo Wenwu Zhenpin (The Golden Age of the Rui State, Zhou Dynasty Treasures from Hancheng, Shaanxi Province)* (Shanghai Shuhua Chubanshe, 2012).

10 These beads were of carnelian and faience, a mixture of powdered clays, lime, soda and silica sand, often of a blue or turquoise colour. Carnelian was popular, most especially in the Indus region and Western Asia, see Jonathan M. Kenoyer, Massimo Vidale and Kuldeep Kumar Bhan, 'Contemporary Stone Beadmaking in Khambhat, India: Patterns of Craft Specialization and Organization of Production as Reflected in the Archaeological Record', *World Archaeology* 23 (1991), pp. 44–63. Faience was most popular also in Western Asia and especially Egypt. The interest in beads among the Rui is a sign of close or more distant contacts with mobile pastoralists who had access to beads in Western Asia and Iran.

11 Other lords of polities to the east and south of Liangdaicun also took up abridged versions of this new style on a much smaller scale. Henansheng Wenwu Kaogusuo and Sanmenxiashi Wenwu Gongsuodui, *Sanmenxia Guoguomu (The Guo State Cemetery in Sanmenxia)*, 2 vols. (Wenwu Chubanshe, 1999), vol. 2, col. pl. 13.

12 These important tombs have been included in several descriptions of steppe culture, as in Hermann Parzinger (ed.), *Im Zeichen des Goldenen Greifen: Königs-gräber der Skythen* (Prestel, 2007); Barry W. Cunliffe, *The Scythians: Nomad Warriors of the Steppe* (Oxford University Press, 2019); St John Simpson and Svetlana Pankova (eds.), *Scythians: Warriors of Ancient Siberia* (Thames & Hudson, 2017). For the excavation of Arzhan I, see Michail P. Grjaznov, *Der*

Grosskurgan von Arzan in Tuva, Südsibirien (Beck, 1984); for Arzhan II, Konstantin V. Chugunov, Hermann Parzinger and Anatoli Nagler, *Der Skythenzeitliche Fürstenkurgan Aržan 2 in Tuva* (Philipp von Zabern, 2010).

13 Jessica Rawson, 'Gold, an Exotic Material in Early China', in Katheryn M. Linduff and Karen S. Rubinson (eds.), *How Objects Tell Stories: Essays in Honor of Emma C. Bunker* (Brepols Publishers, 2018), pp. 109–35.

14 For the full illustration of the gold in the lord's tomb see Sun Bingjun and Cai Qingliang, *Ruiguo Jinyu Xuancui: Shaanxi Hancheng Chunqiu Baozang (Highlights of Rui State Gold and Jade: Spring and Autumn Period Treasures from Shaanxi Hancheng)* (Sanqin Chubanshe, 2007); see also Yang Junchang, Paul Jett and Chen Jianli, *Gold in Ancient China (2000–200 BCE)* (Cultural Relics Press, 2017); see also Rawson, 'Gold, an Exotic Material'.

15 Evidence for riding is fugitive. It is accepted that by the ninth century BC and the building of Arzhan I, in which many horses were sacrificed, mounted warfare was one of the sources of power.

16 See Xie Yaoting, Wang Jinping, Yang Jiyun and Li Yongmin, 'Shanxi Yicheng Dahekou Xizhou Mudi 1017 Hao Mu Fajue' ('The Excavation of the Tomb M1017 at the Dahekou Cemetery of the Western Zhou Dynasty in Yicheng, Shanxi'), *Kaogu Xuebao* 1 (2018), pp. 89–140.

17 For Xinjiang as a possible source of iron-working see Wu Guo, 'From Western Asia to the Tianshan Mountains: On the Early Iron Artefacts Found in Xinjiang', in Jianjun Mei and Thilo Rehren (eds.), *Metallurgy and Civilisation: Eurasia and Beyond* (Archetype Publications, 2009), pp. 107–15. For an overview of the prevalence of iron, especially for weapons, in the steppe see Jeannine Davis-Kimball, Vladimir A. Bashilov and Leonid T. Yablonsky (eds.), *Nomads of the Eurasian Steppes in the Early Iron Age* (Zinat Press, 1995). The routes by which the choice of iron as a valuable metal reached the Central Plains are not clear.

18 For an illustration of the bronze knives with iron blades see Sun et al., 'Shaanxi Hancheng Liangdaicun Yizhi M27', p. 14, fig. 19.1.

19 Exceptionally deep tombs are found among the Peng, settled at Hengshui, Chen Haibo et al., 'Shanxi Jiangxian Hengshui Xizhou Mudi M2055 Fajue Jianbao' ('Report of Excavation at Tomb M2055 from the Western Zhou Cemetery in Hengshui, Jiangxian County of Shanxi Province'), *Jianghan Kaogu* 2 (2022), pp. 38–60; see also Xie Yaoting et al., 'Shanxi Jiangxian Hengshui Xizhou Mudi 1011 Hao Mu Fajue Baogao' ('The Excavation of Tomb M1011 of the Western Zhou Cemetery, Hengshui in Jiangxian, Shanxi'), *Kaogu Xuebao* 1 (2022), pp. 75–148.

20 For further examples see Lothar von Falkenhausen, 'Forerunners of the Houma Bronze Styles: The Shangguo Sequence', *Gugong Xueshu Jikan* 23 (2005), pp. 111–74.

21 Miniature replicas in the Jin tombs are illustrated in Li Xiating and Zhang Kui, 'Tianma-Qucun Yizhi Beizhao Jinhou Mudi Disici Fajue' ('The 4th Season of Excavation of the Graveyard of Marquis of Jin at the Tianma-Qucun Site'), *Wenwu* 8 (1994), pp. 4–21.

22 For ceramics from the north see Xu Tianjin, Meng Yuehu, Li Xiating and Zhang Kui, 'Tianma-Qucun Yizhi Beizhao Jinhou Mudi Diwuci Fajue' ('The 5th Season of Excavation of the Graveyard of Marquis of Jin at the Tianma-Qucun Site'), *Wenwu* 7 (1995), pp. 4–39, Song Jianzhong, Ji Kunzhang, Tian Jianwen and Li Yongmin, 'Shanxi Jiangxian Hengshui Xizhoumu Fajue Jian-bao' ('A Brief Excavation Report on the Tombs of the Western Zhou Located at Hengshui Town, Jiang County, Shanxi Province'), *Wenwu* 8 (2006) pp. 4–18; Khayutina, 'The Tombs of the Rulers of Peng' discusses ceramics from the north found in tombs of women in the region.

23 Discussed above in Chapter 2. See Chen Fang-mei, 'Shang Zhou "Xiyou" Qing-tongqi Lei de Wenhua Yihan: Suowei "Bianyuan" Wenhua Yanjiu de Yiyi' ('The Cultural Connotations of "Rare" Shang and Chou Bronze Types: The Signif-icance of "Marginal" Cultural Research'), *Kuoli Taiwan Tahsüeh Meishushih Yechiu Chik'an* 19 (2005), pp. 1–62; compare Khayutina, 'The Tombs of the Rulers of Peng', pp. 84–96.

24 Maria Khayutina, 'Marital Alliances and Affinal Relatives (Sheng and Hungou) in the Society and Politics of Zhou China in the Light of Bronze Inscriptions', *Early China* 37 (2014), pp. 39–99.

25 These mysterious trapezoidal plaques had lain in storage boxes in museums for decades, their functions unknown. The shape is not a traditional jade form with its straight sides and sharp corners and numerous tiny holes for strings. Earlier ones may have been of wood or bone. For a discussion of the use of these beads within China and possible sources of the tradition in western areas of the steppe see Rawson, 'Ordering the Exotic' and Jessica Rawson, 'Carne-lian Beads, Animal Figures and Exotic Vessels: Traces of Contact Between the Chinese States and Inner Asia, *c.*1000–650 BC', *Archaeologie in China* 1 (2010), pp. 1–42. Further aspects of the origins of these hangings are discussed in Jenny F. So, 'Connecting Friend and Foe: Western Zhou Personal Regalia in Jade and Colored Stones', *Archaeological Research in Asia* 19 (2019), 100108. Full dis-cussions of the use of beads in China are in Huang Tsui-mei, 'Liuguang Yicai, Cuirao Zhuwei: Xizhou Zhi Chuqiu Zaoqi de Tixingpai Lianzhu Chuanshi' ('Gleaming and Exuberant: Bead-strings with Trapezoidal Plaques from West-ern Zhou to the Early Spring and Autumn Period'), in Chen Kwang-tzuu (ed.), *Jinyu Jiaohui: Shang Zhou Kaogu, Yishu yu Wenhua Lunwenji* (*Radiance between Bronze and Jade: Archaeology, Art, and Culture of the Shang and Zhou Dynasties*) (Chungyang Yenchiuyuan Lishih Yuyen Yenchiuso, 2013), pp. 559–600.

26 Recent discussions of carnelian beads in East Asia and the connections west-wards can be followed in Jonathan Mark Kenoyer et al., 'Carnelian Beads in Mongolia: New Perspectives on Technology and Trade', *Archaeological and Anthropological Sciences* 14 (2021).

27 Rawson et al., 'Seeking Horses' argues that the demand for horses also brought materials and technologies to the agricultural basins. Some of the exchanges of fine materials across the steppe made in later centuries are described in William Honeychurch, *Inner Asia and the Spatial Politics of Empire: Archaeology, Mobility, and Culture Contact* (Springer, 2015). The interactions were one of the contributing factors to the later development now called the Silk Road, see Nicola Di Cosmo, 'The "Birth" of the Silk Road between Ecological Frontiers and Military Innovation', in Jeffrey D. Lerner and Yaohua Shi (eds.), *Silk Roads: From Local Realities to Global Narratives* (Oxbow, 2020), pp. 11–20.

28 For both beads and fine jades in the Jin tombs see Sun Hua, Zhang Kui, Chang Chongning and Sun Qingwei, 'Tianma-Qucun Yizhi Beizhao Jinhou Mudi Di'erci Fajue' ('The 2nd Season of Excavation of the Graveyard of Marquis of Jin at the Tianma-Qucun Site'), *Wenwu* 1 (1994), pp. 4–28.

29 For good illustrations of these jades see Sun and Cai, *Ruiguo Jinyu Xuancui.*

30 Auspiciousness emerged from a long practice of various forms of divination and interpretation of natural events. There are very few studies on the early use of auspicious imagery in China, see Wu Hung, 'A Sanpan Shan Chariot Ornament and the Xiangrui Design in Western Han Art', *Archives of Asian Art* 37 (1984), pp. 38–59; Jessica Rawson, 'Cosmological Systems as Sources of Art, Ornament and Design', *Bulletin of the Museum of Far Eastern Antiquities* 72 (2000), pp. 133–89; Jessica Rawson, 'Ornament in China', in Martin J. Powers and Katherine R. Tsiang (eds.), *A Companion to Chinese Art* (John Wiley & Sons, 2016), pp. 371–91.

31 For the protective power of the jade suits see James C. S. Lin, 'Armour for the Afterlife', in Jane Portal (ed.), *The First Emperor: China's Terracotta Army* (British Museum Press, 2007), pp. 181–3; James C. S. Lin (ed.), *The Search for Immortality: Tomb Treasures of Han China* (Yale University Press, 2012).

32 For gifts offered by the Western Zhou see Rawson et al., 'Seeking Horses'; such gifts continued into the ninth and eighth centuries BC, see Cook and Goldin (eds.), *A Source Book*, pp. 213–18, and further discussed in this book in Chapter 8.

33 Nicola Di Cosmo, *Ancient China and Its Enemies: The Rise of Nomadic Power in East Asian History* (Cambridge University Press, 2002).

34 Li, *Landscape and Power*, p. 147; see also Cook and Goldin, *A Source Book*, p. 187.

35 Forging was a process brought into the agricultural lands with peoples from further north-west. For a technical discussion see Chen Kunlong, Mei Jianjun and Sun Bingjun, 'Liangdaicun Liang Zhou Mudi Chutu Qingtongqi Chubu Jiance Fenxi' ('Preliminary Scientific Analysis of Bronze Objects Unearthed from Zhou Cemetery of Liangdaicun'), *Kaogu yu Wenwu* 6 (2009), pp. 91–5.

36 Matyushchenko and Sinitsyna, *Mogil'nik u Derevni Rostovka*.

37 Well-known examples are helmets found in the royal tombs at Anyang, Ts'ai et al., *Shangwang Wuding*, pp. 178–9.

38 Ji Kunzhang, Chang Huaiying and Feng Feng, 'Shanxi Beizhao Jinhou Mudi Yihao Chemakeng Fajue Jianbao' ('Excavation of Chariot-and-horse Pit No. 1 in Graveyard of the Marquis of Jin in Beizhao, Shanxi'), *Wenwu* 2 (2010), pp. 4–22.

39 I have called this change a ritual revolution; see Jessica Rawson, 'A Bronze-casting Revolution in the Western Zhou and Its Impact on Provincial Industries', in Robert Maddin (ed.), *The Beginning of the Use of Metals and Alloys: Papers from the Second International Conference on the Beginning of the Use of Metals and Alloys, Zhengzhou, China, 21–26 October 1986* (MIT Press, 1988), pp. 228–38. Lothar von Falkenhausen, supporting this account, has used the term ritual reform, Falkenhausen, *Chinese Society*, pp. 70–78.

40 Falkenhausen, *Chinese Society*, pp. 98–111.

41 The use of artefacts to realise concepts and practices is described in Jessica Rawson, 'Chinese Burial Patterns: Sources of Information on Thought and Belief', in Colin Renfrew and Christopher Scarre (eds.), *Cognition and Material Culture: The Archaeology of Symbolic Storage* (McDonald Institute for Archaeological Research, 1998), pp. 107–33.

42 Jessica Rawson, 'Ordering the Material World of the Western Zhou', *Archaeological Research in Asia* 19 (2019), 100096.

43 Rawson, 'Ancient Chinese Rituals'.

44 For the hoard found at Zhuangbai in the Zhouyuan area, which illustrates the change, see Rawson, 'Western Zhou Archaeology', pp. 433–40; Jessica Rawson, *Western Zhou Ritual Bronzes from the Arthur M. Sackler Collections* (Arthur M. Sackler Foundation, 1990), pp. 93–114.

45 Li Feng has expressed concern about the concept of changes in the vessels indicating major reforms, planned at the centre, Li, *Early China*, pp. 151–2; see also Paul Vogt, 'Between Kin and King: Social Aspects of Western Zhou Ritual', PhD dissertation (Columbia University, 2012). The suggestions that major ritual changes were made in the tenth century BC do not fit with the introduction of new bronze types from the late ninth century BC.

46 Falkenhausen, *Chinese Society*, pp. 56–64.

47 Jessica Rawson, 'Novelties in Antiquarian Revivals: The Case of the Chinese Ritual Bronzes', *Gugong Xueshu Jikan* 22 (2004), pp. 1–34; Jessica Rawson, 'Reviving Ancient Ornament and the Presence of the Past: Examples from Shang and Zhou Bronze Vessels', in Wu Hung (ed.), *Reinventing the Past: Archaism and Antiquarianism in Chinese Art and Visual Culture* (University of Chicago, 2010), pp. 47–76.

48 Sun et. al., 'Shaanxi Hancheng Liangdaicun', figs. 8, 9.4, 6; Hanchengshi Liangdaicun Yizhi Guanlichu (ed.), *Liangdaicun Yizhi Bowuguan* (*Liangdaicun Museum*) (Shaanxi Kexue Jishu Chubanshe, 2018), pp. 64–5.

49 Unlike the Lord of Rui, his predecessor in tomb M 502 had no access to original ancient pieces, it would seem. Instead he had had small replicas made, which could not be used. They were simple references to his past and mirrored the situation in the Wei Valley, where the family would have had bronzes of different periods on the altars or in use at one and the same time, see Shaanxisheng et al., *Liangdaicun Ruiguo Mudi*, pls. 27–8; for a wider discussion of this phenomenon, see Rawson, 'Novelties in Antiquarian Revivals'.

50 A bronze in a private collection is illustrated in Shouyangzhai, Shanghai Bowuguan and Xianggang Zhongwen Daxue Wenwuguan (eds.), *Shouyang Jijin: Hu Yingying, Fan Jirong Cang Zhongguo Gudai Qingtongqi* (*Ancient Chinese Bronzes from the Shouyang Studio, the Katherine and George Fan Collection*) (Shanghai Guji Chubanshe, 2018), no. 34. See also Khayutina, 'Kinship, Marriage and Politics', pp. 308–10.

51 This comment in the inscription is illustrated in Shaughnessy, *Sources of Western Zhou History*, pp. 1–4, 245–7; Martin Kern, 'Bronze Inscriptions, the *Shijing* and the *Shangshu*: The Evolution of the Ancestral Sacrifice During the Western Zhou', in John Lagerwey and Marc Kalinowski (eds.), *Early Chinese Religion*, Part I: *Shang through Han (1250 BC–220 AD)* (Brill, 2009), p. 153–5.

52 Maria Khayutina, 'The Beginning of Cultural Memory Production in China and the Memory Policy of the Zhou Royal House During the Western Zhou Period (ca. Mid-11th–Early 8th Century BCE)', *Early China* 44 (2021), pp. 19–108.

53 Martin Kern's work is an important complement to a discussion of ritual changes shown in bronze vessels in the late Western Zhou, Kern, 'Bronze Inscriptions'.

54 After Kern, ibid., p. 165.

55 Ibid., pp. 165–9.

56 The Five Proclamations in *The Book of Documents* have in past studies been recognised as early writings of the tenth century BC. The speech on the degeneracy of alcohol, the *Jiu Gao*, is usually listed as one of these early texts, but it is now thought that these may well have been revised or extended from the ninth century BC or later.

57 Kern, 'Bronze Inscriptions', pp. 174–5.

58 A summary of this development is in Bagley, 'Percussion'.

59 Kern, 'Bronze Inscriptions', p. 166.

60 For a discussion of the place of belts in ancient China see Sun Ji, 'Zhongguo Gudai de Daiju' ('Ancient Chinese Belts'), in Sun Ji, *Zhongguo Guyufu Luncong* (*Discussion of Dress in Ancient China*) (Wenwu Chubanshe, 2001), pp. 253–92. Details of the belts as emblems of rank are discussed in Chisako Yoshimura, 'Todai No Choshotai Ni Tsuite' ('Belts with Pendant Thongs of the Tang Period'), *Bijutsushi* 3 (1976), pp. 43–54.

Chapter 7: The Steppe Frontier

1 An account of the continuous interactions with northerners and the horses from the late Shang onwards is set out in Rawson et al., 'Seeking Horses'; see also Ute Luise Dietz, ' "Cimmerian" Bridles: Progress in Cavalry Technology?', in Sandra Lynn Olsen, Mary Aiken Littauer and Ingrid Rea (eds.), *Horses and Humans: The Evolution of Human-Equine Relationships* (Archaeopress, 2006), pp. 157–63.

2 Shaughnessy, 'Western Zhou History', pp. 312–13.

3 For the archaeological report on the cemetery see Beijingshi Wenwu Yanjiusuo, *Liulihe Xizhou Yanguo Mudi: 1973–1977* (*The Western Zhou Yan State Cemetery at Liulihe: 1973–1977*) (Wenwu Chubanshe, 1995). Discussion of the site is in Yitzchak Jaffe, 'Materializing Identity – A Statistical Analysis of the Western Zhou Liulihe Cemetery', *Asian Perspectives* 51 (2012), pp. 47–67.

4 For the four-volume report on the cemetery at Yuhuangmiao see Beijingshi Wenwu Yanjiusuo, *Jundushan Mudi: Yuhuangmiao* (*Yuhuangmiao at the Jundushan Cemeteries*), 4 vols. (Wenwu Chubanshe, 2010). An important discussion is in Peter I. Shulga, *Mogil'nik Yuykhuanmyao v Severnom Kitaye (Vii-Vi Veka Do Nashey Ery)* (*The Cemetery of Yuhuangmiao in Northern China (the 7th–6th Centuries BC)*) (Institute of Archaeology and Ethnography SB RAS, 2015).

5 For an account of the contribution of early writings to our understanding of the history of the period see Shaughnessy, 'Western Zhou History'; we are fortunate to have a full translation of the *Annals* and the Zuo commentary in Durrant et al., *Zuo Tradition*.

6 Durrant et al., *Zuo Tradition*, pp. 228–9.

7 Watson, *Records*, vol. 2, p. 155.

8 Nicola Di Cosmo, 'The Northern Frontier in Pre-imperial China', in Loewe and Shaughnessy (eds.), *The Cambridge History of Ancient China*, pp. 885–966; Nicola Di Cosmo, 'China-Steppe Relations in Historical Perspective', in Jan

Bemmann and Michael Schmauder (eds.), *Complexity of Interaction along the Eurasian Steppe Zone in the First Millennium* CE (Vor- und Frühgeschichtliche Archäologie, Rheinische Friedrich-Wilhelms-Universität, 2015), pp. 49–72.

9 Di Cosmo, *Ancient China and Its Enemies*, pp. 155–8.

10 Reuven Amitai and Michal Biran (eds.), *Nomads as Agents of Cultural Change: The Mongols and Their Eurasian Predecessors* (University of Hawai'i Press, 2014).

11 For accounts of the lives of pastoralists in the past and in more recent times see William Honeychurch, 'Alternative Complexities: The Archaeology of Pastoral Nomadic States', *Journal of Archaeological Research* 22 (2014), pp. 277–326; Anatoly M. Khazanov (trans. Julia Crookenden), *Nomads and the Outside World* (University of Wisconsin Press, 1994). Forms of authority among the pastoralists are discussed in David Sneath, *The Headless State: Aristocratic Orders, Kinship Society, & Misrepresentations of Nomadic Inner Asia* (Columbia University Press, 2007).

12 For further discussion and examples see Chapters 8 and 10 in this book.

13 For an overall history of the steppe peoples, with a concentration on the western steppe, see Anthony, *The Horse, the Wheel, and Language*; a summary looking at the spread of tomb mounds in Europe is in Chris Gosden, Peter N. Hommel and Courtney Nimura, 'Making Mounds: Monuments in Eurasian Prehistory', in Tanja Romankiewicz, Manuel Fernández-Götz, Gary R. Lock and Olivier Büchsenschütz (eds.), *Enclosing Space, Opening New Ground: Iron Age Studies from Scotland to Mainland Europe* (Oxbow Books, 2019), pp. 141–52.

14 A good example is the equipment at a later tomb at Berel in Kazakhstan, Parzinger (ed.), *Im Zeichen des Goldenen Greifen*, pp. 132–47.

15 Dietz, ' "Cimmerian" Bridles'.

16 The only comparable example is in a very unusual tomb in the Wei Valley. There, chariots had been disassembled, with their parts placed around the coffin. Horses were buried at the front, as if to pull the coffin and the tomb owner literally into the afterlife. These were likely tombs of some of the many predecessors of the leader at Yuhuangmiao, who had moved into the Wei Valley and had been drawn into Zhou fighting forces, Shaanxisheng Kaogu Yanjiusuo and Qinshihuang Bingmayong Bowuguan, *Huaxian Dongyang* (*The Dongyang Site in Hua County, Shaanxi*) (Kexue Chubanshe, 2006), pp. 18–114. However, in many late Western Zhou tombs, the wheels of chariots were placed on the secondary ledge as if the coffin chamber formed part of a vehicle with wheels; see Jia Jing and Wang Junxian, 'Fufeng Huangdui Xizhou Mudi Zuantan Qingli Jianbao' ('A Preliminary Report of the Western Zhou Tombs at Huangdui in the Fufeng County'), *Wenwu* 8 (1986), pp. 56–68.

17 Evidence for riding is fugitive and debated. However, the powerful leaders buried at Arzhan in the Tuva Republic from about 800 BC certainly rode,

Grjaznov, *Der Grosskurgan von Arzan in Tuva*; see also Robert Drews, *Early Riders: The Beginnings of Mounted Warfare in Asia and Europe* (Routledge, 2004); William T. T. Taylor et al., 'Understanding Early Horse Transport in Eastern Eurasia through Analysis of Equine Dentition', *Antiquity* 95 (2021), pp. 1478–94.

18 Durrant et al., *Zuo Tradition*, pp. 18–19.

19 Throughout several chapters of this book, the major kurgan, designated at Arzhan II, provides a benchmark for steppe parallels for materials excavated in tombs in China; see Chugunov et al., *Der Skythenzeitliche Fürstenkurgan*. For the cauldrons see pl. 70.

20 Jenny F. So and Emma C. Bunker, *Traders and Raiders on China's Northern Frontier* (Arthur M. Sackler Gallery, Smithsonian Institution, in association with University of Washington Press, 1995).

21 Lead in the smaller of two cauldrons at Arzhan II may be another indication that cauldrons with leaded bronze were made in the south and then offered in some exchanges to steppe groups. Or more likely, that bronze of some sort used in the Loess Plateau reached South Siberia and was recast as a cauldron.

22 As mentioned in Chapter 6, these two bronze types were used widely in the Loess Plateau settlements; see Falkenhausen, *Forerunners of the Houma Bronze Style: The Shangguo sequence* (National Palace Museum, 2005).

23 Beijingshi, *Yuhuangmiao*, vol. 2, pp. 907–9, figs. 569–57. One of these has a flat lid, possibly reproducing wood, a form generally popular also further south in Shanxi and Shandong provinces.

24 Gong Yanxing, Xie Huaying and Hu Xinli, 'Xueguo Gucheng Kancha he Muzang Fajue Baogao' ('Survey and Excavation of the Xue State City and Cemetery'), *Kaogu Xuebao* 4 (1991), pp. 449–95, p. 465, fig. 10, no. 79.

25 Compare Ou Tansheng, 'Chunqiu Zaoqi Huangjun Meng Fufu Mu Fajue Baogao' ('The Excavation of an Early Spring and Autumn Period Tomb Belonging to Huang-state Lord Meng and His Spouse'), *Kaogu* 4 (1984), pp. 302–32.

26 Beijingshi, *Yuhuangmiao*, vol. 2, p. 906, figs. 567, 568, from tomb M2.

27 As Falkenhausen notes, the ancestral cult of the Central Plains could not be taken north in practical terms as it depended on wealth given by the holdings of agricultural land, a settled society with subordinates to work the land, *Chinese Society*, pp. 287–8.

28 There is very little discussion of trade, in the form of barter, in early writings. Although there must always have been exchange and trade, it was not initially studied and researched because in later periods the status of merchants was much lower than that of the literate officials. We can expect to understand more in due course with the publication of Lothar von Falkenhausen's forthcoming work, *Economic Trends in the Age of Confucius (ca. 1000–250 BC): The*

Archaeological Evidence. Some material evidence is presented in So and Bunker, *Traders and Raiders*; see also Honeychurch, *Inner Asia and the Spatial Politics of Empire.* Clearly exchanges were taking place earlier, making possible the Lord of Rui's acquisition of gold. But we have no knowledge of where and how such exchanges happened and who and what was involved. For the Qin and Han period see Mark E. Lewis, *The Early Chinese Empires: Qin and Han* (Harvard Belknap, 2007). The exchanges are part of the foundation of what we call the Silk Road, Di Cosmo, 'The "Birth" of the Silk Road', pp. 11–20.

29 Beijingshi, *Liulihe*, p. 21, fig. 14, p. 30, fig. 20, p. 57, fig. 43, pp. 201–2, figs. 117–18, p. 219, fig. 132.

30 Among many hoards reported north of Beijing, one at Kazuo is a typical example, Beidong Wenwu Fajue Xiaozu, 'Liaoning Kazuoxian Beidongcun Chutu de Yinzhou Qingtongqi' ('Shang–Zhou Period Bronzes Unearthed at Beidong, Kazuo County'), *Kaogu* 6 (1974), pp. 364–72.

31 For excavation reports of tombs of the Upper Xiajiadian see Neimenggu Zizhiqu Wenwu Kaogu Yanjiusuo and Ningchengxian Liao Zhongjing Bowuguan, *Xiaoheishigou: Xiajiadian Shangceng Wenhua Yizhi Fajue Baogao (The Excavation of the Upper Xiajiadian Culture Site at Xiaoheishigou)* (Kexue Chubanshe, 2009) and Liu Guanmin and Xu Guangji, 'Ningcheng Nanshan'gen Yizhi Fajue Baogao' ('The Excavation of Nanshan'gen in Ningcheng County'), *Kaogu Xuebao* 1 (1975), pp. 117–40. For a summary in English see Linduff et al., *Ancient China and Its Eurasian Neighbors*, pp. 75–95.

32 For discussion of bronze compositions see He Tangkun and Jin Fengyi, 'Liaoxi Xiajiadian Shangceng Wenhua Qingtong Hejin Chengfen Chubu Yanjiu' ('Preliminary Study on the Alloying Compositions of Upper Xiajiadian Culture Bronze Objects'), *Kaogu* 1 (2002), pp. 76–83; Hsu Yiu-Kang et al., 'Tracing the Flows of Copper and Copper Alloys in the Early Iron Age Societies of the Eastern Eurasian Steppe', *Antiquity* 90 (2016), pp. 357–75.

33 The movement of vessels, cast on the Central Plains, northwards is shown in Cao, *The Loess Highlands*, and also discussed in Rawson et al., 'Chariotry and Prone Burials'.

34 One of the most distinctive examples is a cup with a horizontal loop as a handle on bronzes in the Upper Xiajiadian tombs; see Neimenggu, *Xiaoheishigou*, p. 373, fig. 303, and for the comparable example at Arzhan II, Chugunov et al., *Der Skythenzeitliche Fürstenkurgan*, pl. 67:1.

35 For the weaponry from the Yuhuangmiao tombs see Beijingshi, *Yuhuangmiao*, vol. 2.

36 Chugunov et al., *Der Skythenzeitliche Fürstenkurgan*, pls. 40–41.

37 Belts have been mentioned in Chapter 3 as part of the essential dress of figures represented on the deer stones in present-day Mongolia and are a prominent

point in Chapter 6, where the Lord of Rui had adopted the gold belts of the steppe. Different forms of belt ornament are illustrated in Beijingshi, *Yuhuangmiao*, pp. 1230–34.

38 For the examples in Arzhan II see Chugunov et al., *Der Skythenzeitliche Fürstenkurgan*, pls. 29–31; and for an example from Tasmola in central Kazakhstan see fig. 287:4, 5. For a Qin state interpretation of this type of belt in jade or another hard stone see Baojishi Kaogu Yanjiusuo, *Qinmu Yizhen: Baoji Yimen Erhao Chunqiumu (Treasures of Qin Tombs: A Spring and Autumn Period Tomb (No. 2) at Yimen, Baoji)* (Kexue Chubanshe, 2016), pp. 156–7, discussed in Chapter 12 in this book. This must have been a quite common adaptation of a steppe belt popular with the Qin; see Tian Yaqi et al., 'Shaanxi Fengxiang Sunjianantou Chuqiu Qinmu Fajue Jianbao' ('The Preliminary Report of the Spring and Autumn Qin Tomb at Sunjianantou, Fengxiang, Shaanxi'), *Kaogu yu Wenwu* 4 (2013), pp. 3–34, p. 10, fig. 6:11.

39 A full account of the major archaeological finds is in Parzinger (ed.), *Im Zeichen des Goldenen Greifen*. A more general description with full maps is in Barry Cunliffe, *By Steppe, Desert and Ocean: The Birth of Eurasia* (Oxford University Press, 2015). For illustrations of recent discoveries in Kazakhstan see Rebecca Roberts (ed.), *Gold of the Great Steppe: People, Power and Production* (Paul Holberton, 2021).

40 Early Scythian tombs were discovered at the Kelermes cemetery in the Kuban region of the Caucasus; see Tatyana V. Ryabkova, 'The Formation of the Early Scythian Cultural Complex of the Kelermes Cemetery in the Kuban Region of the North Caucasus', in: Svetlana Pankova and St John Simpson (eds.), *Masters of the Steppe: The Impact of the Scythians and Later Nomad Societies of Eurasia: Proceedings of a Conference Held at the British Museum, 27–29 October 2017* (Archaeopress Archaeology, 2020), pp. 483–97.

41 Chugunov et al., *Der Skythenzeitliche Fürstenkurgan*. Later developments in the Tuva are described in Konstantin V. Chugunov, 'Der Skythenzeitliche Kulturwandel in Tuva' ('The Scythian Cultural Change in Tuva'), *Eurasia Antiqua* 4 (1998), pp. 273–307.

42 Herodotus (trans. Robin Waterfield), *The Histories* (Oxford University Press, 2008), p. 258. Askoid Ivantchik, 'The Funeral of Scythian Kings: The Historical Reality and the Description of Herodotus (4.71–72)', in Larissa Bonfante (ed.), *The Barbarians of Ancient Europe: Realities and Interactions* (Cambridge University Press, 2011), pp. 71–106.

43 An exhibition catalogue characterises this discussion, Emma C. Bunker, Bruce Chatwin and Ann R. Farkas, *Animal Style Art from East to West* (Asia Society, 1970). See also Emma C. Bunker, *Ancient Bronzes of the Eastern Eurasian Steppes from the Arthur M. Sackler Collections* (Arthur M. Sackler Foundation, 1997). For

an up-to-date assessment of the animal style, see Emma Bunker and Ursula Brosseder, *The Guyuan Mizong Collection: A Study of Inner Asian Steppe Bronzes* (Harrassowitz Verlag, 2022).

44 There is always a reluctance among researchers to consider the wider context of such developments, outside their own domains. However, the earliest imagery of animals, domestic and hunted, and their predators was one of the foundations of representation in Mesopotamia and Iran and crossed into the steppe at Maikop in the Caucasus, among other places, as illustrated in Joan Aruz and Ronald Wellenfelz (eds.), *Art of the First Cities: The Third Millennium b.c. from the Mediterranean to the Indus* (Metropolitan Museum of Art/Yale University Press, 2003); for Maikop see pp. 290–96. Thereafter such subject matter spread widely on cylinder seals, and also across the steppe on petroglyphs, Joan Aruz, Kim Benzel and Jean M. Evans (eds.), *Beyond Babylon: Art, Trade, and Diplomacy in the Second Millennium b.c.* (Metropolitan Museum of Art/Yale University Press, 2008), especially pp. 404–17. On the steppe itself animal imagery was spontaneously depicted in petroglyphs, Jacobson-Tepfer, 'The Emergence of Cultures of Mobility'. As contact continued with Western Asia, new subject matter was continuously available. We do not need to pinpoint where this subject matter originated or how it spread. In the context of ancient China, one important aspect of animal imagery is its general absence from ancient China before the eighth century bc, except in small jade carvings. These were perhaps popular with the Shang and the Zhou as a consequence of their contacts with their neighbours, mentioned in Chapter 5. Small bronze tigers of the eighth century bc from Yicun in Ningxian, Gansu province, are local versions of steppe parallels, as noted by Kim Dong-gil, 'Yuhuangmiao Wenhua Qingtongqi Yanjiu' ('On the Yuhuangmiao Culture Bronze Objects'), PhD dissertation (Jilin University, 2018), pp. 113–15; a similar figure of a tiger was found at Huangdui in Fufeng county, Shaanxisheng, 'Fufeng Huangdui', p. 63, fig. 30. Tigers on bronzes in the tomb of an outsider at Qishan Kongtougou are nice examples of the hybridisation of steppe motifs within a Central Plains framework; see Wang Yang, Zhong Jianrong, Lei Xingshan and Wang Zhankui, 'Shaanxi Qishanxian Kongtougou Yizhi Xizhou Muzang M10 de Fajue' ('The Excavation of the Western Zhou Tomb M10 at Kongtougou, Qishan County, Shaanxi'), *Kaogu* 9 (2021), pp. 24–42, p. 37.

45 Some bronze knives and daggers, and small bronze animal ornaments, have also been found. Collected items are illustrated in Purevjav Erdenechuluun and Diimaajav Erdenebaatar, *The Sword of Heaven: Culture of Bronze Artefacts of the Bronze Age and Hunnu Empire* (Collections of Erdenechuluun Purevjav, 2011).

46 The effects over a longer period are discussed in Gideon Shelach-Lavi, 'Steppe Land Interactions and Their Effects on Chinese Cultures During the Second

and Early First Millennia BCE', in Amitai and Biran (eds.), *Nomads as Agents of Cultural Change*, pp. 10–31.

47 Analysing climate conditions is difficult as data for early periods are elusive. One discussion is in Aleksandr Tairov, 'Rannie Kochevniki Zhaiyk-Irtyshskogo Mezhdurech'ya v VIII–VI vv. do n.e.' ('Early Nomads of the Zhaiyk-Irtysh Interfluve in VIII–VI cc. BC') (Kazakhskiy Nauchno-Issledovatel'skiy Institut Kul'tury, 2017); Nicola di Cosmo gives a later example in Nicola Di Cosmo et al., 'Environmental Stress and Steppe Nomads: Rethinking the History of the Uyghur Empire (744–840) with Paleoclimate Data', *Journal of Interdisciplinary History* 48 (2018), pp. 439–63.

48 Yang Jianhua, 'Differentiation of Two Types of Cultural Remains of the Eastern Zhou Period in North China: On the Relationships among the Rong, Di and the Hu', *Chinese Archaeology* 12 (2012), pp. 136–48; Shan Yueying, 'The Pattern of Archaeological Cultures in Northern China during the Eastern Zhou Period to the Qin Dynasty – Also on the Interactions among the Rong, Di and Hu Ethnic Groups and the Central Plains', *Chinese Archaeology* 16 (2016), pp. 178–88.

49 An extensive account of the different groups who moved into the several regions of northern China down to the Qin period is set out and illustrated in Bunker, *Ancient Bronzes of the Eastern Eurasian Steppes*.

50 Durrant et al., *Zuo Tradition*, p. 55.

51 Poo Mu-chou, *Enemies of Civilization: Attitudes toward Foreigners in Ancient Mesopotamia, Egypt, and China* (State University of New York Press, 2005) gives an interesting comparison of similar attitudes to 'barbarians' among these different cultures. He also examines efforts to assimilate outsiders, pp. 126–8.

Chapter 8: Circling South

1 For one of many accounts of the centuries after the move to Luoyang see Hsu Cho-yun, 'The Spring and Autumn Period', in Loewe and Shaughnessy (eds.), *The Cambridge History of Ancient China*, pp. 545–86.

2 Maxim Korolkov, 'Institutions of State Organised Migration in late Warring States and early Imperial China', paper presented at the Association for Asian Studies 2018 Conference, Washington; 'Convict Labour in the Qin Empire: A Preliminary Study of the "Registers of Convict labourers" from Liye', in Fudan Daxue Lishixue Xi and Fudan Daxue Chutu Wenxian Yu Guwenzi Yanjiu Zhongxin (eds.), *Jianbo Wenxian yu Gudaishi: Di'erjie Chutu Wenxian Qingnian Xuezhe Guoji Luntan Lunwenji* (*Ancient Manuscripts and History: Proceedings of*

the Second International Conference of Excavated Manuscripts) (Zhongxi Shuju, 2015), pp. 132–56.

3 James Cahill, *Fantastics and Eccentrics in Chinese Painting* (Arno Press, 1976).

4 The archaeological report is published in Anhuisheng Wenwu Kaogu Yanjiu-suo and Bengbushi Bowuguan, *Zhonglijun Bai Mu* (*The Tomb of Lord Bai of the Zhongli State*), 3 vols. (Wenwu Chubanshe, 2013). A summary of this report in English is in Kan Xuhang, Zhou Qun and Qian Renfa, 'Spring and Autumn Tomb No. 1 at Shuangdun, Bengbu City, Anhui', *Chinese Archaeology* 10 (2010), pp. 31–7.

5 As well as examples on the steppe, circular tombs in steppe style have been excavated in Xinjiang, Xinjiang Weiwuer Zizhiqu Wenwu Kaogu Yanjiusuo, *Xinjiang Mohuchahan Mudi* (*The Mohuchahan Cemetery in the Hejing County, Xinjiang*) (Kexue Chubanshe, 2016).

6 Anhuisheng Wenwu Kaogu Yanjiusuo and Fengyangxian Wenwu Guanlisuo, *Fengyang Dadongguan yu Bianzhuang* (*The Dadongguan and Bianzhuang Sites in Fengyang, Anhui*) (Kexue Chubanshe, 2018).

7 For an introduction to the state of Chu see Constance A. Cook and John S. Major (eds.), *Defining Chu: Image and Reality in Ancient China* (University of Hawai'i Press, 1999).

8 Early tombs that are attributed to Chu and offer archaeological information have recently been identified in the Han River area; see Zhang Changping, 'Lun Xizhou Shiqi Chuguo de Zhengzhi Zhongxin: Cong Yichang Wanfunao Yizhi Tanqi' ('Political Centre of the Chu State During the Western Zhou Period: On the Wanfunao Site in Yichang'), *Jianghan Kaogu* 6 (2021), pp. 172–83. In the first half of the tenth century BC, the Zhou King Zhao had gone south to restrain the movement of Chu northwards. His attack failed and he is said to have drowned in 978 BC in the River Han.

9 Durrant et al., *Zuo Tradition*, pp. 832–3 give an important comment that the Chu were willing to engage with local peoples to support their military efforts: 'the forces of the Man tribes have joined the army (of Chu) but they do not keep the battle formations'.

10 From another commentary on the *Spring and Autumn Annals* in the *Gongyang zhuan* (trans. Harry Miller), *Commentary of the Gongyuan Zhuan on the Spring and Autumn Annals: A Full Translation* (Palgrave Macmillan, 2015), p. 88.

11 The south-eastern states of Wu and Yue are famous for the production of exceptionally fine swords, one of which found its way into a later Chu tomb, inscribed with the name of Gou Jian, a famous ruler of Yue, Hubeisheng Wenwu Kaogu Yanjiusuo, *Jiangling Wangshan Shazhong Chumu* (*The Chu Cemetery at Shazhong, Wangshan, Jiangling*) (Wenwu Chubanshe, 1996), p. 49, figs. 32:1, 33:1, pl. 14:3.

12 Lothar von Falkenhausen argues in *Chinese Society*, pp. 294–7 that large banquets were now not in the main focused on the ancestral spirits but included a wider company. Considerably more research is required to examine the participants in all such banquets from the Shang to the Han. It is, however, clear from many inscriptions that, as the banquets were directed at an audience to proclaim the virtue of their owner and host, it is likely that the ancestors were always included.

13 Zhang Min and Liu Liwen, 'Jiangsu Dantu Beishanding Chunqiumu Fajue Baogao' ('The Excavation of the Spring and Autumn Period Tomb at Beishanding, Dantu, Jiangsu'), *Dongnan Wenhua* Z1 (1988), pp. 13–50, pls. 1–8.

14 Yang Jiuxia, 'Anhui Shucheng Jiulidun Chunqiumu' ('A Spring and Autumn Period Tomb at Jiulidun, Shucheng, Anhui'), *Kaogu Xuebao* 2 (1982), pp. 229–42; see also Colin Mackenzie, 'Chu Bronze Work: A Unilinear Tradition, or a Synthesis of Diverse Sources?', in Tom Lawton (ed.), *New Perspectives on Chu Culture During the Eastern Zhou Period* (Smithsonian Institution, 1991), pp. 107–58.

15 The bronze vessels seem to have come from several different sources. The same phenomenon has been identified at a Chu tomb in Henan, Alain Thote, 'Intercultural Contacts and Exchanges Illustrated by a Sixth Century B.C. Cemetery in Henan', *Hanxue Yanjiu* 1 (1997), pp. 263–89.

16 Durrant et al., *Zuo Tradition*, p. 823.

17 Ibid., p. 1379.

18 Ibid., p. 1631.

19 It is impossible to overestimate the role of ritual in social interaction among groups, both those who claimed to be part of the Zhou community and newcomers seeking to belong. The quotation is from the version by Simon Leys, *The Analects of Confucius* (W.W. Norton, 1997), p. 3; see also D. C. Lau, *The Analects* (Penguin, 1979).

20 Durrant et al., *Zuo Tradition*, p. 63.

21 Falkenhausen, *Chinese Society*, p. 287: 'the Zhou ancestral cult and the system of lineage organisation to which it was inextricably linked spread to areas and groups formerly outside the Zhou cultural sphere. As lineages of Zhou type became increasingly predominant, other pre-existing social formations were either amalgamated or suppressed, or expelled.'

22 Shaughnessy, *Sources of Western Zhou History*, pp. 75–6.

23 Durrant et al., *Zuo Tradition*, p. 421.

24 The question of how unity under a single ruler was built in ancient China and maintained over centuries, even millennia, is discussed in Pines, *The Everlasting Empire*.

25 For the year 526 BC, see Durrant et al., *Zuo Tradition*, p. 1543.

26 Through the comments in the *Zuo Zhuan* we can explore other ritually based relations, reiterated in the handing over of chariots, Durrant et al., *Zuo Tradition*, p. 125, or in arranging marriages, Durrant et al., *Zuo Tradition*, p. 87, or even in the form precedence should take on formal occasions, Durrant et al., *Zuo Tradition*, p. 481.

27 We have seen this combination of practices typical of the Shang or Zhou rulers engaging with local, often northern customs in Ya Chang's tomb and that of Yu Bo (Ya Chang's jade beads and gold or Yu Bo's miniature vessels, his sword and bird-headed standard were retained and treasured).

28 For the swords of the Upper Xiajiadian see Neimenggu and Ningchengxian, *Xiaoheishigou*, pp. 328, 431.

29 For discussions of swords see Tian Wei, 'Shilun Liang Zhou Shiqi de Qingtongjian' ('On the Bronze Swords of the Zhou Periods'), *Kaogu Xuebao* 4 (2013), pp. 431–68; Zhu Huadong and Tian Weili, 'Qingtong Pingjijian Jianlun' ('On the Flat-ridged Bronze Swords'), *Kaogu yu Wenwu* 4 (2017), pp. 39–44.

30 Li Buqing and Lin Xianting, 'Shandong Penglaixian Liugezhuang Muqun Fajue Jianbao' ('The Excavation of Tombs at Liugezhuang in Penglai, Shandong'), *Kaogu* 9 (1990), pp. 803–10.

31 An early example had been in the tomb of the secondary consort of the Lord of Rui, as we can still see in its outline in an ivory box; see Sun and Cai, *Ruiguo Jinyu Xuancui*, pp. 54–5. A female attachment to these knives, perhaps for cosmetic purposes, is evident from the preservation of fine decorated knives in a purpose-made elegant lacquered box in the tomb of the spouse of the Crown Prince of Wu, buried at Gushi Hougudui, Henansheng Wenwu Kaogu Yanjiusuo, *Gushi Hougudui Yihaomu* (*Tomb M1 at Hougudui, Gushi*) (Daxiang Chubanshe, 2004), pl. 23.

32 Described by Herodotus (trans. Robin Waterfield), *The Histories*, pp. 258–9. The funeral rites are examined in more detail in Ivantchik, 'The Funeral of Scythian Kings'.

33 Armour with foil decoration, gold or tin, was found in several southern tombs, including the Zeng tomb described in Chapter 9, where further examples are described in the notes to that chapter; for sixth-century Chu tombs at Henan province see Henansheng Wenwu Yanjiusuo, Henansheng Danjiang Kuqu Kaogu Fajuedui and Xichuanxian Bowuguan, *Xichuan Xiasi Chunqiu Chumu* (*Chu Tombs at Xiasi, Xichuan*) (Wenwu Chubanshe, 1991), pls. 73–6.

34 For small tigers in gold see Wang Yanmin, Jiang Nan and Jiao Jiantao, 'Henan Dengfeng Gaocheng Dongzhou Mudi Sanhaomu' ('Eastern Zhou No. 3 Tomb at Gaocheng, Dengfeng, Henan Province'), *Wenwu* 4 (2006), pp. 4–16. A pair excavated at Guojiamiao is illustrated in Fang Qin, *Zengguo Lishi yu Wenhua:*

Cong 'Zuoyou Wenwu' Dao 'Zuoyou Chuwang' (Study on the History and Culture of the Zeng State: From 'Zuoyou Wenwu' to 'Zuoyou Chuwang') (Shanghai Guji Chubanshe, 2019), col. pl. 20. Jade versions are numerous in many tombs; see Ou, 'Chunqiu Zaoqi Huangjun Meng Fufu Mu'.

35 Di Cosmo, *Ancient China and Its Enemies* is an essential source for the wider history of these relations. See also Nicola Di Cosmo, 'China-Steppe Relations in Historical Perspective', in Jan Bemmann and Michael Schmauder (eds.), *Complexity of Interaction Along the Eurasian Steppe Zone in the First Millennium CE* (Vor- und Frühgeschichtliche Archäologie, Rheinische Friedrich-Wilhelms-Universität, 2015), pp. 49–72.

36 It is unlikely that there was a direct connection with the Neolithic ceramic makers of the Lower Xiajiadian; however, the connectivity along the eastern seaboard suggests that brilliant painted pottery may have emerged in that region.

37 One of the earliest mounds is identified in the Huang state, Ou, 'Chunqiu Zaoqi Huangjun Meng Fufu Mu'.

38 The excavators suggest that use of the different coloured earths was taken over from ideas of correlative philosophy, of matching of colours, sounds and directions, much more common from the third and second centuries BC onwards, indicating, they argue, that they were already present here in the Huai basin in the late seventh or sixth centuries BC. We have already seen some examples of these later ideas in Chapters 1 and 4. However, while it is certainly probable that local practices inspired the use of earths of different colours, little else about this tomb suggests that we see here early indications of systematic correlative thinking. The *Zuo Zhuan* gives some signs of a growing interest in correlations, but not in the ordered form propagated in the Han period, Durrant et al., *Zuo Tradition*, p. 1545 and p. 1637.

39 These inward-sloping sides were developed further in the south during the Warring States period, as in tombs in Hubei, Li Zhifang et al., 'Hubei Jingzhou Renjiazhong Deng Mudi Zhanguo Muzang Fajue Jianbao' ('Brief Report on the Excavation of the Warring States Tombs in Jingzhou, Hubei Province'), *Jianghan Kaogu* 1 (2022), pp. 15–28.

40 Areas near Fengyang in Anhui are regarded as some of the main sources of quartzite in China, Gao Shuxue et al., 'Woguo Maishiying Chengkuang Qudai Chubu Huafen' ('Preliminary Division of the Quartz Vein Belts in China'), *Zhongguo Feijinshukuang Gongye Daokan* 5 (2020), pp. 5–9.

41 Rawson et al., 'Chariotry and Prone Burials'.

42 Stepped ramps may have been a tradition employed earlier in the Loess Plateau, as we see from an example at Kongtougou at Qishan, Wang et al., 'Shaanxi Qishanxian Kongtougou'.

43 The radiant pattern goes back ultimately to some of the khirigsuurs in Mongolia, discussed in Chapter 3, which seem to have been the inspiration for the arrangements of wooden sections at Arzhan I in the Tuva, Grjaznov, *Der Grosskurgan von Arzan*. This pattern may have attracted different groups for their local reasons, though there may also have been some transmission. It is seen at the khirigsuur-like monument at Huahaizi on the Chinese Altai, Guo Wu et al., 'Xinjiang Qinghexian Huahaizi Sanhao Yizhi Fajue Jianbao' ('The Excavation of the Huahaizi No. 3 Site in Qinghe County, Xinjiang'), *Kaogu* 9 (2016), pp. 25–37. A related arrangement, also in Xinjiang, is described in Ruan Qiurong et al., 'Xinjiang Nileke Wutulan Mudi Fajue Jianbao' ('The Excavation of the Tombs in Wutulan, Nilka, Ili, Xinjiang'), *Wenwu* 12 (2014), pp. 50–63. More likely inspirations for the Zhongli burial are the stone tombs on the Liaodong Peninsula; see Zhongguo Shehui Kexueyuan Kaogu Yanjiusuo, *Shuangtuozi yu Gangshang: Liaodong Shiqian Wenhua de Faxian he Yanjiu* (*Shuangtuozi and Gangshang: Discovery and Study of Prehistoric Culture in the Liaodong Peninsula*) (Kexue Chubanshe, 1996). Mounds on the Liaodong Peninsula can be compared with some in the Tuva, Konstantin V. Chugunov, 'Der Skythenzeitliche Kulturwandel in Tuva' ('The Scythian Cultural Change in Tuva'), *Eurasia Antiqua* 4 (1998), pp. 273–307.

44 Grjaznov, *Der Grosskurgan von Arzan*.

45 For a survey of burials of attendants in tombs see Huang, *Gudai Rensheng Renxun Tonglun*. There are many Shang examples, as discussed in Chapter 3 of this book. There is some indication that even Shang elite tombs may have had some contact with people of the Loess Plateau and taken the practice from there, see Zhao Hui et al., 'Shanxi Lishi Houshi Shangdai Muzang' ('Excavation Report of Shang Tombs at Houshi Village in Lishi, Shanxi'), *Zhongguo Guojia Bowuguan Guankan* 12 (2021), pp. 6–15.

46 For a Rong tomb with attendants neatly buried encircling the principal tomb occupant see Guojia Wenwuju, 'Henan Yichuan Xuyang Mudi' ('The Cemetery at Xuyang, Yichuan County, Henan'), in *2020 Zhongguo Zhongyao Kaogu Faxian* (*Important Archaeological Discoveries in China, 2020*) (Wenwu Chubanshe, 2021), pp. 87–92. For tombs in Shandong with neatly arranged attendants see Shandong Yanshi Tielu Wenwu Kaogu Gongzuodui, *Linyi Fenghuangling Dongzhoumu* (*Eastern Zhou Tomb at Fenghuangling, Linyi*) (Qilu Shushe, 1988); Wu Wenqi and Zhang Qihai, 'Ju'nan Dadian Chunqiu Shiqi Juguo Xunrenmu' ('Spring and Autumn Period Human-Sacrificial Tombs of the Ju State at Dadian, Ju'nan, Shandong'), *Kaogu Xuebao* 3 (1978), pp. 259–88; Gong et al., 'Xueguo Gucheng Kancha'; Shandongsheng Bowuguan, 'Linzi Langjiazhuang Yihao Dongzhou Xunrenmu' ('Excavation of Eastern Zhou Tomb No. 1 with

Human Sacrifices at Langjiazhuang, Linzi, Shandong'), *Kaogu Xuebao* 1 (1977), pp. 73–104.

47 Chugunov et al., *Der Skythenzeitliche Fürstenkurgan.*

48 Xinjiang Weiwner Zizhique, *Xinjiang Mohuchahan.*

49 Konstantin V. Chugunov, 'The Arzhan-2 'Royal' Funerary-Commemorative Complex: Stages of Function and Internal Chronology', in Pankova and Simpson (eds.), *Masters of the Steppe: The Impact of the Scythians*, pp. 80–104.

50 Tombs like that at Fenghuangling, mentioned above in connection with neatly placed attendants, also have the separate frames or chests for other materials as seen at Zhongli.

51 These engagements with the Rong are reported in the *Zuo Zhuan*; see Durrant et al., *Zuo Tradition*, pp. 18–19; 200–201, 218–21, 552–3, 706–7; 212–13; 756–7.

52 Quoted from Durrant et al., *Zuo Tradition*, pp. 915–19.

53 Maria Khayutina, ' "Bi Shi", Western Zhou Oath Texts, and the Legal Culture of Early China', in Martin Kern and Dirk Meyer (eds.), *Origins of Chinese Political Philosophy: Studies in the Composition and Thought of the Shangshu* (Brill, 2017), pp. 416–45. Quoted from Shaughnessy, *Sources of Western Zhou History*, p. 180.

54 Found in the tomb at Shandong, Linyi, Fenghuangling mentioned above, note 46. Compare Nikolai A. Bokovenko, 'The Tagar Culture in the Minusinsk Basin', in Davis-Kimball et al. (eds.), *Nomads of the Eurasian Steppes*, pp. 296–314.

55 Durrant et al., *Zuo Tradition*, pp. 1296–7.

56 For the tomb at Fenghuangling, Linyi in Shandong and also the tombs of the small polities of Ju and Xue see note 46 above. Falkenhausen, *Chinese Society*, p. 254 argues that the Eastern Yi were easily assimilated, and we have seen the use of ritual vessels and names in Chinese characters; but their significance as part of an important line of communication, bringing northern customs south as far as Lord Bai and embedding them, to be taken over by the Qi state and later the Qin state, has not usually been noted.

57 In the southern area of Jiangsu and Zhejiang were mounds often built on to the flat ground with a structure for the burial on, rather than in, the ground. Many have been excavated showing an almost house-like structure over the actual burial made of sloping timbers. The earthen mound was then built over it. Some have small stones below the grave goods. High-fired ceramics, a major local product and forerunner of China's great porcelain industry, made up the major part of the grave goods. These ceramics also made their way in small numbers to the elite Shang and Zhou tombs. Occasionally, some locally made bronzes were interred, and in rare major examples fine bronzes cast at the central workshops were buried. A few reported examples had a number of graves below a single mound, arranged in a radiating pattern; others have only two or three: a late-sixth-century BC tomb at

Pizhou, in Jiangsu, with a tomb mound, has a complex interior plan with numerous attendants and grave goods, described in Kong Lingyuan and Chen Yongqing, 'Jiangsu Pizhoushi Jiunüdun Sanhaodun de Fajue' ('Excavation of the No. 3 Mound at Jiunüdun in Pizhou City, Jiangsu'), *Kaogu* 5 (2002), pp. 19–30. Certainly, the mound at Bengbu might have been stimulated in part by these local examples, but the circular form, the deep pit, the careful arrangements of attendants and the terrace had to have come from elsewhere.

58 Late-seventh-century BC conflicts between the northerners, often called the Di, led to the newcomers creating tombs for themselves with ritual vessels in the Loess Plateau as well as to the south, Tian Jianwen, 'Bianshi Nan Lüliang Baidimu' ('Identifying Baidi Tombs in the South of the Lüliang Mountains'), *Zhongyuan Wenwu* 1 (2021), pp. 73–82.

59 The later Qi tombs also often had separate sections, like the frame or chest in Lord Bai's tomb, for ritual vessels and other burial, see Shandongsheng, 'Linzi Langjiazhuang'; Shandongsheng Wenwu Kaogu Yanjiusuo, *Linzi Qimu 1* (*Linzi Qi Tombs 1*) (Wenwu Chubanshe, 2007). Zhang Xuehai and Luo Xunzhang, 'Qigucheng Wuhao Dongzhoumu ji Daxing Xunmakeng de Fajue' ('The Excavation of the Large Horse Pit No. 5 in the Linzi Site of the Qi State'), *Wenwu* 9 (1984), pp. 14–19. From this development, we can argue that the chest-like structure probably was introduced from the steppe regions and borders and then exploited by a few individuals in eastern China before being more widely used among the Qi.

Chapter 9: The Orchestra of Zeng

1 This flooded landscape fostered the grasses, which, when domesticated, became rice. The earliest rice cultivation is today thought to have been at Liyang to the west of the lake, Zhang Chi, 'The Qujialing–Shijiahe Culture in the Middle Yangzi River Valley', in Underhill (ed.), *A Companion to Chinese Archaeology*, pp. 510–34.

2 Hawkes, *Songs of the South*, p. 110.

3 Lacquer is actually toxic, as discussed in Catharina Blänsdorf, Erwin Emmerling and Michael Petzet (eds.), *Die Terrakottaarmee des Ersten Chinesischen Kaisers Qin Shihuang* (Bayerisches Landesamt für Denkmalpflege, 2001), pp. 391–3.

4 Translated by A. C. Graham in Cyril Birch (ed.) with Donald Keene (assoc. ed.), *Anthology of Chinese Literature* (Penguin, 1967), pp. 385–6.

5 Fang Qin, *Zengguo Lishi yu Wenhua: Cong 'Zuoyou Wenwu' Dao 'Zuoyou Chu-wang (Study on the History and Culture of the Zeng State: From 'Zuoyou Wenwu' to 'Zuoyou Chuwang')* (Shanghai Guji Chubanshe, 2019).

6 Alain Thote, 'Une Tombe Princière Chinoise Du Ve Siècle Avant Notre Ère', *Comptes rendus des séances de – Académie des Inscriptions et Belles-Lettres* 130 (1986), pp. 393–413.

7 For the archaeological report see Hubeisheng Bowuguan, *Zenghou Yi Mu (Tomb of Marquis Yi of State Zeng)*, 2 vols. (Wenwu Chubanshe, 1989).

8 For the copper mines at Tonglüshan see Huangshishi Bowuguan (ed.), *Tonglüshan Gu Kuangye Yizhi (The Ancient Mining Site at Tonglüshan)* (Wenwu Chubanshe, 1999). See also Yang Xiaoneng (ed.), *New Perspectives on China's Past: Chinese Archaeology in the Twentieth Century* (Yale University Press, 2004), pp. 203–5.

9 For the great tombs at Ur see Aruz and Wallenfels (ed.), *Art of the First Cities*, pp. 93–132.

10 For descriptions of Chu see Cook and Major (eds.), *Defining Chu*; Jenny F. So, 'Chu Art: Link between the Old and the New', in Cook and Major (eds.), *Defining Chu*, pp. 33–47; for the wider political context see Lewis, 'Warring States Political History'; Thomas Lawton (ed.), *New Perspectives on Chu Culture during the Eastern Zhou Period* (Arthur M. Sackler Gallery, 1991).

11 The states cannot be seen as having defined boundary-marked land. Instead, they placed settlements in areas they controlled and tried to prevent encroachment.

12 The report of the tomb is in Henansheng Wenwu Kaogu Yanjiusuo, *Gushi Hougudui Yihaomu*.

13 Hubeisheng, *Zenghou Yi Mu*, pp. 19–26.

14 Bronze sections joined wooden beams in the remains of a building in a cemetery at the early Qin capital at Yongcheng; see Yang Xiaoneng, 'Capital Site of the Qin State and the Necropolis of the Dukes of Qin at Fengxiang, Shaanxi Province', in Yang (ed.), *New Perspectives on China's Past*, pp. 181–3.

15 Alain Thote, 'Chinese Coffins from the First Millennium B.C. and Early Images of the Afterworld', *RES: Anthropology and Aesthetics* 61/62 (2012), pp. 22–40; Alain Thote, 'Burial Practices as Seen in Rulers' Tombs of the Eastern Zhou Period: Patterns and Regional Traditions', in John Lagerwey (ed.), *Religion and Chinese Society*, 2 vols. (Chinese University Press/École française d'Extrême-Orient, 2004), vol. 1, pp. 65–107.

16 Hubeisheng, *Zenghou Yi Mu*, pp. 26–45.

17 For a discussion of the issue of a representation understood as an analogue see Chapter 12 in this book.

18 Alain Thote, 'The Double Coffin of Leigudun Tomb No. 1: Iconographic Sources and Related Problems', in Lawton (ed.), *New Perspectives on Chu Culture*, pp. 23–46.

19 Li Ling and Constance Cook, 'Translation of the Chu Silk Manuscript', in Cook and Major (eds.), *Defining Chu*, pp. 171–6.

20 Quotation from Li and Cook, 'Translation of the Chu Silk Manuscript', p. 174.

21 They look like mushrooms but we do not know what these were actually meant to represent. Hubeisheng, *Zenghou Yi Mu*, pp. 356–7 offers more illustrations of these boxes.

22 Alain Thote, 'Aspects of the Serpent on Eastern Zhou Bronzes and Lacquerware', in Whitfield (ed.), *The Problem of Meaning*, pp. 150–60.

23 The equivalent image of a bird on a feline in wood with antler wings is illustrated in Colin Mackenzie, 'Chu Bronze Work: A Unilinear Tradition or a Synthesis of Diverse Sources?', in Lawton (ed.), *New Perspectives on Chu Culture*, pp. 107–57.

24 See a vessel from the Avery Brundage Collection, in the Asian Art Museum, San Francisco, illustrated in Charles D. Weber, *Chinese Pictorial Bronze Vessels of the Late Chou Period* (Artibus Asiae, 1968), fig. 37c. For images of birds swallowing snakes on bronzes in a related style see ibid., figs. 42 and 43.

25 Alain Thote, 'Une Sculpture Chinoise en Bronze du Ve Siècle Avant Notre Ère: Essai D'interprétation', *Arts Asiatiques* 42 (1987), pp. 45–58.

26 For the distribution of antlers in tombs of the Eastern Zhou see Tao Zhenggang and Li Fengshan, 'Shanxi Changzixian Dongzhoumu' ('The Eastern Zhou Tombs at Changzi County in Shanxi'), *Kaogu Xuebao* 4 (1984), pp. 503–29; Shang Qiaoyun et al., 'Luoyang Xigongqu Chunqiumu Fajue Jianbao' ('Excavation of the Spring and Autumn Period Tomb in the Xigong Area at Luoyang'), *Wenwu* 8 (2010), pp. 8–28. See also Zhao Dexiang, 'Dangyang Caojiagang 5 Hao Chumu' ('The No. 5 Chu State Tomb at Caojiagang, Dangyang'), *Kaogu Xuebao* 4 (1988), pp. 455–500, fig. 91; Huang Fengchun and Huang Xuchu, 'Hubei Yunxian Qiaojiayuan Chunqiu Xunrenmu' ('The Human Sacrificial Tombs at Qiaojiayuan in Yunxian, Hubei'), *Kaogu* 4 (2008), pp. 28–50, figs. 6, 7, 28. A very unusual example with small birds mounted on an antler was found in a Xue state tomb in Shandong, Gong et al., 'Xueguo Gucheng Kancha', pl. 15:6. While antlers appear connected with steppe people to the north, they seem like many other northern features, such as stone within tomb construction, to have been adopted piecemeal, moving south down the east coast and into the centre.

27 John S. Major and Jenny F. So, 'Music in Late Bronze Age China', in So (ed.), *Music in the Age of Confucius*, p. 24.

28 Bagley, 'Percussion', pp. 48–52.

29 Lothar von Falkenhausen, 'The Zenghou Yi Finds in the History of Chinese Music', in So (ed.), *Music in the Age of Confucius*, pp. 101–13.

30 Bagley, 'Percussion', p. 41.

31 Quoted from Hawkes, *Songs of the South*, pp. 107–8.

32 Bagley, 'Percussion'. The description that follows in this chapter is based on the account given by Bagley.

33 Hubeisheng, *Zenghou Yi Mu*, pp. 146–7, figs. 66, 67.

34 Bo Lawergren, 'Strings', in So (ed.), *Music in the Age of Confucius*, pp. 65–85; Feng Guangsheng, 'Winds', in So (ed.), *Music in the Age of Confucius*, pp. 87–99.

35 As the bell set has not been exhibited abroad, and probably will never be, there are few very good detailed photographs in major exhibition catalogues. One clear example is in Bagley, 'Percussion', p. 34.

36 Hawkes, *Songs of the South*, p. 49.

37 Hubeisheng, *Zenghou Yi Mu*, pp. 229–30.

38 Lost-wax casting has been researched over a long period, but a clear development has evaded scholars. A discussion of the available knowledge is in Peng Peng, *Metalworking in Bronze Age China: The Lost-Wax Process* (Cambria, 2020).

39 See also Henansheng Wenwu Yanjiusuo, Henansheng Danjiang Kuqu Kaogu Fajuedui and Xichuanxian Bowuguan, *Xichuan Xiasi Chunqiu Chumu (Chu Tombs at Xiasi, Xichuan)* (Wenwu Chubanshe, 1991).

40 Fang Hui and Cui Dayong, 'Changqing Xianrentai Wuhaomu Fajue Jianbao' ('The Excavation of Tomb M5 in Xianrentai, Changqing'), *Wenwu* 9 (1998), pp. 18–30.

41 If lost-wax had been used, or even modified versions of it, full-scale lost-wax casting did not become a widely accepted technology until after the decline of the Han dynasty in the third century AD. See Chapter 12 of this book for important Qin uses of this technology.

42 Jenny F. So, 'Foreign/Eurasian Elements in Pre-imperial Qin Culture: Materials, Techniques and Types', in Liu (ed.), *Beyond the First Emperor's Mausoleum*, pp. 193–211.

43 Hubeisheng, *Zenghou Yi Mu*, pp. 449–52.

44 Xinjiang Wenwu Kaogu Yanjiusuo, *Xinjiang Aletai Diqu Kaogu yu Lishi Wenji (Archaeology and History of the Altay, Xinjiang)* (Wenwu Chubanshe, 2015), pl. 24:2; Chugunov et al., *Der Skythenzeitliche Fürstenkurgan*, pl. 57, no. 6; 'Izzat Allāh Nigahbān, *Marlik: The Complete Excavation Report*, 2 vols. (University Museum, University of Pennsylvania, 1996), vol. 2, pl. 58 (no. 211).

45 Zhao Dexiang, 'Dangyang Caojiagang 5 Hao Chumu' ('The No. 5 Chu State Tomb at Caojiagang, Dangyang'), *Kaogu Xuebao* 4 (1988), pp. 455–500. See also Li Youcheng, 'Yuanpingxian Liuzhuang Tagangliang Dongzhoumu'

('The Eastern Zhou Cemetery at Tagangliang, Liuzhuang Village, Yuanping County'), *Wenwu* 11 (1986), pp. 21–6.

46 Falkenhausen, *Chinese Society*, pp. 294–7.

47 For a lacquered lidded stand, known as a *dou*, in a bronze shape but with lacquer flourishes see Hubeisheng, *Zenghou Yi Mu*, p. 368, fig. 227.

48 For the bamboo-shaped shovel and the incense burners see Hubeisheng, *Zenghou Yi Mu*, p. 247, fig. 144.

49 Lai, *Excavating the Afterlife*, pp. 146–54.

50 For the reconstruction of the tent and the methods of assembly see Zhang Changping, Li Xueting, Guo Changjiang and Hou Jiasheng, 'Hubei Suizhoushi Zenghou Yi Mu Yihao Peizangkeng Fajue Jianbao' ('The Excavation of Accompanying Pit No. 1 of the Tomb of Marquis Yi of the Zeng State in Suizhou, Hubei'), *Kaogu* 11 (2017), pp. 31–44. Fittings for a tent were excavated from a major tomb at Taiyuan; see Shanxisheng Kaogu Yanjiusuo and Taiyuanshi Wenwu Guanli Weiyuanhui, *Taiyuan Jinguo Zhaoqing Mu (Tomb of Jin State Minister Zhao Near Taiyuan)* (Wenwu Chubanshe, 1996). Related fittings were also found in the accompanying deposits with the tomb of the king of Zhongshan (Chapter 10).

51 Patrick McGee, 'How Cook tied Apple's fortunes to China', *Financial Times*, 18 January (2023), www.ft.com/content/d5a80891-b27d-4110-90c9-561b7836f11b.

52 Hubeisheng, *Zenghou Yi Mu*, pp. 358–61.

53 Mark Lewis, *Sanctioned Violence in Early China* (SUNY, 1990), pp. 59–64 illustrates first the great increase in chariot forces, followed by the growing role of huge infantry armies.

54 Wang Yingchen et al., 'Imported or Indigenous? The Earliest Forged Tin Foil Found in China', *Journal of Cultural Heritage* 40 (2019), pp. 177–82.

55 Discussed and illustrated in Rawson et al., 'Seeking Horses'.

56 For a discussion of the use of swords see Alain Thote, 'Origine et Premiers Développements de L'épée En Chine', *Comptes rendus des séances de l'année – Académie des Inscriptions et Belles-Lettres* 147 (2003), pp. 773–802.

57 The Han dynasty, with origins in eastern China, in regions to which Chu had moved, gave a formal courtly style to the visionary poetry of Chu in long poems called *fu*, often translated as rhapsodies. For the full poem see Xiaotong (trans. David Knechtges), *Wen Xuan or Selections of Refined Literature*, vol. 2, *Rhapsodies on Sacrifices, Hunting, Travel, Sightseeing, Palaces and Halls, Rivers and Seas* (Princeton University Press, 1987), quoted from p. 123.

Chapter 10: A Kingdom by Design

1 For a full account in English of the Zhongshan state and its background see Wu Xiaolong, *Material Culture, Power, and Identity in Ancient China* (Cambridge University Press, 2017). For the principal archaeological report see Hebeisheng Wenwu Yanjiusuo, *Cuo Mu: Zhanguo Zhongshanguo Guowang Zhi Mu* (*Tomb of Cuo, the King of the Zhongshan State in the Warring States Period*), 2 vols. (Wenwu Chubanshe, 1995).

2 As illustrated in Bunker, *Ancient Bronzes of the Eastern Eurasian Steppes*; Tian Guangjin and Guo Suxin (eds.), *Erduosi Qingtongqi* (*Bronzes from the Ordos Region*) (Wenwu Chubnashe, 1986). The distribution of belt plaques in the Han period can be followed in Ursula Brosseder, 'Belt-Plaques as Indicator of East-West Relations in the Eurasian Steppe at the Turn of the Millennium', in Ursula Brosseder and Brian Miller (eds.), *Xiongnu Archaeology: Multidisciplinary Perspectives of the First Steppe Empire in Inner Asia* (Friedrich-Wilhelms Universität, 2011), pp. 349–424.

3 The *Zuo Zhuan* commentaries describe a number of Di encounters and victories, Durrant et al., *Zuo Tradition/Zuozhuan*, pp. 220–21, 234–5, 238–9, 298–9. For extensive comments on the activities of the Di first against the Jin state see Di Cosmo, 'The Northern Frontier in Pre-Imperial China', especially pp. 948–9; see also Tao Zhenggang, 'Shanxi Dongzhou Rong Di Wenhua Chutan' ('On the Rong and Di Cultures of Eastern Zhou Period in Shanxi'), in 'Yuanwang Ji' Bianweihui (ed.), *Yuanwang Ji: Shaanxisheng Kaogu Yanjiusuo Huadan Sishi Zhounian Jinian Wenji* (*Papers Prepared for the 40th Anniversary of the Shaanxi Institute of Archaeology*) (Shaanxi Renmin Meishu Chubanshe, 1998), pp. 415–25.

4 Yuri Pines, 'The Warring States Period: Historical Background', in Childs-Johnson (ed.), *The Oxford Handbook of Early China*, pp. 581–94.

5 An account of some Di tombs is in Tian, 'Bianshi Nan Lüliang Baidimu'.

6 For an overview of the tombs that shows the widespread presence of northerners see Yang, 'Differentiation of Two Types of Cultural Remains'; Shan, 'The Pattern of Archaeological Cultures in Northern China'.

7 Zhang Chunchang, Qi Ruipu, Chang Huaiying and Yan Wei, 'Hebei Xingtangxian Gujun Dongzhou Yizhi' ('The Gujun Site of the Eastern Zhou Period in Xingtang County, Hebei'), *Kaogu* 7 (2018), pp. 44–66.

8 For the archaeological report on early tombs in the Lingshou area and the tomb of King Cheng see Hebeisheng Wenwu Yanjiusuo, *Zhanguo Zhongshanguo Lingshoucheng: 1975–1993 Nian Kaogu Fajue Baogao* (*Lingshou City of Zhongshan State of the Warring States Period*) (Wenwu Chubanshe, 2005); Hebeisheng Wenwu Kaogu Yanjiuyuan and Zhongguo Renmin Daxue Kaogu Wenbo Xi, *Shuohuang Tielu Pingshan Duan Gu Zhongshanguo Muzang Fajue Baogao* (*The*

Excavation of Zhongshan State Cemetery in the Pingshan Section of the Shuozhou-Huanghua Railway) (Kexue Chubanshe, 2020).

9 For tombs of outsiders or newcomers that show features brought south from the steppe and enhanced with contact with the central states, including the use of stone, gold and animal heads and unusual bronze vessels see Guojia Wenwuju, 'Shanxi Xiangfen Taosibei Liang Zhou Mudi: 2016–2017 Nian Fajue Shouhuo' ('Major Discoveries at Taosibei Zhou Cemetery in Xiangfen, Shanxi during the 2016–2017 Season'), in Guojia Wenwuju (ed.), *2017 Zhongguo Zhongyao Kaogu Faxian (Important Archaeological Discoveries in China, 2017)* (Wenwu Chubanshe, 2018), pp. 44–9; Wang Jingyan et al., 'Shanxi Xiangfen Taosibei Mudi 2014 Nian I Qu M7 Fajue Jianbao' ('The Excavation of the Tomb M7 at Zone I of the Taosi North Cemetery in Xiangfen, Shanxi in 2014'), *Wenwu* 9 (2018), pp. 4–21; Wang Jingyan et al., 'Shanxi Xiangfen Taosibei Liang Zhou Mudi 2014 Nian Fajue Jianbao' ('The Excavation of the Taosibei Cemetery at Xiangfen, Shanxi'), *Zhongyuan Wenwu* 2 (2018), pp. 4–16; Zheng Shaozong, 'Luanpingxian Hushiha Paotaishan Shanrong Mudi de Faxia' ('The Discovery of Shanrong Cemetery at Paotaishan, Hushiha, Luanping County'), in Wenwu Bianji Weiyuanhui (ed.), *Wenwu Ziliao Congkan* 7 (Cultural Relics Series) (Wenwu Chubanshe, 1983), pp. 67–74.

10 For the history of the Warring States see Lewis, 'Warring States Political History'; Charles Sanft, 'Change and Continuity at the Intersection of Received History and the Material Record in the Warring States Period', in Childs-Johnson (ed.), *The Oxford Handbook of Early China*, pp. 623–36.

11 The Warring States period witnessed a widespread development of walled cities; see Lothar von Falkenhausen, 'Stages in the Development of "Cities" in Pre-imperial China', in Joyce Marcus and Jeremy A. Sabloff (eds.), *The Ancient City: New Perspectives on Urbanism in the Old and New World* (School for Advanced Research Press, 2008), pp. 209–28.

12 Wu, *Material Culture*, p. 35.

13 For a description of Lingshou see ibid., pp. 34–74.

14 In the early centuries described in this book coins did not exist. Some argue that cowries were a form of exchange for transactions. However, while they certainly represented wealth, it is not clear whether they formed any sort of consistent element in trade. They were particularly valued by peoples with northern connections and are found in large quantities in their tombs, for example in the tombs of Fu Hao and Ya Chang at Anyang (Chapter 3). The round coins with which we are familiar were first minted in the Greek colony of Lydia, in today's Turkey. There was no commercial contact with Western Asia in the sixth century BC, as spade and knife coins began to be used. This development is discussed in François Thierry, 'Currency', in Goldin (ed.),

Routledge Handbook of Early Chinese History, pp. 336–66. A full description of Chinese currency is in Peng Xinwei, *A Monetary History of China*, 2 vols. (Western Washington University, 1994). A discussion of possible trade routes is in Wu, *Material Culture*, pp. 130–3.

15 For images of the *banliang* see Thierry, 'Currency', p. 351, figs. 16:11, 16:12.

16 For the inter-state rivalry and competition see Lewis, 'Warring States Political History'.

17 Wu, *Material Culture*, pp. 77–133; Hebeisheng, *Cuo Mu* is a full report on the king's tomb. For the wider context of the city of Lingshou and the tomb of King Cheng see Hebeisheng, *Lingshoucheng*. These reports have been used for information throughout this chapter.

18 Tian Wei, 'Shilun Liang Zhou Shiqi de Jishi Jitan Mu' ('On the Stone and Charcoal in Tombs of the Zhou Period'), *Zhongguo Lishi Wenwu* 2 (2009), pp. 59–67.

19 This stepped profile is one of the most significant and informative features of this tomb. It is discussed in Wu, *Material Culture*, pp. 78–9. An account that differs from my own interpretation of this stepped profile is given in Shi Jie, 'The Hidden Level in Space and Time: The Vertical Shaft in the Royal Tombs of the Zhongshan Kingdom in Late Eastern Zhou (475–221 BCE) China', *Material Religion* 11 (2015), pp. 76–102.

20 The Taihang would have held back the wind-blown loess, while the rock at the base of the tombs is part of the lower slopes of the Taihang.

21 As discussed at the end of Chapter 8, the tombs of the Qi state, which occupied areas originally part of the disparate areas inhabited by the people called at the time the Eastern Yi, took up burial traditions typical of the eastern region, especially the use of mounds and neatly ordered coffins around the central burial. The Qi added stepped sides, some parts above ground, perhaps developing the stepped ramp of the Zhongli tomb, around the sides to provide space for mourners to attend, replacing the terrace at the Zhongli tomb, Shandongsheng, *Linzi Qimu*, pp. 380–82; Shandongsheng, 'Linzi Langjiazhuang'. While the early historians regarded Qi as a state within the Zhou system, their burial patterns show that they also favoured these northern traditions. Zhongshan and states such as Qi were following similar burial patterns despite their different affiliations.

22 Attendance at ritual ancestral ceremonies and access to sacred space are discussed by Khayutina, 'Welcoming Guests'.

23 The remains on the mound and the configuration of the buildings are discussed in Wu, *Material Culture*, pp. 171–9; Wu Hung, 'The Art and Architecture of the Warring States Period', in Loewe and Shaughnessy (eds.), *The Cambridge History of Ancient China*, pp. 651–744.

24 For the examples excavated at Lingshou see Hebeisheng, *Zhanguo Zhong-shanguo*, p. 278, fig. 214, p. 282, figs. 218, 219. The basin with incised designs is probably a southern piece, discussed by Alain Thote in his survey of vessels that carry scenes, 'Intercultural Relations as Seen from Chinese Pictorial Bronzes of the Fifth Century B.C.E', *RES: Anthropology and Aesthetics* 35 (1999), pp. 10–41.

25 A famous example painted in lacquer is of a scene, almost a narrative, on a box excavated at a large Chu period tomb at Baoshan in Hubei province, Hubeisheng Jingsha Tielu Kaogudui, *Baoshan Chumu (The Chu Tombs at Baoshan)*, 2 vols. (Wenwu Chubanshe, 1991), vol. 1, p. 146, fig. 89 (D).

26 This issue has been discussed by Minao Hayashi, 'Concerning the Inscription "May Sons and Grandsons Eternally Use This [Vessel]" ', *Artibus Asiae* 53 (1993), pp. 51–8.

27 See Chapter 8.

28 For the structure of the tomb of King Cheng see Hebeisheng, *Zhanguo Zhong-shanguo*, pp. 122–33, fig. 88.

29 For a translation of the inscriptions on the plan and a discussion of its significance see Wu, *Material Culture*, p. 173, fig. 6.1.

30 Ibid., p. 177.

31 For a translation into English see James I. Crump (trans.), *Chan-Kuo Ts'e (Intrigues of the Warring States)*, (University of Michigan, 1996), Wu, *Material Culture*, p. 178.

32 For a discussion of these arrangements in the first part of the Zhou period see Khayutina, 'Kinship, Marriage and Politics'. For a brief, but wider account see Anne B. Kinney, 'Women in Early China: Views from the Archaeological Record', in Goldin (ed.), *Routledge Handbook of Early Chinese History*, pp. 367–85.

33 Chapter 7 presents the northern and steppe customs of the burial of animals' parts, avoided in the major tombs of the Central Plains. Animal heads have now been found in many of the tombs of the fifth and fourth centuries BC on the Loess Plateau and in the Zhongshan region.

34 As discussed and illustrated in Chapter 5, the northern areas occupied by the Rong and Di were well known as good regions from which to source horses, as described in the *Zuo Zhuan*, Durrant et al., *Zuo Tradition*, p. 1365, see Chapter 5, note 54.

35 A sign of the northern connections of Qi is seen in the burials of large numbers of horses at a few tombs. The exceptional example is Zhang and Luo, 'Qigucheng Wuhao Dongzhoumu'; Shandongsheng, *Linzi Qimu*, colour pl. 22. For an example of a steppe model see Timothy F. Taylor,

'Thracians, Scythians, and Dacians, 800 BC–AD 300', in Barry W. Cunliffe (ed.), *Prehistoric Europe: An Illustrated History* (Oxford University Press, 1998), pp. 373–410.

36 For the violence accompanying the battles of the Warring States period see Lewis, *Sanctioned Violence in Early China*.

37 Hebeisheng, *Zhanguo Zhongshanguo*, Hebeisheng Wenwu Kaogu Yanjiuyuan, Zhongguo Shehui Kexueyuan Kaogu Yanjiusuo, Shijiazhuang Wenwu Yanjiusuo and Xingtangxian Wenwu Baohu Guanlisuo, *Che Chu Zhongshan: Xingtang Gujun Kaogu Faxian* (*Chariots from Zhongshan: The Archaeological Discovery of the Gujun Site, Xingtang*) (Wenwu Chubanshe, 2021).

38 Quoted from Wu, *Material Culture*, p. 108.

39 Ibid., p. 83.

40 For the report on the burial of the goats see Hebeisheng, *Zhanguo Zhongshanguo*, p. 516 and Wu, *Material Culture*, p. 85, fn. 29; the burial of whole animals was rather different from the more usual pastoralist custom of burying animal heads, as at Yuhuangmiao and tombs mentioned above at notes 5 and 9.

41 Hebeisheng, *Zhanguo Zhongshanguo*, described on p. 332.

42 For an overview of iron-working in early China see Donald B. Wagner, *Science and Civilisation in China*, vol. 5, *Chemistry and Chemical Technology, Part 11: Ferrous Metallurgy* (Cambridge University Press, 2008). More recent work on early China is in Wengcheong Lam, 'Iron Technology and Its Regional Development during the Eastern Zhou Period', in Childs-Johnson (ed.), *The Oxford Handbook of Early China*, pp. 595–614; Han Rubin and Chen Jianli, 'Zhongguo Gudai Yetie Tidai Yetong Zhiping' ('A Study on the Transition from Bronze to Iron in Ancient China'), in Cao Wei and Thilo Rehren (eds.), *Qin Shiqi Yejin Kaogu Guoji Xueshu Yantaohui Lunwenji* (*International Symposium on Qin Period Metallurgy and Its Social and Archaeological Context*) (Kexue Chubanshe, 2014), pp. 121–33.

43 Di Cosmo, 'The Northern Frontier in Pre-imperial China', pp. 960–63.

44 For the distribution of vessels in the tomb see Hebeisheng, *Zhanguo Zhongshanguo*. These are listed and discussed in Wu, *Material Culture*, pp. 87–93. For the inscriptions see pp. 150–60.

45 In his discussion of the *ding*, Wu Xiaolong has based his account on the transcriptions and translations in Gilbert L. Mattos, 'Eastern Zhou Bronze Inscriptions', in Edward Shaughnessy (ed.), *New Sources of Early Chinese History: An Introduction to the Reading of Inscriptions and Manuscripts* (The Society for the Study of Early China, and the Institute of East Asian Studies, University of California, 1997), pp. 104–9.

46 For a description of one of the Yan cities from an archaeological perspective see Hebeisheng Wenwu Yanjiusuo, *Yan Xiadu* (*The Lower Capital of the Yan State*), 2 vols. (Wenwu Chubanshe, 1996) and Wu, *Material Culture*, p. 141.

47 After Wu, *Material Culture*, pp. 192–3; in this translation, Wu Xiaolong has followed Constance A. Cook in 'Chungshan Bronze Inscriptions: Introduction and Translation', MA dissertation (University of Washington, 1980).

48 For a brief account of the importance of hierarchy by seniority see Chapter 8 in this book. The relations with Yan are described in Wu, *Material Culture*, p. 141.

49 After Wu, *Material Culture*, p. 152, following Cook, 'Chungshan Bronze Inscriptions'.

50 See ibid., pp. 154–8.

51 After ibid., p. 153, following Cook, 'Chungshan Bronze Inscriptions'.

52 For the rise of the officials given the general name of *Shi* see Pines, *The Everlasting Empire*, pp. 152–4.

53 Li Ling (trans. Lothar von Falkenhausen), 'On the Typology of Chu Bronzes', *Beiträge zur Allgemeinen und Vergleichenden Archäologie* 11 (1991), pp. 57–113.

54 Wu, *Material Culture*, pp. 90–92.

55 Falkenhausen, *Chinese Society*, p. 303, fig. 61.

56 Rawson, *Chinese Jade*; So, *Early Chinese Jades*.

57 For descriptions of the board and some details on the game see Wu, *Material Culture*, pp. 117–21; Rawson (ed.), *Mysteries*, pp. 159–61.

58 Wu, *Material Culture*, p. 142.

59 Winged creatures were part of the object language of areas of the steppe, where people had taken up visual traits from Western Asia and especially from Iran. Beasts with wings and with long horns in silver and more exotic ones in gold have been found in famous sites, such as Issyk in Kazakhstan; see Sören Stark, 'Nomads and Networks: Elites and Their Connections to the Outside World', in Sören Stark and Karen S. Rubinson (eds.), *Nomads and Networks: The Ancient Art and Culture of Kazakhstan* (Institute for the Study of the Ancient World/Princeton University Press, 2012), pp. 106–38; this imagery was widely introduced into the borderlands of northern China and appears in inlaid motifs on bronze vessels reproducing hunting scenes of the pastoralists envisaged in the unknown world of the steppe; see Weber, *Chinese Pictorial Bronzes*, figs. 62–4. Illustrated in this chapter. The wings are often shown as if as felt overlays, as seen at Pazyryk in the Altai, Sergei Rudenko, *Frozen Tombs of Siberia: The Pazyryk Burials of Iron Age Horsemen* (Dent, 1970), pls. 169–70, in carved wood; see p. 166.

60 Domesticated animals and scenes of predators were current in the fourth millennium in Western Asia in many materials and functions, but especially on small engraved cylinder seals, which could be exchanged and passed from hand to hand, see Aruz and Wellenfelz (eds.), *Art of the First Cities*. Along with all the animal tropes described in Chapter 7 in this book, this famous subject crossed into the steppe and was developed in many different regions in a range of materials and styles.

61 A fine example of the incorporation of steppe motifs within the objects of the central states is on a gold sheath ornament from Yan, excavated from tomb M30 at Xinzhuangtou, Yi Country, Heibei province, Wu, *Material Culture*, p. 124, fig. 3:32.

62 The northern imagery of predators and prey was reinterpreted with other, more local creatures in Chu (Chapter 9), as suggested by Wu, illustrated with a wooden screen on which a bird dives to attack snakes, *Material Culture*, pp. 103–14, fig. 3:19.

63 Another lamp, from the tomb of King Cheng, is illustrated and described in Rawson (ed.), *Mysteries*, pp. 156–7, no. 74, where references for other Warring States lamps are cited.

Chapter 11: Catacombs and Chariots

1 For the history of Iran, especially the Achaemenid Empire see Pierre Briant (trans. Peter T. Daniels), *From Cyrus to Alexander: A History of the Persian Empire* (Eisenbrauns, 2002).

2 The Sogdians were an immensely impressive group of merchants, who made major contributions to China's culture and society from the fifth century AD; see Annette L. Juliano and Judith A. Lerner, *Monks and Merchants: Silk Road Treasures from Northwest China. Gansu and Ningxia 4th–7th Century* (Harry N. Abrams with the Asia Society, 2001). For considerable detail on Sogdians in China see Patrick Wertmann, *Sogdians in China: Archaeological and Art Historical Analyses of Tombs and Texts from the 3rd to the 10th Century AD* (Verlag Philipp von Zabern, 2015). For a wider picture see J. Harmatta, Baij Nath Puri and G. F. Etemadi (eds.), *History of Civilizations of Central Asia*, vol. 2, *The Development of Sedentary and Nomadic Civilizations: 700 B.C. to A.D. 250* (UNESCO, 1994).

3 Denis Sinor (ed.), *The Cambridge History of Early Inner Asia* (Cambridge University Press, 1990). For maritime trade see John W. Chaffee, *The Muslim Merchants of Premodern China: The History of a Maritime Asian Trade Diaspora, 750–1400* (Cambridge University Press, 2018).

4 There is no full excavation report for the Majiayuan cemetery, which is in any case, still being unearthed. There are several brief reports. For the central tomb see Zhou Guangji, Zhao Wucheng, Zhao Zhuo, Hua Pingning and Wang Hui, 'Zhangjiachuan Majiayuan Zhanguo Mudi 2007–2008 Nian Fajue Jianbao' ('The Excavation of the Majiayuan Warring States Cemetery in the Zhangjiachuan County, 2007–2008 Seasons'), *Wenwu* 10 (2009), pp. 25–51.

5 It was not possible in the steppe or elsewhere in Eurasia to dig tombs to the depth available in the loess regions. The arrangement of the subordinate tombs has a general resemblance to the deposits and tombs around Arzhan II, as set out in Chapter 8 in this book, following an analysis by Konstantin Chugunov, as discussed in Chugunov, 'The Arzhan-2 Funerary Commemorative Complex'.

6 Liu Bingbing, Xie Yan and Wang Hui, 'Gansu Zhangjiachuan Majiayuan Zhanguo Mudi 2012–2014 Nian Fajue Jianbao' ('Brief Report on the 2012–2014 Excavation of the Majiayuan Cemetery in Zhangjiachuan, of the Warring States Period'), *Wenwu* 3 (2018), pp. 4–25.

7 After Watson, *Records*, vol. 2, p. 155.

8 As Caesar writes, 'They do not pay much attention to agriculture and a large portion of their food consists in milk, cheese and flesh; nor has anyone a fixed quantity of land or his own individual limits', Carolyn Hammond (ed.), *Seven Commentaries on the Gallic War* (Oxford University Press, 2008), pp. 130–31.

9 The wide distribution has puzzled many historians. There have been attempts to suggest that a single Scythian-type society dominated, as if it were almost an empire, as suggested in Pankova and Simpson (eds.), *Scythians* and by some authors in Pankova and Simpson (eds.), *Masters of the Steppe*, pp. 80–104. Such an account is led by the European encounters with the Scythians and underestimates the long chronology and dense and different variations between the many societies across the steppe from Arzhan to Ukraine.

10 Renate Rolle, *Totenkult der Scythen: Teil 1: Das Steppengebiet*, 2 parts (De Gruyter, 1979).

11 Catacombs were found at the central Zhou site of Zhangjiapo, near Xi'an, probably dating to the tenth to ninth centuries BC, evidence of a long engagement with northerners, Zhongguo Shehui Kexueyuan Kaogu Yanjiusuo (ed.), *Zhangjiapo Xizhou Mudi* (*Western Zhou Cemetery at Zhangjiapo*) (Zhongguo Dabai Kechuan Chubanshe, 1999), pp. 68–78. The significance of these non-Zhou clans and newcomers from further away buried in among Zhou cemeteries is discussed in Rawson et al., 'Seeking Horses'.

12 For such tombs see Zhao Xueye, Wang Shan, Tian Songting and Sun Mingxia, 'Gansu Qin'an Wangwa Zhanguo Mudi 2009 Nian Fajue Jianbao' ('Premininary Report on the 2009 Season Excavation of the Warring States Wangwa

Cemetery in Qin'an, Gansu'), *Wenwu* 8 (2012), pp. 27–37. To the north, on the other side of the Liupan Mountains, in what is now Ningxia province, are tombs of what is called the Yanglang culture, Ningxia Wenwu Kaogu Yanjiu-suo, *Wangdahu yu Jiulongshan: Beifang Qingtong Wenhua Mudi* (*Wangdahu and Jiulongshan: Cemeteries of the Northern Bronze Culture*), 2 vols. (Wenwu Chu-banshe, 2016). People there also built catacomb tombs, in which the catacomb itself usually sloped downwards. The main chambers held large numbers of animal heads, Xu Cheng et al., 'Ningxia Guyuan Yanglang Qingtong Wenhua Mudi' ('Bronze Culture Cemetery at Yanglang, Guyuan, Ningxia'), *Kaogu Xuebao* 1 (1993), pp. 13–56.

13 Guo Wu, 'Majiayuan Mudi Suojian Qin Ba Xirong de Wenhua Biaoxiang Jiqi Neiyin' ('The Cultural Representation and Its Internal Cause of Qin's Pre-dominance over the Xirong Seen in Majiayuan Cemetery'), *Sichuan Wenwu* 4 (2019), pp. 46–53; Zhang Yin, 'Dongzhou Xirong Wenhua Majiayuan Leixing Laiyuan Chutan' ('Preliminary Study of the Archaeological Culture of the Western Rong of the Eastern Zhou Period'), *Kaogu yu Wenwu* 2 (2019), pp. 71–6; Liu Yuyang and Wang Hui, 'Xian Qin Shiqi Xibei Youmu Diqu Dongwu Maizang Xisu: Cong Maizang Touti de Xianxiang Tanqi' ('Animal Sacrifices in the Northwestern Region during the Pre-Qin Period: On the Phenomenon of Burying Heads and Hooves'), *Kaogu yu Wenwu* 1 (2017), pp. 62–9.

14 Dai Chunyang, 'Lixian Dabuzishan Qingong Mudi ji Xiangguan Wenti' ('Sev-eral Questions Concerning the Royal Graveyard of the Qin State at Dabuzi, Lixian, Gansu'), *Wenwu* 5 (2000), pp. 74–80; Mao Ruilin, Li Yongning, Zhao Wucheng and Wang Gang, 'Lixian Yuandingshan Chunqiu Qinmu' ('Qin Tombs of the Spring and Autumn Period at Yuandingshan, Lixian, Gansu'), *Wenwu* 2 (2002), pp. 4–30; Li Yongning, Wang Gang, Mao Ruilin and Zhao Wucheng, 'Gansu Lixian Yuandingshan 98LDM2, 2000LDM4 Chunqiu Qinmu' ('Excavation of the Qin Tombs 98LDM2 and 2000LDM4 of the Spring and Autumn Period at Yuandingshan, Lixian, Gansu'), *Wenwu* 2 (2005), pp. 4–27.

15 After Watson, *Records of the Grand Historian: Qin Dynasty* (Columbia Univer-sity Press, 1993), p. 3.

16 After ibid., p. 17.

17 The region was also used in the Tang period for ranching horses; see Jona-than K. Skaff, *Sui-Tang China and its Turko-Mongol Neighbours: Culture, Power and Connections, 580–800* (Oxford University Press, 2012), pp. 262–6.

18 There has been limited discussion on the close links of the Qin with steppe peoples, as in Lothar von Falkenhausen, 'Mortuary Behaviors in Pre-Imperial Qin: A Religious Interpretation', in John Lagerwey (ed.), *Religion and Chinese Society*, 2 vols. (Chinese University Press/École française d'Extrême-Orient,

2004), vol. 1, pp. 109–72. However, there were clearly close relations with north-erners with different burial patterns alongside the Qin, Tian et al., 'Shaanxi Fengxiang Sunjianantou'.

19 Jiao Nanfeng, Sun Weigang and Du Linyuan, 'Qinren de Shige Lingqu' ('On the Ten Cemetery Complexes of the Qin State'), *Wenwu* 6 (2014), pp. 64–76.

20 For the report on the tomb M16, Wang Hui et al., 'Zhangjiachuan Majiayuan Zhanguo Mudi 2008–2009 Nian Fajue Jianbao' ('Brief Report on the 2008–2009 Excavation of the Majiayuan Cemetery in Zhangjiachuan, of the Warring States Period'), *Wenwu* 10 (2010), pp. 4–26.

21 While Wu Xiaolong, in 'Cultural Hybridity and Social Status: Elite Tombs on China's Northern Frontier during the Third Century BC', *Antiquity* 87 (2013), pp. 121–36, suggests the steps are signs of hybridity and used to display hierarchical rank, it is probably more appropriate to compare them with the stepped ramp of the tomb of Lord Bai of Zhongli (Chapter 8) and a long-standing northern tradition.

22 This suggestion has been made by Raphael Wong, 'Steppe and Local Identities on the Frontier of the State and Empire of Qin during the 7th to 3rd Centuries BC', DPhil thesis (University of Oxford, 2019).

23 Chugunov et al., *Der Skythenzeitliche Fürstenkurgan*, pl. 35.

24 Wong, 'Steppe and Local Identities', figs. 4:26, 4:27. Later examples persisted among the north-eastern tribes of the Xianbei, Jilinsheng Wenwu Kaogu Yanjiusuo (ed.), *Yushu Laohesheng (The Excavation of Laohesheng, Yushu, Jilin)* (Wenwu Chubanshe, 1987).

25 Honeychurch, *Inner Asia and the Spatial Politics of Empire*, pp. 278–88.

26 Extensive illustrations of belts and other gold and silver ornaments are found in Gansusheng Wenwu Kaogu Yanjiusuo, *Xirong Yizhen: Majiayuan Zhanguo Mudi Chutu Wenwu (The Legacy of Xirong: Artefacts from the Warring State Period Cemetery at Majiayuan, Gansu)* (Wenwu Chubanshe, 2014).

27 The vessels are discussed and illustrated in Chapters, 3, 5 and 6 in this book.

28 This famous material was reported in K. A. Akishev, *Kurgan Issyk: Iskusstvo Sakov Kazahstana (Kurgan Issyk: Art of the Sakas of Kazakhstan)* (Iskusstvo, 1978); see also Parzinger (ed.), *Im Zeichen des Goldenen Greifen*, pp. 106–7; Yang Jianhua and Katheryn M. Linduff, 'A Contextual Explanation for "Foreign" or "Step-pic" Factors Exhibited in Burials at the Majiayuan Cemetery and the Opening of the Tianshan Mountain Corridor', *Asian Archaeology* 1 (2013), pp. 73–84.

29 Wang et al., 'Zhangjiachuan', p. 24, fig. 62.

30 A jade sole was found in a third-century BC tomb at Fanjiacun in Linzi, Shan-dong province, almost certainly a central Chinese adaptation of a steppe practice, Li Dongjiang et al., 'Shandong Linzi Fanjiacun Mudi 2012 Nian Fajue

Jianbao' ('The Excavation of the Fanjiacun Cemetery, Linzi, Shandong, in 2012'), *Wenwu* 4 (2015), pp. 9–27, fig. 24.

31 Briant, *From Cyrus to Alexander.*

32 John Curtis and Nigel Tallis (eds.), *Forgotten Empire: The World of Ancient Persia* (British Museum Press, 2005), p. 13, fig. 2.

33 Material from many of these sites is illustrated in Parzinger (ed.), *Im Zeichen des Goldenen Greifen.*

34 For the discussion of the technical processes see So, 'Foreign/Eurasian Elements in Pre-imperial Qin Culture'; Liu Yan, 'Exotica as Prestige Technology: The Production of Luxury Gold in Western Han Society', *Antiquity* 91 (2017), pp. 1588–602.

35 Michael D. Frachetti, 'Multiregional Emergence of Mobile Pastoralism and Nonuniform Institutional Complexity across Eurasia', *Current Anthropology* 53 (2012), pp. 2–38.

36 Zhou Guangji, Fang Zhijun, Xie Yan and Ma Mingyuan, '2006 Niandu Gansu Zhangjiachuan Huizu Zizhixian Majiayuan Zhanguo Mudi Fajue Jianbao' ('Preliminary Report on the 2006 Season Excavation of the Warring States Majiayuan Cemetery in Zhangjiachuan Hui Autonomous County, Gansu'), *Wenwu* 9 (2008), pp. 4–28, fig. 19.

37 Huang Xiaojuan, Wang Hui and Zhao Xichen, 'Gansu Zhangjiachuanxian Majiayuan Zhanguo Mudi M4 Muguan Shiyanshi Kaogu Jianbao' ('Laboratory Report on the Warring States Wooden Coffin from M4 from the Majiayuan Cemetery in Zhangjiachuan County, Gansu'), *Kaogu* 8 (2013), pp. 25–35.

38 Related, less numerous groups have been identified in other local cemeteries.

39 Quoted from David Morgan and Peter Jackson (trans.), *The Mission of Friar William of Rubruck: His Journey to the Great Khan Möngke, 1253–1255* (Hackett Publishing Company Inc., 1990, repr. 2009), p. 248; also described in Marie Favereau, *The Horde: How the Mongols Changed the World* (Harvard Belknap, 2021), p. 112.

40 Chugunov et al., *Der Skythenzeitliche Fürstenkurgan*, pl. 68; compare with a cup from Pazyryk, Rudenko, *Frozen Tombs of Siberia*, pl. 54.

41 For a full overview of the tombs see Rudenko, *Frozen Tombs of Siberia*; for a review of recent research see Katheryn M. Linduff and Karen S. Rubinson, *Pazyryk Culture up in the Altai* (Routledge, 2021). For the relationship with Majiayuan see Wu Hsiao-yun, 'Shandian Shang de Xionglu, Menghu yu Yeshanyang: Majiayuan Mache Caoyuan Zhuangshi de Laiyuan yu Chuanbo Tujing' ('Stags, Tigers and Ibexes in the Mountains: The Origins and Transmission of Steppe Patterns seen on Chariots Found at Majiayuan in Zhangjiachuan, Gansu'), *Gugong Xueshu Jikan* 34 (2016), pp. 1–51.

42 Rudenko, *Frozen Tombs of Siberia*, pl. 154.

43 Such comparisons are fundamental in conveying the closely interconnected societies from Kazakhstan to Gansu province. Examples of this type of harness from Berel are illustrated in Roberts (ed.), *Gold of the Great Steppe*, p. 125. For an example at Pazyryk see Rudenko, *Frozen Tombs of Siberia*, p. 130, fig. 66. The Qin harness is illustrated in this book, Chapter 12.

44 For the numerous sites with similar motifs and materials see Parzinger, *Im Zeichen Des Goldenen Greifen.*

45 Motifs that we associate with the Mediterranean and Western Asia are some of the startling finds at both Pazyryk and Majiayuan; see Rudenko, *Frozen Tombs of Siberia*, pp. 144–71; for bridles see figs. 79–92. Scrolls derived from the running scrolls of the Mediterranean are abundant at Majiayuan; see Wang et al., 'Zhangjiachuan', p. 7, fig. 6. For Berel see Parzinger (ed.), *Im Zeichen des Goldenen Greifen*, pp. 132–47; Roberts (ed.), *Gold of the Great Steppe*, pp. 118–28.

46 Rudenko, *Frozen Tombs of Siberia*, pls. 119–20.

47 Stark and Rubinson (eds.), *Nomads and Networks*, p. 110.

48 Ibid., pp. 113–16.

49 Rudenko, *Frozen Tombs of Siberia*, pls. 174, 177; Stark and Rubinson, *Nomads and Networks*, figs. 7:5, 7:6; Wu Xin, 'Persian and Central Asian Elements in the Social Landscape of the Early Nomads at Pazyryk, Southern Siberia', in Popova et al. (eds.), *Social Orders and Social Landscapes*, pp. 120–49.

50 Rudenko, *Frozen Tombs of Siberia*, p. 175, fig. 89, p. 115, fig. 55.

51 Valerie Hansen, *The Silk Road: A New History* (Oxford University Press, 2012).

52 Described as 'tribute', in AD 707 the Turkic Khan delivered 5,000 horses, 200 camels and over 100,000 cattle and sheep, Skaff, *Sui-Tang China*, p. 267. In 734 or 735 the emperor Xuanzong calculated that he owed 500,000 bolts of silk for 14,000 horses, Skaff, *Sui-Tang China*, p. 269.

53 William Honeychurch, 'From Steppe Roads to Silk Roads: Inner Asian Nomads and Early Interregional Exchange', in Amitai and Biran (eds.), *Nomads as Agents of Cultural Change*, pp. 50–87; Di Cosmo, 'China-Steppe Relations in Historical Perspective'.

54 Two English versions of articles by Zhao Wucheng describe the detailed structures and decoration of the chariots, 'The Restoration of the Chariots of the Warring-States Period in Majiayuan, Gansu', *Chinese Archaeology* 13 (2013), pp. 176–85, and 'The Restoration of the Chariots of the Warring-States Period in Majiayuan, Gansu (continued) – the Designing and Making Skills of Chariots and Modifying and Designing Ideas of Oxcarts', *Chinese Archaeology* 19 (2019), pp. 169–81.

55 Zhao Wucheng, 'Gansu Majiayuan Zhanguo Mu Mache de Fuyuan: Jiantan Zushu Wenti' ('The Reconstruction of the Chariots from the Warring States

Tombs at Majiayuan, Gansu, with a Discussion of Ethnicity'), *Wenwu* 6 (2010), pp. 75–83, fig. 3 illustrates the two additional struts. See also above note 54.

56 The chariots have steppe rather than Zhou features, Wu, 'Shandian Shang de Xionglu'. The numerous-spoked wheels can be compared with a highly unusual chariot excavated at Pazyryk, Rudenko, *Frozen Tombs of Siberia*, fig. 131.

57 Zhao, 'Gansu Majiayuan', fig. 2 and Wang et al., 'Zhangjiachuan', fig. 49.

58 The several categories are set out in Zhao Wucheng, 'The Restoration of Chariots'.

59 For illustrations of the most elaborate chariots and many of the iron sections with gold and silver overlay see Gansusheng, *Xirong*.

60 Discussed in many of Thomas Allsen's works, *Culture and Conquest in Mongol Eurasia* (Cambridge University Press, 2001); see also Favereau, *The Horde*.

61 This identification made by Raphael Wong in *Steppe and Local Identities* is of profound importance to our understanding of many features of the tomb of the First Emperor, discussed in the next chapter.

62 This significant observation has been made by Raphael Wong, ' "Steppe Style" in Southeast Gansu Province (China) in the 4th and 3rd Centuries BC', in Pankova and Simpson (eds.), *Masters of the Steppe*, pp. 650–59; Raphael Wong, 'Carpets, Chariots and the State of Qin', *Orientations* 48 (2017), pp. 60–70.

63 Rudenko, *Frozen Tombs of Siberia*, pl. 174.

64 The example from Nineveh in the British Museum is object 185,0909.57, dated to 645 BC.

65 Rudenko, *Frozen Tombs of Siberia*, pl. 162.

66 For the Pazyryk cheekpiece in wood see Rudenko, *Frozen Tombs of Siberia*, pl. 94B.

67 Stark and Rubinson (eds.), *Nomads and Networks*, p. 102, figs. 6–9.

68 This comparison is illustrated in Jessica Rawson and Huan Limin, 'Cong Mabiao Xingzhi de Yanbian Kan Zhongyuan yu Ouya Caoyuan de Zaoqi Jiaoliu' ('On the Cultural Exchange between the Central Plains and the Steppe through the Typological Changes of Early Cheek Pieces'), in Beijing Daxue Chutu Wenxian Yanjiusuo (ed.), *Qingtongqi yu Jinwen* 8 (Shanghai Guji Chubanshe, 2022), pp. 167–204.

69 As discussed in a preliminary survey, Cai Dawei, Zhu Siqi, Hu Songmei, Tian Yaqi, Sun Yang, Chen Xi and Zhou Hui, 'Shaanxi Fengxiang Qingong Yihao Damu Chemakeng Magu Yihai Gu DNA Yanjiu' ('Mitochondrial DNA Analysis of Horse Remains from the Chariot Burial Pits of No. 1 Qingong Mausoleum in Fengxiang, Shaanxi Province'), *Kaogu yu Wenwu* 3 (2018), pp. 106–12.

70 B. van Geel et al., 'Climate Change and the Expansion of the Scythian Culture after 850 BC: A Hypothesis', *Journal of Archaeological Science* 31 (2004), pp. 1735–42; Ganna I. Zaitseva et al., 'Chronology and Possible Links Between Climatic and Cultural Change During the First Millennium BC in Southern Siberia and Central Asia', *Radiocarbon* 46 (2004), pp. 259–76.

Chapter 12: The Everlasting Army

1 Mentioned in Chapter 5.

2 Described in Chapter 11.

3 The movement of the Qin eastwards and the archaeological material that confirms the stages in this move are described in Teng Mingyu, 'From Vassal State to Empire: An Archaeological Examination of Qin Culture', in Pines et al. (eds.), *Birth of an Empire*, pp. 71–112. See also Maria Khayutina (ed.), *Qin: The Eternal Emperor and His Terracotta Warriors* (Neue Zürcher Zeitung Publishing, 2013); Portal (ed.), *The First Emperor*; Edward Burman, *Terracotta Warriors: History, Mystery and the Latest Discoveries* (Weidenfeld & Nicolson, 2018).

4 Other tombs of lesser Qin lords in the same cemetery also have large ramps, made possible by the deep deposits of loess in the Western Wei Valley.

5 The tomb and the early history of the Qin at Yongcheng are discussed in Alain Thote, 'Tombs of the Principality of Qin: Elites and Commoners', in Khayutina (ed.), *Qin: The Eternal Emperor*, pp. 37–45.

6 Watson, *Records: Qin Dynasty*, pp. 8 and 17.

7 Carol Michaelson, *Gilded Dragons: Buried Treasures from China's Golden Ages* (British Museum, 1999), p. 25, nos. 1, 2.

8 Khayutina (ed.), *Qin: The Eternal Emperor*, p. 43. Tian Renxiao and Lei Xingshan, 'Baojishi Yimencun Erhao Chunqiumu Fajue Jianbao' ('The Tomb No. 2 of the Qin State at Yimencun, Baoji'), *Wenwu* 10 (1993), pp. 1–14; Baojishi Kaogu Yanjiusuo, *Qinmu Yizhen: Baoji Yimen Erhao Chunqiumu (Treasures of Qin Tombs: A Spring and Autumn Period Tomb (No. 2) at Yimen, Baoji)* (Kexue Chubanshe, 2016).

9 Khayutina (ed.), *Qin: The Eternal Emperor*, p. 42, fig. 13.

10 For the Qin exploitation of mega-sized structures see Gideon Shelach-Lavi, 'Collapse or Transformation? Anthropological and Archaeological Perspectives on the Fall of the Qin', in Yuri Pines et al. (eds.), *Birth of an Empire*, pp. 113–38.

11 The steppe models for mounded tombs, with neatly arranged coffins around a central one, are discussed in Chapter 8, where the steppe prototypes described by Herodotus and the kurgans at Arzhan are considered.

12 For flexed burials see Han Jianye, 'Zhongguo Gudai Quzhizang Puxi Shuli' ('The Development of the Flexed Burial Tradition in Early China'), *Wenwu* 1 (2006), pp. 53–60. A good example in which the attendants are neatly arranged, with flexed legs, is at Fengxiang, Tian et al., 'Shaanxi Fengxiang Sunjianan-tou'. Lothar von Falkenhausen, 'Mortuary Behavior in Pre-Imperial Qin: A Religious Interpretation', in John Lagerwey (ed.), *Religion and Chinese Society*, 2 vols. (Chinese University Press/École française d'Extrême-Orient, 2004), vol. 1, pp. 109–72; Falkenhausen, *Chinese Society*, pp. 213–21.

13 Sima Qian describes relations between the people he calls the Rong and the Qin in his chapter 'The Basic Annals of the Qin', Watson, *Records: Qin Dynasty*, pp. 15–16.

14 Cai Dawei et al., 'Shaanxi Fengxiang Qingong Yihao Damu Chemakeng Magu Yihai Gu DNA Yanjiu', pp. 106–12.

15 Watson, *Records: Qin Dynasty*, pp. 159–78.

16 Ibid., p. 63. The translation has been modified, taking out the words 'replicas', 'imitations' and 'representations' as they are not in the original Chinese.

17 Ibid., pp. 63–4, modified to translate the character for *xiang* as analogue.

18 We tend, when writing and thinking in English, to see the tomb as a model or at least symbolic, as described by Wu Hung, *The Art of the Yellow Springs: Understanding Chinese Tombs* (Reaktion Books, 2020), pp. 19–20. However, the huge expenditure in labour and materials to create the whole complex suggests that we should understand that the emperor expected to dwell there in his afterlife.

19 This account is directly based on the work of Duan Qingbo, described in Duan Qingbo, 'Qinshihuangdi Ling de Wutan Kaogu Diaocha: "863" Jihua Qinshi-huang Ling Wutan Kaogu Jinzhan Qingkuang de Baogao' ('The Geophysical Exploration of the Mausoleum of Emperor Qin Shihuang: The New Archae-ological Discovery of the National 863 Project'), *Xibei Daxue Xuebao* 1 (2005), pp. 80–86. Duan Qingbo, 'Qinshihuang Ling Fengtu Jianzhu Tantao: Jianshi "Zhongcheng Guanyou"' ('On the Buildings on Top of the First Emperor's Tomb Mound'), *Kaogu* 5 (2006), pp. 70–76. I am grateful for the work of Dr Limin Huan in creating a very illuminating cross-section of the tomb below the mound following Duan's account. As Duan's description is based upon remote sensing and not on excavation, there are many details and measure-ments that remain to be confirmed. At present the section used here is merely provisional.

20 In a talk in honour of Professor Lothar Ledderose at Heidelberg University on 12 July 2022, Professor Lukas Nickel drew attention to a large masonry-prepared stone at the site of the tomb of the First Emperor that might have been cut to install in such a position. It is possible that it was intended for the

wall in the deep chamber. See also Wu, 'Persian and Central Asian Elements in the Social Landscape and Duan Qingbo, 'Sino-Western Cultural Exchange as Seen through the Archaeology of the First Emperor's Necropolis', *Journal of Chinese History* (2022), pp. 1–52.

21 A full description is given in Jie Shi, 'Incorporating All for One: The First Emperor's Tomb Mound', *Early China* 37 (2014), pp. 359–91. His work is based upon Duan Qingbo, 'Qinshihuangdi Ling de Wutan Kaogu Diao-cha', and Shaanxisheng Kaogu Yanjiuyuan and Qinshihuang Bingmayong Bowuguan, *Qinshihuangdi Lingyuan Kaogu Baogao (2001–2003) (The Excavation of the Mausoleum of the First Qin Emperor (2001–2003 Seasons))* (Wenwu Chu-banshe, 2007).

22 For a description of the site and full map of the tomb deposits see Armin Selbitschka, 'The Tomb Complex and its Hidden Secrets', in Khayutina (ed.), *Qin: The Eternal Emperor*, pp. 144–53.

23 A wide-ranging report, including these small figures, is in Yuan Zhongyi, *Qin-shihuangdi Ling de Kaogu Faxian yu Yanjiu (Archaeological Discoveries and Research on the Emperor Qin Shihuang's Mausoleum)* (Shaanxi Renmin Chubanshe, 2002), pp. 210–15.

24 Cao Wei, 'The Discovery of a Century: The Terracotta Army of the First Emperor of China', in Khayutina (ed.), *Qin: The Eternal Emperor*, pp. 140–43.

25 This view is proposed in Jessica Rawson, 'The Power of Images: The Model Universe of the First Emperor and Its Legacy', *Historical Research* 75 (2002), pp. 123–54; this approach has been taken up by Barbieri-Low, *Ancient Egypt and Early China*, pp. 185–91. For discussion of the background to the creation of models of people see Armin Selbitschka, 'Miniature Tomb Figurines and Models in Pre-imperial and Early Imperial China: Origins, Development and Significance', *World Archaeology* 47 (2015), pp. 20–44. For examples from Shan-dong see Li Yuexun, 'Shandong Zhangqiu Nülangshan Zhanguomu Chutu Yuewu Taoyong ji Youguan Wenti' ('On the Ceramic Dancing Figurines Unearthed from the Warring States Tomb at Nülangshan, Zhangqiu, Shan-dong'), *Wenwu* 3 (1993), pp. 1–6.

26 Detailed drawings of the figures and information on many other aspects of the site are described in Yuan, *Qinshihuangdi Ling*.

27 Armin Selbitschka, 'The Terracotta Men and Their Roles', in Khayutina (ed.), *Qin: The Eternal Emperor*, pp. 156–63.

28 For illustrations of the variety of hairstyles and beards and different shapes of face and head see Catharina Blänsdorf, Erwin Emmerling and Michael Petzet (eds.), *Die Terrakottaarmee Des Ersten Chinesischen Kaisers Qin Shihuang* (Bayer-isches Landesamt für Denkmalpflege, 2001), pp. 157–71.

29 Lothar Ledderose, *Ten Thousand Things: Module and Mass Production in Chinese Art* (Princeton University Press, 2000), discusses the system by which this depiction of an army was achieved.

30 Extensive report of research and discussion on colour is presented in Blänsdorf et al., *Die Terrakottaarmee.*

31 Other steppe groups, such as the tribes called the Xiongnu, were also attacking from the north.

32 Khayutina (ed.), *Qin: The Eternal Emperor*, p. 35; Maxim Korolkov, *The Imperial Network in Ancient China: The Foundation of Sinitic Empire in Southern East Asia* (Routledge, 2021).

33 This explanation for the creation of the army in clay was offered as early as 1989 in Hiroshi Sofukawa (trans. Chang Feng), 'Lingmu Zhidu yu Linghun Guan', ('The Funerary Rituals and the Idea of the Immaterial Spirit') *Wenbo* 2 (1989), pp. 34–8.

34 Korolkov, *The Imperial Network in Ancient China.*

35 Lewis, 'Warring States Political History'; Falkenhausen, *Chinese Society*; Robin D. S. Yates, 'The Rise of Qin and the Military Conquest of the Warring States', in Portal (ed.), *The First Emperor*, pp. 30–57.

36 Yuri Pines, 'King Zheng of Qin, the First Emperor of China', in Khayutina (ed.), *Qin: The Eternal Emperor*, pp. 105–15.

37 Differences between the earlier Qin boundary and the newly acquired territories, which were less loyal, are described in Korolkov, *The Imperial Network in Ancient China*, pp. 92–5.

38 Armin Selbitschka, 'Physical Exercise vs. Acrobatic Performance: A Reevaluation of the So-called "Acrobat Figures" from Pit 9901 at the First Emperor's Mausoleum', in Lillian Lan-ying Tseng (ed.), *Art, Archaeology and the First Emperor: A Global Approach* (Global Institute for Advanced Studies, New York University / Open Book Publishers, forthcoming).

39 Quotation from Selbitschka, 'Physical Exercise'.

40 A figure marked with the acupuncture points was excavated at Sichuan; see Xie Tao, Wu Jiabi, Suo Dehao and Liu Xiangyu, 'Chengdushi Tianhuizhen Laoguanshan Hanmu' ('The Han Period Tomb at Laoguanshan, Chengdu'), *Kaogu* 7 (2014), pp. 59–70.

41 Duan Qingbo, *Qinshihuangdi Lingyuan Kaogu Yanjiu* (*Archaeological Research of the Qin First Emperor's Mausoleum Complex*) (Beijing Daxue Chubanshe, 2011). His proposals have been examined and presented in English by Anthony Barbieri-Low in Duan Qingbo, 'Sino-Western Cultural Exchange as Seen through the Archaeology of the First Emperor's Necropolis'.

42 Rachel Mairs, *The Archaeology of the Hellenistic Far East: A Survey* (Archaeopress, 2011); *The Hellenistic Far East: Archaeology, Language, and Identity in Greek Central Asia* (University of California Press, 2014).

43 In his article 'The First Emperor and Sculpture in China', *Bulletin of the School of Oriental and African Studies* 76 (2013), pp. 413–47, Lukas Nickel has made an argument that we can find signs of an interest in sculpture of human figures and he selects also the quotation from Watson, *Qin Dynasty*, p. 45, given here.

44 It is not possible to retrieve a plan guiding the form in which the mausoleum was created. Lothar Ledderose has suggested that there must have been such a blueprint and has then analysed methods of manufacture, Ledderose, *Ten Thousand Things*, pp. 51–73.

45 Lothar Ledderose builds his presentation of the ways in which the figures were put together and realised in the use of modular structures overall in China, Ledderose, *Ten Thousand Things*.

46 For the report see Shaanxisheng and Qinshihuang, *Qinshihuangdi Lingyuan Kaogu Baogao (2001–2003) (Report of the Excavation at the Tomb of the First Emperor (2001-2003))* (Wenwu Chubanshe 2007), pp. 109–85.

47 Research by Dr Shao is fundamental to understanding the innovative technologies at the tomb of the First Emperor, Shao Anding, *Qinshihuangdi Lingyuan Chutu Caihui Qingtong Shuiqin Zhizuo Gongyi ji Xiangguan Wenti Yanjiu (Study on the Painted Bronze Waterfowls Unearthed from the Mausoleum of the First Emperer of Qin: Their Manufacturing Techniques and Related Issues)* (Kexue Chubanshe, 2019).

48 Shao Anding et al., 'Qinshihuangdi Lingyuan Chutu Qingtong Shuiqin de Buzhui Gongyi ji Xiangguan Wenti Chutan' ('On the Patch-Repairing Technique of the Bronze Waterfowls from the Mausoleum of the First Qin Emperor'), *Kaogu* 7 (2014), pp. 96–104; for the context in which material and artefacts from Central Asia reached the western borders of the Qin state see So, 'Foreign/Eurasian Elements in Pre-imperial Qin Culture'.

49 Wong, "Steppe Style".

50 Zhao, Dingxin, *The Confucian-Legalist State: A New Theory of Chinese History* (Oxford University Press, 2015), p. 258.

51 Much less elegant but very evocative stone sculpture, remaining on the mound at the Maoling, second to first century BC, also shows that contacts with the West stimulated their creation, Ann Paludan, *The Chinese Spirit Road: The Classical Tradition of Stone Tomb Statuary* (Yale University Press, 1991). Paludan, *Chinese Sculpture*.

52 For a full discussion of the smaller versions in Han period tombs of the imperial princes see Allison R. Miller, *Kingly Splendor; Court Art and Materiality in Han China* (Columbia University Press, 2021).

53 This much larger vision, stimulated by contact with Iran, was first proposed by Duan Qingbo, embracing many areas, in Duan Qingbo, *Qinshihuangdi Lingyuan Kaogu Yanjiu*. See also Alain Thote, 'Defining Qin Artistic Traditions: Heritage, Borrowing and Innovation', in Liu (ed.), *Beyond the First Emperor's Mausoleum*, pp. 13–29; Wang Hui, 'Archaeological Finds of the Majiayuan Cemetery and Qin's Interaction with Steppe Culture', in Liu (ed.), *Beyond the First Emperor's Mausoleum*, pp. 213–39; Yang and Linduff, 'A Contextual Explanation for "Foreign" or "Steppic" Factors'.

54 These features are recognised and discussed in Rawson and Huan, 'Cong Mabiao Xingzhi'. For the almost identical saddles at Berel see Roberts (ed.), *Gold of the Great Steppe*, p. 125. The rider displayed on a felt hanging at Pazyryk is illustrated in plate 31.

55 Durrant et al., *Zuo Tradition* in the year 538 BC, p. 1365; see also Di Cosmo, 'The Northern Frontier in Pre-imperial China'.

56 This stable building is surprisingly little-reported and almost never discussed. The pit also has no number, suggesting that its presence has not been explored. Brief mentions are in Selbitschka, 'The Tomb Complex', pp. 148–9, with reference to Yuan Zongyi, *Qin Shi Huang Ling Bingma Yong Yanjiu* (*Study of the Terracotta Warriors at the Tomb of the First Emperor*) (Wenwu Press, 1990), p. 33.

57 For the report see Shaanxisheng Kaogu Yanjiuyuan and Qinshihuang Bingmayong Bowuguan, *Qinshihuangdi Lingyuan Kaogu Baogao (2000)* (*The Excavation of the Mausoleum of the First Qin Emperor (2000 Season)*) (Wenwu Chubanshe, 2000).

58 Ibid., pp. 65–94. Li Yue et al., 'Horses in Qin Mortuary Practice: New Insights from Emperor Qin Shihuang's Mausoleum', *Antiquity* 96 (2022), pp. 903–19.

59 While Duan Qingbo argued that much of the emperor's organisation of his empire and of his tomb was founded on Achaemenid practice, Anthony J. Barbieri-Low, who has translated a paper in which this argument is made, suggests that not all Duan's suggestions can be substantiated. However, he and Robin D. S. Yates support the suggestion of the Persian origins of the messenger system in *Law, State, and Society in Early Imperial China: A Study with Critical Edition and Translation of the Legal Texts from Zhangjiashan Tomb Numbers 247*, 2 vols. (Brill, 2015), pp. 736–7.

60 Tian Yaqi et al., 'Shaanxi Fengxiang Yongshan Xuechi Qin Han Jisi Yizhi Kaogu Diaocha yu Fajue Jianbao' ('The Survey and Excavation of the Qin and Han Period Sacrificial Site at Xuechi, Yongshan, Fengxiang County, Shaanxi'), *Kaogu yu Wenwu* 6 (2020), pp. 3–49; Burman, *Terracotta Warriors*, pp. 18–19.

61 Watson, *Records*, vol. 2, p. 160.

62 For a report on the excavation and reconstruction of the suits of armour, helmets and horse armour see Shaanxisheng and Qinshihuang, *Qinshihuangdi Lingyuan Kaogu Baogao (2000)*, pp. 95–247 and Shaanxisheng and Qinshihuang, *Qinshihuangdi Lingyuan Kaogu Baogao (2001–2003)*, pp. 237–305.

63 Lin, 'Armour for the Afterlife'.

64 For discussion of the manufacture of the weaponry see Marcos Martinón-Torres et al., 'Making Weapons for the Terracotta Army', *Archaeology International* 13 (2011), pp. 65–75; Xiuzhen Janice Li et al., 'Crossbows and Imperial Craft Organisation: The Bronze Triggers of China's Terracotta Army', *Antiquity* 88 (2014), pp. 126–40; Xiuzhen Janice Li, *Bronze Weapons of the Qin Terracotta Warriors: Standardisation, Craft Specialisation and Labour Organisation* (BAR Publishing, 2020). Lothar Ledderose has taken the analysis of subdivision of labour, one of early China's major strengths, much further, and discusses the modular underpinning of this development in *Ten Thousand Things*. For inscribed weapons see Yuan, *Qinshihuangdi Ling*, pp. 248–62.

65 Among the early descriptions of the army that rejected the notion of the army as a portrait is Ladislav Kesner, 'Likeness of No One: (Re)Presenting the First Emperor's Army', *The Art Bulletin* 77 (1995), pp. 115–32.

66 Portal (ed.), *The First Emperor*, p. 132, figs. 133 and 134.

67 Yuan, *Qinshihuangdi Ling*, pp. 342–51. For the widespread recruitment of convict labour for many different tasks see Maxim Korolkov, 'Convict Labor in the Qin Empire: A Preliminary Study of the "Registers of Convict Laborers" from Liye', in Fudan Daxue Lishixue Xi and Fudan Daxue Chutu Wenxian Yu Guwenzi Yanjiu Zhongxin (eds.), *Jianbo Wenxian yu Gudaishi: Di'erjie Chutu Wenxian Qingnian Xuezhe Guoji Luntan Lunwenji (Ancient Manuscripts and History: Proceedings of the Second International Conference of Excavated Manuscripts)* (Zhongxi Shuju, 2015), pp. 132–56.

68 Convict labour may have been in use for a long time. It was a notable feature of Qin management, not just to build walls or the tomb, but also to spread Qin authority into new areas, Korolkov, 'Convict Labor in the Qin Empire'.

69 Liu (ed.), *Beyond the First Emperor's Mausoleum*.

70 The longer history of regulations and laws is set out in Ernest Caldwell, *Writing Chinese Laws: The Form and Function of Legal Statutes Found in the Qin Shuihudi Corpus* (Routledge, 2018).

71 Yuri Pines (trans. and ed.), *The Book of Lord Shang: Apologetics of State Power in Early China* (Columbia University Press, 2017), provides a full account of Lord Shang's ambitions.

72 Yuri Pines, 'Qin: From Principality to Kingdom to Empire', in Khayutina (ed.), *Qin: The Eternal Emperor*, pp. 27–35.

73 The extension of punishment to families was established by Lord Wen of Qin in the late eighth century BC, Watson, *Records: Qin Dynasty*, p. 6. For the detailed legal texts that survive see Barbieri-Low and Yates, *Law, State, and Society in Early Imperial China*.

74 A translation and discussion of the bamboo-slip regulations from Shuihudi is in A. F. P. Hulsewé, *Remnants of Ch'in Law: An Annotated Translation of the Ch'in Legal and Administrative Rules of the 3rd Century B.C., Discovered in Yün-Meng Prefecture, Hu-Pei Province, in 1975* (Brill, 1985). A full account of other discoveries and a translation of the major Han dynasty regulations are in Barbieri-Low and Yates, *Law, State, and Society in Early Imperial China*.

75 For the reform of the characters see Ch'en Chao-jung, 'The Standardization of Writing', in Khayutina (ed.), *Qin: The Eternal Emperor*, pp. 130–37.

76 For the wider impact of such inscriptions reinforcing, through repetition, the emperor's unification and control see Charles Sanft, *Communication and Cooperation in Early Imperial China: Publicizing the Qin Dynasty* (State University of New York Press, 2014); Michael Loewe, 'The First Emperor and the Qin Empire', in Portal (ed.), *The First Emperor*, pp. 60–79.

77 Quotation from Khayutina (ed.), *Qin: The Eternal Emperor*, p. 185, no. 115.

78 Yuri Pines, 'Contested Sovereignty: Heaven, the Monarch, the People, and the Intellectuals in Traditional China', in Zvi Ben-Dor Benite, Stefanos Geroulanos and Nicole Jerr (eds.), *The Scaffolding of Sovereignty: Global and Aesthetic Perspectives on the History of a Concept* (Columbia University Press, 2017), pp. 80–101, discusses the period and includes this quotation from the *Lüshi Chunqiu*, a third-century BC text usually attributed to Lü Buwei. As Yuri Pines also argues, Jia Yi (200–168 BC) recognised that the promise of unity and a new ruler may have attracted many: 'The masses hoped that they would obtain peace and security and there was no one who did not whole-heartedly look up in reverence', Pines, *The Everlasting Empire*, p. 20.

79 After Watson, *Records: Qin Dynasty*, p. 45.

80 After ibid., p. 56.

81 For a discussion of the possible cosmology behind the emperor's thinking and projects see David W. Pankenier, 'Qin Cosmography and the First Cosmic Capital: Xianyang', in Liu (ed.), *Beyond the First Emperor's Mausoleum*, pp. 45–57.

82 Korolkov and Hein, 'State-induced Migration and the Creation of State Spaces'.

83 For a discussion of the roads and many other aspects of the Qin expansion see Korolkov, *Empire-Building and Market-Making*, p. 451.

84 This discovery was made by Shao Anding, *Qinshihuangdi Lingyuan*, and has been followed up by Yang Huan, 'Qinshihuangdi Ling Chutu Qingtong Mache Zhuzao Gongyi Xintan' ('Rethinking the Casting Techniques on the Bronze

Chariots from the Mausoleum of the First Qin Emperor'), *Wenwu* 4 (2019), pp. 88–96. Yang, taking over materials from Shao, argues that the use of an armature within the structures, and also core-pins and patching, are all features of lost-wax casting and are never seen in China's indigenous piece-mould casting.

85 Wong, 'Steppe Style'.

86 Ibid.

87 The two chariots are among the most popular exhibits at the Museum of the Terracotta Warriors. The archaeological discovery is reported in Qinshihuang Bingmayong Bowuguan and Shaanxisheng Kaogu Yanjiusuo, *Qinshihuang Ling Tongchema Fajue Baogao* (*The Excavation of Bronze Chariots and Horses in the Mausoleum of the First Qin Emperor*) (Wenwu Chubanshe, 1998). For features that can be compared with Iran see Wong, 'Steppe Style'.

88 Martin Kern, 'Imperial Tours and Mountain Inscriptions', in Portal (ed.), *The First Emperor*, p. 110. Martin Kern, *The Stele Inscriptions of Ch'in Shih-Huang: Text and Ritual in Early Chinese Imperial Representation* (American Oriental Society, 2000).

89 Kern, 'Imperial Tours', p. 112, fn. 19.

90 Wu Hung, *The Art of the Yellow Springs*, pp. 53–64.

Epilogue

1 Hansen, *The Silk Road*; see also Peter Frankopan, *The Silk Roads: A New History of the World* (Bloomsbury, 2015).

2 Andrew Sherratt, 'The Trans-Eurasian Exchange: The Prehistory of Chinese Relations with the West', in Victor Mair (ed.), *Contact and Exchange in the Ancient World* (University of Hawai'i Press, 2006), pp. 30–61.

Further Reading

Amitai, Reuven and Michal Biran (eds.). *Nomads as Agents of Cultural Change: The Mongols and Their Eurasian Predecessors*. Honolulu: University of Hawai'i Press, 2014.

Bagley, Robert W. (ed.). *Ancient Sichuan: Treasures from a Lost Civilization*. Seattle, WA / Princeton, NJ: Seattle Art Museum / Princeton University Press, 2001.

Bunker, Emma C. (ed.). *Ancient Bronzes of the Eastern Eurasian Steppes from the Arthur M. Sackler Collections*. New York: Arthur M. Sackler Foundation, 1997.

Campbell, Roderick B. *Violence, Kinship and the Early Chinese State: The Shang and Their World*. Cambridge: Cambridge University Press, 2018.

Chang, Kwang-chih. *Shang Civilization*. New Haven, CT: Yale University Press, 1980.

Childs-Johnson, Elizabeth (ed.). *The Oxford Handbook of Early China*. Oxford: Oxford University Press, 2020.

Chugunov, Konstantin V., Hermann Parzinger and Anatoli Nagler. *Der Skythenzeitliche Fürstenkurgan Aržan 2 in Tuva*. Mainz: Philipp von Zabern, 2010.

Cook, Constance A. and John S. Major (eds.). *Defining Chu: Image and Reality in Ancient China*. Honolulu: University of Hawai'i Press, 1999.

Di Cosmo, Nicola. *Ancient China and Its Enemies: The Rise of Nomadic Power in East Asian History*. Cambridge: Cambridge University Press, 2002.

Durrant, Stephen W., Wai-yee Li and David Schaberg. *Zuo Tradition / Zuozhuan: Commentary on the 'Spring and Autumn Annals'*. 3 vols. Seattle, WA: University of Washington Press, 2016.

von Falkenhausen, Lothar. *Chinese Society in the Age of Confucius (1000–250 BC): The Archaeological Evidence*. Los Angeles: Cotsen Institute of Archaeology, University of California, 2006.

Goldin, Paul Rakita (ed.). *Routledge Handbook of Early Chinese History*. London / New York: Routledge, 2017.

Graham, Angus Charles. *Disputers of the Tao: Philosophical Argument in Ancient China*. La Salle, IL. Open Court, 1989.

Grebnev, Yegor. *Mediation of Legitimacy in Early China: A Study of the Neglected Zhou Scriptures and the Grand Duke Traditions*. New York: Columbia University Press, 2022.

Hawkes, David. *Ch'u Tz'u: The Songs of the South, an Ancient Chinese Anthology.* Oxford: Clarendon Press, 1959.

Keightley, David N. *The Ancestral Landscape: Time, Space, and Community in Late Shang China (ca. 1200–1045 B.C.)* Berkeley, CA: Institute of East Asian Studies, University of California, Berkeley, 2000.

Keightley, David N. *Working for His Majesty: Research Notes on Labor Mobilization in Late Shang China (ca. 1200–1045 B.C.), as Seen in the Oracle-Bone Inscriptions, with Particular Attention to Handicraft Industries, Agriculture, Warfare, Hunting, Construction, and the Shang's Legacies.* China Research Monograph 67. Berkeley, CA: Institute of East Asian Studies, University of California, Berkeley, 2012.

Kern, Martin. *The Stele Inscriptions of Ch'in Shih-Huang: Text and Ritual in Early Chinese Imperial Representation.* New Haven, CT: American Oriental Society, 2000.

Kern, Martin, 'Bronze Inscriptions, the *Shijing* and the *Shangshu*: The Evolution of the Ancestral Sacrifice During the Western Zhou', in J. Lagerwey and M. Kalinowski (eds.), *Early Chinese Religion, Part 1: Shang through Han (1250 BC– 220 AD).* Leiden: Brill, 2009, pp. 143–200.

Khayutina, Maria (ed.). *Qin: The Eternal Emperor and His Terracotta Warriors.* Zurich: Neue Zürcher Zeitung Publishing, 2013.

Korolkov, Maxim. *The Imperial Network in Ancient China: The Foundation of Sinitic Empire in Southern East Asia.* London and New York: Routledge, 2022.

Ledderose, Lothar. *Ten Thousand Things: Module and Mass Production in Chinese Art.* Princeton, NJ: Princeton University Press, 2000.

Legge, James. *The Chinese Classics.* 5 vols. London: Trübner, 1861–72.

Lewis, Mark Edward. *The Early Chinese Empires: Qin and Han.* Cambridge, MA: Harvard University Press, 2007.

Li Feng. *Landscape and Power in Early China: The Crisis and Fall of the Western Zhou, 1045–771 BC.* Cambridge: Cambridge University Press, 2006.

Linduff, Katheryn M., Sun Yan, Cao Wei and Liu Yuanqing. *Ancient China and Its Eurasian Neighbors: Artifacts, Identity and Death in the Frontier, 3000–700 BCE.* Cambridge: Cambridge University Press, 2017.

Liu Bin, Qin Ling and Zhuang Yijie (eds.). *Liangzhu Culture: Society, Belief and Art in Neolithic China.* Abingdon/New York: Routledge, 2020.

Liu Li and Chen Xingcan. *The Archaeology of China: From the Late Paleolithic to the Early Bronze Age.* Cambridge: Cambridge University Press, 2012.

Liu, Yang (ed.). *Beyond the First Emperor's Mausoleum: New Perspectives on Qin Art.* Minneapolis, MN: Minneapolis Institute of Arts, 2014.

Loewe, Michael (ed.). *Early Chinese Texts: A Bibliographical Guide.* Berkeley, CA: Society for the Study of Early China and the Institute of East Asian Studies, 1993.

Further Reading

Loewe, Michael and Edward L. Shaughnessy (eds.). *The Cambridge History of Ancient China: From the Origins of Civilization to 221 B.C.* Cambridge: Cambridge University Press, 1999.

Mei, Jianjun. 'Cultural Interaction between China and Central Asia during the Bronze Age', *Proceedimgs of the British Academy*, vol. 121, 2003, pp. 1–39.

Nylan, Michael. *The Five 'Confucian' Classics*. New Haven, CT: Yale University Press, 2001.

Pines, Yuri. *The Everlasting Empire: The Political Culture of Ancient China and Its Imperial Legacy*. Princeton, NJ: Princeton University Press, 2012.

Pines, Yuri, Gideon Shelach-Lavi, Lothar von Falkenhausen and Robin D. S. Yates (eds.). *Birth of an Empire: The State of Qin Revisited*. Berkeley, CA: University of California Press, 2014.

Portal, Jane (ed.). *The First Emperor: China's Terracotta Army*. London: British Museum Press, 2007.

Rawson, Jessica (ed.). *Mysteries of Ancient China: New Discoveries from the Early Dynasties*. London: British Museum Publications, 1996.

Rawson, Jessica 'Chinese Burial Patterns: Sources of Information on Thought and Belief', in A. C. Renfrew and C. Scarre (eds.), *Cognition and Material Culture: The Archaeology of Symbolic Storage*. Cambridge: McDonald Institute for Archaeological Research, 1998, pp. 107–33.

Sanft, Charles. *Communication and Cooperation in Early Imperial China: Publicizing the Qin Dynasty*. Albany, NY: State University of New York Press, 2014.

Shaughnessy, Edward L. *Sources of Western Zhou History: Inscribed Bronze Vessels*. Berkeley, CA: University of California Press, 1991.

So, Jenny F. (ed.). *Music in the Age of Confucius*. Washington DC: Freer Gallery of Art and Arthur M. Sackler Gallery, 2000.

—. *Early Chinese Jades in the Harvard Art Museums*. Cambridge, MA: Harvard Art Museums, 2019.

Steinke, Kyle and Dora C. Y. Ching (eds.). *Art and Archaeology of the Erligang Civilization*. Princeton, NJ: P. Y. and Kinmay W. Tang Center for East Asian Art, Department of Art and Archaeology, Princeton University, 2014.

Sterckx, Roel. *Chinese Thought: From Confucius to Cook Ding*. London: Pelican, 2019.

Sun, Yan. *Many Worlds under One Heaven: Material Culture, Identity, and Power in the Northern Frontiers of the Western Zhou, 1045–771 BCE*. New York: Columbia University Press, 2021.

Sun, Zhouyong et al. 'The First Neolithic Urban Center on China's North Loess Plateau: The Rise and Fall of Shimao', *Archaeological Research in Asia* 14 (2018), pp. 33–45.

Underhill, Anne P. *Craft Production and Social Change in Northern China*. New York/London: Kluwer Academic/Plenum Publishers, 2002.

Further Reading

Underhill, Anne P. (ed.). *A Companion to Chinese Archaeology*. Hoboken, NJ: Wiley-Blackwell, 2013.

Watson, Burton. *Records of the Grand Historian of China. Translated from the Shih Chi of Ssu-Ma Ch'ien*. 2 vols. New York/London: Columbia University Press, 1961.

Wu, Xiaolong. *Material Culture, Power, and Identity in Ancient China*. Cambridge/New York: Cambridge University Press, 2017.

Yang, Jianhua, Shao Huiqiu and Pan Ling. *The Metal Road of the Eastern Eurasian Steppe: The Formation of the Xiongnu Confederation and the Silk Road*. Singapore: Springer, 2020.

Index

Aelianus (Greek author), 317

Afghanistan, 342, 343

afterlife: abandonment of ancestors, 145; alcohol consumption in, 47, 75, 130, 131, 132, 165–6, 260, 261, 293–4; analogies governing, xxxii, xxxiii, 241–3, 274; art objects as essential bonds with, xxii, 41, 48–9, 50, 73, 157; attendant burial at Arzhan, 199, 225–6; attendant burial introduced by newcomers, 222, 225–6, 229; attendants buried in Taosi, 39; attendants in tombs of Qi lords, 230; attendants in tombs of Zhongshan kings, 271, 272, 280; attendants in Wu state tomb, Henan, 239, 241; attendants of leader at Majiayuan, 306; attendants of Lord Bai, 208, *218*, 218, 223; attendants of Marquis Yi of Zeng, *234*, 239, 241, 248, 266; attendants of Qin rulers, 330, 331; attendants of Ya Chang, 64, 81, 85; in catacombs, 308; chariots as status symbols in, 88, 141–7, 152–3, 161–2, 192, 219, 230, 282, 308, 319–23, 324–5; and displays of wealth, xxvi, xxx, 12–15, 37, 48–51, 140–7, 152–8, 174–5, 187–99, 207–10, 237–40, 248–66, 273–99, 310–15, 319–25; and the family, xxvii, xxx–xxxi, 42–3, 73, 124–6, 157, 221, 276–7; female attendants in, 237, 238, 239, 241, 248, 249, 253, 266, 280; female companions in, 123–4, 126, 131, 152, 156, 159–60, 163, 165, 207, 209, 218, 239, 279, 280; females accompanying First Emperor, 332, 336; of the First Emperor, xxvii, 327, 330, 335–42, 343–7, 350–3, 355, 356–60; hunting expeditions in, 261, 262, 281, 284; inauguration of in architecture, 275–6; jade's associations with, 12, 18, 19–25, 29, 80, 154–5, 158–60, 218, 265; King Cuo's plan for, 273–85, 287–99; local preferences, 200, 229–30, 265; miniatures as mementos in, 126–7; mirrors world of living, 77; and musical communication, 51–2, 173–4, 237–8, 248–57; need for nourishment in, xxix, 37, 41–7, 49, 52–3, 67, 75–6, 130–1, 165–6, 221; new fashions conferring status in, 220, 258–9, 265, 284; Qin state rituals, 330–1; as real, not symbolic, xxvii, 42–3, 51, 109–10, 337; realised by painted analogies, 241–2, 274; stables/horses for, 184, 187, 188, 192, 199, 226, 281–8, 306, 323, 331, 335, 336, 347; status of consorts in, 279; of strange creatures in the south, 266; tomb as dwelling for eternity, 44–5, 237; tomb as vehicle drawn by horses into, 188; tombs as palaces/mansions for, xxvi, xxvii, 38–9, 42–4, 124, 152, 208–9, 238–50,

475

Yangtze River – *cont'd.*
 delta, xxiv, xxvii, 2, 5–10,
 11–15, 20, 25–7, 31, 36, 95, 210; flood
 plain, 233; flooding of, 25–7, 97,
 98; and Pacific Monsoon, xxi, 361;
 rising of on Tibetan Plateau, 93;
 Three Gorges, xx, xxi, 93,
 96–7
Yao (mythical emperor), 35
Yazi River, 98
Yellow Emperor, 35
Yellow River, *118*, *148*; and climate,
 xxi, 93, 179, 233; colour of, xxiii;
 course of, xx, 31–3, 34, 59; the
 Dragons' Gate, 33; Fen as tributary
 of, 31–3, 35, 36, 140, 151; flooding of,
 27; Great Bend of, 33, 156, 349; and
 Huai River, 207; levees on Central
 Plains, xx, 59; Liangdaicun on, 149;
 movement of horses down,
 88–9; rich silt of, xxiii, 31, 33, 36, 44,
 59; Wei as main tributary, ix,
 33, 35
Yellow River basin, ix, xxxiii, xxxiv;
 bronze-casting tradition in, 103, 104,
 111, 156, 162, 248; Chu expansion
 north into, 217; continuous
 movement of people into, xxxiv,
 35, 88–9, 121–2, 179–84; dialogue /
 encounters with northern
 pastoralists, 35, 57, 63, 157–8;
 polities / cities across, xxii–xxiii,
 10–11, 17, 31, 88, 97, 128, 205, 210, 214,
 265; ritual traditions in, xxiv, xxxiv,
 77–8, 244, 255, 259, 265; routes into,
 34–5, 54, 181–2; vast size of, 61; Zhou
 authority in weakens, 170, 181–2,
 210, 217 *see also* Anyang, city of;
 Taosi, ancient city of; Xi'an, city of
the Yi, x, 228, 229, 230, 273

Yi (ruler of Zeng), 236–7
Yi, Mount, *359*
Yimencun near Xi'an, *330*
Yongcheng, *326*, 329–31, 340, 347–8
Yu, Emperor, 27, 360
Yu Bo, tomb of, Baoji: bells in, 124, 130,
 131; bird-headed staff, *139*, *140*, 141;
 east–west alignment of bodies, 123;
 as joint burial, 123–4; objects in, *120*,
 124–8, 130–1, 134, 135, 138–41, *139*,
 146–7, 157, 173, 308, 312; tombs
 nearby, 125, *125*
Yu clan / lineage, 129–30, 136–40, 141;
 and ancestral cult, 123–5, 130, 135, 166;
 at Baoji, 123–8, 129–32, 139–40, 143,
 144, 146–7, 151, 181–2; disappearance
 of, 145–7, 192; and horses, 142–3,
 147; military role of, 138–45, 147;
 northern heritage of, 124, 125, 126,
 127–8, 139–40, 146, 147; tomb of last
 Yu lord, *142*, 147; and the willow-
 leaf sword, 139–40, 141, 147; Yu Bo as
 leader, 123, 124, 125–6, 181–2; Yu Bo
 Ge, 136–7, *137*, 138, *142*, 143; and Zhou
 dynasty, 123–8, 129–30, 132, 135,
 136–40, 141, 144, 145–7, 181–2
the Yuan, Mongol dynasty of,
 181, 325
Yuhuangmiao, *178*, 182, 184–5, *186*,
 187–8, 189–90, 192, 193, 194–7, 200,
 201; burial of animal heads at, *180*,
 184, 187, 221; gold tiger at, 196–7, *197*,
 220–1; growing wealth / authority of
 the steppe lords, 202; objects valued
 for their bronze at, 192, 193–4, 308;
 spirals of gold at, 197, 258 *see also*
 Mountain Rong leader, tomb of
 (Yuhuangmiao)
Yunmeng Marsh, xx, 210, 233, 265
Yunnan province, 109